WOMEN, CULTURE AND MEDIA

WOMEN, CULTURE AND MEDIA

TANUJA TRIVEDI

ISHA

Women, Culture and Media
Rs. 950

ISBN: 978-81-8205-532-2

Published in 2013 in India by
Isha Books,
B-63, 1st Floor, New Gupta Colony,
Near DDA Market,
Delhi-110009

Laser Typesetting: Durga Print Media, Delhi

Printed at: G. Print Process, Delhi

Contents

Preface

In many prehistoric cultures, women assumed a particular cultural role. In gatherer-hunter societies, women were generally the gatherers of plant foods, small animal foods and fish, while men hunted meat from large animals. In more recent history, the gender roles of women have changed greatly. Traditionally, middle class women were involved in domestic tasks emphasizing child care. For poorer women, especially working class women, although this often remained an ideal, [specify] economic necessity compelled them to seek employment, outside the home. The occupations that were available to them were, however, lower in pay than those available to men. As changes in the labour market for women came about, availability of employment changed from only "dirty", long hour factory jobs to "cleaner", more respectable office jobs where more education was demanded, women's participation in the U.S. labour force rose from 6 per cent in 1900 to 23 per cent in 1923. These shifts in the labour force led to changes in the attitudes of women at work, allowing for the revolution which resulted in women becoming career and education oriented. Movements advocate equality of opportunity for both sexes and equal rights irrespective of gender. Through a combination of economic changes and the efforts of the feminist movement, in recent decades women in most societies now have access to careers beyond the traditional homemaker. Although a greater number of women are seeking higher education, salaries are often claimed to be less than those of men. CBS News claims that in the United States women who are ages 30 to 44 and hold a university degree make only 62 per cent of what similarly qualified men do, a lower rate than in all but three of the 19 countries for which numbers are available. The nations with greater inequity in pay are Germany, New Zealand and Switzerland.

Feminism is a collection of movements aimed at defining, establishing, and defending equal political, economic, and social rights for women. In addition, feminism seeks to establish equal opportunities for women in education and employment. A feminist is "an advocate or supporter of the rights and equality of women". Feminist theory, which emerged from these feminist movements, aims to understand the nature of gender inequality by examining women's social roles and lived experience; it has developed theories in a variety of disciplines in order to respond to issues such as the social construction of sex and gender. Some of the earlier forms of feminism have been criticized for taking into account only white, middle-class, educated perspectives. This led to the creation of ethnically specific or multiculturalist forms of feminism. Feminist activists campaign for women's rights - such as in contract law, property, and voting - while also promoting 'bodily integrity, autonomy, and reproductive rights for women. Feminist campaigns have changed societies, particularly in the West, by achieving women's suffrage, gender neutrality in English, equal pay for women, reproductive rights for women (including access to contraceptives and abortion), and the right to enter into contracts and own property. Feminists have worked to protect women and girls from domestic violence, sexual harassment, and sexual assault. They have also advocated for workplace rights, including maternity leave, and against forms of discrimination against women. Feminism is mainly focused on women's issues, but because feminism seeks gender equality, some feminists argue that men's liberation is a necessary part of feminism, and that men are also harmed by sexism and gender roles.

Gender equality, also known as sex equality or sexual equality, is the goal of the equality of the genders, stemming from a belief in the injustice of myriad forms of gender inequality. This goal includes making women's rights equal to men's and also making men's rights equal to women's. Women's rights are entitlements and freedoms claimed for women and girls of all ages in many societies. The idea is that women should have equal rights with men. In some places these rights are institutionalized or supported by law, local custom, and behaviour, whereas in others they may be ignored or suppressed. They differ from broader notions of human rights through claims of an inherent historical and traditional bias against the exercise of rights by women and girls in favour of men and boys. Issues commonly associated with notions of women's rights include, though are not limited to, the right: to bodily integrity and autonomy; to vote (suffrage); to hold public office; to work; to fair wages or equal pay; to own property; to education; to serve in the military or be conscripted; to enter into legal contracts; and to have marital, parental and religious rights.

Women empowerment refers to increasing the spiritual, political, social or economic strength of women. Empowerment is probably the totality of the following or similar capabilities:

- Having decision-making power of their own
- Having access to information and resources for taking proper decision
- Having a range of options from which you can make choices (not just yes/no, either/or)
- Ability to exercise assertiveness in collective decision making
- Having positive thinking on the ability to make change
- Ability to learn skills for improving one's personal or group power
- Ability to change others' perceptions by democratic means
- Involving in the growth process and changes that is never ending and self-initiated
- Increasing one's positive self-image and overcoming stigma.

This book, "Women, Culture and Media" provides an introductory overview issues related to women, culture and media with focus on contemporary women and gender studies; culture and communication studies; and media studies. A critical overview of womanism, feminity, feminine psychology and feminism is also given. This book attempts firstly towards understanding the relevance of sexism, gender gap and gender apartheid and secondly towards understanding major issues related to gender sociology, gender role and gender equality. An overview of select case studies and concerned customs involved with role of sex selection, sex segregation and gender segregation are given. This book also attempts towards understanding major elements w.r.t. women, role of gender equality and religion. Focus also lies on women rights and status of women related case studies, problems and challenges. An analysis of language and gender neutrality is done. The book is user-friendly.

1

Introductory Overview of Women, Culture and Media

Introduction

Women's portrayal in the media has been a point of strong international debate, and is also a highly-sensitised topic in our country. The issue of media sociology also comes up subsequently as an important element in this scenario, rendering it difficult to determine whether it is the media that affects and shapes the trends of society or vice versa. Most would agree that it is a two-way propensity, where the media and the masses influence and modify each other in an open-ended and undetermined way. And since women constitute half the society, their own role in ascertaining how the fairer sex is projected in the media cannot be overlooked either. At an interesting discussion recently organised on the issue by a Lahore-based NGO, there was a lot of brainstorming on the subject. Hardcore feminists present at the session insisted that our patriarchal, male-domineering set-up influences the conjuring up of women's negative and stereotypical images in the print as well as the electronic media. A few others had a more open approach to the problem. They were honest enough to point a finger at their ownselves, too, arguing that the coverage extended to women's issues and their portrayal also stems from women's own rather confounded and ambiguous thought process. And that they have not as yet been able to determine where their liberty, or so-called 'independence' lies.

"We are a confused and a confounded lot, partially borrowing ideologies and slogans from the West, without taking the trouble to adapt them to the indigenous requirements, and partially generating our own on the basis of long-held beliefs and shallow research." After all, it is mostly women denying rights to other women in so many cases, in their various roles in our society. It is the mother who puts aside the best portion of a meaty meal for the son, and lets the daughter nibble on a cartilaginous bit. Often mothers are behind decisions regarding the education, marriage and careers of their daughters, disallowing them to gain higher education or work outside home, though more so in the urban areas. In rural areas, a majority of the fathers mostly make such choices. "We might say that these decisions are again nurtured by a patriarchal set-up, and women having themselves gone through the system, follow it blindly with little arguments or questioning. But the same excuse can also be brought forward for men, who have also gone through the same system. Many men might be blindly following the culture, too, without challenging the normative pattern or age-old norms," argues an open-approach participant. Whether we say that it is this normative society that is mirrored by the media, or that media is conjuring up images of women in which it wants to see them fitted — in either case women cannot be totally abdicated from holding responsibility for the mannerism in which the media projects them. Blaming the media alone for making women objects of beauty or symbols of sexual derision for the male eye might be a little unfair. Many women entering the glamorous world of films, television or advertising want to be considered as sex-symbols or queens of physical perfection themselves. Most would rather be known more for their looks than acting potentials or skills.

Another argument that is put forward at this point is that women do not mostly enjoy top positions in the print and electronic media, to enable them to check the tendency of women's negative projection. With a female heading PTV Lahore centre, this may not hold true. But even in the absence of female leadership, women working within the media can take a stand to undertake factual roles, in which they are portrayed as conscious, useful citizens. Why do they have to be always depicted as vulnerable belles, drowned in a sea of pathos and melodrama? Feryal Ali Gauhar is one of the few television stars who takes a stand against such projection, and refuses to star in a play that would portray her as a persecuted, ignored first wife. "Women's real liberation lies in the realization of their individuality and independent thought process, not in stripping themselves or taking to the streets," observes the eminent writer, Bano Qudsia. Why do our actresses allow themselves to be painted in garish, exposing dresses, with overblown anatomy, or in baffled, terrorized poses on film billboards that pollute the skyline of Lahore? There is a dearth of educated women from respectable backgrounds willing to enter the world of acting, but if those already in the media put their foot down against negative stereotypical roles, the story writers, directors and producers would be left with no choice but to grant respect to women which is their due. It is also wrong to assume that our public likes to see only dramatic or glamorous images of women. We can cite many examples of films and television plays sans all this that made it to the top.

Women employed in the print media, specially the vernacular press, should watch against the sensationalism to which news concerning women are subjected. Crime against women, in particular, is covered in a way that becomes a crime in its own right. Eye-catching headlines, accompanied by dramatic descriptions of the crime and equally appalling pictures, fail to fulfil the purpose that lies behind the media's role in fighting infraction. But since it's mostly the male reporters who cover crime, their training in gender sensitization and gender reporting is very important. What kind of message does an Urdu daily give that describes the murder of a young woman by placing a headline that reads, 'Fashionable woman murdered in train'? The subheads say, 'Polished nails and henna on hands'. If the reporter was trying to tell the readers that the victim was probably a newlywed, he could have simply called her one, instead of creating ambiguity and suspense in the minds of the readers by resorting to this type of embellished and unnecessary description lacking in 'objectivity and impartiality', the essential features of a good news story.

One may, therefore, infer that while women's projection in the media constitutes a major concern with the women, it's not only men who need be gender sensitised in a positive way. Even women need to be clear about what they want to adopt as the insignia of their identity, ensuring that this conviction comes from within the women directly involved 'in the media and with the media', because these are the women who are eventually in a position to direct change by their firm stance. Any amount of undetermined debating and slogan-chanting from outside alone would not guarantee healthy and positive images of women in the media.

As far as, media coverage of women and women's issues are concerned, globally women professionals and athletes continue to be under- represented in news coverage, and are often stereotypically portrayed when they are included. Although there has been a steady increase in the number of women professionals over the past 20 years, most mainstream press coverage continues to rely on men as experts in the fields of business, politics and economics. Women in the news are more likely to be featured in stories about accidents, natural disasters, or domestic violence than in stories about their professional abilities or expertise.

Women in politics are similarly sidelined. Canadian journalist Jenn Goddu studied newspaper and magazine coverage of three women's lobby groups over a 15-year period. She discovered that journalists tend to focus on the domestic aspects of the politically active woman's life (such as "details about the high heels stashed in her bag, her habit of napping in the early evening, and her lack of concern about whether or not she is considered ladylike") rather than her position on the issues. Quebec political analyst Denis Monière uncovered similar patterns. In 1998, Monière analysed 83 late evening newscasts on three national networks—the Canadian Broadcasting Corporation, Radio-Canada (the French-language public broadcaster) and TVA. He observed that women's views were solicited mainly in the framework of "average citizens" and rarely as experts, and that political or economic success stories were overwhelmingly masculine. Monière also noted that the number of female politicians interviewed was disproportionate to their number in Parliament or in the Quebec National Assembly; nor, he noted, was this deficiency in any way compensated for by the depth and quality of coverage.

Inadequate women's coverage seems to be a worldwide phenomenon. In 2000, the Association of Women Journalists (Association des femmes journalistes – AFJ) studied news coverage of women and women's issues in 70 countries. It reported that only 18 per cent of stories quote women, and that the number of women-related stories came to barely 10 per cent of total news coverage. News talk shows are equally problematic. The White House Project reports that only 9 per cent of the guests on Sunday morning news shows such as *Meet the Press* and *Face the Nation* are women, and even then they only speak 10 per cent of the time—leaving 90 per cent of the discussion to the male guests. Project president Marie Wilson warns that the lack of representation for women will have profound consequences on whether or not women are perceived as competent leaders, because "authority is not recognized by these shows. It is created by these shows." Professor Caryl Rivers notes that politically active women are often disparaged and stereotyped by the media. When Hillary Clinton was still first lady, she was referred to as a "witch" or "witchlike" at least 50 times in the press. Rivers writes, "male political figures may be called mean and nasty names, but those words don't usually reflect superstition and dread. Did the press ever call Presidents Carter, Reagan, Bush, or Clinton warlocks?"

Women athletes are also given short shrift in the media. Margaret Carlisle Duncan and Michael Messner studied sports coverage on three network affiliates in Los Angeles. They report that only nine per cent of airtime was devoted to women's sports, in contrast to the 88 per cent devoted to male athletes. Female athletes fared even worse on ESPN's national sports show *Sports Center*, where they occupied just over two per cent of airtime. And, according to the Canadian Association for the Advancement of Women, Sports and Physical Activity, women athletes receive just three per cent of sports coverage in major Canadian dailies. Margaret Carlisle Duncan notes that commentators (97 per cent of whom are men) use different language when they talk about female athletes. Whereas men are described as "big," "strong," "brilliant," "gutsy" and "aggressive," women are more often referred to as "weary," "fatigued," "frustrated," "panicked," "vulnerable" and "choking." Commentators are also twice as likely to call men by their last names only, and three times as likely to call women by their first names only. Duncan argues that this "reduces female athletes to the role of children, while giving adult status to white male athletes."

The Prix Déméritas (Brickbat Prize) for sexist reporting was awarded by Quebec's *Gazette des femmes* to the journalists who covered the 2000 International Women's Tennis Cup. The *Gazette* noted in particular the journalists' keen interest in any of the athletes' poses that could be seen as suggestive, as well as the excessive attention accorded to Anna Kournikova— for her beauty rather than her game. Media images of women in sports are also very different from the familiar pictures of male athletes in action. Female athletes are increasingly photographed in what Professor Pat Griffin calls "hyper-sexualised poses." Griffin notes, "When it was once enough to feminize women athletes, now it is necessary to sexualise them for men. Instead of hearing, 'I am woman, hear me roar,' we are hearing 'I am hetero-sexy, watch me strip.'"

When well-respected news-show host Greta Van Susteren moved from CNN to Fox in early 2002, she not only had a makeover; she surgically altered her face to appear younger and more "beautiful." When her new show, On the Record, premiered, her hair was perfectly coiffed and she sat behind a table so viewers could see her short skirt and legs.

Robin Gerber notes that, "Before her surgery, Van Susteren had been an increasingly visible beacon projecting the hope that women had made progress. You believed that she had made it in television because she was so darn smart, clearly the best legal analyst on the air." However, her surgery symbolizes what many analysts have argued for decades: that the way a woman looks is far more important than what she has to say. Gerber concludes that Van Susteren "has become a painful reminder of women's inequality... Being smart, smarter, smartest isn't enough. By trying to become just another pretty face, Van Susteren instead became another cultural casualty."

2

Towards Understanding Women, Culture and Media in a Broader Perspective

Woman

A woman, is a female human. The term woman is usually reserved for an adult, with the term girl being the usual term for a female child or adolescent. However, the term *woman* is also sometimes used to identify a female human, regardless of age, as in phrases such as "Women's rights."

The Old English wifman meant "female human" (werman meant "male human". Man or mann had a gender neutral meaning of "human", corresponding to Modern English "one" or "someone". However in around 1000 AD "man" started to be used more to refer to "male human", and in the late 1200s began to inevitably displace and eradicate the original word "werman"). The medial labial consonants coalesced to create the modern form "woman"; the initial element, which meant "female," underwent semantic narrowing to the sense of a married woman ("wife").

A very common Indo-European root for woman, **gen-*, is the source of English queen (Old English *cwēn* primarily meant woman, highborn or not; this is still the case in Danish, with the modern spelling *kvinde*, as well as in Swedish *kvinna*), as well as gynaecology (from Greek γυνη *gynē*), banshee fairy woman (from Irish *bean* woman, *sí* fairy) and zenana (from Persian *zan*). The Latin *fēmina*, whence female, is likely from the root in *fellā re* (to suck), referring to breastfeeding. The symbol for the planet Venus is the sign also used in biology for the female sex. It is a stylized representation of the goddess Venus's hand mirror or an abstract symbol for the goddess: a circle with a small equilateral cross underneath (Unicode: ⁺O). The Venus symbol also represented femininity, and in ancient alchemy stood for copper.

Alchemists constructed the symbol from a circle (representing spirit) above an equilateral cross (representing matter).

Womanhood is the period in a female's life after she has transitioned through childhood and adolescence, generally age 18. Puberty generally begins at about age 10, followed by menarche at age 12 to 13. Many cultures have rites of passage to symbolise a *girl*'s coming of age, such as confirmation in some branches of Christianity, bat mitzvah in Judaism, or even just the custom of a special celebration for a certain birthday (generally between 12 and 21), like the Quinceañera of Latin America. The word woman can be used generally, to mean any female human, or specifically, to mean an adult female human as contrasted with *girl*. The word *girl* originally meant "young person of either sex" in English; it was only around the beginning of the 16th century that it came to mean specifically a female child. The term *girl* is sometimes used colloquially to refer to a young or unmarried woman, however during the early 1970s feminists challenged such use because the use of the word to refer to a fully grown woman may cause offence. In particular, previously common terms such as office *girl* are no longer used. Conversely, in certain cultures which link family honour with female virginity, the word *girl* is still used to refer to a never-married woman; in this sense it is used in a fashion roughly analogous to the obsolete English maid or *maiden*. Referring to an unmarried female as a woman may, in such a culture, imply that she is sexually experienced, which would be an insult to her family. There are various words used to refer to the quality of being a woman. The term "womanhood" merely means the state of being a woman, having passed the menarche; "femininity" is used to refer to a set of supposedly typical female qualities associated with a certain attitude to gender roles; "womanliness" is like "femininity", but is usually associated with a different view of gender roles; "femaleness" is a general term, but is often used as shorthand for "human femaleness"; "distaff" is an archaic adjective derived from women's conventional role as a spinner, now used only as a deliberate archaism; "muliebrity" is a neologism (derived from the Latin) meant to provide a female counterpart of "virility", but used very loosely, sometimes to mean merely "womanhood", sometimes "femininity" and sometimes even as a collective term for women.

The earliest women whose names are known were:

- Enheduanna, born c. 2285 BCE, was the high priestess of the temple of the Moon God in the Sumerian city-state of Ur and possibly the first poet and first named author of either gender.
- Tashlultum, in late 24th-early 23rd centuries BCE, Akkadian queen, wife of Sargon of Akkad, and mother of Enheduanna.
- Peseshet, c. 2600 BCE, was a physician in ancient Egypt.
- Merit-Ptah, c. 2700 BCE, also lived in Egypt and is the earliest known female physician and scientist.

- Merneith, c. 3000 BCE was a consort and a regent of ancient Egypt during the first dynasty. She may have been ruler of Egypt in her own right.
- Neithhotep, c. 3200 BCE, was the wife of Narmer and the first queen of ancient Egypt.

Understanding the Aspects Biology and Gender

In terms of biology, the female sex organs are involved in the reproductive system, whereas the secondary sex characteristics are involved in nurturing children or, in some cultures, attracting a mate. The ovaries, in addition to their regulatory function producing hormones, produce female gametes called eggs which, when fertilised by male gametes (sperm), form new genetic individuals. The uterus is an organ with tissue to protect and nurture the developing foetus and muscle to expel it when giving birth. The vagina is used in copulation and birthing (although the word vagina is often colloquially and incorrectly used for the vulva or external female genitalia, which also includes the labia, the clitoris, and the female urethra). The breast evolved from the sweat gland to produce milk, a nutritious secretion that is the most distinctive characteristic of mammals, along with live birth. In mature women, the breast is generally more prominent than in most other mammals; this prominence, not necessary for milk production, is probably at least partially the result of sexual selection. (For other ways in which men commonly differ physically from women.) An imbalance of maternal hormonal levels and some chemicals (or drugs) may alter the secondary sexual characteristics of fetuses. Most women have the karyotype 46, XX, but around one in a thousand will be 47, XXX, and one in 2500 will be 45, X. This contrasts with the typical male karotype of 46, XY; thus, the X and Y chromosomes are known as female and male, respectively. Because humans inherit mitochondrial DNA only from the mother's ovum, genetic studies of the female line tend to focus on mitochondrial DNA. Biological factors are not sufficient determinants of whether a person considers herself a woman or is considered a woman. Intersex individuals, who have mixed physical and/or genetic features, may use other criteria in making a clear determination. There are also transgender or transsexual women, who were born or physically assigned as male at birth, but identify as women; there are varying social, legal and individual definitions with regard to these issues. Although fewer females than males are born (the ratio is around 1:1.05), due to a longer life expectancy there are only 81 men aged 60 or over for every 100 women of the same age. Women typically have a longer life expectancy than men. This is due to a combination of factors: genetics (redundant and varied genes present on sex chromosomes in women); sociology (such as not being expected in most countries to perform military service); health- impacting choices (such as suicide or the use of cigarettes, and alcohol); the presence of the female hormone estrogen, which has a cardioprotective effect in premenopausal women; and the effect of high levels of androgens in men. Out of the total human population, there are 101.3 men for every 100 women (source: 2001 World Almanac). Most women go through menarche and are then able to become pregnant and bear children. This generally requires internal fertilisation of her eggs with the sperm of a man through sexual intercourse, though artificial insemination or the surgical implantation of an existing embryo is also possible. The study of female reproduction and reproductive organs is called gynaecology. There are some diseases that primarily affect women, such as lupus. Also, there are some sex-related illnesses that are found more frequently or exclusively in women, e.g., breast cancer, cervical cancer, or ovarian cancer. Women and men may have different symptoms of an illness and may also respond differently to medical treatment. This area of medical research is studied by gender-based medicine.

During early foetal development, embryos of both sexes appear gender-neutral; the release of hormones is what changes physical appearance male or female. As in cases without two sexes, such as species that reproduce asexually, the gender-neutral appearance is closer to female than to male.

Understanding the Culture and Gender Roles

In many prehistoric cultures, women assumed a particular cultural role. In hunter-gatherer societies, women were generally the gatherers of plant foods, small animal foods, fish, and learned to use dairy products, while men hunted meat from large animals. These tasks were often given to the women because they were not only seen as safe, but also as easy. Men had a hard time relying on women for food. Because the hunger and survival of the society trumped anything else, men decided that women could not be trusted with feeding an entire society. Other anthropologists however have suggested that women only began to follow this behaviour after permanent settlement had been made, thus making these gender roles a result of civilisation rather than evolution. In more recent history, the gender roles of women have changed greatly. Traditionally, middle-class women were typically involved in domestic tasks emphasising child care. For poorer women, especially working class women, although this often remained an ideal, economic necessity compelled them to seek employment outside the home. The occupations that were available to them were, however, lower in pay than those available to men. As changes in the labour market for women came about, availability of employment changed from only "dirty", long houred factory jobs to "cleaner", more respectable office jobs where more education was demanded, women's participation in the U.S. labour force rose from 6 per cent in 1900 to 23 per cent in 1923. These shifts in the labour force led to changes in the attitudes of women at work, allowing for the revolution which resulted in women becoming career and education oriented. Movements advocate equality of opportunity for both sexes and equal rights irrespective of gender. Through a combination of economic changes and the efforts of the feminist movement, in recent decades women in most societies now have access to careers beyond the traditional homemaker. Although a greater number of women are seeking higher education, salaries often continue to be less than those of men. In the United States women who are aged 30 to 44 years and hold a university degree make only 62 per cent of what similarly qualified men do, a lower rate than in all but three of the 19 countries for which numbers are available. The nations with greater inequity in pay are Germany, New Zealand and Switzerland.

Understanding Contemporary Women Education

The educational gender gap in Organisation for Economic Cooperation and Development (OECD) countries has been reduced over the last 30 years. Younger women today are far more likely to have completed a tertiary qualification: in 19 of the 30 OECD countries, more than twice as many women aged 25 to 34 have completed tertiary education than have women aged 55 to 64 years. In 21 of 27 OECD countries with comparable data, the number of women graduating from university-level programmes is equal to or exceeds that of men. Fifteen-year-old girls tend to show much higher expectations for their careers than boys of the same age.While women account for more than half of university graduates in several OECD countries, they receive only 30 per cent of tertiary degrees granted in science and engineering fields, and women account for only 25 per cent to 35 per cent of researchers in most OECD countries.

Reflections on Women's History

Women's history is the study of the role that women have played in history, together with the methods needed to study women. It includes the study of the history of the growth (and decline) of women's rights throughout recorded history, the examination of individual women of historical significance, and the effect that historical events have had on women. Inherent in the study of women's history is the belief that more traditional recordings of history have minimized or ignored the contributions of women and the effect that historical events had on women as a whole; in this respect, woman's history is often a form of historical revisionism, seeking to challenge or expand the traditional historical consensus. The main centres of scholarship have been the U.S. and Britain, where second-wave feminist historians, influenced by the new approaches promoted by social history, led the way. As activists in women's liberation, discussing and analysing the oppression and inequalities they experienced as women, they felt it imperative to find out about the lives of their foremothers—and found very little scholarship in print. History was written mainly by men and about men's activities in the public sphere—war, politics, diplomacy and administration. Women are usually excluded and, when mentioned, are usually portrayed in sex-stereotypical roles, such as wives, mothers, daughters and mistresses. History is value-laden in regard to what is considered historically 'worthy'.

Western Europe

Britain

In the 21st century women still don't have the same rights as men, although some changes came about in the 19th and 20th centuries, for example women cannot yet fight in direct combat units and although the right to equal pay is enshrined in law, in reality women earn less than men even when doing the same job. Women ran the household, bore the children, were nurses, mothers, wives, neighbours, friends and teachers, but very little of their activities were formally recorded. During periods of war women were drafted in to undertake work that had been traditionally restricted to men. Following the wars they invariably lost their jobs in industry and had to return to domestic and service roles during the late 19th century and early 20th century, Scottish women's history did not really develop as a field until the 1980s, with most work on women before 1700 appearing in the last two decades. Several recent studies have taken a biographical approach, but other work has drawn on the insights from research elsewhere to examine such issues as work, family, religion, crime, and images of women. Scholars are also uncovering women's voices in their letters, memoirs, poetry, and court records. Because of the late development of the field, much recent work has been recuperative, but increasingly the insights of gender history both in other countries and in Scottish history after 1700 are being used to frame the questions that are asked. Future work should contribute both to a reinterpretation of the current narratives of Scottish history and also to a deepening of the complexity of the history of women in late medieval and early modern Britain and Europe.

France

French historians have taken a unique approach with a great deal of scholarship in women's and gender history despite the lack of women's and gender study programmes or departments at the university level. The high level of research and publication in women's and gender history is due to the high interest within French society. This structural discrimination against the study of gender history in France is changing due to international studies increasing with the formation of the European Union and more F ench scholars seeking appointments outside Europe. In the Ancient Régime in

France very few women held any formal power—some queens did, as did the heads of Catholic Convents. In the Enlightenment the writings of philosopher Jean Jacques Rousseau gave political programme for reform of the ancient régime, founded on a reform of domestic mores. Rousseau's conception of the relations between private and public spheres is more unified than that found in modern sociology. Rousseau argued that the domestic role of women is a structural precondition for a "modern" society. Salic law prohibited women from rule; however, the laws for the case of a regency, when the king was too young to govern by himself, brought the queen into the centre of power. The queen could assure the passage of power from one king to another—from her late husband to her young son—while simultaneously assuring the continuity of the dynasty. Educational aspirations were on the rise and were becoming increasingly institutionalised in order to supply the church and state with the functionaries to serve as their future administrators. Girls were schooled too, but not to assume political responsibility. Girls were ineligible for leadership positions and were generally considered to have an inferior intellect to their brothers. France had many small local schools where working-class children - both boys and girls - learned to read, the better "to know, love, and serve God." The sons and daughters of the noble and bourgeois elites, however, were given quite distinct educations: boys were sent to upper school, perhaps a university, while their sisters - if they were lucky enough to leave the house - would be sent to board at a convent with a vague curriculum. The Enlightenment challenged this model, but no real alternative presented itself for female education. Only through education at home were knowledgeable women formed, usually to the sole end of dazzling their salons.

Germany

Historians have paid special attention to the efforts by Nazi Germany to reverse the gains women made before 1933, especially in the relatively liberal Weimar Republic. It appears the role of women in Nazi Germany changed according to circumstances. Theoretically the Nazis believed that women must be subservient to men, avoid careers, devote themselves to childbearing and child-rearing, and be a helpmate of the traditional dominant father in the traditional family. However, before 1933, women played important roles in the Nazi organisation and were allowed some autonomy to mobilise other women. After Hitler came to power in 1933, the activist women were replaced by bureaucratic women who emphasised feminine virtues, marriage, and childbirth. As Germany prepared for war, large numbers were incorporated into the public sector and with the need for full mobilisation of factories by 1943, all women were required to register with the employment office. Hundreds of thousands of women served in the military as nurses, and support personnel, and another hundred thousand served in the Luftwaffe helping to operate the anti-aircraft systems. Women's wages remained unequal and women were denied positions of leadership or control. More than two million women were murdered in the Holocaust. The Nazi ideology viewed women generally as agents of fertility. Accordingly, it identified the Jewish woman as an element that must be exterminated in order to thwart the rise of future generations. For these reasons, the Nazis treated women as prime targets for annihilation in the Holocaust.

Eastern Asia

Interest in the study of women's history in Eastern Europe has been delayed. Representative is Hungary, where the historiography has been explored by Petö and Szapor (2007). Academia resisted incorporating this specialised field of history, primarily because of the political atmosphere and a lack of institutional support. Before 1945, historiography dealt chiefly with nationalist themes that supported the antidemocratic political agenda of the state. After 1945, academia reflected a Soviet model. Instead of providing an atmosphere in which women could be the subjects of history, this era ignored the role of the women's rights movement in the early 20th century. The collapse of Communism in 1989 was followed by a decade of promising developments in which biographies of prominent Hungarian women were published and important moments of women's political and cultural history were the subjects of research. However, the quality of this scholarship was uneven and failed to take advantage of the methodological advances in research in the West. In addition, institutional resistance continued, as evidenced by the lack of undergraduate or graduate programmes dedicated to women's and gender history at Hungarian universities.

Japan

Japanese women's history was marginal to historical scholarship until the late 20th century. The subject hardly existed before 1945 and even after that date many academic historians were reluctant to accept women's history as a part of Japanese history. However, the social and political climate of the 1980s in particular, favourable in many ways to women, gave opportunities for Japanese women's historiography to promote itself and also brought the subject fuller academic recognition. Exciting and innovative research on Japanese women's history began in the 1980s. Much of this has been conducted not only by academic women's historians, but also by freelance writers, journalists, and amateur historians; that is, by people who have been less saddled with traditional historical methods and expectations. The study of Japanese women's history has now reached the point where the subject no longer requires justification.

China

Much of the published work deals with women as visible participants in revolution, revolution and employment as women's liberation, Confucianism and the family as sources of women's oppression. While rural marriage rituals, such as bride price and dowry, have remained the same in form their function has changed, reflecting the nuclearisation of family and the growth in women's agency in the marriage transaction. (Gail Hershatter, *Women in China's Long Twentieth Century* (2007)). In recent scholarship on China, the concept of gender has yielded a bounty of new knowledge in English and Chinese-language writings. Mann (2009) explores how Chinese biographers have depicted women over two millennia (221 BCE to 1911), especially during the Han dynasty. Zhang Xuecheng, Sima Qian, and Zhang Huiyan and other writers often portrayed domestic scenes featuring women of the governing class, and they appear in death scenes in the narratives and in the role of martyrs.

Tibet

The historiography of women in the history of Tibet confronts the suppression of women's histories in the social narratives of an exiled community. McGranahan (2010) examines the role of women in the 20th century, especially during the Chinese invasion and occupation of Tibet. She studies women in the Tibetan resistance army, menstrual blood as a contaminating agent, and the subordination of women in a Buddhist society.

United States

The serious studies of women written by amateur women scholars were ignored by the male-dominated history profession until the 1960s, when the first breakthroughs came. The field of women's history exploded dramatically after 1970, along with the growth of the new social history and the acceptance of women into graduate programmes in history departments. An important development is to integrate women into the history of race and slavery. A pioneer effort was Deborah Gray White's 'Are'nt I a Woman? Female Slaves in the Plantation South (1985), which helped to open up analysis of race, slavery, abolitionism and feminism, as well as resistance, power, and activism, and themes of violence, sexualities, and the body. A major trend in recent years has been to emphasise a global perspective.

Women's Rights and Gender Equality

Women's rights refers to the social and human rights of women. In the United States, the abolition movements sparked an increased wave of attention on the status of women, but the history of feminism reaches far back before the 18th century. The advent of the reformist age during the 19th century meant that those invisible minorities or marginalised majorities were to find a catalyst and a microcosm in such new tendencies of reform. The earliest works on the so-called "woman question" criticised the restrictive role of women, without necessarily claiming that women were disadvantaged or that men were to blame. In Britain, the Feminism movement began in the 19th century and continues in the present day. In the early 20th century, Simone de Beauvouir wrote a detailed analysis of women's oppression. In the late 1960s and early 1970s, feminist movements, such as the one in the United States substantially changed the condition of women in the Western world. The trigger for the revolution was the development of the birth control pill in 1960, which gave women access to easy and reliable contraception.

Employment

The 1870 US Census was the first to count "Females engaged in each and every occupation" and provides an intriguing snapshot of women's history. It reveals that, contrary to popular belief, not all American women of the Victorian period were either idle in their middle class homes or working in sweatshops. Women were 15 per cent of the total work force (1.8 million out of 12.5). They made up one-third of factory "operatives," to be sure, but teaching and the more gentle occupations of dressmaking, millinery, and tailoring played a larger role. Two-thirds of teachers were women. And they could be found in such unexpected places as iron and steel works (495), mines (46), sawmills (35), oil wells and refineries (40), gas works (4), and charcoal kilns (5), and held such surprising jobs as ship rigger (16), teamster (196), turpentine labourer (185), brass founder/worker (102), shingle and lathe maker (84), stock-herder (45), gun and locksmith (33), hunter and trapper (2). There were five lawyers, 24 dentists, and 2000 doctors.

Sex and Reproduction

In the history of sex, the social construction of sexual behaviour - its taboos, regulation and social and political impact - has had a profound effect on women in the world since prehistoric times. The history of abortion dates back to ancient times and has impacted men and women in a variety of ways in different times and places. Historically, it is unclear how often the ethics of abortion (induced abortion) was discussed. In the later half of the 20th century some nations began to legalise abortion. This controversial subject has sparked heated debate and in some cases even violence. Women have been exposed to various tortuous sexual conditions and have been discriminated against in various fashions in history. An example are the comfort women, women who were forced to work as prostitutes in military brothels in Japanese-occupied countries during World War II.

Clothing

The social aspects of clothing have revolved around traditions regarding certain items of clothing intrinsically suited different gender roles. In particular, the wearing of skirts and trousers has given rise to common phrases expressing implied restrictions in use and disapproval of offending behaviour. For example, ancient Greeks often considered the wearing of trousers by Persian men as a sign of an effeminate attitude. Women's clothing in Victorian fashion was used as a means of control and admiration. Reactions to the elabourate confections of French fashion led to various calls for reform on the grounds of both beauty (Artistic and Aesthetic dress) and health (dress reform; especially for undergarments and lingerie). Although trousers for women did not become fashionable until the later 20th century, women began wearing men's trousers (suitably altered) for outdoor work a hundred years earlier. In the 1960s, André Courrèges introduced long trousers for women as a fashion item, leading to the era of the pantsuit and designer jeans and the gradual eroding of the prohibitions against girls and women wearing trousers in schools, the workplace, and fine restaurants. Corsets also have long been used for fashion, and body modification, such as waistline reduction. There were, and are, many different styles and types of corsets, varying depending on the intended use, corset maker's style, and the fashions of the era.

Status of Women

The status of women in the Victoria Era is often seen as an illustration of the striking discrepancy between the nation's power and richness and what many, then and now, consider its appalling social conditions. Victorian morality was full of many contradictions. A plethora of social movements concerned with improving public morals co-existed with a class system that permitted harsh living conditions for many, such as women. There is an apparent contradiction between the widespread cultivation of an outward appearance of dignity and restraint and the prevalence of social phenomena that included prostitution. In the Victorian era, the bathing machine was developed. It was a device that flourished in the 19th century to allow people to wade in the ocean at beaches without violating Victorian notions of modesty. The bathing machine was part of sea-bathing etiquette that was more rigorously enforced upon women than men.

Understanding Culture in a Broader Perspective

Culture is a term that has many different inter-related meanings. For example, in 1952, Alfred Kroeber and Clyde Kluckhohn compiled a list of 164 definitions of "culture" in *Culture: A Critical Review of Concepts and*

Definitions. However, the word "culture" is most commonly used in three basic senses:

- Excellence of taste in the fine arts and humanities, also known as high culture.
- An integrated pattern of human knowledge, belief, and behaviour that depends upon the capacity for symbolic thought and social learning.
- The set of shared attitudes, values, goals, and practices that characterises an institution, organisation, or group.

When the concept first emerged in eighteenth- and nineteenth- century Europe, it connoted a process of cultivation or improvement, as in agriculture or horticulture. In the nineteenth century, it came to refer first to the betterment or refinement of the individual, especially through education, and then to the fulfillment of national aspirations or ideals. In the mid-nineteenth century, some scientists used the term "culture" to refer to a universal human capacity. For the German nonpositivist sociologist Georg Simmel, culture referred to "the cultivation of individuals through the agency of external forms which have been objectified in the course of history". In the twentieth century, "culture" emerged as a concept central to anthropology, encompassing all human phenomena that are not purely results of human genetics. Specifically, the term "culture" in American anthropology had two meanings: (1) the evolved human capacity to classify and represent experiences with symbols, and to act imaginatively and creatively; and (2) the distinct ways that people living in different parts of the world classified and represented their experiences, and acted creatively. Following World War II, the term became important, albeit with different meanings, in other disciplines such as cultural studies, organisational psychology, the sociology of culture and management studies.

The etymology of the modern term "culture" has a classical origin. In English, the word "culture" is based on a term used by Cicero, in his *Tusculan Disputations*, wrote of a cultivation of the soul or *"cultura animi"*, thereby using an agricultural metaphor to describe the development of a philosophical soul, which was understood teleologically as the one natural highest possible ideal for human development. Samuel Pufendorf took over this metaphor in a modern context, meaning something similar, but no longer assuming that philosophy is man's natural perfection. His use, and that of many writers after him "refers to all the ways in which human beings overcome their original barbarism, and through artifice, become fully human".

As described by Velkley.

The term "culture," which originally meant the cultivation of the soul or mind, acquires most of its later modern meanings in the writings of the eighteenth-century German thinkers, who on various levels were developing on Rousseau's criticism of modern liberalism and Enlightenment. Thus, a contrast between "culture" and "civilisation" is usually implied in these authors, even when not expressed as such. Two primary meanings of culture emerge from this period: culture as the folk-spirit having a unique identity, and culture as cultivation of inwardness or free individuality. The first meaning is predominant in our current use of the term "culture," although the second still plays a large role in what we think culture should achieve, namely the full "expression" of the unique "authentic" self.

Understanding the Early Modern Discourses

German Romanticism

The German philosopher Immanuel Kant (1724–1804) formulated an individualist definition of "enlightenment" similar to the concept of *bildung*: "Enlightenment is man's emergence from his self-incurred immaturity." He argued that this immaturity comes not from a lack of understanding, but from a lack of courage to think independently. Against this intellectual cowardice, Kant urged: *Sapere aude*, "Dare to be wise!" In reaction to Kant, German scholars such as Johann Gottfried Herder (1744–1803) argued that human creativity, which necessarily takes unpredictable and highly diverse forms, is as important as human rationality. Moreover, Herder proposed a collective form of *bildung*: "For Herder, Bildung was the totality of experiences that provide a coherent identity, and sense of common destiny, to a people." In 1795, the great linguist and philosopher Wilhelm von Humboldt (1767–1835) called for an anthropology that would synthesize Kant's and Herder's interests. During the Romantic era, scholars in Germany, especially those concerned with nationalist movements—such as the nationalist struggle to create a "Germany" out of diverse principalities, and the nationalist struggles by ethnic minorities against the Austro-Hungarian Empire—developed a more inclusive notion of culture as "worldview." According to this school of thought, each ethnic group has a distinct worldview that is incommensurable with the worldviews of other groups. Although more inclusive than earlier views, this approach to culture still allowed for distinctions between "civilised" and "primitive" or "tribal" cultures. In 1860, Adolf Bastian (1826–1905) argued for "the psychic unity of mankind". He proposed that a scientific comparison of all human societies would reveal that distinct worldviews consisted of the same basic elements. According to Bastian, all human societies share a set of "elementary ideas" (*Elementargedanken*); different cultures, or different "folk ideas" (*Völkergedanken*), are local modifications of the elementary ideas. This view paved the way for the modern understanding of culture. Franz Boas (1858–1942) was trained in this tradition, and he brought it with him when he left Germany for the United States.

English Romanticism

In the nineteenth century, humanists such as English poet and essayist Matthew Arnold (1822–1888) used the word "culture" to refer to an ideal of individual human refinement, of "the best that has been thought and said in the world." This concept of culture is comparable to the German concept of *bildung*: "... culture being a pursuit of our total perfection by means of getting to know, on all the matters which most concern us, the best which has been thought and said in the world." In practice, culture referred to an élite ideal and was associated with such activities as art, classical music, and haute cuisine. As these forms were associated with urban life, "culture" was identified with "civilisation" (from lat. *civitas*, city). Another facet of the Romantic movement was an interest in folklore, which led to identifying a "culture" among non-elites. This distinction is often characterized as that between "high culture", namely that of the ruling social group, and "low culture." In other words, the idea of "culture" that developed in Europe during the 18th and early 19th centuries reflected inequalities within European societies. Matthew Arnold contrasted "culture" with "anarchy;" other Europeans, following philosophers Thomas Hobbes and Jean-Jacques Rousseau, contrasted "culture" with "the state of nature". According to Hobbes and Rousseau, the Native Americans who were being conquered by Europeans from the 16th centuries on were living in a state of nature; this opposition was expressed through the contrast between "civilised" and "uncivilised." According to this way of thinking, one could classify some countries and nations as more civilised than others and some people as more cultured than others. This contrast led to Herbert Spencer's theory of Social Darwinism and Lewis Henry Morgan's theory of cultural evolution. Just as some critics have argued that the distinction between high and low cultures is really an expression of the conflict between European elites and non-elites, some critics have argued that the distinction between civilised and uncivilised people is really an expression of the conflict between European colonial powers and their colonial subjects. Other 19th century critics, following Rousseau, have accepted this differentiation between higher and lower culture, but have seen the refinement and sophistication of high culture as corrupting and unnatural developments that obscure and distort people's essential nature. These critics considered folk music (as produced by working-class people) to honestly express a natural way of life, while classical music seemed superficial and decadent. Equally, this view often portrayed indigenous peoples as "noble savages" living authentic and unblemished lives, uncomplicated and uncorrupted by the highly stratified capitalist systems of the West. In 1870, Edward Tylor (1832–1917) applied these ideas of higher versus lower culture to propose a theory of the evolution of religion. According to this theory, religion evolves from more polytheistic to more monotheistic forms. In the process, he redefined culture as a diverse set of activities characteristic of all human societies. This view paved the way for the modern understanding of culture.

Understanding the 20th Century Discourses

American anthropology

Although anthropologists worldwide refer to Tylor's definition of culture, in the 20th century "culture" emerged as the central and unifying concept of American anthropology, where it most commonly refers to the universal human capacity to classify and encode their experiences symbolically, and communicate symbolically encoded experiences socially. American anthropology is organised into four fields, each of which plays an important role in research on culture: biological anthropology, linguistics, cultural anthropology and archaeology. Research in these fields have influenced anthropologists working in other countries to different degrees.

Understanding Biological Anthropology: The Evolution of Culture

Discussion concern culture among biological anthropologists centres around two debates. First, is culture uniquely human or shared by other species (most notably, other primates)? This is an important question, as the theory of evolution holds that humans are descended from (now extinct) non-human primates. Second, how did culture evolve among human beings? Gerald Weiss noted that although Tylor's classic definition of culture was restricted to humans, many anthropologists take this for granted and thus elide that important qualification from later definitions, merely equating culture with any learned behaviour. This slippage is a problem because during the formative years of modern primatology, some primatologists were trained in anthropology (and understood that culture refers to learned behaviour among humans), and others were not. Notable non-anthropologists, like Robert Yerkes and Jane Goodall thus argued that since chimpanzees have learned behaviours, they have culture. Today, anthropological primatologists are divided, several arguing that non-human primates have culture, others arguing that they do not. This scientific debate is complicated by ethical concerns. The subjects of primatology are non-human primates, and whatever culture these primates have is threatened by human activity. After reviewing the research on primate culture, W.C. McGrew concluded, "[a] discipline requires subjects, and most species of nonhuman primates are endangered by their human cousins. Ultimately, whatever its merit, cultural primatology must be committed to cultural survival [i.e. to the survival of primate cultures]." McGrew suggests a definition of culture that he finds scientifically useful for studying primate culture. He points out that scientists do not have access to the subjective thoughts or knowledge of non-human primates. Thus, if culture is defined in terms of knowledge, then scientists are severely limited in their attempts to study primate culture. Instead of defining culture as a kind of knowledge, McGrew suggests that we view culture as a process. He lists six steps in the process:

1. A new pattern of behaviour is invented, or an existing one is modified.
2. The innovator transmits this pattern to another.
3. The form of the pattern is consistent within and across performers, perhaps even in terms of recognisable stylistic features.
4. The one who acquires the pattern retains the ability to perform it long after having acquired it.
5. The pattern spreads across social units in a population. These social units may be families, clans, troops, or bands.
6. The pattern endures across generations.

McGrew admits that all six criteria may be strict, given the difficulties in observing primate behaviour in the wild. But he also insists on the need to be as inclusive as possible, on the need for a definition of culture that "casts the net widely":

> Culture is considered to be group-specific behaviour that is acquired, at least in part, from social influences. Here, group is considered to be the species-typical unit, whether it be a troop,.lineage, subgroup, or so on. *Prima facie* evidence of culture comes from within species but across-group variation in behaviour, as when a pattern is persistent in one community of chimpanzees but is absent from another, or when different communities perform different versions of the same pattern. The suggestion of culture in action is stronger when the difference across the groups cannot be explained solely by ecological factors.

As Charles Frederick Voegelin pointed out, if "culture" is reduced to "learned behaviour," then all animals have culture. Certainly all specialists agree that all primate species evidence common cognitive skills: knowledge of object-permanence, cognitive mapping, the ability to categorise objects, and creative problem solving. Moreover, all primate species show evidence of shared social skills: they recognise members of their social group; they form direct relationships based on degrees of kinship and rank; they recognise third-party social relationships; they predict future behaviour; and they cooperate in problem-solving.

Nevertheless, the term "culture" applies to non-human animals only if we define culture as any or all learned behaviour. Within mainstream physical anthropology, scholars tend to think that a more restrictive definition is necessary. These researchers are concerned with how human beings evolved to be different from other species. A more precise definition of culture, which excludes non-human social behaviour, would allow physical anthropologists to study how humans evolved their unique capacity for "culture".

Chimpanzees (*Pan troglodytes* and *Pan paniscus*) are humans' (*Homo sapiens*) closest living relative; both are descended from a common ancestor which lived around five or six million years ago. This is the same amount of time it took for horses and zebras, lions and tigers to diverge from their respective common ancestors. The evolution of modern humans is rapid: *Australopithicenes* evolved four million years ago and modern humans in past several hundred thousand years. During this time humanity evolved three distinctive features:

(a) the creation and use of conventional symbols, including linguistic symbols and their derivatives, such as written language and mathematical symbols and notations;
(b) the creation and use of complex tools and other instrumental technologies; and
(c) the creation and participation in complex social organisation and institutions.

According to developmental psychologist Michael Tomasello, "where these complex and species-unique behavioural practices, and the cognitive skills that underlie them, came from" is a fundamental anthropological question. Given that contemporary humans and chimpanzees are far more different than horses and zebras, or rats and mice, and that the evolution of this great difference occurred in such a short period of time, "our search must be for some small difference that made a big difference – some adaptation, or small set of adaptations, that changed the process of primate cognitive evolution in fundamental ways." According to Tomasello, the answer to this question must form the basis of a scientific definition of "human culture."

In a recent review of the major research on human and primate tool-use, communication, and learning strategies, Tomasello argues that the key human advances over primates (language, complex technologies, complex social organisation) are all the results of humans pooling cognitive resources. This is called "the ratchet effect:" innovations spread and are shared by a group, and mastered "by youngsters, which enables them to remain in their new and improved form within the group until something better comes along." The key point is that children are born good at a particular kind of social learning; this creates a favored environment for social innovations, making them more likely to be maintained and transmitted to new generations than individual innovations. For Tomasello, human social learning—the kind of learning that distinguishes humans from other primates played a decisive role in human evolution—is based on two elements: first, what he calls "imitative learning," (as opposed to "emulative learning" characteristic of other primates) and second, the fact that humans represent their experiences symbolically (rather than iconically, as is characteristic of other primates). Together, these elements enable humans to be both inventive, and to preserve useful inventions. It is this combination that produces the ratchet effect.

The kind of learning found among other primates is "emulation learning," which "focuses on the environmental events involved – results or changes of state in the environment that the other produced – rather than on the actions that produced those results." Tomasello emphasises that emulation learning is a highly adaptive strategy for apes because it focuses on the effects of an act. In labouratory experiments, chimpanzees were shown two different ways for using a rake-like tool to obtain an out-of-reach-object. Both methods were effective, but one was more efficient than the other. Chimpanzees consistently emulated the more efficient method.

Examples of emulation learning are well documented among primates. Notable examples include Japanese macaque potato washing, Chimpanzee tool use, and Chimpanzee gestural communication. In 1953, an 18-month-old female macaque monkey was observed taking sandy pieces of sweet potato (given to the monkeys by observers) to a stream (and later, to the ocean) to wash off the sand. After three months, the same behaviour was observed in her mother and two playmates, and then the playmates' mothers. Over the next two years seven other young macaques were observed washing their potatoes, and by the end of the third year 40 per cent of the troop had adopted the practice. Although this story is popularly represented as a straightforward example of human-like learning, evidence suggests that it is not. Many monkeys naturally brush sand off from food; this behaviour had been observed in the macaque troop prior to the first observed washing. Moreover, potato washing was observed in four other separate macaque troops, suggesting that at least four other individual monkeys had learned to wash off sand on their own. Other monkey species in captivity quickly learn to wash off their food. Finally, the spread of learning among the Japanese macaques was fairly slow, and the rate at which new members of the troop learned did not keep pace with the growth of the troop. If the form of learning were imitation, the rate of learning should have been exponential. It is more likely that the monkeys' washing behaviour is based on the common behaviour of cleaning of food, and that monkeys that spent time by the water independently learned to wash, rather than wipe their food. This explains both why those monkeys that kept company with the original washer, and who thus spent a good deal of time by the water, also figured out how to wash their potatoes. It also explains why the rate at which this behaviour spread was slow.

Chimpanzees exhibit a variety of population-specific tool use: termite-fishing, ant-fishing, ant-dipping, nut-cracking, and leaf-sponging. Gombe chimpanzees fish for termites using small, thin sticks, but chimpanzees in Western Africa use large sticks to break holes in mounds and use their hands to scoop up termites. Some of this variation may be the result of "environmental shaping" (there is more rainfall in western Africa, softening termite mounds and making them easier to break apart, than in the Gombe reserve in eastern Africa. Nevertheless it is clear that chimpanzees are good at emulation learning. Chimpanzee children independently know how to roll over logs, and know how to eat insects. When children see their mothers rolling over logs to eat the insects beneath, they quickly learn to do the same. In other words, this form of learning builds on activities the children already know.

The kind of learning characteristic of human children is "Imitative learning," which "means reproducing an instrumental act understood intentionally." Human infants begin to display some evidence of this form of learning between the ages of nine and twelve months, when infants fix their attention not only on an object, but on the gaze of an adult which enables them to use adults as points of reference and thus "act on objects in the way adults are acting on them." This dynamic is well documented and has also been termed "joint engagement" or "joint attention." Essential to this dynamic is the infant's growing capacity to recognise others as "intentional agents:" people "with the power to control their spontaneous behaviour" and who "have goals and make active choices among behavioural means for attaining those goals."

The development of skills in joint attention by the end of a human child's first year of life provides the basis for the development of imitative learning in the second year. In one study 14-month old children imitated an adult's over-complex method of turning on a light, even when they could have used an easier and more natural motion to the same effect. In another study, 16-month old children interacted with adults who alternated between a complex series of motions that appeared intentional and a comparable set of motions that appeared accidental; they imitated only those motions that appeared intentional. Another study of 18-month old children revealed that children imitate actions that adults intend, yet in some way fail, to perform. Tomasello emphasises that this kind of imitative learning "relies fundamentally on infants' tendency to identify with adults, and on their ability to distinguish in the actions of others the underlying goal and the different means that might be used to achieve it." He calls this kind of imitative learning "cultural learning because the child is not just learning about things from other persons, she is also learning things through them — in the sense that she must know something of the adult's perspective on a situation to learn the active use of this same intentional act." He concludes that the key feature of cultural learning is that it occurs only when an individual "understands others as intentional agents, like the self, who have a perspective on the world that can be followed into, directed and shared."

Emulation learning and imitative learning are two different adaptations that can only be assessed in their larger environmental and evolutionary contexts. In one experiment, chimpanzees and two-year-old children were separately presented with a rake-like-tool and an out-of-reach object. Adult humans then demonstrated two different ways to use the tool, one more efficient, one less efficient. Chimpanzees used the same efficient method following both demonstrations. Most of the human children, however, imitated whichever method the adult was demonstrating. Were chimps and humans to be compared on the basis of these results, one might think that Chimpanzees are more intelligent. From an evolutionary perspective they are equally intelligent, but with different kinds of intelligence adapted to different environments. Chimpanzee learning strategies are well-suited to a stable physical environment that requires little social cooperation (compared to humans). Human learning strategies are well-suited to a complex social environment in which understanding the intentions of others may be more important than success at a specific task. Tomasello argues that this strategy has made possible the "ratchet effect" that enabled humans to evolve complex social systems that have enabled humans to adapt to virtually every physical environment on the surface of the earth. Tomasello further argues that cultural learning is essential for language-acquisition. Most children in any society, and all children in some, do not learn all words through the direct efforts of adults. "In general, for the vast majority of words in their language, children must find a way to learn in the ongoing flow of social interaction, sometimes from speech not even addressed to them." This finding has been confirmed by a variety of experiments in which children learned words even when the referent was not present, multiple referents were possible, and the adult was not directly trying to teach the word to the child. Tomasello concludes that "a linguistic symbol is nothing other than a marker for an intersubjectively shared understanding of a situation." Tomasello's 1999 review of the research contrasting human and non-human primate learning strategies confirms biological anthropologist Ralph Holloway's 1969 argument that a specific kind of sociality linked to symbolic cognition were the keys to human evolution, and constitute the nature of culture. According to Holloway, the key issue in the evolution of *H. sapiens*, and the key to understanding "culture," "is how man organizes his experience." Culture is "the imposition of arbitrary form upon the environment." This fact, Holloway argued, is primary to and explains what is distinctive about human learning strategies, tool-use, and language. Human tool-making and language express "similar, if not identical, cognitive processes" and provide important evidence for how humankind evolved.

In other words, whereas McGrew argues that anthropologists must focus on behaviours like communication and tool-use because they have no access to the mind. Holloway argues that human language and tool-use, including the earliest stone tools in the fossil record, are highly suggestive of cognitive differences between humans and non-humans, and that such cognitive differences in turn explain human evolution. For Holloway, the question is not whether other primates communicate, learn or make tools, but the *way* they do these things. "Washing potatoes in the ocean … stripping branches of leaves to get termites," and other examples of primate tool-use and learning "are iconic, and there is no feedback from the environment to the animal ." Human tools, however, express an independence from natural form that manifests symbolic thinking. "In the preparation of the stick for termite-eating, the relation between product and raw material is iconic. In the making of a stone tool, in contrast, there is no necessary relation between the form of the final product and the original material." In Holloway's view, our non-human ancestors, like those of modern chimpanzees and other primates, shared motor and sensory skills, curiosity, memory, and intelligence, with perhaps differences in degree. "It is when these are integrated with the unique attributes of arbitrary production (symbolisation) and imposition that cultural man appears."

> I have suggested above that whatever culture may be, it includes "the imposition of arbitrary forms upon the environment." This phrase has two components. One is a recognition that the relationship between the coding process and the phenomenon (be it a tool, social network, or abstract principle) is non-iconic. The other is an idea of man as a creature who can make delusional systems work—who imposes his fantasies, his non-iconic constructs (and constructions), upon the environment. The altered environment shapes his perceptions, and these are again forced back on the environment, are incorporated into the environment, and press for further adaptation.

This is comparable to the "ratcheting" aspect suggested by Tomasello and others that enabled human evolution to accelerate. Holloway concludes that the first instance of symbolic thought among humans provided a "kick-start" for brain development, tool complexity, social structure, and language to evolve through a constant dynamic of positive feedback. "This interaction between the propensity to structure the environment arbitrarily and the feedback from the environment to the organism is an emergent process, a process different in kind from anything that preceded it."

Linguists Charles Hockett and R. Ascher have identified thirteen design-features of language, some shared by other forms of animal communication. One feature that distinguishes human language is its tremendous productivity; in other words, competent speakers of a language are capable of producing an exponential number of original utterances. This productivity seems to be made possible by a few critical features unique to human language. One is "duality of patterning," meaning that human language consists of the articulation of several distinct processes, each with its own set of rules: combining phonemes to produce morphemes, combining morphemes to produce words, and combining words to produce sentences. This means that a person can master a relatively limited number of signals and sets of rules, to create infinite combinations. Another crucial element is that human language is symbolic: the sound of words (or their shape, when written) typically bear no relation to what they represent. In other words, their meaning is arbitrary. That words have meaning is a matter of convention. Since the meaning of words are arbitrary, any word may have several meanings, and any object may be referred to using a variety of words; the actual word used to describe a particular object depends on the context, the intention of the speaker, and the ability of the listener to judge these appropriately. As Tomasello notes,

> An individual language user looks at a tree and, before drawing the attention of her interlocutor to that tree, must decide, based on her assessment of the listener's current knowledge and expectations, whether to say "that tree over there," "it," "the oak," "that hundred-year-oak," "the tree," "the bagswing tree," "that thing in the front yard," "the ornament," "the embarrassment," or any of a number of other expressions. ... And these decisions are not made on the basis of the speaker's direct goal with respect to the object or activity involved, but rather that they are made on the basis of her goal with respect to the listener's interest and attention to that object or activity.

This is why symbolic cognition and communication and imitative learning go hand-in-hand.

Holloway argues that the stone-tools associated with genus *Homo* have the same features of human language:

> Returning to matter of syntax, rules, and concatenated activity mentioned above, almost any model which describes a language process can also be used to describe tool-making. This is hardly surprising. Both activities are concatenated, both have rigid rules about the serialization of unit activities (the grammar, syntax), both are hierarchical systems of activity (as is any motor activity), and both produce arbitrary configurations which thence become part of the environment, either temporarily or permanently.
>
> Productivity can be seen in the facts that basic types were probably used for multiple purposes, that tool industries tend to expand with time, and that a slight variation on a basic pattern may be made to meet some new functional requisite. Elements of a basic "vocabulary" of motor operations—flakes, detachment, rotation, preparation of striking platform, etc.—are used in different combinations to produce dissimilar tools, with different forms,

> and supposedly, different uses. . . . Taking each motor event alone, no one action is complete; each action depends on the prior one and requires a further one, and each is dependent on another act on the original plan. In other words, at each point of the action except the last, the piece is not "satisfactory" in structure. Each unit action is meaningless by itself in the sense of the use of the tool; it is meaningful only in the context of the whole completed set of actions culminating in the final product. This exactly parallels language.

As Tomasello has demonstrated, symbolic thought can operate only in a particular social environment:

> Arbitrary symbols enforce consensus to perceptions, which not only allows members to communicate about the same objects in terms of space and time (as in hunting) but it also makes it possible for social relationships to be standardized and manipulated through symbols. It means that idiosyncrasies are smoothed out and perceived within classes of behaviour. By enforcing perceptual invariance, symbols also enforce social behavioural constancy, and enforcing social behavioural constancy is a prerequisite to differential task-role sectors in a differentiated social group adapting not only to the outside environment but to its own membership.

Biological anthropologist Terrence Deacon, in a synthesis of over twenty years of research on human evolution, human neurology, and primatology, describes this "ratcheting effect" as a form of "Baldwinian Evolution." Named after psychologist James Baldwin, this describes a situation in which an animal's behaviour has evolutionary consequences when it changes the natural environment and thus the selective forces acting on the animal.

> Once some useful behaviour spreads within a population and becomes more important for subsistence, it will generate selection pressures on genetic traits that support its propagation ... Stone and symbolic tools, which were initially acquired with the aid of flexible ape-learning abilities, ultimately turned the tables on their users and forced them to adapt to a new niche opened by these technologies. Rather than being just useful tricks, these behavioural prostheses for obtaining food and organising social behaviours became indispensable elements in a new adaptive complex. The origin of "humanness" can be defined as that point in our evolution where these tools became the principle [*sic?*] source of selection on our bodies and brains. It is the diagnostic of *Homo symbolicus*.

According to Deacon, this occurred between 2 and 2.5 million years ago, when we have the first fossil evidence of stone tool use and the beginning of a trend in an increase in brain size. But it is the evolution of symbolic language which is the cause—and not the effect—of these trends. More specifically, Deacon is suggesting that *Australopithecines*, like contemporary apes, used tools; it is possible that over the millions of years of *Australopithecine* history, many troops developed symbolic communication systems. All that was necessary was that one of these groups so altered their environment that "it introduced selection for very different learning abilities than affected prior species." This troop or population kick-started the Baldwinian process (the "ratchet effect") that led to their evolution to genus *Homo*.

The question for Deacon is, what behavioural-environmental changes could have made the development of symbolic thinking adaptive? Here he emphasises the importance of distinguishing humans from all other species, not to privilege human intelligence but to problematize it. Given that the evolution of *H. sapiens* began with ancestors who did not yet have "culture," what led them to move away from cognitive, learning, communication, and tool-making strategies that were and continued to be adaptive for most other primates (and, some have suggested, most other species of animals)? Learning symbol systems is more time consuming than other forms of communication, so symbolic thought made possible a different communication strategy, but not a more efficient one than other primates. Nevertheless, it must have offered some selective advantage to *H. sapiens* to have evolved. Deacon starts by looking at two key determinants in evolutionary history: foraging behaviour, and patterns of sexual relations. As he observes competition for sexual access limits the possibilities for social cooperation in many species; yet, Deacon observes, there are three consistent patterns in human reproduction that distinguish them from other species:

1. Both males and females usually contribute effort towards the rearing of their offspring, though often to differing extents and in very different ways.
2. In all societies, the great majority of adult males and females are bound by long-term, exclusive sexual access rights and prohibitions to particular individuals of the opposite sex.
3. They maintain these exclusive sexual relations while living in modest to large-sized, multi-male, multi-female, cooperative social groups.

Moreover, there is one feature common to all known human foraging societies (all humans prior to ten or fifteen thousand years ago), and markedly different from other primates: "the use of meat. . . . The appearance of the first stone tools nearly 2.5 million years ago almost certainly correlates with a radical shift in foraging behaviour to gain access to meat." Deacon does not believe that symbolic thought was necessary for hunting or tool-making (although tool-making may be a reliable index of symbolic thought); rather, it was necessary for the success of distinctive social relations.

The key is that while men and women are equally effective foragers, mothers carrying dependent children are not effective hunters. They must thus depend on male hunters. This favors a system in which males have exclusive sexual access to females, and females can predict that their sexual partner will provide food for them and their children. In most mammalian species the result is a system of rank or sexual competition that results in either polygyny, or life-long pair-bonding between two individuals who live relatively independent of other adults of their species; in both cases male aggression plays an important role in maintaining sexual access to mate(s). What is unique about humans?

> Human reliance on resources that are relatively unavailable to females with infants selects not only for cooperation between a child's father and mother but also for the cooperation of other relatives and friends, including elderly individuals and juveniles, who can be relied upon for assistance. The special demands of acquiring meat and caring for infants in our own evolution together contribute to the underlying impetus for the third characteristic feature of human reproductive patterns: cooperative group living.

What is uniquely characteristic about human societies is what required symbolic cognition, which consequently leads to the evolution of culture: "cooperative, mixed-sex social groups, with significant male care and provisioning of offspring, and relatively stable patterns of reproductive exclusion." This combination is relatively rare in other species because it is "highly susceptible to disintegration." Language and culture provide the glue that holds it together.

Chimpanzees also, on occasion, hunt meat; in most cases, however, males consume the meat immediately, and only on occasion share with females who happen to be nearby. Among chimpanzees, hunting for meat increases when other sources of food become scarce, but under these conditions, sharing decreases. The first forms of symbolic thinking made stone-tools possible, which in turn made hunting for meat a more dependable source of food for our nonhuman ancestors while making possible forms of social communication that make sharing—between males and females, but also among males, decreasing sexual competition:

> So the socio-ecological problem posed by the transition to a meat-supplemented subsistence strategy is that it cannot be utilised without a social structure which guarantees unambiguous and exclusive mating and is sufficiently egalitarian to sustain cooperation via shared or parallel reproductive interests. This problem can be solved symbolically.

Symbols and symbolic thinking thus make possible a central feature of social relations in every human population: reciprocity. Evolutionary scientists have developed a model to explain reciprocal altruism among closely related individuals. Symbolic thought makes possible reciprocity between distantly related individuals.

Understanding the Archeological Approaches to Culture

In the 19th century archeology was often a supplement to history, and the goal of archeologists was to identify artifacts according to their typology and stratigraphy, thus marking their location in time and space. Franz Boas established that archeology be one of American anthropology's four fields, and debates among archeologists have often paralleled debates among cultural anthropologists. In the 1920s and 1930s, Australian-British archeologist V. Gordon Childe and American archeologist W.C. McKern independently began moving from asking about the date of an artifact, to asking about the people who produced it — when archeologists work alongside historians, historical materials generally help answer these questions, but when historical materials are unavailable, archeologists had to develop new methods. Childe and McKern focused on analysing the relationships among objects found together; their work established the foundation for a three-tiered model:

1. An individual artifact, which has surface, shape, and technological attributes (e.g. an arrowhead).
2. A sub-assemblage, consisting of artifacts that are found, and were likely used, together (e.g. an arrowhead, bow and knife).
3. An assemblage of sub-assemblages that together constitute the archeological site (e.g. the arrowhead, bow and knife; a pot and the remains of a hearth; a shelter).

Childe argued that a "constantly recurring assemblage of artifacts" to be an "archaeological culture." Childe and others viewed "each archeological culture ... the manifestation in material terms of a specific people."

In 1948 Walter Taylor systematized the methods and concepts that archeologists had developed and proposed a general model for the archeological contribution to knowledge of cultures. He began with the mainstream understanding of culture as the product of human cognitive activity, and the Boasian emphasis on the subjective meanings of objects as dependent on their cultural context. He defined culture as "a mental phenomenon, consisting of the contents of minds, not of material objects or observable behaviour." He then devised a three-tiered model linking cultural anthropology to archeology, which he called conjunctive archeology:

1. Culture, which is unobservable and nonmaterial.
2. Behaviours resulting from culture, which are observable and nonmaterial.

3. Objectifications, such as artifacts and architecture, which are the result of behaviour and material.

That is, material artifacts were the material residue of culture, but not culture itself. Taylor's point was that the archeological record could contribute to anthropological knowledge, but only if archeologists reconceived their work not just as digging up artifacts and recording their location in time and space, but as inferring from material remains the behaviours through which they were produced and used, and inferring from these behaviours the mental activities of people. Although many archeologists agreed that their research was integral to anthropology, Taylor's programme was never fully implemented. One reason was that his three-tier model of inferences required too much fieldwork and labouratory analysis to be practical. Moreover, his view that material remains were not themselves cultural, and in fact twice-removed from culture, in fact left archeology marginal to cultural anthropology.

In 1962 Leslie White's former student Lewis Binford proposed a new model for anthropological archeology, called "the New Archeology" or "Processual Archeology," based on White's definition of culture as "the extra-somatic means of adaptation for the human organism." This definition allowed Binford to establish archeology as a crucial field for the pursuit of the methodology of Julian Steward's cultural ecology:

> The comparative study of cultural systems with variable technologies in a similar environmental range or similar technologies in differing environments is a major methodology of what Steward (1955: 36–42) has called "cultural ecology," and certainly is a valuable means of increasing our understanding of cultural processes. Such a methodology is also useful in elucidating the structural relationships between major cultural sub-systems such as the social and ideological sub-systems.

In other words, Binford proposed an archeology that would be central to the dominant project of cultural anthropologists at the time (culture as non-genetic adaptations to the environment); the "new archeology" was the cultural anthropology (in the form of cultural ecology or ecological anthropology) of the past.

In the 1980s, there was a movement in the United Kingdom and Europe against the view of archeology as a field of anthropology, echoing Radcliffe-Brown's earlier rejection of cultural anthropology. During this same period, then-Cambridge archeologist Ian Hodder developed "post-processual archeology" as an alternative. Like Binford (and unlike Taylor) Hodder views artifacts not as objectifications of culture but as culture itself. Unlike Binford, however, Hodder does not view culture as an environmental adaptation. Instead, he "is committed to a fluid semiotic version of the traditional culture concept in which material items, artifacts, are full participants in the creation, deployment, alteration, and fading away of symbolic complexes." His 1982 book, Symbols in Action, evokes the symbolic anthropology of Geertz, Schneider, with their focus on the context dependent meanings of cultural things, as an alternative to White and Steward's materialist view of culture. In his 1991 textbook, Reading the Past: Current Approaches to Interpretation in Archaeology, Hodder argued that archeology is more closely aligned to history than to anthropology.

Understanding Relationship between Language and Culture

The connection between culture and language has been noted as far back as the classical period and probably long before. The ancient Greeks, for example, distinguished between civilised peoples and bárbaros "those who babble", i.e. those who speak unintelligible languages. The fact that different groups speak different, unintelligible languages is often considered more tangible evidence for cultural differences than other less obvious cultural traits. The German romanticists of the 19th century such as Herder, Wundt and Humbolt, often saw language not just as one cultural trait among many but rather as the direct expression of a people's national character, and as such as culture in a kind of condensed form. Herder, for example, suggests, "*Denn jedes Volk ist Volk; es hat seine National Bildung wie seine Sprache*" (Since every people is a People, it has its own national culture expressed through its own language). Franz Boas, founder of American anthropology, like his German forerunners, maintained that the shared language of a community is the most essential carrier of their common culture. Boas was the first anthropologist who considered it unimaginable to study the culture of a foreign people without also becoming acquainted with their language. For Boas, the fact that the intellectual culture of a people was largely constructed, shared and maintained through the use of language, meant that understanding the language of a cultural group was the key to understanding its culture. At the same time, though, Boas and his students were aware that culture and language are not directly dependent on one another. That is, groups with widely different cultures may share a common language, and speakers of completely unrelated languages may share the same fundamental cultural traits. Numerous other scholars have suggested that the form of language determines specific cultural traits. This is similar to the notion of Linguistic determinism, which states that the form of language determines individual thought. While Boas himself rejected a causal link between language and culture, some of his intellectual heirs entertained the idea that habitual patterns of speaking and thinking in a particular language may influence the culture of the linguistic group. Such belief is related to the theory of Linguistic relativity. Boas, like most modern anthropologists, however, was more inclined to relate the interconnectedness between language and culture to the fact that, as B.L. Whorf put it, "they have grown up together".

Indeed, the origin of language, understood as the human capacity of complex symbolic communication, and the origin of complex culture is often thought to stem from the same evolutionary process in early man. Evolutionary anthropologists suppose that language evolved as early humans began to live in large communities which required the use of complex communication to maintain social coherence. Language and culture then both emerged as a means of using symbols to construct social identity and maintain coherence within a social group too large to rely exclusively on pre-human ways of building community such as, for example, grooming. Since language and culture are both in essence symbolic systems, twentieth century cultural theorists have applied the methods of analysing language developed in the science of linguistics to also analyze culture. Particularly the structural theory of Ferdinand de Saussure, which describes symbolic systems as consisting of signs (a pairing of a particular form with a particular meaning), has come to be applied widely in the study of culture. But also post-structuralist theories, that nonetheless still rely on the parallel between language and culture as systems of symbolic communication, have been applied in the field of semiotics. The parallel between language and culture can then be understood as analog to the parallel between a linguistic sign, consisting, for example, of the sound [kau] and the meaning "cow", and a cultural sign, consisting, for example, of the cultural form of "wearing a crown" and the cultural meaning of "being king". In this way it can be argued that culture is itself a kind of language. Another parallel between cultural and linguistic systems is that they are both systems of practice, that is they are a set of special ways of doing things that is constructed and perpetuated through social interactions. Children, for example, acquire language in the same way as they acquire the basic cultural norms of the society they grow up in – through interaction with older members of their cultural group. However, languages, now understood as the particular set of speech norms of a particular community, are also a part of the larger culture of the community that speak them. Humans use language as a way of signalling identity with one cultural group and difference from others. Even among speakers of one language, several different ways of using the language exist, and each is used to signal affiliation with particular subgroups within a larger culture. In linguistics such different ways of using the same language are called "varieties". For example, the English language is spoken differently in the USA, the UK and Australia, and even within English-speaking countries there are hundreds of dialects of English that each signal a belonging to a particular region and/or subculture. For example, in the UK the cockney dialect signals its speakers' belonging to the group of lower class workers of east London.

Differences between varieties of the same language often consist in different pronunciations and vocabulary, but also sometimes of different grammatical systems and very often in using different styles (e.g. cockney Rhyming slang or Lawyers' jargon). Linguists and anthropologists, particularly sociolinguists, ethnolinguists and linguistic anthropologists have specialised in studying how ways of speaking vary between speech communities. A community's ways of speaking or signing are a part of the community's culture, just as other shared practices are. Language use is a way of establishing and displaying group identity. Ways of speaking function not only to facilitate communication, but also to identify the social position of the speaker. Linguists call different ways of speaking language varieties, a term that encompasses geographically or socioculturally defined dialects as well as the jargons or styles of subcultures. Linguistic anthropologists and sociologists of language define communicative style as the ways that language is used and understood within a particular culture.

The differences between languages does not consist only in differences in pronunciation, vocabulary or grammar, but also in different "cultures of speaking". Some cultures, for example have elabourate systems of "social deixis", systems of signalling social distance through linguistic means. In English, social deixis is shown mostly though distinguishing between addressing some people by first name and others by surname, but also in titles such as "Mrs.", "boy", "Doctor" or "Your Honour", but in other languages such systems may be highly complex and codified in the entire grammar and vocabulary of the language. In several languages of east Asia, for example Thai, Burmese and Javanese, different words are used according to whether a speaker is addressing someone of higher or lower rank than oneself in a ranking system with animals and children ranking the lowest and gods and members of royalty as the highest. Other languages may use different forms of address when speaking to speakers of the opposite gender or in-law relatives and many languages have special ways of speaking to infants and children. Among other groups, the culture of speaking may entail not speaking to particular people, for example, many indigenous cultures of Australia have a taboo against talking to one's in-law relatives, and in some cultures speech is not addressed directly to children. Some languages also require different ways of speaking for different social classes of speakers, and often such a system is based on gender differences, as in Japanese and Koasati.

Understanding the Role of Cultural Anthropology

The modern anthropological understanding of culture has its origins in the 19th century with German anthropologist Adolf Bastian's theory of the "psychic unity of mankind," which, influenced by Herder and von Humboldt, challenged the identification of "culture" with the way of life of European elites, and British anthropologist Edward Burnett Tylor's attempt to define culture as inclusively as possible. Tylor in 1874 described culture in the following way: "Culture or civilisation, taken in its wide ethnographic sense, is that complex whole which includes knowledge, belief, art, morals, law, custom, and any other capabilities and habits acquired by man as a member of society." Although Tylor was not aiming to propose a general theory of culture (he explained his understanding of culture in the course of a larger argument about the nature of religion), American anthropologists have generally presented their various definitions of culture as refinements of Tylor's. Franz Boas's student Alfred Kroeber (1876–1970) identified culture with the "superorganic," that is, a domain with ordering principles and laws that could not be explained by or reduced to biology. In 1973, Gerald Weiss reviewed various definitions of culture and debates as to their parsimony and power, and proposed as the most scientifically useful definition that "culture" be defined "as our generic term for all human nongenetic, or metabiological, phenomena" (italics in the original).

Franz Boas, founded modern American anthropology with the establishment of the first graduate programme in anthropology at Columbia University in 1896. At the time the dominant model of culture was that of cultural evolution, which posited that human societies progressed through stages of savagery to barbarism to civilisation; thus, societies that for example are based on horticulture and Iroquois kinship terminology are less evolved than societies based on agriculture and Eskimo kinship terminology. One of Boas's greatest accomplishments was to demonstrate convincingly that this model is fundamentally flawed, empirically, methodologically, and theoretically. Moreover, he felt that our knowledge of different cultures was so incomplete, and often based on unsystematic or unscientific research, that it was impossible to develop any scientifically valid general model of human cultures. Instead, he established the principle of cultural relativism and trained students to conduct rigorous participant observation field research in different societies. Boas understood the capacity for culture to involve symbolic thought and social learning, and considered the evolution of a capacity for culture to coincide with the evolution of other, biological, features defining genus Homo. Nevertheless, he argued that culture could not be reduced to biology or other expressions of symbolic thought, such as language. Boas and his students understood culture inclusively and resisted developing a general definition of culture. Indeed, they resisted identifying "culture" as a thing, instead using culture as an adjective rather than a noun. Boas argued that cultural "types" or "forms" are always in a state of flux. His student Alfred Kroeber argued that the "unlimited receptivity and assimilativeness of culture" made it practically impossible to think of cultures as discrete things.

Boas's students dominated cultural anthropology through World War II, and continued to have great influence through the 1960s. They were especially interested in two phenomena: the great variety of forms culture took around the world, and the many ways individuals were shaped by and acted creatively through their own cultures. This led his students to focus on the history of cultural traits: how they spread from one society to another, and how their meanings changed over time—and the life histories of members of other societies. Others, such as Ruth Benedict (1887–1948) and Margaret Mead (1901–1978), produced monographs or comparative studies analysing the forms of creativity possible to individuals within specific cultural configurations. Essential to their research was the concept of "context": culture provided a context that made the behaviour of individuals understandable; geography and history provided a context for understanding the differences between cultures. Thus, although Boasians were committed to the belief in the psychic unity of humankind and the universality of culture, their emphasis on local context and cultural diversity led them away from proposing cultural universals or universal theories of culture.

There is a tension in cultural anthropology between the claim that culture is a universal (the fact that all human societies have culture), and that it is also particular (culture takes a tremendous variety of forms around the world). Since Boas, two debates have dominated cultural anthropology. The first has to do with ways of modeling particular cultures. Specifically, anthropologists have argued as to whether "culture" can be thought of as a bounded and integrated thing, or as a quality of a diverse collection of things, the numbers and meanings of which are in constant flux. Boas's student Ruth Benedict suggested that in any given society cultural traits may be more or less "integrated," that is, constituting a pattern of action and thought that gives purpose to people's lives, and provides them with a basis from which to evaluate new actions and thoughts, although she implies that there are various degrees of integration; indeed, she observes that some cultures fail to integrate. Boas, however, argued that complete integration is rare and that a given culture only appears to be integrated because of observer bias. For Boas, the appearance of such patterns—a national culture, for example- was the effect of a particular point of view.

The first debate was effectively suspended in 1934 when Ruth Benedict published *Patterns of Culture*, which has continuously been in print. Although this book is well known for popularising the Boasian principle of cultural relativism, among anthropologists it constituted both an imporıant summary of the discoveries of Boasians, and a decisive break from Boas's emphasis on the mobility of diverse cultural traits. "Anthropological work has been overwhelmingly devoted to the analysis of cultural traits," she wrote "rather than to the study of cultures as articulated wholes." Influenced by

Polish-British social anthropologist Bronisław Malinowski, however, she argued that "The first essential, so it seems today, is to study the living culture, to know its habits of thought and the functions of its institutions" and that "the only way in which we can know the significance of the selected detail of behaviour is against the background of the motives and emotions and values that are institutionalised in that culture." Influenced by German historians Wilhelm Dilthey and Oswald Spengler, as well as by Gestalt psychology, she argued that "the whole determines its parts, not only their relation but their very nature," and that "cultures, likewise, are more than the sum of their traits." "Just as each spoken language draws very selectively from an extensive, but finite, set of sounds any human mouth (free from defect) can make, she concluded that in each society people, over time and through both conscious and unconscious processes, selected from an extensive but finite set of cultural traits which then combine to form a unique and distinctive pattern."

> The significance of cultural behaviour is not exhausted when we have clearly understood that it is local and man-made and hugely variable. It tends to be integrated. A culture, like an individual, is a more or less consistent pattern of thought and action. Within each culture there come into being characteristic purposes not necessarily shared by other types of society. In obedience to their purposes, each people further and further consolidates its experience, and in proportion to the urgency of these drives the heterogeneous items of behaviour take more and more congruous shape. Taken up by a well-integrated culture, the most ill-assorted acts become characteristic of its particular goals, often by the most unlikely metamorphoses.

Although Benedict felt that virtually all cultures are patterned, she argued that these patterns change over time as a consequence of human creativity, and therefore different societies around the world had distinct characters. The book *Patterns of Culture* contrasts Zuñi, Dobu and Kwakiutl cultures as a way of highlighting different ways of being human. Benedict observed that many Westerners felt that this view forced them to abandon their "dreams of permanence and ideality and with the individual's illusions of autonomy" and that for many, this made existence "empty." She argued however that once people accepted the results of scientific research, people would "arrive then at a more realistic social faith, accepting as grounds of hope and as new bases for tolerance the coexisting and equally valid patterns of life which mankind has created for itself from the raw materials of existence."

This view of culture has had a tremendous impact outside of anthropology, and dominated American anthropology until the Cold War, when anthropologists like Sidney Mintz and Eric Wolf rejected the validity and value of approaching "each culture" as "a world in itself" and "relatively stable."

They felt that, too often, this approach ignored the impact of imperialism, colonialism, and the world capitalist economy on the peoples Benedict and her followers studied (and thus re-opened the debate on the relationship between the universal and the particular, in the form of the relationship between the global and the local). In the meantime, its emphasis on metamorphosing patterns influenced French structuralism and made American anthropologists receptive to British structural-functionalism.

The second debate has been over the ability to make universal claims about all cultures. Although Boas argued that anthropologists had yet to collect enough solid evidence from a diverse sample of societies to make any valid general or universal claims about culture, by the 1940s some felt ready. Whereas Kroeber and Benedict had argued that "culture"—which could refer to local, regional, or trans-regional scales—was in some way "patterned" or "configured," some anthropologists now felt that enough data had been collected to demonstrate that it often took highly structured forms. The question these anthropologists debated was, were these structures statistical artifacts, or were they expressions of mental models? This debate emerged full-fledged in 1949, with the publication of George Murdock's *Social Structure*, and Claude Lévi-Strauss's *Les Structures Élémentaires de la Parenté*.

Opposing Boas and his students was Yale anthropologist George Murdock, who compiled the Human Relations Area Files. These files code cultural variables found in different societies, so that anthropologists can use statistical methods to study correlations among different variables. The ultimate aim of this project is to develop generalisations that apply to increasingly larger numbers of individual cultures. Later, Murdock and Douglas R. White developed the standard cross-cultural sample as a way to refine this method.

French anthropologist Claude Lévi-Strauss's structuralist anthropology brought together ideas of Boas (especially Boas's belief in the mutability of cultural forms, and Bastian's belief in the psychic unity of humankind) and French sociologist's Émile Durkheim's focus on social structures (institutionalised relationships among persons and groups of persons). Instead of making generalisations that applied to large numbers of societies, Lévi-Strauss sought to derive from concrete cases increasingly abstract models of human nature. His method begins with the supposition that culture exists in two different forms: the many distinct structures that could be inferred from observing members of the same society interact (and of which members of a society are themselves aware), and abstract structures developed by analysing shared ways (such as myths and rituals) members of a society represent their social life (and of which members of a society are not only not consciously aware, but which moreover typically stand in opposition to, or negate, the social structures of which people are aware). He then sought to develop one universal mental structure that could only be inferred through the systematic comparison of particular social and cultural structures. He argued that just as there are laws through which a finite and relatively small number of chemical elements could be combined to create a seemingly infinite variety of things, there were a finite and relatively small number of cultural elements which people combine to create the great variety of cultures, anthropologists observe. The systematic comparison of societies would enable an anthropologist to develop this cultural "table of elements," and once completed, this table of cultural elements would enable an anthropologist to analyze specific cultures and achieve insights hidden to the very people who produced and lived through these cultures. Structuralism came to dominate French anthropology and, in the late 1960s and 1970s, came to have great influence on American and British anthropology. Murdock's HRAF and Lévi-Strauss's structuralism provide two ambitious ways to seek the universal in the particular, and both approaches continue to appeal to different anthropologists. However, the differences between them reveal a tension implicit in the heritage of Tylor and Bastian. Is culture to be found in empirically observed behaviours that may form the basis of generalisations? Or does it consist of universal mental processes. which must be inferred and abstracted from observed behaviour? This question has driven debates among biological anthropologists and archeologists as well.

In the United Kingdom, the creation of structural functionalism was anticipated by Raymond Firth's (1901–2002) *We the Tikopia*, published in 1936, and marked by the publication of *African Political Systems*, edited by Meyer Fortes (1906–1983) and E.E. Evans-Pritchard (1902–1973) in 1940. In these works these anthropologists forwarded a synthesis of the ideas of their mentor, Bronisław Malinowski (1884–1942), and his rival, A. R. Radcliffe-Brown (1881–1955). Both Malinowski and Radcliffe-Brown viewed anthropology—what they call "social anthropology"—as that branch of sociology that studied so-called primitive societies. According to Malinowski's theory of functionalism, all human beings have certain biological needs, such as the need for food and shelter, and the biological need to reproduce. Every society develops its own institutions, which function to fulfill these needs. In order for these institutions to function, individuals take on particular social roles that regulate how they act and interact. Although members of any given society may not understand the ultimate functions of their roles and institutions, an ethnographer can develop a model of these functions through the careful observation of social life. Radcliffe-Brown rejected Malinowski's notion of function, and believed that a general theory of primitive social life could only be built up through the careful comparison of different societies. Influenced by the work of French sociologist Émile Durkheim (1858–1917), who argued that primitive and modern societies are distinguished by distinct social structures, Radcliffe-Brown argued that anthropologists first had to map out the social structure of any given society before comparing the structures of different societies. Firth, Fortes, and Evans-Pritchard found it easy to combine Malinowski's attention to social roles and institutions with Radcliffe-Brown's concern with social structures. They distinguished between "social organisation" (observable social interactions) and "social structure" (rule-governed patterns of social interaction), and shifted their attention from biological functions to social functions. For example, how different institutions are functionally integrated, and the extent to, and ways in, which institutions function to promote social solidarity and stability. In short, instead of culture (understood as all human non-genetic or extra-somatic phenomena) they made "sociality" (interactions and relationships among persons and groups of people) their object of study. (Indeed, Radcliffe-Brown once wrote "I should like to invoke a taboo on the word culture.")

Coincidentally, in 1946 sociologist Talcott Parsons (1902–1979) founded the Department of Social Relations at Harvard University influenced by such European sociologists like Émile Durkheim and Max Weber, Parsons developed a theory of social action that was closer to British social anthropology than to Boas's American anthropology, and which he also called "structural functionalism." Parson's intention was to develop a total theory of social action (why people act as they do), and to develop at Harvard an inter-disciplinary programme that would direct research according to this theory. His model explained human action as the result of four systems:

1. The "behavioural system" of biological needs.
2. The "personality system" of an individual's characteristics affecting their functioning in the social world.
3. The "social system" of patterns of units of social interaction, especially social status and role.
4. The "cultural system" of norms and values that regulate social action symbolically.

According to this theory, the second system was the proper object of study for psychologists; the third system for sociologists, and the fourth system for cultural anthropologists. Whereas the Boasians considered all of these systems to be objects of study by anthropologists, and "personality" and "status and role" to be as much a part of "culture" as "norms and values," Parsons envisioned a much narrower role for anthropology and a much narrower definition of culture.

Although Boasian cultural anthropologists were interested in norms and values, among many other things, it was only with the rise of structural functionalism that people came to identify "culture" with "norms and values."

Many American anthropologists rejected this view of culture (and by implication, anthropology). In 1980, anthropologist Eric Wolf wrote:

> As the social sciences transformed themselves into "behavioural" science, explanations for behaviour were no longer traced to culture: behaviour was to be understood in terms of psychological encounters, strategies of economic choice, strivings for payoffs in games of power. Culture, once extended to all acts and ideas employed in social life, was now relegated to the margins as "world view" or "values."

Nevertheless, several of Talcott Parsons' students emerged as leading American anthropologists. At the same time, many American anthropologists had a high regard for the research produced by social anthropologists in the 1940s and 1950s and found structural-functionalism to provide a very useful model for conducting ethnographic research.

The combination of American cultural anthropology theory with British social anthropology methods has led to some confusion between the concepts of "society" and "culture." For most anthropologists, these are distinct concepts. Society refers to a group of people; culture refers to a pan- human capacity and the totality of non-genetic human phenomena. Societies are often clearly bounded; cultural traits are often mobile, and cultural boundaries, such as they are, can be typically porous, permeable, and plural. During the 1950s and 1960s anthropologists often worked in places where social and cultural boundaries coincided, thus obscuring the distinction. When disjunctures between these boundaries become highly salient, for example during the period of European de-colonisation of Africa in the 1960s and 1970s, or during the post-Bretton Woods realignment of globalisation, however, the difference often becomes central to anthropological debates.

Parsons' students Clifford Geertz and David M. Schneider, and Schneider's student Roy Wagner, went on to important careers as cultural anthropologists and developed a school within American cultural anthropology called "symbolic anthropology," the study of the social construction and social effects of symbols. Since symbolic anthropology easily complemented social anthropologists' studies of social life and social structure, many British structural-functionalists (who rejected or were uninterested in Boasian cultural anthropology) accepted the Parsonian definition of "culture" and "cultural anthropology." British anthropologist Victor Turner (who eventually left the United Kingdom to teach in the United States) was an important bridge between American and British symbolic anthropology.

Attention to symbols, the meaning of which depended almost entirely on their historical and social context, appealed to many Boasians. Leslie White asked of cultural things, "What sort of objects are they? Are they physical objects? Mental objects? Both? Metaphors? Symbols?

Reifications?" In *Science of Culture* (1949), he concluded that they are objects "*sui generis*"; that is, of their own kind. In trying to define that kind, he hit upon a previously unrealised aspect of symbolisation, which he called "the symbolate"—an object created by the act of symbolisation. He thus defined culture as "symbolates understood in an extra-somatic context."

Nevertheless, by the 1930s White began turning away from the Boasian approach. He wrote,

> In order to live man, like all other species, must come to terms with the external world.... Man employs his sense organs, nerves, glands, and muscles in adjusting himself to the external world. But in addition to this he has another means of adjustment and control.... This mechanism is culture.

Although this view echoes that of Malinowski, the key concept for White was not "function" but "adaptation." Whereas the Boasians were interested in the history of specific traits, White was interested in the cultural history of the human species, which he felt should be studied from an evolutionary perspective. Thus, the task of anthropology is to study "not only how culture evolves, but why as well.... In the case of man ... the power to invent and to discover, the ability to select and use the better of two tools or ways of doing something— these are the factors of cultural evolution." Unlike 19th century evolutionists, who were concerned with how civilised societies rose above primitive societies. White was interested in documenting how, over time, humankind as a whole has through cultural means discovered more and more ways for capturing and harnessing energy from the environment, in the process transforming culture.

At the same time that White was developing his theory of cultural evolution, Kroeber's student Julian Steward was developing his theory of cultural ecology. In 1938 he published *Basin-Plateau Aboriginal Socio- Political Groups* in which he argued that diverse societies— for example, the indigenous Shoshone or White farmers on the Great Plains— were not less or more evolved; rather, they had adapted differently to different environments. Whereas Leslie White was interested in culture understood holistically as a property of the human species, Julian Steward was interested in culture as the property of distinct societies. Like White he viewed culture as a means of adapting to the environment, but he criticised Whites "unilineal" (one direction) theory of cultural evolution and instead proposed a model of "multilineal" evolution in which (in the Boasian tradition) each society has its own cultural history.

When Julian Steward left a teaching position at the University of Michigan to work in Utah in 1930, Leslie White took his place; in 1946 Julian Steward was made Chair of the Columbia University Anthropology Department. In the 1940s and 1950s their students, most notably Marvin Harris,

Sidney Mintz, Robert Murphy, Roy Rappaport, Marshall Sahlins, Elman Service, Andrew P. Vayda and Eric Wolf dominated American anthropology. Most promoted materialist understandings of culture in opposition to the symbolic approaches of Geertz and Schneider. Harris, Rappaport, and Vayda were especially important for their contributions to cultural materialism and ecological anthropology, both of which argued that "culture" constituted an extra-somatic (or non-biological) means through which human beings could adapt to life in drastically differing physical environments.

The debate between symbolic and materialist approaches to culture dominated American Anthropologists in the 1960s and 1970s. The Vietnam War and the publication of Dell Hymes' *Reinventing Anthropology*, however, marked a growing dissatisfaction with the then dominant approaches to culture. Hymes argued that fundamental elements of the Boasian project such as holism and an interest in diversity were still worth pursuing: "interest in other peoples and their ways of life, and concern to explain them within a frame of reference that includes ourselves." Moreover, he argued that cultural anthropologists are singularly well-equipped to lead this study (with an indirect rebuke to sociologists like Parsons who sought to subsume anthropology to their own project):

> In the practice there is a traditional place for openness to phenomena in ways not predefined by theory or design – attentiveness to complex phenomena, to phenomena of interest, perhaps aesthetic, for their own sake, to the sensory as well as intellectual, aspects of the subject. These comparative and practical perspectives, though not unique to formal anthropology, are specially husbanded there, and might well be impaired, if the study of man were to be united under the guidance of others who lose touch with experience in concern for methodology, who forget the ends of social knowledge in elabourating its means, or who are unwittingly or unconcernedly culture-bound.

It is these elements, Hymes argued, that justify a "general study of man," that is, "anthropology".

During this time notable anthropologists such as Mintz, Murphy, Sahlins, and Wolf eventually broke away, experimenting with structuralist and Marxist approaches to culture, they continued to promote cultural anthropology against structural functionalism.

Media

- Media (communication), tools used to store and deliver information or data
  - ➢ Advertising media, various media, content, buying and placement for advertising.
  - ➢ Broadcast media, communications delivered over mass electronic communication networks.

- Digital media, electronic media used to store, transmit, and receive digitised information.
- Electronic media, communications delivered via electronic or electromechanical energy.
- Hypermedia, media with hyperlinks.
- Mass media, all means of mass communications.
- Multimedia, communications that incorporate multiple forms of information content and processing.
- New media, a broad term encompassing the amalgamation of traditional media with the interactive power of computer and communications technology.
- News media, mass media focused on communicating news.
- News media (United States), the news media of the United States of America.
- Print media, communications delivered via paper or canvas.
- Published media, any media made available to the public.
- Recording media, devices used to store information.
- Social media, media disseminated through social interaction.
- MEDIA Programmeme, a European Union initiative to support the European audiovisual sector.

Understanding Mass Media and its Role

Mass media refers collectively to all media technologies which are intended to reach a large audience via mass communication. Broadcast media (also known as electronic media) transmit their information electronically and comprise of television, film and radio, movies, CDs, DVDs and some other gadgets like cameras or video consoles. Alternatively, print media uses a physical object as a means of sending their information, such as a newspaper, magazines, brochures, newsletters, books, leaflets and pamphlets. Photography can also be included under this subheading as it is a medium communicated through visual representations. The term also refers to the organisations which control these technologies, such as television stations or publishing companies. Mobile phones, computers and Internet are sometimes referred to as New-age Media. Internet media is able to achieve mass media status in its own right, due to the many mass media services it provides, such as email, websites, blogging, Internet and TV. For this reason, many mass media outlets have a presence on the web, by such things as having TV ads which link to a website, or having games in their sites to entice gamers to visit their website. In this way, they can utilise the easy accessibility that the Internet has, and the outreach that Internet affords, as information can easily be broadcast to many different regions of the world simultaneously and cost-efficiently. Outdoor media is a form of mass media which comprises billboards, signs, placards placed inside and outside of commercial buildings/objects like shops/ buses, flying billboards (signs in tow of airplanes), blimps, and skywriting. Public speaking and event organising can also be considered as a form of mass media.

Until recent time, mass media was clearly defined and consisted of eight mass media industries: books, newspapers, magazines, recordings, radio, movies, television and the Internet. With the explosion of digital communication technology in the late 20th and early 21st centuries, the question of what forms of media should be classified as "Mass Media" has become more prominent. For example, it is controversial whether to include cell phones, video games and computer games (such as MMORPGs) in the definition. Currently, mass media is classified into the "seven mass media": print, recordings, cinema, radio, television, Internet, mobile phones. While a telephone is a two way communication device, mass media refers to medium which can communicate a message to a large group, often simultaneously. However, modern cell phones are no longer a single use device. Most cell phones are equipped with Internet access and capable of connecting to the web which is itself a mass medium. A question arises of whether this makes cell phones a mass medium or simply a device used to access a mass medium (the Internet).There is currently a system where marketers and advertisers are able to tap into satellites, and broadcast commercials and advertisements directly to cell phones, unsolicited by the phone's user. This transmittion of mass advertising to millions of people is a form of mass communication. Video games may also be evolving into a mass medium. Video games convey the same messages and ideologies to all their users. Users sometimes share the experience with each other by playing online. Excluding the Internet however, it is questionable whether players of video games are sharing a common experience when they play the game separately. It is possible to discuss in great detail the events of a video game with a friend you have never played with because the experience was identical to you both. The question is if this is then a form of mass communication. MMORPGS such as Runescape provide a common gaming experience to millions of users throughout the globe. It is arguable that the users are receiving the same message, i.e., the game is mass communicating the same messages to the various players.

Mass vs. Mainstream

Mass media is also sometimes referred to as the "mainstream media" (although it is in fact something different), due to the tendency of media choosing to select prominent, yet trivial, stories which will be of interest to a general audience (such as celebrity break-ups), whilst ignoring controversial or intellectually stimulating news. This trend is attributed to the fact that media, though used to provide a service to the public to keep them updated, is essentially a business and will naturally do what it must to sell. Mass media has become one of the main sources of news and entertainment for the general public, and over the past century, has become a globally huge industry.

Mass vs. Local

Mass media is distinguished from local media by the notion that whilst the former aims to reach a very large market such as the entire population of a country, the latter broadcasts to a much smaller population and area, and generally focuses on regional news rather than global events. A third type of media, speciality media, provides for specific demographics, such as specialty channels on TV (sports channels, porn channels, etc.). These definitions are not set in stone, and it is possible for a media outlet to be promoted in status from a local media outlet to a global media outlet. Some local media, which takes an interest in state or provincial news can rise to prominence due to their investigative journalism, and to the local region's preference of updates in national politics rather than regional news. *The Guardian*, formerly known as the Manchester Guardian is an example of one such media outlet. Once a regional daily newspaper, *The Guardian* is currently a nationally-respected paper.

Broadcast and New-Age vs. Print

Despite the view that broadcast media and new age media have made print media obsolete, there exists a majority of audiences who prefer the print media for various communication purposes.

Criticism

One major criticism of the mass media is that it can be too topical. A mass media is often forced to cover national and international news due to it having to cater for and be relevant for a wide demography. As such, it has to skip over many interesting or important local stories because they simply do not interest the large majority of their viewers. An example given by the website *WiseGeek* is that "the residents of a community might view their fight against development as critical, but the story would only attract the attention of the mass media if the fight became controversial or if precedents of some form were set".

Whilst some elitists refer to mass media as the "opiate of the masses", others argue that is a vital aspect of human societies. By understanding mass media, one is then able to analyse and find a deeper understanding of one's population and culture. This valuable and powerful ability is one reason why the field of media studies is popular. As WiseGeek says, "watching, reading, and interacting with a nation's mass media can provide clues into how people think, especially if a diverse assortment of mass media sources are perused".

Since the 1950s, in the countries that have reached a high level of industrialization, the mass media of cinema, radio and TV have a key role in political power.

Contemporary research demonstrates an increasing level of concentration of media ownership, with many media industries already highly concentrated and dominated by a very small number of firms.

History

The history of mass media can be traced back to the days when dramas were performed in various ancient cultures. This was the first time when a form of media was "broadcast" to a wider audience. The first dated printed book known is the *Diamond Sutra*, printed in China in 868 AD, although it is clear that books were printed earlier. Movable clay type was invented in 1041 in China. However, due to the slow spread of literacy to the masses in China, and the relatively high cost of paper there, the earliest printed mass-medium was probably European popular prints from about 1400. Although these were produced in huge numbers, very few early examples survive, and even most known to be printed before about 1600 have not survived. The term "mass media" was coined with the creation of print media, which is notable for being the first example of mass media, as we use the term today. This form of media started in Europe in the Middle Ages. Johannes Gutenberg's invention of the printing press allowed the mass production of books to sweep the nation. He printed the first book on a printing press with movable type in 1453. *The Gutenberg Bible*, one of the books he published, was translated into many different languages and printed throughout the continent. The invention of the printing press in the late 15th century gave rise to some of the first forms of mass communication, by enabling the publication of books and newspapers on a scale much larger than was previously possible. The invention also transformed the way the world received printed materials, although books remained too expensive really to be called a mass-medium for at least a century after that. Newspapers developed from about 1612, with the first example in English in 1620; but they took until the 19th century to reach a mass-audience directly. The first high-circulation newspapers arose in London in the early 1800s, such as *The Times*, and were made possible by the invention of high-speed rotary steam printing presses, and railroads which allowed large-scale distribution over wide geographical areas. The increase in circulation, however, led to a decline in feedback and interactivity from the readership, making newspapers a more one-way medium.

The phrase "the media" began to be used in the 1920s. The notion of "mass media" was generally restricted to print media up until the post-Second World War, when radio, television and video were introduced. The audio-visual facilities became very popular, because they provided both information and entertainment, because the colour and sound engaged the viewers/listeners and because it was easier for the general public to passively watch TV or listen to the radio than to actively read. In recent times, the Internet became the latest and most popular mass medium. Information has become readily available through websites, and easily accessible through search engines. One can do many activities at the same time, such as playing games, listening to music, and social networking, irrespective of location. Whilst other forms of mass media are restricted in the type of information they can offer, the Internet comprises a large percentage of the sum of human knowledge through such things as *Google Books*. Modern day mass media consists of the Internet, mobile phones, blogs, podcasts and RSS feeds.

During the 20th century, the growth of mass media was driven by technology, including that which allowed much duplication of material. Physical duplication technologies such as printing, record pressing and film duplication allowed the duplication of books, newspapers and movies at low prices to huge audiences. Radio and television allowed the electronic duplication of information for the first time. Mass media had the economics of linear replication: a single work could make money. An example of Riel and Neil's theory: proportional to the number of copies sold, and as volumes went up, unit costs went down, increasing profit margins further. Vast fortunes were to be made in mass media. In a democratic society, the media can serve the electorate about issues regarding government and corporate entities (see Media influence). Some consider the concentration of media ownership to be a threat to democracy.

Major Professions Involving Mass Media

Journalism

Journalism is the discipline of collecting, analysing, verifying and presenting information regarding current events, trends, issues and people. Those who practice journalism are known as journalists. News-oriented journalism is sometimes described as the "first rough draft of history" (attributed to Phil Graham), because journalists often record important events, producing news articles on short deadlines. While under pressure to be first with their stories, news media organisations usually edit and proofread their reports prior to publication, adhering to each organisation's standards of accuracy, quality and style. Many news organisations claim proud traditions of holding government officials and institutions accountable to the public, while media critics have raised questions about holding the press itself accountable.

Public relations

Public relations is the art and science of managing communication between an organisation and its key publics to build, manage and sustain its positive image. Examples include:

- Corporations use marketing public relations to convey information about the products they manufacture or services they provide to potential customers to support their direct sales efforts. Typically, they support sales in the short and long term, establishing and burnishing the corporation's branding for a strong, ongoing market.
- Corporations also use public relations as a vehicle to reach legislators and other politicians, seeking favourable tax, regulatory, and other treatment, and they may use public relations to portray themselves as enlightened employers, in support of human-resources recruiting programmes.
- Nonprofit organisations, including schools and universities, hospitals, and human and social service agencies, use public relations in support of awareness programmes, fund-raising programmes, staff recruiting, and to increase patronage of their services.
- Politicians use public relations to attract votes and raise money, and, when successful at the ballot box, to promote and defend their service in office, with an eye to the next election or, at career's end, to their legacy.

Publishing

Publishing is the industry concerned with the production of literature or information – the activity of making information available for public view. In some cases, authors may be their own publishers. Traditionally, the term refers to the distribution of printed works such as books and newspapers. With the advent of digital information systems and the Internet, the scope of publishing has expanded to include websites, blogs, and the like. As a business, publishing includes the development, marketing, production, and distribution of newspapers, magazines, books, literary works, musical works, software, other works dealing with information. Publication is also important as a legal concept: (1) as the process of giving formal notice to the world of a significant intention, for example, to marry or enter bankruptcy, and; (2) as the essential precondition of being able to claim defamation; that is, the alleged libel must have been published.

Software Publishing

A software publisher is a publishing company in the software industry between the developer and the distributor. In some companies, two or all three of these roles may be combined (and indeed, may reside in a single person, especially in the case of shareware). Software publishers often license software from developers with specific limitations, such as a time limit or geographical region. The terms of licensing vary enormously, and are typically secret. Developers may use publishers to reach larger or foreign markets, or to avoid focussing on marketing. Or publishers may use developers to create software to meet a market need that the publisher has identified.

Forms

Today, mass media is generally categorised into seven branches. These "seven mass media", in order of their introduction are:

1. Print (books, pamphlets, newspapers, magazines, etc.) from the late 15th century.
2. Recordings (gramophone records, magnetic tapes, cassettes, cartridges, CDs, DVDs) from the late 19th century.
3. Cinema from about 1900.
4. Radio from about 1910.
5. Television from about 1950.
6. Internet from about 1990.
7. Mobile phones from about 2000.

Each mass media has its own content types, its own creative artists and technicians, and its own business model. The sixth and seventh media, Internet and mobile, are often called collectively as digital media; and the fourth and fifth, radio and TV, as broadcast media.

Broadcast

The sequencing of content in a broadcast is called a schedule. With all technological endeavours a number of technical terms and slang are developed please see the list of broadcasting terms for a glossary of terms used. Television and radio programmes are distributed through radio broadcasting over frequency bands that are highly regulated by the Federal Communications Commission. Such regulation includes determination of the width of the bands, range, licencing, types of receivers and transmitters used, and acceptable content. Cable programmes are often broadcast simultaneously with radio and television programmes, but have a more limited audience. By coding signals and having decoding equipment in homes, cable also enables subscription-based channels and pay-per-view services. A broadcasting organisation may broadcast several programmes at the same time, through several channels (frequencies), for example, BBC One and Two. On the other hand, two or more organisations may share a channel and each use it during a fixed part of the day. Digital radio and digital television may also transmit multiplexed programmeming, with several channels compressed into one ensemble. When broadcasting is done via the Internet the term webcasting is often used. In 2004 a new phenomenon occurred when a number of technologies combined to produce podcasting. Podcasting is an asynchronous broadcast/narrowcast medium, with one of the main proponents being Adam Curry and his associates the Podshow.

Film

'Film' encompasses motion pictures as individual projects, as well as the field in general. The name comes from the photographic film (also called filmstock), historically the primary medium for recording and displaying motion pictures. Many other terms exist — motion pictures (or just pictures and "picture"), the silver screen, photoplays, the cinema, picture shows, flicks — and commonly movies. Films are produced by recording people and objects with cameras, or by creating them using animation techniques and/or special effects. They comprise a series of individual frames, but when these images are shown rapidly in succession, the illusion of motion is given to the viewer. Flickering between frames is not seen due to an effect known as persistence of vision — whereby the eye retains a visual image for a fraction of a second after the source has been removed. Also of relevance is what causes the perception of motion; a psychological effect identified as beta movement. Film is considered by many to be an important art form; films entertain, educate, enlighten and inspire audiences. Any film can become a worldwide attraction, especially with the addition of dubbing or subtitles that translate the film message. Films are also artifacts created by specific cultures, which reflect those cultures, and, in turn, affect them.

Video Games

A video game is a computer-controlled game where a video display such as a monitor or television is the primary feedback device. The term "computer game" also includes games which display only text (and which can therefore theoretically be played on a teletypewriter) or which use other methods, such as sound or vibration, as their primary feedback device, but there are very few new games in these categories. There always must also be some sort of input device, usually in the form of button/joystick combinations (on arcade games), a keyboard and mouse/trackball combination (computer games), or a controller (console games), or a combination of any of the above. Also, more esoteric devices have been used for input. Usually there are rules and goals, but in more open-ended games the player may be free to do whatever they like within the confines of the virtual universe. In common usage, a "computer game" or a "PC game" refers to a game that is played on a personal computer. "Console game" refers to one that is played on a device specifically designed for the use of such, while interfacing with a standard television set. "Arcade game" refers to a game designed to be played in an establishment in which patrons pay to play on a per-use basis. "Video game" (or "videogame") has evolved into a catchall phrase that encompasses the aforementioned along with any game made for any other device, including, but not limited to, mobile phones, PDAs, advanced calculators, etc.

Audio Recording and Reproduction

Sound recording and reproduction is the electrical or mechanical re-creation and/or amplification of sound, often as music. This involves the use of audio equipment such as microphones, recording devices and loudspeakers. From early beginnings with the invention of the phonograph using purely mechanical techniques, the field has advanced with the invention of electrical recording, the mass production of the 78 record, the magnetic wire recorder followed by the tape recorder, the vinyl LP record. The invention of the compact cassette in the 1960s, followed by Sony's Walkman, gave a major boost to the mass distribution of music recordings, and the invention of digital recording and the compact disc in 1983 brought massive improvements in ruggedness and quality. The most recent developments have been in digital audio players. An album is a collection of related audio recordings, released together to the public, usually commercially. The term record album originated from the fact that 78 RPM Phonograph disc records were kept together in a book resembling a photo album. The first collection of records to be called an "album" was Tchaikovsky's *Nutcracker Suite*, release in April 1909 as a four-disc set by Odeon records. It retailed for 16 shillings — about £15 in modern currency. A music video (also promo) is a short film or video that accompanies a complete piece of music, most commonly a song. Modern music videos were primarily made and used as a marketing device intended to promote the sale of music recordings. Although the origins of music videos go back much further, they came into their own in the 1980s, when Music Television's format was based on them. In the 1980s, the term "rock video" was often used to describe this form of entertainment, although the term has fallen into disuse.

Music videos can accommodate all styles of filmmaking, including animation, live action films, documentaries, and non-narrative, abstract film.

Understanding the New-Age Media

Internet

The Internet (also known simply as "the Net" or less precisely as "the Web") is a more interactive medium of mass media, and can be briefly described as "a network of networks". Specifically, it is the worldwide, publicly accessible network of interconnected computer networks that transmit data by packet switching using the standard Internet Protocol (IP). It consists of millions of smaller domestic, academic, business, and governmental networks, which together carry various information and services, such as e-mail, online chat, file transfer, and the interlinked Web pages and other documents of the World Wide Web. Contrary to some common usage, the Internet and the World Wide Web are not synonymous: the Internet is the system of interconnected computer networks, linked by copper wires, fiber-optic cables, wireless connections etc.; the Web is the contents, or the interconnected documents, linked by hyperlinks and URLs. The World Wide Web is accessible through the Internet, along with many other services including e-mail, file sharing and others described below. Toward the end of the 20th century, the advent of the World Wide Web marked the first era in which most individuals could have a means of exposure on a scale comparable to that of mass media. Anyone with a web site has the potential to address a global audience, although serving to high levels of web traffic is still relatively expensive. It is possible that the rise of peer-to-peer technologies may have begun the process of making the cost of bandwidth manageable. Although a vast amount of information, imagery, and commentary (i.e. "content") has been made available, it is often difficult to determine the authenticity and reliability of information contained in web pages (in many cases, self-published). The invention of the Internet has also allowed breaking news stories to reach around the globe within minutes. This rapid growth of instantaneous, decentralized communication is often deemed likely to change mass media and its relationship to society. "Cross-media" means the idea of distributing the same message through different media channels. A similar idea is expressed in the news industry as "convergence". Many authors understand cross-media publishing to be the ability to publish in both print and on the web without manual conversion effort. An increasing number of wireless devices with mutually incompatible data and screen formats make it even more difficult to achieve the objective "create once, publish many". The Internet is quickly becoming the center of mass media. Everything is becoming accessible via the Internet. Instead of picking up a newspaper, or watching the 10 o'clock news, people can log onto the Internet to get the news they want, when they want it. For example, many workers listen to the radio through the Internet while sitting at their desk. Even the education system relies on the Internet. Teachers can contact the entire class by sending one e-mail. They may have web pages where students can get another copy of the class outline or assignments. Some classes have class blogs in which students are required to post weekly, with students graded on their contributions.

Blogs (web logs)

Blogging, too, has become a pervasive form of media. A blog is a website, usually maintained by an individual, with regular entries of commentary, descriptions of events, or interactive media such as images or video. Entries are commonly displayed in reverse chronological order, with most recent posts shown on top. Many blogs provide commentary or news on a particular subject; others function as more personal online diaries. A typical blog combines text, images and other graphics, and links to other blogs, web pages, and related media. The ability for readers to leave comments in an interactive format is an important part of many blogs. Most blogs are primarily textual, although some focus on art (artlog), photographs (photoblog), sketchblog, videos (vlog), music (MP3 blog), audio (podcasting) are part of a wider network of social media. Microblogging is another type of blogging which consists of blogs with very short posts.

RSS feeds

RSS is a format for syndicating news and the content of news-like sites, including major news sites like Wired, news-oriented community sites like *Slashdot*, and *personal blogs*. It is a family of Web feed formats used to publish frequently updated content such as blog entries, news headlines, and podcasts. An RSS document (which is called a "feed" or "web feed" or "channel") contains either a summary of content from an associated web site or the full text. RSS makes it possible for people to keep up with web sites in an automated manner that can be piped into special programmes or filtered displays.

Podcast

A podcast is a series of digital-media files which are distributed over the Internet using syndication feeds for playback on portable media players and computers. The term podcast, like broadcast, can refer either to the series of content itself or to the method by which it is syndicated; the latter is also called podcasting. The host or author of a podcast is often called a podcaster.

Mobile

Mobile phones were introduced in Japan in 1979 but became a mass media only in 1998 when the first downloadable ringing tones were introduced in Finland. Soon most forms of media content were introduced on mobile phones, and today the total value of media consumed on mobile towers over that of Internet content, and was worth over 31 billion dollars in 2007 (source Informa). The mobile media content includes over 8 billion dollars worth of mobile music (ringing tones, ringback tones, truetones, MP3 files, karaoke, music videos, music streaming services etc.); over 5 billion dollars worth of mobile gaming; and various news, entertainment and advertising services. In Japan mobile phone books are so popular that five of the ten best-selling printed books were originally released as mobile phone books. Similar to the Internet, mobile is also an interactive media, but has far wider reach, with 3.3 billion mobile phone users at the end of 2007 to 1.3 billion Internet users (source ITU). Like e-mail on the Internet, the top application on mobile is also a personal messaging service, but SMS text messaging is used by over 2.4 billion people. Practically all Internet services and applications exist or have similar cousins on mobile, from search to multiplayer games to virtual worlds to blogs. Mobile has several unique benefits which many mobile media pundits claim make mobile a more powerful media than either TV or the Internet, starting with mobile being permanently carried and always connected. Mobile has the best audience accuracy and is the only mass media with a built-in payment channel available to every user without any credit cards or paypal accounts or even an age limit. Mobile is often called the 7th Mass Medium and either the fourth screen (if counting cinema, TV and PC screens) or the third screen (counting only TV and PC).

Print Media

Book

A book is a collection of sheets of paper, parchment or other material with a piece of text written on them, bound together along one edge within covers. A book is also a literary work or a main division of such a work. A book produced in electronic format is known as an e-book.

Magazine

A magazine is a periodical publication containing a variety of articles, generally financed by advertising and/or purchase by readers.

Magazines are typically published weekly, biweekly, monthly, bimonthly or quarterly, with a date on the cover that is in advance of the date it is actually published. They are often printed in colour on coated paper, and are bound with a soft cover.

Magazines fall into two broad categories: consumer magazines and business magazines. In practice, magazines are a subset of periodicals, distinct from those periodicals produced by scientific, artistic, academic or special interest publishers which are subscription-only, more expensive, narrowly limited in circulation, and often have little or no advertising.

Magazines can be classified as:

- General interest magazines (e.g. *Frontline*, *India Today*, *The Week*, *The Sunday Times* etc.).
- Special interest magazines (women's, sports, business, scuba diving, etc.)

Newspaper

A newspaper is a publication containing news and information and advertising, usually printed on low-cost paper called newsprint. It may be general or special interest, most often published daily or weekly. The first printed newspaper was published in 1605, and the form has thrived even in the face of competition from technologies such as radio and television. Recent developments on the Internet are posing major threats to its business model, however. Paid circulation is declining in most countries, and advertising revenue, which makes up the bulk of a newspaper's income, is shifting from print to online; some commentators, nevertheless, point out that historically new media such as radio and television did not entirely supplant existing.

Outdoor Media

Outdoor media is a form of mass media which comprises billboards, signs, placards placed inside and outside of commercial buildings/objects like shops/buses, flying billboards (signs in tow of airplanes), blimps, and skywriting. Many commercial advertisers use this form of mass media when advertising in sports stadiums. Tobacco and alcohol manufacturers used billboards and other outdoor media extensively. However, in 1998, the Master Settlement Agreement between the US and the tobacco industries prohibited the billboard advertising of cigarettes. In a 1994 Chicago-based study, Diana Hackbarth and her colleagues revealed how tobacco- and alcohol-based billboards were concentrated in poor neighbourhoods. In other urban centers, alcohol and tobacco billboards were much more concentrated in African-American neighbourhoods than in white neighbourhoods.

Personal Media

Non-mass or "personal" media (point-to-point and person-to-person communication) can include:

- Gestures
- Letter
- Telephony

Understanding Mass Media's Influences and Effects

There are three theories to describe the influence of mass media. The website CliffNotes explains in detail the theories which examine the role that mass media plays in modern society. The limited-effects theory, which was originally tested in the 1940s and 1950s, states that "because people usually choose what media to interact with based on what they already believe, media exerts a negligible influence". The class-dominant theory states that "the media reflects and projects the view of a minority elite, which controls it". It continues by explaining that the people who own and control the corporations that produce media comprise this elite. The culturalist theory, which was developed in the 1980s and 1990s, combines the other two theories and claims that "people interact with media to create their own meanings out of the images and messages they receive". This theory states that audience members play an active, rather than passive role in relation to mass media. In an article entitled *Mass Media Influence on Society*, Rayuso argues that the media is dominated by five major companies (Time Warner, VIACOM, Vivendi Universal, Walt Disney and News Corp) which own 95 per cent of all mass media including theme parks, movie studios, television and radio broadcast networks and programming, video news, sports entertainment, telecommunications, wireless phones, video games software, electronic media and music companies. Whilst historically, there was more diversity in companies, they have recently merged to form an elite which have the power to shape the opinion and beliefs of people. People buy after seeing thousands of advertisements by various companies in TV, newspapers or magazines, which are able to affect their purchasing decisions. The definition of what is acceptable by society is dictated by the media. This power can be used for good, for example encouraging children to play sport. However, it can also be used for bad, for example children being influenced by cigars smoked by film stars, their exposure to sex images, their exposure to images of violence and their exposure to junk food ads. The documentary *Supersize Me* describes how companies like McDonalds have been sued in the past, the plaintiffs claiming that it was the fault of their liminal and subliminal advertising that "forced" them to purchase the product. The Barbie and Ken dolls of the 1950s are sometimes cited as the main cause for the obsession in modern day society for women to be skinny and men to be buff. After the attacks of 9/11, the media gave extensive coverage of the event and exposed Osama's guilt for the attack, information they were told by the authorities. This shaped the public opinion to support the war on terrorism, and later, the war on Iraq. A main concern is that due to this immense power of the mass media (being able to drive the public opinion), media receiving inaccurate information could cause the public opinion to support the wrong cause. In his book *The Commercialization of American Culture*, Matthew P. McAllister says that "a well-developed media system, informing and teaching its citizens, helps democracy move toward its ideal state."

In 1997, J. R. Finnegan Jr. and K. Viswanath identified three main effects or functions of mass media.

1. *The Knowledge Gap:* The mass media influences knowledge gaps due to factors including "the extent to which the content

is appealing, the degree to which information channels are accessible and desirable, and the amount of social conflict and diversity there is in a community".

2. *Agenda Setting:* People are influenced in how they think about issues due to the selective nature of what media choose for public consumption. After publicly disclosing that he had prostate cancer prior to the 2000 New York senatorial election, Rudolph Giuliani, the mayor of New York City (aided by the media) sparked a huge priority elevation of the cancer in people's consciousness. This was because news media began to report on the risks of prostate cancer, which in turn prompted a greater public awareness about the disease and the need for screening. This ability for the media to be able to change how the public thinks and behaves has occurred on other occasions. In mid-1970s when Betty Ford and Happy Rockefeller, wives of the then-President and then-Vice President respectively, were both diagnosed with breast cancer. J. J. Davis states that "when risks are highlighted in the media, particularly in great detail, the extent of agenda setting is likely to be based on the degree to which a public sense of outrage and threat is provoked". When wanting to set an agenda, framing can be invaluably useful to a mass media organisation. Framing involves "taking a leadership role in the organisation of public discourse about an issue". The media is influenced by the desire for balance in coverage, and the resulting pressures can come from groups with particular political action and advocacy positions. Finnegan and Viswanath say, "groups, institutions, and advocates compete to identify problems, to move them onto the public agenda, and to define the issues symbolically" (1997, p. 324).

3. *Cultivation of Perceptions:* The extent to which media exposure shapes audience perceptions over time is known as cultivation. Television is a common experience, especially in places like the United States, to the point where it can be described as a "homogenising agent" (S. W. Littlejohn). However, instead of being merely a result of the TV, the effect is often based on socio-economic factors. Having a prolonged exposure to TV or movie violence might affect a viewer to the extent where they actively think community violence is a problem, or alternatively find it justifiable. The resulting belief is likely to be different depending on where people live however. Since the '50s, when cinema, radio and TV began to be the primary or the only source of information for a larger and larger percentage of the population, these media began to be considered as central instruments of mass control.

Up to the point that it emerged the idea that when a country has reached a high level of industrialisation, the country itself "belongs to the person who controls communications." Mass media play a significant role in shaping public perceptions on a variety of important issues, both through the information that is dispensed through them, and through the interpretations they place upon this information. They also play a large role in shaping modern culture, by selecting and portraying a particular set of beliefs, values, and traditions (an entire way of life), as reality. That is, by portraying a certain interpretation of reality, they shape reality to be more in line with that interpretation.

Relationship between Mass Media and Racism

Mass media has played a large role in the way white Americans perceive African-Americans. The media focus on African-Americans in the contexts of crime, drug use, gang violence, and other forms of anti-social behaviour has resulted in a distorted and harmful public perception of African-Americans. African-Americans have been subjected to oppression and discrimination for the past few hundred years. According to Stephen Balkaran in his article Mass Media and Racism, "The media has played a key role in perpetuating the effects of this historical oppression and in contributing to African-Americans' continuing status as second-class citizens". This has resulted in an uncertainty among white Americans as to what the genuine nature of African-Americans really is. Despite the resulting racial divide, the fact that these people are undeniably American has "raised doubts about the white man's value system". This means that there is a somewhat "troubling suspicion" among some Americans that their white America is tainted by the black influence.

Trends

In an article by Peter R. Kann, Chairman of Dow Jones, he explains the ten "disturbing trends in mass media:"

1. The blurring of the lines between journalism and entertainment.
2. The blurring of lines between news and opinion.
3. The blending of news and advertising, sponsorships or other commercial relationships.
4. The problems and pitfalls inherent in pack journalism.
5. The issue of conflict and context.
6. The exaggerated tendency toward pessimism.
7. The growing media fascination with the bizarre, the perverse and the pathological — John Mark Karr journalism.
8. Social orthodoxy, or political correctness.

9. The media's short attention span.
10. The matter of [the media's] power.

Future

In 2002, Arnold Kling wrote that "the newspaper business is going to die within the next twenty years. Newspaper publishing will continue, but only as a philanthropic venture." Jim Pinkerton said in 2006 of the future of mass media, "Every country with ambitions on the international stage will soon have its own state-supported media."

Leo Laporte, founder of the TWiT network of podcasts, says that "there will always be a need for storytellers, people who dig up facts and explain them".

Purposes

Mass media encompasses much more that just news, although it is sometimes misunderstood in this way. It can be used for various purposes:

- Advocacy, both for business and social concerns. This can include advertising, marketing, propaganda, public relations, and political communication.
- Entertainment, traditionally through performances of acting, music, sports, and TV shows along with light reading; since the late 20th century also through video and computer games.
- Public service announcements and emergency alerts (that can be used as political device to communicate propaganda to the public).

Technologies

The electronic and print medias use a wide range of mediums. These include broadcasting (in the narrow sense, for radio and television); film (mostly used for entertainment, but also for documentaries); the Internet, blogs or podcasts (such as news, music, pre-recorded speech, and video); publishing (including electronic publishing). Many instances of various types of recorded discs or tapes —in the 20th century, these were mainly used for music; video and computer uses followed, video games themselves having developed into a mass form of media. Other devices, such as mobile phones, can be used for rapid breaking news and short clips of entertainment like jokes, horoscopes, alerts, games, music, and advertising.

3

Contemporary Women and Gender Studies, Cultural and Communication Studies and Media Studies

Defining Women's Studies

Women's studies, also known as feminist studies, is an interdisciplinary academic field which explores politics, society and history from an intersectional, multicultural women's perspective. It critiques and explores societal norms of gender, race, class, sexuality, and other social inequalities.

Women's studies were first conceived as an academic rubric apart from other departments in the late 1970s, as the second wave of feminism gained political influence in the academy through student and faculty activism. As an academic discipline, it was modeled on the American studies and ethnic studies (such as Afro-American studies) and Chicano Studies programmes that had arisen shortly before it. The first two Women's Studies Programmes in the United States were established in 1970 at San Diego State College (now San Diego State University) and SUNY-Buffalo. The SDSU programme was initiated after a year of intense organising of women's consciousness raising groups, rallies, petition circulating, and operating unofficial or experimental classes and presentations before seven committees and assemblies. Carol Rowell Council was the student co-founder along with Dr. Joyce Nower, a literature instructor. The SUNY-Buffalo programme was also the result of intense debate and feminist organising led by Elizabeth Lapovsky Kennedy, and it was eventually birthed out of the American Studies department. In 1972,

Sarah Lawrence College became the first institution to grant Masters degrees to Women's History. Throughout the later 1970s many universities and colleges created departments and programmes in women's studies, and professorships became available in the field which did not require the sponsorship of other departments. By the late twentieth century, women's studies courses were available at many universities and colleges around the world. A 2007 survey conducted by the National Women's Studies Association included 576 institutions offering women's studies or gender studies at some level. Currently there are 678 listed in their online searchable database, of institutions offering women's/gender studies courses and degrees with 15 institutions offering a Ph.D. in the United States. Courses in the United Kingdom can be found through the Universities and Colleges Admissions Service.

Women's studies faculty practice a diverse array of pedagogies, though there are some common themes to the way many Women's Studies courses are taught. Women's studies curricula often encourage students to engage in hands-on activities, including discussion and reflection upon course materials. The development of critical reading, writing, and oral expression are often key to these courses. The decentralisation of the professor as the source of knowledge and wisdom is also common. Courses are often more egalitarian, stressing critical analysis of texts, and the development of critical writing. Some courses offer pedagogical methods of teaching which involves in-depth participation from both instructor and students of the course. Like gender studies, Women's Studies employs feminist, queer, and critical theories. Since the 1970s, Women's Studies has taken a post-modern approach to understanding gender and how it intersects with race, class, ethnicity, religion, age, and (dis)ability to produce and maintain power structures within society that ensure social inequality. With this, there has been a focus on language, subjectivity, and social hegemony, and how the lives of subjects, however they identify, are constituted. At the core of these theories is the notion that however one identifies, gender, sex, and sexuality are not intrinsic, but are socially constructed. Women studies programmes are involved in social justice and design curriculums that are embedded with theory and also activism outside of the classroom. Some Women Studies programmes offer internships that are community- based allowing students the opportunity to gain a better understanding of how oppression directly affects women's lives. This experience, informed by theory from feminist studies, queer theory, black feminist theory, African studies, and many other theoretical frameworks, allows students the opportunity to critically analyze experience as well as evolve creative solutions for issues on a local level. However, Daphne Patai, from the University of Massachusetts Amherst, has criticised this aspect of women's studies programmes, arguing that they place politics over education, arguing that "the strategies of faculty members in these programmes have included policing insensitive language, championing research methods deemed congenial to women (such as qualitative over quantitative methods), and conducting classes as if they were therapy sessions." It is important to note, however, that many Women's Studies curricula engage with a variety of different epistemological and methodological practices. Feminist scholarship is diverse and utilises positivism, critical realism, and standpoint theory in its interdisciplinary scholarship.

Feminist activism not only focuses on women's issues but has spread throughout many other movements including (but not limited to) environmental issues, body politics, feminist art, identity, issues, reproductive rights, gender issues, animal rights, homosexual rights, and ethnic minority rights. These forms of activism can include letter writing, boycotting, protesting, the visual arts, bodily demonstrations, education, and leafleting. In current feminism, the focus has shifted to encompass an outlook and desire for equality for all—identifying oppressive systems and forces around the world that affect all types of beings. Feminist activism explores the intersections of social, political, and cultural histories (among various others denominators), their implications. It dedicates time and energy to the liberation of all people from injustices. Simply studying or being a student of women's studies can be seen as activism in itself. Therefore, for most students of women's studies, an activism status is already engaged. To foster the growth of the study body, one of the key aspects of women's studies classes and programmes is to connect the classroom to social change. Women's studies classes and programmes focus on power structures, oppression, inequality, and social suffering. Within these categories, women's studies students learn through a humanistic/multicultural approach, questioning the world we live in and envisioning alternative realities. Learning is through educative experiences, linking the outside world to the classroom. Students are encouraged to bridge their learning and community involvement and take action in the world to foster positive social transformation. Students and feminist activists not only learn about oppression in society but also look at the possibility for a global unity in difference.

Defining Gender Studies

Gender studies is a field of interdisciplinary study which analyses race, ethnicity, sexuality and location. Gender study has many different forms. One view exposed by the philosopher Simone de Beauvoir said: "One is not born a woman, one becomes one". This view proposes that in gender studies, the term "gender" should be used to refer to the social and cultural constructions of masculinities and femininities, not to the state of being male or female in its entirety. However, this view is not held by all gender theorists. Other areas of gender study closely examine the role that the biological states of being male or female have on social constructs of gender. Specifically, in what way gender roles are defined by biology and how they are defined by cultural trends. The field emerged from a number of different areas: the sociology of the 1950s and later (see Sociology of gender); the theories of the psychoanalyst Jacques Lacan; and the work of feminists such as Judith Butler. Gender is an important area of study in many disciplines, such as literary theory, drama studies, film theory, performance theory, contemporary art history, anthropology, sociology, psychology and psychoanalysis. These disciplines sometimes differ in their approaches to how and why they study gender. For instance in anthropology, sociology and psychology, gender is often studied as a practice, whereas in cultural studies representations of gender are more often examined. Gender studies is also a discipline in itself: an interdisciplinary area of study that incorporates methods and approaches from a wide range of disciplines. Each field came to regard "gender" as a practice, sometimes referred to as something that is performative. Feminist theory of psychoanalysis, articulated mainly by Julia Kristeva (the "semiotic" and "abjection") and Bracha Ettinger (the "matrixial trans-subjectivity" and the "primal mother-phantasies"), and informed both by Freud, Lacan and the Object relations theory, is very influential in gender studies.

Gender Studies and Psychoanalytic Theory

Sigmund Freud

Some feminist critics have dismissed the work of Sigmund Freud as sexist, because of his view that women are 'mutilated and must learn to accept their lack of a penis' (in Freud's terms a "deformity"). On the other hand, feminist theorists such as Juliet Mitchell, Nancy Chodorow, Jessica Benjamin, Jane Gallop, Bracha Ettinger, Shoshana Felman, Griselda Pollock and Jane Flax have argued that psychoanalytic theory is vital to the feminist project and must, like other theoretical traditions, be adapted by women to free it from vestiges of sexism. Shulamith Firestone, in "Freudianism: The Misguided Feminism", discusses how Freudianism is almost completely accurate, with the exception of one crucial detail: everywhere that Freud writes "penis", the word should be replaced with "power".

Jacques Lacan

Lacan's theory of sexuation organises femininity and masculinity according to different unconscious structures. Both male and female subjects participate in the "phallic" organisation, and the feminine side of sexuation is "supplementary" and not opposite or complementary. Sexuation (sexual situation) — the development of gender-roles and role-play in childhood — breaks down concepts of gender identity as innate or biologically determined (clarify-refutes? challenges?) Critics like Elizabeth Grosz accuse Jacques

Lacan of maintaining a sexist tradition in psychoanalysis. Others, such as Judith Butler, Bracha Ettinger and Jane Gallop have used Lacanian work, though in a critical way, to develop gender theory.

Julia Kristeva

Julia Kristeva has significantly developed the field of semiotics. In her work on abjection, she structures subjectivity upon the abjection of the mother and argues that the way in which an individual excludes (or abjects) their mother as means of forming an identity is similar to the way in which societies are constructed. She contends that patriarchal cultures, like individuals, have had to exclude the maternal and the feminine so that they can come into being.

Mark Blechner

Mark Blechner expanded psychoanalytic views of sex and gender, calling psychoanalysis "the once and future queer science". He has argued that there is a "gender fetish" in western society, in which the gender of sexual partners is given enormously disproportionate attention over other factors involved in sexual attraction, such as age and social class. He proposes that the words "homosexuality" and "heterosexuality" be given prefixes, depending on the dimension that is the same or different between partners. "Age heterosexuality" would indicate an attraction between people of different ages, for example. What is conventionally called "heterosexuality" (attraction between a man and a woman) would be called "gender heterosexuality". Cultures can have very different norms of maleness and masculinity. Blechner identifies the terror, in Western males, of penetration. Yet in many societies, being gay is defined only by being a male who lets himself be penetrated. Males who penetrate other males are considered masculine and not gay and are not the targets of prejudice. In other cultures, however, 'receptive fellatio' is the norm for early adolescence and seen as a requirement for developing normal manliness.

Literary Theory

Psychoanalytically oriented French feminism focused on visual and literary theory all along. Virginia Woolf's legacy as well as "Adrienne Rich's call for women's revisions of literary texts, and history as well, has galvanised a generation of feminist authors to reply with texts of their own". Griselda Pollock and other femininsts have articulated Myth and Poetry and literature, from the point of view of gender.

Post-modern Influence

The emergence of post-feminism affected gender studies, causing a movement in theories identity away from the concept of fixed or essentialist gender identity, to post-modern fluid or multiple identities.

More recently, the relation between post-modernism or post-structuralism and masculinity has been considered. Masculinity can be taken as always in movement and never fixed or stable. See Reeser, *Masculinities in Theory* (2010) for a comprehensive overview of this approach.

Women's Studies

Women's studies is an interdisciplinary academic field devoted to topics concerning women, feminism, gender, and politics. It often includes feminist theory, women's history (e.g. a history of women's suffrage) and social history, women's fiction, women's health, feminist psychoanalysis and the feminist and gender studies-influenced practice of most of the humanities and social sciences.

Judith Butler

The concept of gender performativity is at the core of Butler's work, notably in *Gender Trouble*. In Butler's terms the performance of gender, sex, and sexuality is about power in society. She locates the construction of the "gendered, sexed, desiring subject" in "regulative discourses". A part of Butler's argument concerns the role of sex in the construction of "natural" or coherent gender and sexuality. In her account, gender and heterosexuality are constructed as natural because the opposition of the male and female sexes is perceived as natural in the social imaginary.

Historian and theorist Bryan Palmer argues that gender studies current reliance on post-structuralism — with its reification of discourse and avoidance of the structures of oppression and struggles of resistance — obscures the origins, meanings, and consequences of historical events and processes, and he seeks to counter the current gender studies with an argument for the necessity to analyze lived experience and the structures of subordination and power. Pope Benedict XVI has denounced some of the gender theories, warning that they blur the distinction between male and female and could thus lead to the "self-destruction" of the human race. Rosi Braidotti has criticized gender studies as: "the take-over of the feminist agenda by studies on masculinity, which results in transferring funding from feminist faculty positions to other kinds of positions. There have been cases...of positions advertised as 'gender studies' being given away to the 'bright boys'. Some of the competitive take-over has to do with gay studies. Of special significance in this discussion is the role of the mainstream publisher Routledge who, in our opinion, is responsible for promoting gender as a way of deradicalising the feminist agenda, re-marketing masculinity and gay male identity instead." Calvin Thomas countered that, "as Joseph Allen Boone points out, 'many of the men in the academy who are feminism's most supportive allies' are gay," and that it is "disingenuous" to ignore the ways in which mainstream publishers such as Routledge have promoted feminist theorists.

Understanding Cultural Studies

Cultural studies is an academic field grounded in critical theory and literary criticism. It concerns the political nature of contemporary culture, as well as its historical foundations, conflicts, and defining traits. It is distinguished from cultural anthropology and ethnic studies in both objective and methodology. Researchers concentrate on how a particular medium or message relates to ideology, social class, nationality, ethnicity, sexuality, and/or gender, rather than investigating a particular culture or area of the world. Cultural studies approaches subjects holistically, combining feminist theory, social theory, political theory, history, philosophy, literary theory, media theory, film/video studies, communication studies, political economy, translation studies, museum studies and art history/criticism to study cultural phenomena in various societies. Thus, cultural studies seeks to understand the ways in which meaning is generated, disseminated, and produced through various practices, beliefs, institutions, and political, economic, or social structures within a given culture.

The term was coined by Richard Hoggart in 1964 when he founded the Birmingham Centre for Contemporary Cultural Studies or CCCS. It has since become strongly associated with Stuart Hall, who succeeded Hoggart as Director. From the 1970s onward, Stuart Hall's pioneering work, along with his colleagues Paul Willis, Dick Hebdige, Tony Jefferson, and Angela McRobbie, created an international intellectual movement. Many cultural studies scholars employed Marxist methods of analysis, exploring the relationships between cultural forms (the superstructure) and that of the political economy (the base). By the 1970s, however, the politically formidable British working classes were in decline. Britain's manufacturing industries were fading and union rolls were shrinking. Yet, millions of working class Britons backed the rise of Margaret Thatcher. For Stuart Hall and other Marxist theorists, this shift in loyalty from the Labour Party to the Conservative Party was antithetical to the interests of the working class and had to be explained in terms of cultural politics. In order to understand the changing political circumstances of class, politics, and culture in the United Kingdom, scholars at the CCCS turned to the work of Antonio Gramsci, an Italian thinker of the 1920s and 30s. Gramsci had been concerned with similar issues: why would Italian labourers and peasants vote for fascists? Why, in other words, would working people vote to give more control to corporations, and see their own rights and freedoms abrogated? Gramsci modified classical Marxism in seeing culture as a key instrument of political and social control. In this view, capitalists use not only brute force (police, prisons, repression, military) to maintain control, but also penetrate the everyday culture of working people. Thus, the key rubric for Gramsci and for cultural studies is that of cultural hegemony.

Scott Lash writes,

> In the work of Hall, Hebdige and McRobbie, popular culture came to the fore... What Gramsci gave to this was the importance of consent and culture. If the fundamental Marxists saw power in terms of class versus class, then Gramsci gave to us a question of class alliance. The rise of cultural studies itself was based on the decline of the prominence of fundamental class-versus-class politics.

Edgar and Sedgwick write,

> The theory of hegemony was of central importance to the development of British cultural studies [particularly the CCCS]. It facilitated analysis of the ways in which subordinate groups actively resist and respond to political and economic domination. The subordinate groups need not be seen merely as the passive dupes of the dominant class and its ideology.

This line of thinking opened up fruitful work exploring agency, a theoretical outlook which reinserted the active, critical capacities of all people. Notions of agency have supplanted much scholarly emphasis on groups of people (e.g. the working class, primitives, colonised peoples, women) whose political consciousness and scope of action was generally limited to their position within certain economic and political structures. In other words, many economists, sociologists, political scientists, and historians have traditionally deprived everyday people of a role in shaping their world or outlook, although anthropologists since the 1960s have foregrounded the power of agents to contest structure, first in the work of transactionalists like Fredrik Barth, and then in works inspired by resistance theory and post-colonial theory. At times, cultural studies' romance with agency nearly excluded the possibility of oppression, overlooks the fact that the subaltern have their own politics, and romanticises agency, overblowing its potentiality and pervasiveness. In work of this kind, popular in the 1990s, many cultural studies scholars discovered in consumers ways of creatively using and subverting commodities and dominant ideologies. This orientation has come under fire for a variety of reasons. Cultural studies concerns itself with the meaning and practices of everyday life. Cultural practices comprise the ways people do particular things (such as watching television, or eating out) in a given culture. In any given practice, people use various objects (such as iPods or crucifixes). Hence, this field studies the meanings and uses people attribute to various objects and practices. Recently, as capitalism has spread throughout the world (a process associated with globalisation), cultural studies has begun to analyse local and global forms of resistance to Western hegemony.

In his book *Introducing Cultural Studies*, Ziauddin Sardar lists the following five main characteristics of cultural studies:

- Cultural studies aims to examine its subject matter in terms of cultural practices and their relation to power. For example, a study of a subculture (such as white working class youth in London) would consider the social practices of the youth as they relate to the dominant classes.
- It has the objective of understanding culture in all its complex forms and of analysing the social and political context in which culture manifests itself.
- It is both the object of study and the location of political criticism and action. For example, not only would a cultural studies scholar study an object, but she/he would connect this study to a larger, progressive political project.
- It attempts to expose and reconcile the division of knowledge, to overcome the split between tacit cultural knowledge and objective (universal) forms of knowledge.
- It has a commitment to an ethical evaluation of modern society and to a radical line of political action.

Scholars in the United Kingdom and the United States developed somewhat different versions of cultural studies after the field's inception in the late 1970s. The British version of cultural studies was developed in the 1950s and 1960s mainly under the influence first of Richard Hoggart, E.P. Thompson, and Raymond Williams, and later Stuart Hall and others at the Centre for Contemporary Cultural Studies at the University of Birmingham. This included overtly political, left-wing views, and criticisms of popular culture as 'capitalist' mass culture; it absorbed some of the ideas of the Frankfurt School critique of the "culture industry" (i.e. mass culture). This emerges in the writings of early British cultural-studies scholars and their influences: see the work of for example, Raymond Williams, Stuart Hall, Paul Willis, and Paul Gilroy. In contrast, "cultural studies was grounded in a pragmatic, liberal-pluralist tradition" in the United States (Lindlof & Taylor, 2002, p. 60). The American version of cultural studies initially concerned itself more with understanding the subjective and appropriative side of audience reactions to, and uses of, mass culture; for example, American cultural-studies advocates wrote about the liberatory aspects of fandom. The distinction between American and British strands, however, has faded. In Canada, cultural studies has sometimes focused on issues of technology and society, continuing the emphasis in the work of Marshall McLuhan and others. In Australia, there has sometimes been a special emphasis on cultural policy. In South Africa, human rights and Third World issues are among the topics treated. There were a number of exchanges between Birmingham and

Italy, resulting in work on Italian leftism, and theories of postmodernism. On the other hand, there is a debate in Latin America about the relevance of cultural studies, with some researchers calling for more action-oriented research. Cultural studies is relatively undeveloped in France, where there is a stronger tradition of semiotics, as in the writings of Roland Barthes. Also in Germany it is undeveloped, probably due to the continued influence of the Frankfurt School, which has developed a body of writing on such topics as mass culture, modern art and music. Some researchers, especially in early British cultural studies, apply a Marxist model to the field. This strain of thinking has some influence from the Frankfurt School, but especially from the structuralist Marxism of Louis Althusser and others. The main focus of an orthodox Marxist approach concentrates on the production of meaning. This model assumes a mass production of culture and identifies power as residing with those producing cultural artifacts. In a Marxist view, those who control the means of production (the economic base) essentially control a culture. Other approaches to cultural studies, such as feminist cultural studies and later American developments of the field, distance themselves from this view. They criticize the Marxist assumption of a single, dominant meaning, shared by all, for any cultural product. The non-Marxist approaches suggest that different ways of consuming cultural artifacts affect the meaning of the product. This view is best exemplified by the book *Doing Cultural Studies: The Case of the Sony Walkman* (by Paul du Gay et al.), which seeks to challenge the notion that those who produce commodities control the meanings that people attribute to them. Feminist cultural analyst, theorist and art historian Griselda Pollock contributed to cultural studies from viewpoints of art history and psychoanalysis. The writer Julia Kristeva was an influential voice in the turn of the century, contributing to cultural studies from the field of art and psychoanalytical French feminism. Ultimately, this perspective criticizes the traditional view assuming a passive consumer, particularly by underlining the different ways people read, receive, and interpret cultural texts. On this view, a consumer can appropriate, actively reject, or challenge the meaning of a product. These different approaches have shifted the focus away from the production of items. Instead, they argue that consumption plays an equally important role, since the way consumers consume a product gives meaning to an item. Some closely link the act of consuming with cultural identity. Stuart Hall and John Fiske have become influential in these developments. In the context of cultural studies, the idea of a text not only includes written language, but also films, photographs, fashion or hairstyles: the texts of cultural studies comprise all the meaningful artifacts of culture. Similarly, the discipline widens the concept of "culture". "Culture" for a cultural studies researcher not only includes traditional high culture (the culture of ruling social groups) and popular culture, but also everyday meanings and practices.

The last two, in fact, have become the main focus of cultural studies. A further and recent approach is comparative cultural studies, based on the discipline of comparative literature and cultural studies.

Contemporary Cultural Studies

Sociologist Scott Lash has recently putforth the idea that cultural studies is entering a new phase. Arguing that the political and economic milieu has fundamentally altered from that of the 1970s, he writes, "I want to suggest that power now... is largely post-hegemonic... Hegemony was the concept that de facto crystallised cultural studies as a discipline. Hegemony means domination through consent as much as coercion. It has meant domination through ideology or discourse..." He writes that the flow of power is becoming more internalised, that there has been "a shift in power from the hegemonic mode of 'power over' to an intensive notion of power from within (including domination from within) and power as a generative force." Resistance to power, in other words, becomes complicated when power and domination are increasingly (re)produced within oneself, within subaltern groups, within exploited people.

On the same subject, American feminist theorist and author of *Gender Trouble*, Judith Butler wrote in the scholarly journal *Diacritics* an essay entitled "Further Reflections on the Conversions of Our Time", in which she described the shift in these terms:

"The move from a structuralist account in which capital is understood to structure social relations in relatively homologous ways to a view of hegemony in which power relations are subject to repetition, convergence, and rearticulation brought the question of temporality into the thinking of structure, and marked a shift from a form of Althusserian theory that takes structural totalities as theoretical objects to one in which the insights into the contingent possibility of structure inaugurate a renewed conception of hegemony as bound up with the contingent sites and strategies of the rearticulation of power."

In response, however, Richard Johnson argues that Lash appears to have misunderstood the most basic concept of the discipline. 'Hegemony', even in the writings of Antonio Gramsci, is not understood as a mode of domination at all, but as a form of political leadership which involves a complex set of relationships between various groups and individuals and which always proceeds from the immanence of power to all social relations. This complex understanding has been taken much further in the work of Stuart Hall and that of political theorist Ernesto Laclau, who has had some influence on Cultural Studies. It is, therefore, unclear as to why Lash claims that Cultural Studies has understood hegemony as a form of domination, or where the originality of his theory of power is actually thought to lie.

Institutionally, the discipline has undergone major shifts. The Department of Cultural Studies at the University of Birmingham, which was descended from the Centre for Contemporary Cultural Studies, closed in 2002, although by this time the intellectual centre of gravity of the discipline had long since shifted to other universities throughout the world. Strong cultural studies programmes can be found in the United Kingdom, North and South America, Europe, Australia, and Asia, and there are a host of journals and conferences where cultural studies research is published and presented.

Critical Views

Cultural studies is not a unified theory but a diverse field of study encompassing many different approaches, methods, and academic perspectives; as in any academic discipline, cultural studies academics frequently debate among themselves. However, some academics from other fields have criticised the discipline as a whole. It has been popular to dismiss cultural studies as an academic fad. Yale literature professor Harold Bloom has been an outspoken critic of the cultural studies model of literary studies. Critics such as Bloom see cultural studies as it applies to literary scholarship as a vehicle of careerism by academics, instead promoting essentialist theories of culture, mobilising arguments that scholars should promote the public interest by studying what makes beautiful literary works beautiful.

Bloom stated his position during the 3 September 2000 episode of C-SPAN's Booknotes:

[T]here are two enemies of reading now in the world, not just in the English-speaking world. One [is] the lunatic destruction of literary studies... and its replacement by what is called cultural studies in all of the universities and colleges in the English-speaking world, and everyone knows what that phenomenon is. I mean, the...now-weary phrase 'political correctness' remains a perfectly good descriptive phrase for what has gone on and is, alas, still going on almost everywhere and which dominates, I would say, rather more than three-fifths of the tenured faculties in the English-speaking world, who really do represent a treason of the intellectuals, I think, a 'betrayal of the clerks'.

Literary critic Terry Eagleton is not wholly opposed to cultural studies theory like Bloom, but has criticised certain aspects of it, highlighting what he sees as its strengths and weaknesses in books such as After Theory (2003). For Eagleton, literary and cultural theory have the potential to say important things about the "fundamental questions" in life, but theorists have rarely realised this potential. Whereas sociology was founded upon various historic works which purposefully set out to distinguish the subject as distinct from philosophy or psychology, cultural studies lacks any fundamental literature explicitly founding a new discipline. A relevant criticism comes from Pierre

Bourdieu who, working in the sociological tradition, wrote on similar topics such as photography, art museums, and modern literature. Bourdieu's point is that cultural studies lacks scientific method. His own work makes innovative use of statistics and in-depth interviews. Cultural studies is relatively unstructured as an academic field. It is difficult to hold researchers accountable for their claims because there is no agreement on method and validity.

The Sokal Affair

One of the most prominent critiques of cultural studies came from physicist Alan Sokal, who submitted an article to a cultural-studies journal, *Social Text*. This article was what Sokal thought would be a parody of what he perceived to be the "fashionable nonsense" of postmodernists working in cultural studies. As the paper was coming out, Sokal published an article in a self-described "academic gossip" magazine *Lingua Franca*, revealing the hoax. His explanation for doing this was:

> Politically, I'm angered because most (though not all) of this silliness is emanating from the self-proclaimed Left. We're witnessing here a profound historical volte-face. For most of the past two centuries, the Left has been identified with science and against obscurantism; we have believed that rational thought and the fearless analysis of objective reality (both natural and social) are incisive tools for combating the mystifications promoted by the powerful — not to mention being desirable human ends in their own right. The recent turn of many "progressive" or "leftist" academic humanists and social scientists toward one or another form of epistemic relativism betrays this worthy heritage and undermines the already fragile prospects for progressive social critique. Theorising about "the social construction of reality" won't help us find an effective treatment for AIDS or devise strategies for preventing global warming. Nor can we combat false ideas in history, sociology, economics and politics if we reject the notions of truth and falsity.

Communication Studies

Communication studies is an academic field that deals with processes of communication, commonly defined as the sharing of symbols over distances in space and time. Hence, communication studies encompasses a wide range of topics and contexts ranging from face-to-face conversation to speeches to mass media outlets such as television broadcasting. Communication studies, as a discipline, is also often interested in how audiences interpret information and the political, cultural, economic, and social dimensions of speech and language in context. Communication is institutionalised under many different names at different universities and in various countries, including "communication", "communication studies", "speech communication", "rhetorical studies", "communications science", "media studies", "communication arts", "mass communication", "media ecology,", "communication and media science" and sometimes even "mediology" although the latter is a different area of study. Communication studies often overlaps with academic programmes in journalism, film and cinema, radio and television, advertising and public relations and performance studies. Recently, institutions have migrated towards the common term of "communication studies" to encapsulate and cohere the vast depth and breadth of the field. In the United States, the National Communication Association (NCA) recognises nine distinct but often overlapping sub-disciplines within the broader communication discipline: Communication and Technology, Critical-Cultural, Health, Intercultural-International, Interpersonal-Small Group, Mass Communication, Organisational, Political, and Rhetorical. The International Communication Association (ICA) recognises a much larger and evolving list of sections, including among others Communication History; Communication Law and Policy; Ethnicity and Race in Communication; Feminist Scholarship; Gay, Lesbian, Bisexual and Transgender Studies; Global Communication and Social Change; Information Systems; Instructional/ Developmental Communication; Journalism Studies; Language and Social Interaction; Organisational Communication; Philosophy of Communication; Political Communication; Popular Communication; Public Relations; and Visual Communication Studies.

Communication studies is often considered a part of both the social sciences and the humanities, drawing heavily on fields such as sociology, psychology, anthropology, biology, political science, and economics as well as rhetoric, literary studies, linguistics, and semiotics. The field can incorporate and overlap with the work of other disciplines as well, however, including engineering, architecture, mathematics, computer science, gender and sexuality studies. The vast breadth and interdisciplinary nature of communication studies has understandably made it difficult for both students and institutions to place it within the broader educational system. Despite intellectual incoherence, the field attracts and sustains large numbers of students, scholarly journals, professional associations, and lively discussions across the academy for researchers, educators, lawmakers, businesses, and reformers. Broadly understood, the contemporary study of communication per se interfaces and overlaps with areas such as business, organisational development, philosophy, languages, composition, theatre, debate (often called "forensics"), literary criticism, sociology, psychology, history, anthropology, semiotics, international policy, economics and political science, among others. The breadth and the primacy of communication in many areas of life is responsible for the ubiquity of communication studies, as well as for the resulting confusion about what does and does not constitute communication. Ongoing debates rage whether communication studies can best be understood as a discipline, a field, or simply a topic. Most US graduate programmes in Communication today trace their history through speech to ancient rhetoric. Programmes in Communication, Communication Arts or Communication Sciences often include Organisational Communication, Interpersonal Communication, Speech Communication (or Rhetoric), Mass Communication, and sometimes Journalism, Film criticism, Theatre, Political science (e.g., political campaign strategies, public speaking, effects of media on elections), or Radio, Television or Film production. Graduates of formal communication programmes can be found in a wide range of fields working as university professors, marketing researchers, media editors and designers, journalists, human resources managers, corporate trainers, public relations practitioners, and media managers and consultants in a variety of fields including, media production, life coaching, public speaking, organisational, political campaign/issue management and public policy.

Various aspects of communication have long been the subject of human study. In ancient Greece and Rome, the study of rhetoric, the art of oratory and persuasion, was a vital subject for students. One significant ongoing debate was whether one could be an effective speaker in a base cause (Sophists) or whether excellent rhetoric came from the excellence of the orator's character (Socrates, Plato, Cicero). Through the European Middle Ages and Renaissance, grammar, rhetoric, and logic constituted the entire trivium, the base of the system of classical learning in Europe.

History of Communication Studies in North America

1900s–1920s

Though the study of communication reaches back to antiquity and beyond, early twentieth-century work by Charles Horton Cooley, Walter Lippmann, and John Dewey has been of particular importance for the academic discipline as it stands today in the United States. In his 1909 *Social Organisation: a Study of the Larger Mind*, Cooley defines communication as "the mechanism through which human relations exist and develop—all the symbols of the mind, together with the means of conveying them through space and preserving them in time." This view, which has subsequently been largely marginalised in sociology, gave processes of communication a central and constitutive place in the study of social relations. *Public Opinion*, published in 1922 by Walter Lippmann, couples this view of the constitutive importance of communication with a fear that the rise of new technologies and institutions of mass communication allowed for the manufacture of consent and generated dissonance between what he called 'the world outside and the pictures in our heads' on a scale that made democracy as classically conceived almost impossible to realise. John Dewey's 1927 *The Public and its Problems* drew on the same view of communications, but coupled it instead with an optimistic progressive and democratic reform agenda, arguing famously "communication can alone create a great community". Cooley, Lippmann, and Dewey capture themes like the central importance of communication in social life, the rise of large and potentially powerful media institutions and the development of new communications technologies in societies undergoing rapid transformation, and questions regarding the relationship between communication, democracy, and community. All these remain central to the discipline of communication studies. Many of these concerns are also central to the work of writers such as Gabriel Tarde and Theodor W. Adorno, which has been central to the development of communication studies elsewhere. The first decades of the twentieth century also saw the development of parallel currents of cultural criticism that drew less on the social sciences and more on the humanities. Though trained as a sociologist, the work of W. E. B. Du Bois on art and spirituals stands out here. The study of American public address began during this time frame. In 1925, Herbert A. Wichelns published the essay "The Literary Criticism of Oratory" in the book *Studies in Rhetoric and Public Speaking in Honor of James Albert Winans.* Wicheln's essay attempted to "put rhetorical studies on par with literary studies as an area of academic interest and research." Wichelns wrote that oratory should be taken as seriously as literature, and therefore, it should be subject to criticism and analysis. Although the essay is now standard reading in most rhetorical criticism courses, it had little immediate impact (from 1925–1935) on the field of rhetorical studies.

1930s–1950s

The institutionalisation of communication studies in U.S. higher education and research has often been traced to Columbia University, the University of Chicago, and the University of Illinois Urbana-Champaign, where early pioneers and institutionalisers like Paul F. Lazarsfeld, Harold Lasswell, and Wilbur Schramm worked. The work of Samuel Silas Curry, who founded the School of Expression in 1879 in Boston, is also noted in early communication research. Today, the School of Expression is known as Curry College, located in Milton, MA, which houses one of the nation's oldest Communication programmes. The Bureau of Applied Social Research was established in 1944 at Columbia University by Paul F. Lazarsfeld. It was a continuation of the Rockefeller Foundation-funded Radio Project that he had led at various institutions (University of Newark, Princeton) from 1937, which had been at Columbia as the Office of Radio Research since 1939. In its various incarnations, the

Radio Project had involved Lazarsfeld himself, and people like Adorno, Hadley Cantril, Herta Herzog, Gordon Allport, and Frank Stanton (who went on to be president of CBS). Lazarsfeld and the Bureau mobilized substantial sums for research, and produced, with various co-authors, a series of books and edited volumes that helped define the discipline, such as *Personal Influence* (1955) which remains a classic in what is called the 'media effects'-tradition. At Columbia, communications studies have traditionally been closely aligned with sociology, and people like Robert Merton and others from the sociology programme were at times involved. The university did only recently, in the 1990s, establish an actual degree-granting graduate programme in communications, illustrating how much important research on communications continues to take place outside the discipline that carries the name. The Bureau, and Lazarsfeld's research more generally, exemplifies the close relations that have sometimes existed between communication studies and the media industries. From the 1940s and onwards, the University of Chicago was home to several temporary but important committees and commissions on communications, programmes that also educated several leading communication scholars.

In contrast to what took place at Columbia, these programmes explicitly claimed the name 'communications' for themselves. The Committee on Communication and Public Opinion, also funded by the Rockefeller Foundation, was staffed with, in addition to Lasswell, people such as Douglas Waples, Samuel A. Stouffer, Louis Wirth, and Herbert Blumer, all of whom held positions elsewhere at the university. They formed a committee that essentially served as a scholarly and educational extension of the federal government's increasing interest in communications during times of war, and was in particular closely linked to the Office of War Information. The committee is a reminder of connection as important as the Bureau's with the industry, namely the connection between communication studies and government interests and funding. Chicago later provided an institutional home for The Hutchins Commission on the Freedom of the Press and the Committee on Communication (1947–1960). The latter was a degree-granting programme that counted Elihu Katz, Bernard Berelson, Edward Shils, and David Riesman amongst its faculty, and produced graduates like Herbert J. Gans and Michael Gurevitch. The committee also produced publications like Berelson and Janowitz, *Public Opinion and Communication* (1950) and the journal *Studies in Public Communication*.

The Institute for Communications Research was founded at the University of Illinois at Urbana-Champaign in 1947 by Wilbur Schramm, who was a key figure in the post-war institutionalisation of communication studies in the US. Like the various Chicago committees, the Illinois programme claimed the name 'communications' and granted graduate degrees in the subject. Schramm, who, in contrast to the more social science-inspired figures at Columbia and Chicago, had a background in English literature, developed communication studies partly by merging existing programmes in speech communication, rhetoric, and, especially, journalism under the aegis of communication. He also edited a textbook *The Process and Effects of Mass Communication* (1954) that helped define the field, partly by claiming the Lazarsfeld, Lasswell, Carl Hovland, and Kurt Lewin as its founding fathers. He also wrote several other manifestos for the discipline, including *The Science of Human Communication* 1963. Schramm and the Institute moved on to Stanford University in 1955. Many of Schramm's students, such as Everett Rogers, went on to make important contributions of their own.

1950s–1960s

From the 1950s onwards, communications studies branched out in several new and often very different directions. Numerous new programmes opened up at various universities, and new journals were established. The work of what has been called 'medium theorists', arguably defined by Harold Innis '(1950) *Empire and Communications* grew increasingly important, and was popularized by Marshall McLuhan in his *Understanding Media* (1964). This perspective informs the later work of Joshua Meyrowitz (*No Sense of Place*, 1986). Two developments in the 1940s shifted the paradigm of communication studies in the 1950s and thereafter toward a more-quantitative orientation, or at least the inescapable need to consider such an orientation. One was cybernetics, as formulated by Norbert Wiener in his *Cybernetics: Or the Control and Communication in the Animal and the Machine*. The other was information theory, as recast in quantitative terms by Claude E. Shannon and Warren Weaver in their *Mathematical Theory of Communication*. These works were widely appropriated to, and offered for some the prospect of, a general theory of society. The tradition of critical theory associated with the Frankfurt School was, as in Europe, an important source of influence for many researchers. While done out of sociology departments, the work of Jürgen Habermas, the US-based Leo Löwenthal, Herbert Marcuse, and Siegfried Kracauer, as well as earlier figures like Adorno and Max Horkheimer continued to inform a whole tradition of cultural criticism that often focused both empirically and theoretically on the culture industry. In 1953, to address growing needs in industry, Rensselaer Polytechnic Institute began offering a master of science degree in technical writing. In the 1960s, partly because of the need to represent that the degree incorporated training in oral and audiovisual communication, the degree title became technical communication. It was the brainchild of longtime RPI professor and administrator Jay R. Gould.

1960s–1970s

In the 1960s Gould and his colleagues experienced increasing demand for doctoral-level studies in technical and business communication. As a result, in 1965 RPI began its Ph.D. programme in Communication and Rhetoric. This Ph.D. degree programme became a prototype for other technologically oriented programmes in the United States and other industrialised countries. The 1960s and 1970s saw the development of Cultivation Theory, pioneered by George Gerbner at the Annenberg School for Communication at the University of Pennsylvania. This approach shifted emphasis from the short-term effects that had been the central interest of many earlier works on the media, and instead tried to track the effect of exposure to, for instance, television over time on viewers' perceptions of reality.

1970s–1980s

Neil Postman founded the media ecology programme at New York University in 1971. Media ecologists draw on a wide range of inspirations in their attempts to study entire media environments in an even broader and more cultural fashion than the work done in the Canadian medium theory tradition. This perspective is the basis of a separate professional association, the Media Ecology Association. In 1972, Maxwell McCombs and Donald Shaw published a path-breaking article that offered an agenda-setting theory of media effects that gave new ways of conceptualising the short-term media effects that earlier work had generally deemed limited. This approach, organised around additional ideas such as framing, priming, and gatekeeping, has been highly influential, especially in the study of political communication and news coverage. The 1970s also saw the development of what became known as uses and gratifications research, developed by scholars such as Elihu Katz, Jay G. Blumler, and Michael Gurevitch. Instead of looking at communications processes simply as a one-way flow from senders to receivers, this approach began scrutinising what audiences get out of communications, what they do with it, why they engage with it—especially with mass media.

Defining Cultural Bias

Cultural bias is the phenomenon of interpreting and judging phenomena by standards inherent to one's own culture. The phenomenon is sometimes considered a problem central to social and human sciences, such as economics, psychology, anthropology, and sociology. Some practitioners of the aforementioned fields have attempted to develop methods and theories to compensate for or eliminate cultural bias. Cultural bias occurs when people of a culture make assumptions about conventions, including conventions of language, notation, proof and evidence. They are then accused of mistaking these assumptions for laws of logic or nature. Numerous such biases exist, concerning cultural norms for colour, location of body parts, mate selection, concepts of justice, linguistic and logical validity, acceptability of evidence, and taboos.

Examples

People who read English often assume that it is natural to scan a visual field from left to right and from top to bottom. In the United States it is typical for the "on" position of a toggle switch to be "up", whereas in the UK, Australia, and New Zealand it is "down." Also, in these countries, North is the top of a map, up is usually the larger quantity and better, as well. As another example, Japanese do not place an X in a check-box to indicate acceptance—this indicates refusal.

These conventions are generally useful, as once one is used to light switches behaving a certain way one does not need to learn a per-light switch rule but just a general rule. Unfortunately, when people move between cultures or design something for a different group they often do not attend to which conventions remain and which change. Linguistic and ethnic groups often do not share these notational assumptions. Notational and operative assumptions can change control systems if the users implement, from a different culture than the designers, funnel interpretations from their original world view. Safety-critical systems, according to Seidner, become responses to threats of control. Through the emergence of majority and minority categories in society, cultural biases ensue.

Role of Cross-cultural Communication

Cross-cultural communication (also frequently referred to as intercultural communication, which is also used in a different sense, though) is a field of study that looks at how people from differing cultural backgrounds communicate, in similar and different ways among themselves, and how they endeavour to communicate across cultures.

During the Cold War, the United States economy was largely self- contained because the world was polarized into two separate and competing powers: the east and west. However, changes and advancements in economic relationships, political systems, and technological options began to break down old cultural barriers. Business transformed from individual- country capitalism to global capitalism. Thus, the study of cross-cultural communication was originally found within businesses and the government both seeking to expand globally. Businesses began to offer language training to their employees. Businesses found that their employees were ill equipped for overseas work in the globalising market. Programmes were developed to train employees to understand how to act when abroad. With this also came the development of the Foreign Service Institute, or FSI, through the Foreign Service Act of 1946, where government employees received trainings and prepared for overseas posts. There began also implementation of a "world view" perspective in the curriculum of higher education. In 1974, the International Progress Organisation, with the support of UNESCO and under the auspices of Senegalese President Léopold Sédar Senghor, held an international conference on "The Cultural Self-comprehension of Nations" (Innsbruck, Austria, 27–29 July 1974) which called upon United Nations member states "to organise systematic and global comparative research on the different cultures of the world" and "to make all possible efforts for a more intensive training of diplomats in the field of international cultural co-operation ... and to develop the cultural aspects of their foreign policy."

In the past decade, there has become an increasing pressure for universities across the world to incorporate intercultural and international understanding and knowledge into the education of their students. International literacy and cross-cultural understanding have become critical to a country's cultural, technological, economic, and political health. It has become essential for universities to educate, or more importantly, "transform", to function effectively and comfortably in a world characterised by close; multi-faceted relationships and permeable borders. Students must possess a certain level of global competence to understand the world they live in and how they fit into this world. This level of global competence starts at ground level- the university and its faculty- with how they generate and transmit cross-cultural knowledge and information to students.

Cross-cultural communication endeavours to bring together such relatively unrelated areas as cultural anthropology and established areas of communication. Its core is to establish and understand how people from different cultures communicate with each other. Its charge is to also produce some guidelines with which people from different cultures can better communicate with each other. Cross-cultural communication, as in many scholarly fields, is a combination of many other fields. These fields include anthropology, cultural studies, psychology and communication. The field has also moved both toward the treatment of interethnic relations, and toward the study of communication strategies used by co-cultural populations, i.e., communication strategies used to deal with majority or mainstream populations. The study of languages other than one's own can not only serve to help us understand what we as human beings have in common, but also assist us in understanding the diversity which underlies not only our languages, but also our ways of constructing and organising knowledge, and the many different realities in which we all live and interact. Such understanding has profound implications with respect to developing a critical awareness of social relationships. Understanding social relationships and the way other cultures work is the groundwork of successful globalisation business efforts. Language socialisation can be broadly defined as "an investigation of how language both presupposes and creates anew, social relations in cultural context". It is imperative that the speaker understands the grammar of a language, as well as how elements of language are socially situated in order to reach communicative competence. Human experience is culturally relevant, so elements of language are also culturally relevant. One must carefully consider semiotics and the evaluation of sign systems to compare cross-cultural norms of communication. There are several potential problems that come with language socialisation, however. Sometimes people can over-generalise or label cultures with stereotypical and subjective characterisations. Another primary concern with documenting alternative cultural norms revolves around the fact that no social actor uses language in ways that perfectly match normative characterisations. A methodology for investigating how an individual uses language and other semiotic activity to create and use new models of conduct and how this varies from the cultural norm should be incorporated into the study of language socialisation.

However, with the process of globalisation, especially the increasing of global trade, it is unavoidable that different cultures will meet, conflict, and blend together. People from different cultures find it hard to communicate not only due to language barrier but also affected by culture styles. For instance, in independent cultures, such as in the United States, Canada, and Western Europe, an independent figure of self is dominant. This independent figure is characterised by a sense of self relatively distinct from others and the environment. In interdependent cultures, usually identified as Asian as well as many Latin American, African, and Southern European cultures, an interdependent figure of self is dominant. There is a much greater emphasis on the interrelatedness of the individual to others and the environment, the self is meaningful only (or primarily) in the context of social relationships, duties, and roles. In some degree, the effect brought by cultural difference override the language gap. And this culture style difference contributes to one of the biggest challenge for cross-culture communication. Effective communication with people of different cultures is especially challenging. Cultures provide people with ways of thinking—ways of seeing, hearing, and interpreting the world. Thus, the same words can mean different things to people from different cultures, even when they talk the "same" language. When the languages are different, and translation has to be used to communicate, the potential for misunderstandings increases. The study of cross-cultural communication is fast becoming a global research area. As a result, cultural differences in the study of cross-cultural communication can already be found. For example, cross-cultural communication is generally considered to fall within the larger field of communication studies in the US, but it is emerging as a sub-field of applied linguistics in the UK. As the application of cross-cultural communication theory to foreign language education is increasingly appreciated around the world, cross-cultural communication classes can be found within foreign language departments of some universities, while other schools are placing cross-cultural communication programmes in their departments of education.

Incorporation into College Programmes

With the increasing pressures and opportunities of globalisation, the incorporation of international networking alliances has become an "essential mechanism for the internationalisation of higher education". Many universities from around the world have taken great strides to increase intercultural understanding through processes of organisational change and innovations. In general, university processes revolve around four major dimensions which include: organisational change, curriculum innovation, staff development, and student mobility. Ellingboe emphasises these four major dimensions with his own specifications for the internationalisation process. His specifications include: (1) college leadership; (2) faculty members' international involvement in activities with colleagues, research sites, and institutions worldwide; (3) the availability, affordability, accessibility, and transferability of study abroad programmes for students; (4) the presence and integration of international students, scholars, and visiting faculty into campus life; and (5) international co-curricular units (residence halls, conference planning centers, student unions, career centers, cultural immersion and language houses, student activities, and student organisations). Above all, universities need to make sure that they are open and responsive to changes in the outside environment.

In order for internationalisation to be fully effective, the university (including all staff, students, curriculum, and activities) needs to be current with cultural changes, and willing to adapt to these changes. As stated by Ellingboe, internationalisation "is an ongoing, future-oriented, multidimensional, interdisciplinary, leadership-driven vision that involves many stakeholders working to change the internal dynamics of an institution to respond and adapt appropriately to an increasingly diverse, globally focused, ever-changing external environment". New distance learning technologies, such as interactive teleconferencing, enable students located thousands of miles apart to communicate and interact in a virtual classroom.

Research has indicated that certain themes and images such as children, animals, life cycles, relationships, and sports can transcend cultural differences, and may be used in international settings such as traditional and online university classrooms to create common ground among diverse cultures (Van Hook, 2011). The main theories for cross-cultural communication are based on the work done looking at value differences between different cultures, especially the works of Edward T. Hall, Richard D. Lewis, Geert Hofstede, and Fons Trompenaars. Clifford Geertz was also a contributor to this field. Also Jussi V. Koivisto's model on cultural crossing in internationally operating organisations elaborates from this base of research. These theories have been applied to a variety of different communication theories and settings, including general business and management (Fons Trompenaars and Charles Hampden-Turner) and marketing (Marieke de Mooij, Stephan Dahl). There have also been several successful educational projects which concentrate on the practical applications of these theories in cross-cultural situations. These theories have also been criticised mainly by management scholars (e.g. Nigel Holden) for being based on the culture concept derived from 19th century cultural anthropology and emphasising on culture-as-difference and culture-as-essence. Another criticism has been the uncritical way Hofstede's dimensions are served up in textbooks as facts (Peter W. Cardon). There is a move to focus on 'cross-cultural interdependence' instead of the traditional views of comparative differences and similarities between cultures. Cross-cultural management is increasingly seen as a form of knowledge management. Cross-cultural communication gives opportunities to share ideas, experiences, and different perspectives and perception by interacting with local people.

Aspects of Cross Cultural Communication

There are several parameters that may be perceived differently by people of different cultures. These may include:

- *High and Low Context Cultures*: Context is the most important cultural dimension and also immensely difficult to define. The idea of context in culture was an idea put forth by an anthropologist by the name of Edward T Hall. Hall breaks up culture into two main groups: High and Low context cultures. He refers to context as the stimuli, environment or ambiance surrounding the environment. Depending on how a culture relies on the three points to communicate their meaning, will place them in either High or Low context cultures. For example, Hall goes on to explain that low-context cultures assume that the individuals know very little about what they are being told, and therefore must be given a lot of background information. High-context cultures assume the individual is knowledgeable about the subject and has to be given very little background information.
- *Non Verbal, Oral and Written*: The main goal behind improving intercultural audiences is to pay special attention to specific areas

of communication to enhance the effectiveness of the intercultural messages. These specific areas are broken down into three sub categories; Non-verbal, Oral and Written messages. Non-verbal contact involves everything from something as obvious as eye contact and facial expressions to more discrete forms of expression such as the use of space. Experts have labeled the term Kinesics to mean communicating through body movement. Huseman, author of Business Communication, explains that the two most prominent ways of communication through Kinesics is eye contact and facial expressions. Eye contact, Huseman goes on to explain, is the key factor in setting the tone between two individuals and greatly differs in meaning between cultures. In the Americas and Western Europe eye contact is interpreted the same way, conveying interest and honesty. People who avoid eye contact when speaking are viewed in a negative light, withholding information and lacking in general confidence. However, in the Middle East, Africa, and especially Asia eye contact is seen as disrespectful and even challenging of one's authority. People who make eye contact, but only briefly, are seen as respectful and courteous. Facial expressions are their own language by comparison, and universal throughout all cultures. Dale Leathers, for example, states that facial expression can communicate ten basic classes of meaning. The final part to Non-verbal communication lies in our gestures, and can be broken down into five subcategories; Emblems, illustrators, Regulators, Affect Displays, and Adaptors. Emblems and Illustrators are the easiest to communicate since Emblems refer to sign language (such as the "Thumbs Up" which is one of the most recognised symbols in the world) and Illustrators mimic what we speak (such as gesturing how much time is left by holding up a certain amount of fingers). Regulators act as a way of conveying meaning through gestures (raising up one's hand for instance indicates that one has a certain question about what was just said) and become more complicated since the same regulator can have different meanings across different cultures (making a circle with ones hand for instance in the Americas means OK but in Japan the gesture is symbolic for money, and in France conveys the notion of worthlessness). The last two, Affect Displays and Adaptors, are the two the individual has very little to no control over. Affect Displays reveal emotions such as happiness (through a smile) or sadness (mouth trembling, tears) where Adaptors are more subtle such as a yawn or clenching fists in anger. The last Non-verbal type of communication deals with communication through the space around us, or Proxemics.

Huseman goes on to explain that Hall identifies three types of space; Feature-fixed Space, Semifixed Feature Space and Informal Space. Feature-fixed space deals with how cultures arrange their space on a large scale, such as buildings and parks. Semifixed Feature Space deals with how we arrange our space inside said buildings, such as the placement of our desks, chairs and plants. Informal space is the space that we place importance on. Talking distance, how close people sit to one another and office space are all examples. A production line worker will often have to make an appointment to see his supervisor however the supervisor is free to visit the production line workers at will.

Oral and written communication is generally easier to learn, adapt and deal with in the business world for the simple fact that each language is unique. The one difficulty that comes into play is Paralanguage, "Language refers to what is said, Paralanguage refers to how it is said. Even though, logically, the same words should convey the same meaning the volume, rate, and emphasis placed on those words can change the meaning of the phrase. The example given by Huseman took the sentence "I would like to help you" and simply by placing the emphases on the words I, Like, Help, You in four different sentences changes the meaning of the phrase.

Towards Understanding Intercultural Communication Principles

Intercultural communication principles guide the process of exchanging meaningful and unambiguous information across cultural boundaries, in a way that preserves mutual respect and minimises antagonism. For these purposes, culture is a shared system of symbols, beliefs, attitudes, values, expectations, and norms of behaviour. It refers to coherent groups of people whether resident wholly or partly within state territories, or existing without residence in any particular territory. Hence, these principles may have equal relevance when a tourist seeks help, where two well-established independent corporations attempt to merge their operations, and where politicians attempt to negotiate world peace. Two factors have raised the importance of this topic:

- Improvements in communication and transportation technology have made it possible for previously stable cultures to meet in unstructured situations, e.g. the internet opens lines of communication without mediation, while budget airlines transplant ordinary citizens into unfamiliar milieux. Experience proves that merely crossing cultural boundaries can be considered threatening, while positive attempts to interact may provoke defensive responses. Misunderstanding may be compounded by either an exaggerated sensitivity to possible slights, or an exaggerated and over-protective fear of giving offence;

- Some groups believe that the phenomenon of globalisation has reduced cultural diversity and so reduced the opportunity for misunderstandings, but characterising people as a homogeneous market is simplistic. One product or brand only appeals to the material aspirations of one self-selecting group of buyers, and its sales performance will not affect the vast multiplicity of factors that may separate the cultures.

People from different cultures encode and decode messages differently, increasing the chances of misunderstanding, so the safety-first consequence of recognising cultural differences should be to assume that everyone's thoughts and actions are not just like ours. Such assumptions stem from potentially devastating ignorance and can lead to much frustration for members of both cultures. Entering a culture with this type of ethnocentrism, the assumption your own culture is correct, is another by product of ignorance and cultural misunderstanding. Main types of misunderstanding are:

Some cultural characteristics will be easy to identify, e.g. whether people are conscious of status or make displays of material wealth. But many rights are assumed, values are implied, and needs are unspoken, (e.g. for safety, security, love, a sense of belonging to a group, self-esteem, and the ability to attain one's goals).

For example, issues of personal security, dignity, and control will be very different as between an abled and a disabled person. Similarly, there may be problems of respect when a person from a rigidly class-based culture meets a meritocrat, or where there is racism, sexism or religious intolerance in play. In such situations, identity is fundamental when disputing the proper role or "place" of the other, about who is in control of their lives, and how they present themselves to the outside world. But the reality is more deeply rooted in power relationships: about who is on top of the social, economic, and/or political hierarchy. Family members or long term rivals may be obsessed with their mutual competition. The relationships between racial or ethnic groups may be affected by economic jealousy. Nations may assert that their political systems are superior. Such conflicts are difficult to resolve because no-one wants to be the loser, and few are willing to share the winnings. Stereotyping can aggravate these problems and prevent people from realising that there is another way to interpret a situation, or that other groups may define their rights in a different way. Hence, what may appear just or fair to one group can often seem unjust to an opposing group.

People may misinterpret each other's motives. For example, one group may assume that they are simply exchanging information about what they believe, but the other believes that they are negotiating a change in behavior. This is must likely to arise when the parties are not completely honest with each other from the outset. Individuals may wish to protect their privacy, corporations may be concerned about industrial espionage, and politicians may be bound by requirements of secrecy in the national interest. Nevertheless, clarifying the purpose of the interaction is essential to eliminating confusion, particularly if vested interests are involved.

If time is not a factor and those interacting approach their meetings with goodwill and patience, effective communication is more likely. But, if the parties are under pressure (whether generated by external circumstances or internal needs), emotions may colour the exchange. Prejudice is a short-cut decision- making tool. In a crisis, fear and anger may trigger more aggressive tactics, particularly if the meeting is being staged under the gaze of the news media.

Towards Improving Intercultural Communication

It is essential that people research the cultures and communication conventions of those whom they propose to meet. This will minimise the risk of making the elementary mistakes. It is also prudent to set a clear agenda so that everyone understands the nature and purpose of the interaction. When language skills are unequal, clarifying one's meaning in five ways will improve communication:

1. Avoid using slang and idioms, choosing words that will convey only the most specific denotative meaning;
2. Listen carefully and, if in doubt, ask for confirmation of understanding (particularly important if local accents and pronunciation are a problem);
3. Recognise that accenting and intonation can cause meaning to vary significantly; and
4. Respect the local communication formalities and styles, and watch for any changes in body language;
5. Investigate their culture's perception of your culture by reading literature about your culture through their eyes before entering into communication with them. This will allow you to prepare yourself for projected views of your culture you will be bearing as a visitor in their culture.

If it is not possible to learn the other's language, it is expedient to show some respect by learning a few words. In all important exchanges, a translator can convey the message. When writing, the choice of words represent the relationship between the reader and the writer so more thought and care should be invested in the text since it may well be thoroughly analysed by the recipient.

Content and Scope of Media Studies

Media studies is an academic discipline and field of study that deals with the content, history and effects of various media; in particular, the 'mass media'. Media studies may draw on traditions from both the social sciences and the humanities, but mostly from its core disciplines of mass communication, communication, communication sciences and communication studies. Researchers may also develop and employ theories and methods from disciplines including cultural studies, rhetoric, philosophy, literary theory, psychology, political science, political economy, economics, sociology, anthropology, social theory, art history and criticism, film theory, feminist theory, and information theory.

In addition to the interdisciplinary nature of the academic field, popular understandings of media studies encompass:

- Online communication
- Electronic media
- Journalism
- Mass communication
- Media influence
- Creative industries
- Political economy
- Cultural studies
- Media production (Television production, Filmmaking)
- Media psychology

Foundational Media theories include: Media effects theory; agenda setting, priming, framing, political economy, discourse analysis, content analysis, hyperpersonal theory, representation theory, imagined community, public sphere, theories of persuasion, attention, and control, etc.

Most production and journalism courses incorporate media studies content, but academic institutions often establish separate departments. Media studies students may see themselves as observers of media, not creators or practitioners. These distinctions vary across national boundaries. The essential definition of media studies involves the study of media effects. Specific programmes in media studies that focus on the study of media effects have emerged at Fielding Graduate University, Penn State UCLA, and Touro University Worldwide.

Separate strands exist within media studies, such as television studies. Film studies is often considered a separate discipline, though television and video games studies grew out of it, as made evident by the application of basic critical theories such as psychoanalysis, feminism and Marxism.

Critical media theory looks at how the corporate ownership of media production and distribution affects society, and provides a common ground to social conservatives (concerned by the effects of media on the traditional family) and liberals and socialists (concerned by the corporatisation of social discourse). The study of the effects and techniques of advertising forms a cornerstone of media studies.

Contemporary media studies includes the analysis of new media with emphasis on the internet, video games, mobile devices, interactive television, and other forms of mass media which developed from the 1990s. Because these new technologies allow instant communication across the world (chat rooms and instant messaging, online video games, video conferencing), interpersonal communication is an important element in new media studies.

It has been argued that media studies has not fully acknowledged the changes which the internet and digital interactive media have brought about, seeing these as an 'add-on'. David Gauntlett has argued for a 'Media Studies 2.0' which fully recognises the ways in which media has changed, and that traditional boundaries between 'audiences' and 'producers' has collapsed.

Political Communication and Political Economy

From the beginning, media studies are closely related to politics and wars such as campaign research and war propaganda. Political communication mainly studies the connections among politicians, voters and media. It focused on the media effects. There are four main media influence theories: hypodermic needle model (1930s behaviourism), two-step flow model (Katz and Lazarsfeld, 1955), limited effects (Klapper, 1960), and the spiral of silence (Noelle-Neumann, 1984). Also, many scholars studied the technique of political communication such as rhetoric, symbolism etc. Much of this research has been developed in journals of mass communication and public opinion scholarship. In the last quarter century, political economy has played a major part in media studies literature. The theory gained notoriety in media studies particularly with the publication of Edward S. Herman and Noam Chomsky's *Manufacturing Consent*, published in 1988. In the book, the authors discuss a theory of how the United States' media industry operates, which they term a "propaganda model." The model describes a "decentralised and non-conspiratorial market system of control and processing, although at times the government or one or more private actors may take initiatives and mobilise co-ordinated elite handling of an issue."

News Gathering and Distribution

This links to another key theme: not so much the normative theories of how news should come about, but rather the empirical practice of how it does really come about. An early emphasis was on 'gatekeeping': what are the criteria an editor uses to select items from the stream of information at hand, for instance from material provided by the news agencies? Later, emphasis shifted to the entire process of news gathering and distribution. Classical studies were *Making news – A study in the construction of reality* by Gaye Tuchman. (1978), Deciding what's news (at CBS & NBC, Time and Newsweek) by Herbert J. Gans (1979) in the US, and putting reality together – BBC news by Philip Schlesinger (1987). Another influential early study was *The media are American* by British scholar Jeremy Tunstall (1977). It discussed the reasons behind the Anglophone dominance of the industry. Sean McBride, a former Irish minister and co-founder of Amnesty International, led a major study for Unesco: Many voices, One world – Towards a new more just and more efficient world information and communication order (1983). Various legal aspects of this debate were summarised in *The politics of world communication* by Cees Hamelink (1994), *Social and Psychological Ones in Understanding global news* by Jaap van Ginneken (1998).

Media Studies in Australia

Media is studied as a broad subject in most states in Australia, with the state of Victoria being a world leader in curriculum development. Media studies in Australia was first developed as an area of study in Victorian universities in the early 1960s, and in secondary schools in the mid 1960s. Today, all Australian universities teach media studies. According to the Government of Australia's 'Excellence in Research for Australia' report, the leading universities in the country for media studies (which were ranked well above World standards by the report's scoring methodology) are Monash University, QUT, RMIT, University of Melbourne, University of Queensland and UTS. In secondary schools, an early "film studies" course first began being taught as part of the Victorian junior secondary curriculum during the mid 1960s. And, by the early 1970s, an expanded "media studies" course was being taught. The course became part of the senior secondary curriculum (later known as the Victorian Certificate of Education or "VCE") in the 1980s. It has since become, and continues to be, a strong component of the VCE. Notable figures in the development of the Victorian secondary school curriculum were the media artist and director Peter Greenaway, Trevor Barr (who authored one of the first media text books *Reflections of Reality*) and later John Murray (who authored *The Box in the Corner*, *In Focus*, and *10 Lessons in Film Appreciation*). Today, Australian states and territories that teach media studies at a secondary level are Australian Capital Territory, Northern Territory, Queensland, South Australia, Victoria and Western Australia. Media studies does not appear to be taught in the state of New South Wales at a secondary level. In Victoria, the VCE media studies course is structured as: Unit 1 - Representation, Technologies of Representation, and New Media; Unit 2 - Media Production, Australian Media Organisations; Unit 3 - Narrative Texts, Production Planning; and Unit 4 - Media Process, Social Values, and Media Influence. Media studies also form a major part of the primary and junior secondary curriculum, and includes areas such as photography, print media and television. Victoria also hosts the peak media teaching body known as ATOM which publishes Metro, and Screen Education magasines.

Media Studies in Germany

In Germany two main streams of Media Theory or Media Studies can be identified. The first large flow of media theory based in humanities and cultural sciences as the Theater scholarship ("Theaterwissenschaft") and German language and literature studies widens since the 1960s. In this orientation, the Media studies in Germany today mainly developed and established. As one of the first publications to this new direction is by Helmut Kreuzer, published the study Literature Studies - Media Studies (Literaturwissenschaft – Medienwissenschaft), summed up the units of the "Düsseldorfer Germanistentag" 1976. The second stream is comparable to Communication Studies. Pioneered by Elisabeth Noelle-Neumann in the 1940s this stream studies mass media, its institutions and its effects on society and individuals. The term Wissenschaft however, cannot be translated as studies straightforwardly, as both science and humanities equally fall under it. Accordingly, German media theory combines philosophy, psychoanalysis, history, and science studies with the media specific research. Medienwissenschaften is currently one of the most popular university courses in Germany, with many applicants mistakenly assuming that studying it will automatically lead them to a career in TV or other media. This has led to widespread disillusionment, with students blaming the universities for offering highly theoretical course content. The universities maintain that practical journalistic training is not the aim of the academic studies they offer.

Media Studies in India

The media industry is growing in India at the rate of 20 per cent per annum. Together, entertainment and media form the country's sixth biggest industry, with 3.5 million people working in it. Within the next 4–5 years, the industry is expected to gross eighty thousand crores (800 billion rupees) annually.

With a view to making the best use of communication facilities for information, publicity and development, the Government of India in 1962-63 sought the advice of the Ford Foundation/UNESCO team of internationally known mass communication specialists who recommended the setting up of a national institute for training, teaching and research in mass communication.

Media Studies in the Netherlands

In the Netherlands, media studies are split into several academic courses such as (applied) communication sciences, communication- and information sciences, communication and media, media and culture or theater, film and television sciences. Whereas communication sciences focuses on the way people communicate, be it mediated or unmediated, media studies tends to narrow the communication down to just mediated communication. However, it would be a mistake to consider media studies a specialism of communication sciences, since media make up just a small portion of the overall course. Indeed, both studies tend to borrow elements from one another. Communication sciences (or a derivative thereof) can be studied at Erasmus University Rotterdam, Radboud University, Tilburg University, University of Amsterdam, University of Groningen, University of Twente, Roosevelt Academy, University of Utrecht, VU University Amsterdam and Wageningen University and Research Centre. Media studies (or something similar) can be studied at the University of Amsterdam, VU University Amsterdam, Erasmus University Rotterdam and the University of Utrecht.

Media Studies in New Zealand

Media Studies in New Zealand is very healthy, especially due to the NZ film industry and is taught at both secondary and tertiary education institutes. One of the main features of the industry, Weta Digital can be credited with the popularity of Media Studies in NZ. Media Studies in NZ can be regarded as a singular success, with the subject well-established in the tertiary sector (such as Screen and Media Studies at the University of Waikato; Media Studies, Victoria University of Wellington; Film, Television and Media Studies, University of Auckland; Media Studies, Massey University; Communication Studies, University of Otago).

Media Studies in UK

In the UK media studies developed in the 1960s from the academic study of English, and from literary criticism more broadly. The key date, according to Andrew Crisell, is 1959:

When Joseph Trenaman left the BBC's Further Education Unit to become the first holder of the Granada Research Fellowship in Television at Leeds University. Soon after in 1966, the Centre for Mass Communication Research was founded at Leicester University, and degree programmes in media studies began to sprout at polytechnics and other universities during the 1970s and 1980s.

Media Studies is now taught all over the UK. It is taught at Key Stages 1– 3, Entry Level, GCSE and at A level and the Scottish Qualifications Authority offers formal qualifications at a number of different levels. It is offered through a large area of exam boards including AQA and WJEC.

Media Studies in USA

Mass communication, communication studies or simply communication may be more popular names than "media studies" for academic departments in the United States. However, the focus of such programmes sometimes excludes certain media—film, book publishing, video games, etc. The title "media studies" may be used alone, to designate film studies and rhetorical or critical theory, or it may appear in combinations like "media studies and communication" to join two fields or emphasize a different focus.

Examples: The New School in New York City (the first media studies programme in the country, created in 1975), The Paley Center for Media in New York City, Comparative Media Studies at MIT, Cinema and Media Studies at the University of Chicago, Media and Cultural Studies at the University of California, Riverside, Rhetoric and Media Studies at Willamette University, Media Studies in Communication at Kennesaw State University, the Instructional Technology and Media Program at Columbia University, and The Department of Modern Culture and Media at Brown University.

Formerly an interdisciplinary major at the University of Virginia the Department of Media Studies was officially established in 2001 and has quickly grown to wide recognition. This is partly thanks to the acquisition of Professor Siva Vaidhyanathan, a well known cultural historian and media scholar Siva Vaidhyanathan, as well as the Inaugural Verklin Media Policy and Ethics Conference, endowed by the CEO of Canoe Ventures and UVA alumnus David Verklin . In 2010 a group of undergraduate students in the Media Studies Department established the Movable Type Academic Journal the first ever undergraduate academic journal of its kind. The department is expanding rapidly and doubled in size in 2011.

Brooklyn College, part of the City University of New York, has been offering graduate studies in television and media since 1961. Currently, the Department of Television and Radio administers an MS in Media Studies, and hosts the Center for the Study of World Television.

The University of Southern California has three distinct centers for media studies: the Center for Visual Anthropology (founded in 1984), the Institute for Media Literacy at the School of Cinematic Arts (founded in 1998) and the Annenberg School for Communication and Journalism (founded in 1971).

University of California, Berkeley has three institutional structures within which media studies can take place: the department of Film and Media (formerly Film Studies Program), including famous theorists as Mary Ann Doane and Linda Williams, the Center for New Media, and a long established interdisciplinary programme formerly titled Mass Communications, which recently changed its name to Media Studies, dropping any connotations which accompany the term "Mass" in the former title. Until recently, Radford University in Virginia used the title "media studies" for a department that taught practitioner-oriented major concentrations in journalism, advertising, broadcast production and Web design. In 2008 those programmes were combined with a previous department of communication (speech and public relations) to create a School of Communication. (A "media studies major" at Radford still means someone concentrating on journalism, broadcasting, advertising or Web production).

The University of Denver has a renowned programme for digital media studies. It is an interdisciplinary programme combining communications, computer science, and the arts.

In 2004 Bernard Luskin of Fielding Graduate University established an EdD programme in Media Studies and a PhD programme in Media Psychology with a concentration in Media Studies. Courses in Media Studies were started at Touro University Worldwide in 2009.

4

Womanism, Femininity, Feminine Psychology and Feminism

Womanism

The word *womanism* was adapted from Pulitzer Prize winning author Alice Walker's use of the term in her book *In Search of Our Mothers' Gardens: Womanist Prose*. In her book, Walker used the word to describe the perspective and experiences of "women of colour".

Although most Womanist scholarship centers on the African American woman's experience, other non-white theorists identify themselves with this term.

The roots of theological womanism grew out of the theology of Jacquelyn Grant, Delores Williams, and James Hal Cone.

Grant responded by claiming that Cone did not attend to the fullness of black experience — specifically that of black women. She argued that the oppression of black women is different from that of black men. She believes that Jesus is a "divine co-sufferer" who suffered in his time like black women today.

Delores Williams took the work of theologians such as Cone and Grant and expanded upon them. In her book *Sisters in the Wilderness*, she defines womanism in the following way:

> "Womanist theology is a prophetic voice concerned about the well- being of the entire African American community, male and female, adults and children. Womanist theology attempts to help black women see, affirm, and have confidence in the importance of their experience and faith for determining the character of the Christian religion in the African American community. Womanist theology challenges all oppressive forces impeding black women's

> struggle for survival and for the development of a positive, productive quality of life conducive to women's and the family's freedom and well-being. Womanist theology opposes all oppression based on race, sex, class, sexual preference, physical ability, and caste" (67).

Womanism in Education

Some examples of educational institutions that incorporate womanism in their graduate coursework are Interdenominational Theological Seminary, ITC in Atlanta, Georgia (where Dr. Jacquelyn Grant is a professor), Eden Theological Seminary in Saint Louis, Missouri, Vanderbilt Divinity School in Nashville, Tennessee Memphis Theological Seminary in Memphis, Tennessee, and Chicago Theological Seminary in Chicago, Illinois.

Womanism and Feminism

Womanism is a term commonly used in the context of academic theological studies. Some authors use womanism and black feminism almost interchangeably, as they have much overlap and share heroines and foremothers. Other experts make a distinction based on the prioritization of men. Both black and white feminists are primarily concerned with women, in contrast to women's roles in what they consider as male-centred society.

Womanists are black women who are, in a traditional communal sense, concerned very much with both black women and black men. Men, and their welfare, are sometimes claimed to be a higher priority to womanists than to feminists. Some feminists consider this a subversion of the feminist critique of androcentrism and corrective/constructive focus on women.

"White" feminism (as it is sometimes referred to by Womanists) is also called upon to remember that black women (and all women of minority race/ethnicity and/or low socio-economic status) were ignored and silenced by "white" feminism through its second wave.

Womanists have argued that the gains of second wave feminism and beyond were largely built around the lifestyles and options of highly educated, upper-middle class white women. Some womanists have also argued that negative unintended consequences resulting from feminist reforms have fallen heavily upon women of colour - specifically in regard to the structure of the black family unit.

Africana Womanism

"Africana Womanism" is a term coined in the late 1980s by Clenora Hudson-Weems intended as an ideology applicable to all women of African descent. It is grounded in African culture and Afrocentrism and focuses on the experiences, struggles, needs, and desires of Africana women of the African diaspora. It distinguishes itself from feminism, or Alice Walker's womanism. The Africana Womanism Society lists eighteen characteristics of the The

Africana womanist, including self-naming, self-defining, family-centred, flexible and desiring positive male companionship.

Clenora Hudson-Weems, Professor of English, University of Missouri, author of *Africana Womanism: Reclaiming Ourselves*, coined the concept Africana Womanism in the late 1980s (Africana is the feminine form of the Latin *Africanus*, meaning of Africa, and appears to be preferred by the movement over African). Hudson-Weems argues that "Africana Womanism is not an addendum to feminism, Black feminism, African feminism or Alice Walker's womanism" According to Patricia Collins, "Although some Africana women may support the very ideas on which feminism rests, however, many of them reject the term "feminism" because of what they perceive as its association with white women's cause. They see feminism as operating exclusively within the terms white and American and perceive its opposite as being Black and American." Further many African men and women do not accept the ideology of feminism. According to Hudson-Weems, she states that "there is a general consensus in the Africana community that the feminist movement, by and large, is the White woman's movement for two reason. First, the Africana woman does not see the man as her primary enemy as does the White feminist, who is carrying out an age-old battle with her White male counterpart for subjugating her as his property. Africana men have never had the same institutionalised power to oppress Africana women as White men have had to oppress White women."

Africana Womanism contrasts feminist/womanist ideology and many Africana women (and men) have come to embrace it. Hudson-Weems (1998), *Africana Womanism: Reclaiming Ourselves*, explains the development of Africana Womanism:

> Africana Womanism is a term I coined and defined in 1987 after nearly two years of publicly debating the importance of self-naming for Africana women. Why the term 'Africana Womanism'? Upon concluding that the term 'Black Womanism' was not quite the terminology to include the total meaning desired for this concept, I decided that 'Africana Womanism,' a natural evolution in naming, was the ideal terminology for two basic reasons. The first part of the coinage, *Africana*, identifies the ethnicity of the woman being considered, and this reference to her ethnicity, establishing her cultural identity, relates directly to her ancestry and land base—Africa. The second part of the term Womanism, recalls Sojourner Truth's powerful impromptu speech 'Ain't I a Woman?', one in which she battles with the dominant alienating forces in her life as a struggling Africana Woman, questioning the accepted idea of womanhood. Without question she is the flip side of the coin, the co-partner in the struggle for her people, one who, unlike the white woman, has received no special privileges in American society.

Africana Womanist ideology contributes to Afrocentric discourse. Africana womanism fundamental foundation is built on traditional Africana philosophy and values, and Afrocentric theories:

Lastly, Nah Dove (1998) *African Womanism: An Afrocentric Theory*, credits Hudson-Weems and other scholars in shaping the Africana womanist model. Dove asserts:

A concept [Africana Womanism] that has been shaped by the work of women such as Clenora Hudson-Weems, Ifi Amadiume, Mary E. Modupe Kolawole, and others. African womanism may be viewed as fundamental to the continuing development of Afrocentric theory. Africana womanism brings to the forefront the role of African mothers as leaders in the struggle to regain, reconstruct, and create a cultural integrity that espouses the ancient Maatic principles of reciprocity, balance, harmony, justice, truth, righteousness, order, and so forth. (p. 535)

Values

The Africana Womanist concept was best exemplified in Brenda Verner's (1994) article, *The Power and Glory of Africana Womanism*:

> Africana Womanism in essence says: We love men. We like being women. We love children. We like being mothers. We value life. We have faith in God and the Bible. We want families and harmonious relationships. We are not at war with our men seeking money, power and influence through confrontation. Our history is unique. We are the inheritors of African-American women's history, and as such we shall not redefine ourselves nor that history to meet some politically correct image of a popular culture movement, which demands the right to speak for and redefine the morals and mores of all racial, cultural and ethnic groups. Nor shall we allow the history to be "shanghied" to legitimatise the "global political agenda" of others. We reject the status of victim. Indeed, we are victors, Sisters in Charge of our own destiny. We are Africana culture-keepers: Our primary obligation is to the progress of our cultural way of life through the stability of family and the commitment to community. The practice of cultural womanism is not limited to Africana women. Italian, Japanese, Hispanic, East Indian, Arab, Jewish women, etc., all utilise this approach to decision-making, and know the value of maintaining indigenous cultural autonomy. The rite of passing generation-to-generation knowledge free from outside manipulation, coercion or intimidation insures traditional integrity, which fosters a climate of cultural security. Traditional cultures should not be obligated to bow to redefinitions foisted upon them by elitist entities that gain their authority via the drive of well-organised "media hype."

Male-womanist

Africana men can embrace a Africana womanist approach. According to Tolagbe Ogunlege (1998), "Referring to a man as a male-womanist is not an anomaly or rarity, and bestowing gender-specific title on individuals of the opposite sex has been practiced by Africana peoples for millennia. For example, among the Yoruba, an exceptional woman who has made significant contributions to the educational, socioeconomic, and/or spiritual growth and development of her family and community is referred to as a man-woman or obinrin bi okunrin. Ogunlege further explains that among the Lebou people of Senegal, a man who governs according to ancient customs is referred to as the "Mother of the Country". An example of a Male Womanist or Male African Womanist would be Rev. Majadi Baruti of Udja Temple Ministries. Although taking a slightly different approach, Rev. Baruti states that Africana Womanism is one of the historical antecedents for his creation of what he calls "Black Goddess Consciousness". "The term Black Goddess Consciousness can be defined as the spiritual study of and/or acceptance of the divinity, sacredness and holiness of the Divine Afrikan Feminine, the perpetuation of such Consciousness for the salvation of Afrikan people through its Saviour Messiah. The Afrikan Woman." Rev. Majadi Baruti. His Udja Temple Ministries hosts two programmes found on Blogtalkradio.com. One called The Roof Garden is co-hosted and produced by Rev. Susan Mitchell, Executive Complement for Udja Temple Ministries. The other simply called Udja Temple Presents: Rev. Majadi Baruti. Rev. Baruti refers to himself as a Black Goddess Evangelist, Pan-Afrikan Nationalist. He and his Co-Host Rev. Mitchell purport that Udja Temple Ministries has the singular purpose of restoring the image and worship of the Afrikan Woman as a Goddess in the spirits of Afrikan People.

Womanism in African Education

The Africana Womanist concept was adopted by many faculties in higher education. According to Daphne W. Ntiri (2001), Associate Professor of Social Science, Wayne State University, "Since Clenora Hudson-Weems broke new ground with her 1993 book *Africana Womanism: Reclaiming Ourselves*, discourse on the place and agenda of Africana women in the women's movement reflects the text's influence. In only six years, this work is in the second printing of its third revised edition. It has been adopted by faculty in several higher education institutions in as far away places as Africa, Brazil, Japan, and the Caribbean Islands. Adoption at national universities includes California State University-Long Beach, Florida A&M, Indiana State University, Northern Illinois University, San Francisco State University, Temple University, the University of Missouri, and the University of Utah to name a few" (p. 163).

Examples of Womanism in African Literature

1. Five Africana Womanist novels: Zora Neale Hurston, *Their Eyes Were Watching God.* Hudson-Weems states that the character Janie is a protagonists to name and define herself. Also, a protagonist of family-centeredness (pp. 81–82); Mariama Ba, a renowned Senegalese writer, *So Long a Letter*, Ba's attack on polygamous society that subjugates women, and her interests in the rights of Africana women are reflected in her novel. According to Hudson-Weems "the novel does not justify categorizing it as a feminist novel, which the author dedicates the book 'To all women and men of good will,' thereby demonstrating her natural inclination to include men as a very important part of women's lives" (Hudson-Weems, pp. 93–94); Paule Marshall, a prominent African-Caribbean writer, *Praisesong for the Widow*, which the character "Reena" bears the historical nuances of so-called shortcomings of the Africana woman in relationship with her male companion. Pauline, the narrator, advocates a solution to the deteriorating relationship between the Africana man and woman (Hudson-Weems, p. 105); Toni Morrison, *Beloved*. Hudson-Weems asserts that "From Morrison first novel, *The Bluest Eye*, to *Sula*, *Song of Solomon*, *Tar Baby*, and finally to her fifth novel, *Beloved*, the author develops the roles of the male and the female in this collective struggle" (p. 119); and Terry McMillan, *Diasppearing Acts*. Hudson-Weems explains that the character Zora Banks is self-naming and self-defining, family-centered and compatible, flexible with her roles and ambitions, demanding of respect and strong, reverence of elders and authentic, and last but not least, nurturing and mothering (pp. 133–134). Africana Womanist literature also consists of Africana family dynamics, Africana women and men—their interrelationship, and experiences within their communities, and religion. For instance: Russell J. Rickford (2003) *Betty Shabazz: Surviving Malcolm X: A Journey of Strength from Wife to Widow to Heroine*; Ilyasah Shabazz (2002), *Growing Up X: A Memoir by the Daughter of Malcolm X*; Sonsyrea Tate (1997) *Growing Up in the Nation of Islam*; Yvonne S. Thornton, M.D. (1995), *The Ditchdigger's Daughters: A Black Family's Astonishing Success Story*; Alex Haley (1976) *Roots: The Saga of an American Family*; Coretta Scott King (1969), *My Life with Martin Luther King, Jr.* In addition to Regina Jennings (2001), *Africana Womanism in The Black Panther Party: A Personal Story*, published in *The Western Journal of Black Studies*. Jennings describes her experiences as a young woman who joined the Black Panther Party in Oakland, California using the theory of Africana Womanism.

Towards Understanding Femininity

Femininity (also called womanliness or womanhood) is a set of attributes, behaviours, and roles generally associated with girls and women. Though socially constructed, femininity is made up of both socially defined and biologically created factors. This makes it distinct from the simple definition of the biological female sex, as women, men, and transgender people can all exhibit feminine traits. Traits associated with femininity include a variety of social and cultural factors, and often vary depending on location and context. Behavioural traits that are considered feminine include gentleness, empathy, and sensitivity. The counterpart to femininity is masculinity.

The English word feminine is derived from the Latin *femina* meaning "woman" or "female," and literally "she who suckles". Modern notions of femininity began during the English medieval period at the time of the bubonic plague in the 1300s. Women in the Middle Ages were referred to simply as maiden, wife, or widow. After the Black Death in England wiped out approximately half of the population, traditional gender roles of wife and mother changed, and opportunities opened up for women in society. The concept of "woman" changed in a number of ways and new language had to be created to describe these roles, with words like femininity and womanhood.

Role of Behaviour and Personality

While the defining characteristics of femininity are not universally identical, some patterns exist. Gentleness, empathy, sensitivity, caring, compassion, tolerance, nurturance, deference, self-abasement, and succorance are behaviours generally considered feminine. Femininity is sometimes linked with sexual objectification and sexual appeal. Sexual passiveness, or sexual reception, is sometimes considered feminine while sexual assertiveness and sexual desire is sometimes considered masculine. Ann Oakley's sex/gender dichotomy has had a considerable influence on sociologists defining masculine and feminine behaviour as regulated, policed, and reproduced in our society, as well as the power structures relating to the concepts. Some queer theorists and other postmodernists, however, have rejected the sex (biology)/gender (culture) dichotomy as a "dangerous simplification". An ongoing debate with regards to sex and psychology concerns the extent to which gender identity and gender-specific behaviour is due to socialisation versus inborn factors. According to Diane F. Halpern, both factors play a role, but the relative importance of each must still be investigated. The nature versus nurture question, for example, is extensively debated and is continually revitalised by new research findings. Some hold that feminine identity is partly a 'given' and partly a goal to be sought. In 1959, researchers such as John Money and Anke Erhardt proposed the prenatal hormone theory. Their research argues that sexual organs bathe the embryo with hormones in the womb, resulting in the birth of an individual with a distinctively male or female brain; this was suggested by some to "predict future Behavioural development in a masculine or feminine direction". This theory, however, has been criticised on theoretical and empirical grounds and remains controversial. In 2005, scientific research investigating sex and psychology showed that gender expectations and stereotype threat affect behaviour, and a person's gender identity can develop as early as three years of age. Money also argued that gender identity is formed during a child's first three years. Mary Vetterling-Braggin argues that all characteristics associated with femininity arose from early human sexual encounters which were mainly male-forced and female-unwilling, because of male and female anatomical differences. Others, such as Carole Pateman, Ria Kloppenborg, and Wouter J. Hanegraaff, argue that the definition of femininity is the result of how females must behave in order to maintain a patriarchal social system. In Carl Jung's school of analytical psychology, the anima and animus are the two primary anthropomorphic archetypes of the unconscious mind. The anima and animus are described by Jung as elements of his theory of the collective unconscious, a domain of the unconscious that transcends the personal psyche. In the unconscious of the male it finds expression as a feminine inner personality: anima; equivalently, in the unconscious of the female it is expressed as a masculine inner personality: animus.

Role of Clothing and Appearance

In Western cultures, the ideal of feminine appearance has traditionally included long, flowing hair, light skin, a narrow waist, and little or no body hair or facial hair. In other cultures, however, these standards may vary. For example, in many parts of the world, underarm hair is not considered unfeminine. These feminine ideals of beauty have been criticised by some feminists and others as restrictive, unhealthy, and discriminatory. In particular, the prevalence of anorexia and other eating disorders in Western countries has frequently been blamed on the feminine ideal of thinness.

Cultural standards vary a great deal on what is considered feminine. For example, in 16th century France, high heels were considered a masculine type of shoe, though they are currently considered feminine. In Ancient Egypt, sheath and beaded net dresses were considered female clothing, while wraparound dresses, perfumes, cosmetics, and elabourate jewelry were worn by both men and women. In Ancient Persia, clothing was generally unisex, though women wore veils and headscarves. Women in Ancient Greece wore himations; and in Ancient Rome women wore the *palla*, a rectangular mantle, and the maphorion. The typical feminine outfit of aristrocratic women of the Renaissance was an undershirt with a gown and a high-waisted overgown, and a plucked forehead and beehive or turban-style hairdo.

Body alteration is the deliberate altering of the human body for aesthetic or non-medical purpose. One such purpose has been to induce perceived feminine characteristics in women. For centuries in Imperial China, smaller feet were considered to be a more aristocratic characteristic in women. The practice of foot binding was intended to enhance this characteristic, though it often made walking difficult and painful. In a few parts of Africa and Asia, neck rings are worn in order to elongate the neck. In these cultures, a long neck characterises feminine beauty. The Padaung of Burma and Tutsi women of Burundi, for instance, practice this form of body deformation.

Ideal feminine

What is considered as the *ideal feminine* is defined by each individual culture based on what that culture considers valuable, and is often the subject of heated debate.

In politics

In international politics, female leaders of nations embody feminine expectations of national identity in their society. They use their femininity to appeal to ordinary people and gain strategic advantage over their male opponents. Some famous examples in political leadership and the ideal in femininity are represented by Hillary Rodham Clinton, USA; Yulia Tymoshenko, Ukraine; Isabel Martínez de Perón, Argentina; Michelle Bachelet, Chile; Ellen Johnson Sirleaf, Liberia Yingluck Shinawatra, Thailand; Laura Chinchilla, Costa Rica; and Ekaterina Furtseva, Soviet Union.

In men's view

Men's perceptions of feminine beauty range widely among different cultures. In 1883, Francis Galton first noticed that averageness or koinophilia is a strong indicator of physical beauty. Today, a multi-billion-dollar industry exists around what men find feminine. Studies show that men in Indo-European cultures find ideal feminine proportions that fit a 0.7 waist–hip ratio as most attractive. Physiologists have shown that women with hourglass figures are more fertile than other women due to higher levels of certain female hormones, a fact that may subconsciously condition males choosing mates.

In popular culture

In 1876, Horatio Alger, Jr. proclaimed women of Cape Cod as the ideal feminine beauty. Specifically, because they were blond, tan, physically fit and educated.

In 1959, the Barbie fashion doll was introduced as a feminine ideal of modern aesthetic beauty by Mattel, in the United States. While there are those who hold Barbie to be the feminine ideal, Barbie's anatomical proportions are exaggerated and do not, for example, meet the aesthetic proportions that men in Indo-European cultures find most attractive. This icon of femininity, in the views of some, attracts a wide international audience of women and men. She has been used as a teaching tool for femininity. One of the most common criticisms of Barbie is that she promotes an unrealistic and unattainable idea of feminine beauty and fits the weight criteria for anorexia. In China, female consumers rejected Barbie's ideal of feminine beauty and its image for women as extraneously sexy. In Iran, the feminine ideals and independent lifestyle represented by Barbie are considered a threat to Iranian values, "more harmful than an American missile." In Saudi Arabia Barbie was banned for the same reason, by the religious police as a moral threat to Islam.

Traditional Roles

Gender stereotypes influence traditional feminine occupations, resulting in micro aggression toward women who break traditional gender roles. These stereotypes include that women have a caring nature, have skill at household-related work, have greater manual dexterity than men, are more honest than men, and have a more attractive physical appearance. Occupational roles associated with these stereotypes include: midwife, teacher, accountant, data entry clerk, cashier, salesperson, receptionist, housekeeper, cook, maid, social worker, and nurse. Occupational segregation maintains gender inequality and gender pay gap. Early computer programmers were women. This has reversed in recent decades, however, with programming being perceived as a masculine occupation. In the field of medicine, the role of physician was traditionally seen as masculine, while the role of nurse was considered feminine. These associations are now considered outdated in much of the world, although certain specialisations, such as surgery and emergency medicine, are dominated by a masculine culture and have a higher salary.

Leadership is associated with masculinity in Western cultures, and women are perceived less favourably as potential leaders. However, some people have argued that the "feminine"-style leadership, which is associated with leadership that focuses on help and cooperation, is advantageous over "masculine" leadership, which is associated with focusing on tasks and control. Female leaders are more often described by Western media using characteristics associated with femininity, such as emotion. Role Congruity Theory, which proposes that people tend to view deviations from expected gender roles negatively, is sometimes used to explain why people have a tendency to evaluate behaviour that fulfills the prescriptions of a leader role less favourably when it is enacted by a woman.

Explanations for Occupational Imbalance

It has been argued that primary sex characteristics of men and women, such as the ability to bear children, caused a historical sexual division of labour and gender stereotypes evolved culturally to perpetuate this division.

The practice of bearing children tends to interrupt the continuity of employment. According to human capital theory, this retracts from the female investment in higher education and employment training. Richard Anker of the International Labour Office argues human capital theory does not explain the sexual division of labour because many occupations tied to feminine roles, such as administrative assistance, require more knowledge, experience, and continuity of employment than unskilled masculinised occupations, such as truck driving. Anker argues the feminisation of certain occupations limits employment options for women.

Role Congruity Theory, which proposes that people tend to view deviations from expected roles negatively, supports the empirical evidence that gender discrimination exists in areas traditionally associated with one gender or the other.

Religion

Asian Religions

Shamanism may have originated as early as the paleolithic period, predating all organised religions. Archeological finds have suggested that the earliest known shamans were female. Among Altaic peoples, shamanic roles continue to be filled primarily by women. In Korea, for example, the mudang is usually female, acting as an intercessor between the human and spirit worlds.

In Hindu traditions, Devi is the female aspect of the divine. Shakti is the divine feminine creative power, the sacred force that moves through the entire universe and the agent of change. She is the female counterpart without whom the male aspect, which represents consciousness or discrimination, remains impotent and void. As the female manifestation of the supreme lord, she is also called Prakriti, the basic nature of intelligence by which the Universe exists and functions. In Hinduism, the universal creative force Yoni is feminine, with inspiration being the life force of creation.

In Taoism, the concept of **yin** represents the primary force of the female half of yin and yang. The yin is also present, to a smaller proportion, in the male half. The yin can be characterised as slow, soft, yielding, diffuse, cold, wet, and passive.

In Judaeo-Christian Theology

The *Book of Genesis* describes divine creation of the world out of nothing or *ex nihilo.* In Wisdom literature and in the wisdom tradition, wisdom is the feminine aspect of God. According to the Book of Job, "Wisdom comes from nothingness." In the *Book of Wisdom*, wisdom is "the fashioner of all things" (v. 22). Because wisdom is God's "creative agent," she must be intimately identified with God. The Wisdom of God is feminine in Hebrew: *Chokhmah*, in Arabic: *Hikmah*, in Greek: *Sophia*, and in Latin: *Sapientia*. In Hebrew, both Shekhinah (the Holy Spirit and divine presence of God) and Ruach HaKodesh (divine inspiration) are feminine.

In the Kabbalah, Chokhmah (wisdom and intuition) is the force in the creative process that God used to create the heavens and the earth. Binah (understanding and perception) is the great mother, the feminine receiver of energy and giver of form. Binah receives the intuitive insight from Chokhmah and dwells on it in the same way that a mother receives the seed from the father, and keeps it within her until it's time to give birth. The intuition, once received and contemplated with perception, leads to the Creation of the Universe.

Femininity in Men

Men who behave in ways associated with femininity may be called effeminate. Men who wear clothing associated with femininity are cross-dressers. A drag queen is a man who wears women's clothing and behaves in an extremely feminine manner for entertainment purposes.

Femininity is not necessarily related to a man's sexuality, though male femininity is often associated with homosexuality in modern Western culture. The terms *femiphobia*, *effeminophobia*, and *sissyphobia* are sometimes used to describe a generally negative attitude displayed in many societies towards feminine men.

Feminist Views

Feminist philosophers such as Judith Butler and Simone de Beauvoir contend that femininity and masculinity are created through repeated performances of gender. These performances reproduce and define the traditional categories of sex and/or gender. Many second-wave feminists reject what they regard as constricting standards of female beauty, created for the subordination and objectifying of women and self-perpetuated by reproductive competition and women's own aesthetics. Others, such as third-wave feminists and lipstick feminists, argue that feminism shouldn't devalue feminine culture and identity, and that symbols of feminine identity such as make-up, suggestive clothing and having a sexual allure can be valid and empowering personal choices for both sexes.

Feminine Psychology

Feminine psychology is a term used to describe issues concerning the gender of psychology of female human identity, and the issues that women face throughout their lives. Karen Horney "began work on her version of feminine psychology in 1922, when she became the first woman to present a paper on the topic at an international psychoanalytic congress" (Schultz, 170). She countered Sigmund Freud's concept of penis envy with what she called womb envy.

Understanding Womb Envy

Womb envy is a term originating from Karen Horney, a neo-Freudian feminist and pioneering theorist in personality, psychoanalysis, and feminine psychology (Boeree, 24). Horney was critical of Freud's theory on penis envy, which she felt arose from inadequate evidence. "Freud offered descriptions and interpretations of this alleged phenomenon from a male point of view in a place and time when women were considered second-class citizens (Schultz, 170). Freud felt that women were victims of their anatomy and were jealous of men for possessing a penis (Schultz, 170). Horney argued that men envied women for their ability to be mothers. This idea was based on the pleasure she experienced in childbirth. "When one begins, as I did, to analyse men only after a fairly long experience of analysing women, one receives a most surprising impression of the intensity of this envy of pregnancy, childbirth, and motherhood" (Horney, 1967, pp. 60–61). She claimed that womb envy occurs just as much in men as penis envy occurs for neurotic women. "The degree to which men are driven to succeed and to have their names live on," she said, "is mere compensation for their inability to more directly extend themselves into the future by means of carrying, nurturing, and bearing children" (Boeree, 26). Horney felt that men had to overcompensate for their womb envy by searching for achievement in their work. The womb envy and the resentment that comes along with it are "manifested unconsciously in behaviours designed to disparage and belittle women and to reinforce their inferior status" (Schultz, 171). "Men strive to be the superior sex because of this womb envy." Horney did not deny that "many women believe themselves to be inferior to men" (Schultz, 171). What she did deny was the fact that some women felt so due to societal reasons, not because they were born female. The idea of feeling unworthy derives from the ways women have been treated in male-dominated cultures. "After generations of social, economic, and cultural discrimination, it is understandable that many women see themselves in this light" (Schultz, 171).

Motherhood vs. Career

For hundreds of years, women have battled with the conflicts of choosing between the more traditional role of motherhood and the more modern concept of career woman, often fighting to strike a balance between the two in order to satisfy both the need for personal achievement and the need for love and emotional security. If a mother works, she misses her children and feels guilty for not spending time with them. However, if she stays home, then she misses the personal fulfillment of work, interaction with other adults, and the financial security of her income. The additional income also relieves some stress and gives the mother the ability to provide advantages to her children they may not have otherwise—for example, better education or better healthcare. Working also allows women to feel as though they are making a contribution to society beyond the family. A more fulfilled mother, in most cases, will be a better mother. However, women will often neglect their own needs so that they can satisfy the demands of their careers, motherhood, and relationships. They will neglect their health and allow less time for sleep. Women will often take on the full responsibility for the care of their children as well as the care of their relationship, when in reality it is just as much the responsibility of the father to provide for the emotional needs of his children and partner, as well as their financial needs (Hansen *et al.*, 2002). According to a study conducted by Dr. Jennifer Stuart, sometimes the past history of the woman affects her decision to work or to stay home with her children, or to try to find a balance between the two. "Whether or not her mother worked outside the home has little impact on a woman's comfort with choices around work and motherhood. Rather, her experience of comfort or conflict with her own choices is strongly influenced by the quality of her relationship with her mother. Women whose mothers fostered feelings of both warm attachment and confident autonomy may find ways to enjoy their children and/or work, often modifying work and family environments in ways that favour both" (Stuart, 2008). Some women have no choice other than to work while raising children because of financial need. Others work for personal fulfillment. In either case, women are making compromises in their careers so that they can balance paid work and motherhood responsibilities. They are cutting back hours and accepting lower pay or a lower job status. In order to make the compromise, they have chosen to be satisfied with being average rather than being a top performer in the workplace (Kapur, 2004).

What mothers have to remember, according to Dr. Ramon Resa, is that "children are fairly resilient and will adapt to whatever changes are required. They are also astute at sensing unhappiness, disappointment and apathy" (Resa, 2009). There is no harm in trying any path in order to find fulfillment, because no decision is permanent and can be changed as the situation warrants.

Cultural Influences on Women

Throughout history, women have been regarded as the weaker of the sexes and afforded fewer rights, which include but are not limited to education, legal and career opportunities. For women, being a wife and a mother has long been regarded their most significant and only important profession. It was only in the 20th century that widespread countries finally saw women as sex object with a persuasive voice. In the 20th century, most women were afforded the right to go to school beyond elementary education and the opportunity to go to college, opening the door to more career opportunities than becoming a teacher or nurse. In that century, feminism also opened the door to women gaining a voice in politics with the right to vote, which in turn gave women the right to run for office. The cultural shifts and changes in attitude toward women began in the 20th century in almost every nation and continued into the 21st century, as the traditional roles of women in society continued to be rewritten. The old school of thought was that women were the weaker of the two sexes and therefore inferior to men. Under the common law of England in the 19th century, an unmarried woman could own property, make a contract, or sue and be sued, but a married woman, defined as being one with her husband, gave up her name and virtually all her property, inherited or otherwise, and came under her husband's control (Brinjikji, 1999). In early America, life for a woman was much different from that in England. In early America, a man more or less owned his wife and children as if they were material possessions. If a poor man decided to send his children to the poor house, the mother had no legal grounds and, by all accounts, was defenseless. It was only in the 19th century that things began to change significantly in America. In the early to mid-19th century, some local governments began modifying the laws to allow women to act as lawyers, to own property in their own names if their husbands saw fit, and sue for property (Lambert). As of the early 21st century in America and throughout many nations, married or not, a woman can buy, sell, or own her own property, go into contractual relationships, sue and be sued, act in her own defense, and protect her children. In 1848, when the Seneca Falls Convention for women's rights was held in New York State, one of the complaints documented in the Declaration of Sentiments was that the "history of mankind is a history of repeated injuries and usurpations on the part of man toward woman, having in direct object the establishment of an absolute tyranny over her... He has denied her the facilities for obtaining a thorough education, all colleges being closed against her." One of the outcomes of the convention was a demand for higher education (Lowe, 1989). For women, formal education had always been second in importance and subpar to that for men, and colonial America was no exception. In colonial America, girls usually learned to read and write at dame schools and could only attend the master schools for boys when there was room, which was usually during the summer months when most boys were working (Lowe, 1989). In fact, women did not begin to go to college until after the Civil War, and for the most part they went to co-educational institutions. The newly established land grant colleges in the Midwest opened as coeducational facilities, while the more established institutions of the northeast resisted the move to coeducation (Lowe, 1989).

Being denied the opportunity to be fully educated meant that women had to learn from their mother's example that cooking, cleaning, and caring for children was the behaviour expected of them when they grew up uneducated. Beginning in colonial times and extending as late as 1900, the only jobs available to women were seamstress work or keeping boardinghouses. Some women did work in professions available mostly to men, becoming doctors, lawyers, preachers, teachers, writers, and singers. By the end of the 19th century and due to increasing need for education in the above fields, the only acceptable occupations for working women were limited to factory labour or domestic work. Women were excluded from the professions, except for writing and teaching (Lowe, 1989). As of the early 21st century in most nations, there has been progress such that women are allowed to complete as much education as they want and to choose what profession they wish. Though the glass ceiling still exists in some industries, women are making great advances in every area from working in coal mines to working on the front lines.

Feminism and its Typology

Feminism is a collection of movements aimed at defining, establishing, and defending equal political, economic, and social rights and equal opportunities for women. Its concepts overlap with those of women's rights. Feminism is mainly focused on women's issues, but because feminism seeks gender equality, some feminists argue that men's liberation is a necessary part of feminism, and that men are also harmed by sexism and gender roles. Feminists are "person[s] whose beliefs and behaviour[s] are based on feminism." Feminist theory, emerging from these feminist movements, aims to understand the nature of gender inequality by examining women's social roles and lived experience, developing theories in a variety of disciplines in order to respond to issues such as the social construction of sex and gender. Some of the earlier forms of feminism have been criticised for being geared towards white, middle-class, educated perspectives. This led to the creation of ethnically-specific or multiculturalist forms of feminism.

Feminist activists campaign for women's rights – such as in contract law, property, and voting – while also promoting bodily integrity and autonomy and reproductive rights for women. Feminist campaigns have changed societies, particularly in the West, by achieving women's suffrage, gender neutrality in English, equal pay for women, reproductive rights for women (including access to contraceptives and abortion), and the right to enter into contracts and own property. Feminists have struggled to protect women and girls from domestic violence, sexual harassment, and sexual assault. They have also advocated for workplace rights, including maternity leave, and against forms of discrimination against women.

History

Depending on time, culture and country, feminists around the world have had different causes and goals. Most western feminist historians assert that all movements that work to obtain women's rights should be considered feminist movements, even when they did not (or do not) apply the term to themselves. Other historians assert that the term should be limited to the modern feminist movement and its descendants. Those historians use the label "protofeminist" to describe earlier movements. The history of the modern western feminist movements is divided into three "waves". Each wave dealt with different aspects of the same feminist issues. The first wave comprised women's suffrage movements of the nineteenth and early twentieth centuries, promoting women's right to vote. The second wave was associated with the ideas and actions of the women's liberation movement beginning in the 1960s. The second wave campaigned for legal and social equality for women. The third wave is a continuation of, and a reaction to, the perceived failures of second-wave feminism, beginning in the 1990s.

Feminism in Nineteenth and Early Twentieth Centuries

First-wave feminism was a period of activity during the nineteenth century and early twentieth century. In the U.K. and US, it focused on the promotion of equal contract, marriage, parenting, and property rights for women. By the end of the nineteenth century, activism focused primarily on gaining political power, particularly the right of women's suffrage, though some feminists were active in campaigning for women's sexual, reproductive, and economic rights at this time.

Women's suffrage was achieved in Britain's Australasian colonies at the close of the 19th century, with the self-governing colonies of New Zealand and South Australia granting women the right to vote in 1893 and 1895 respectively. It was followed by Australia permitting women to stand for parliamentary office and granting women's' right to vote. In Britain the Suffragettes and the Suffragists campaigned for the women's vote, and in 1918 the Representation of the People Act was passed granting the vote to women over the age of 30 who owned houses. In 1928 this was extended to all women over twenty-one. In the US, notable leaders of this movement included Lucretia Mott, Elizabeth Cady Stanton, and Susan B. Anthony, who each campaigned for the abolition of slavery prior to championing women's right to vote and were strongly influenced by Quaker thought. In the United States, first-wave feminism is considered to have ended with the passage of the Nineteenth Amendment to the United States Constitution (1919), granting women the right to vote in all states. The term 'first wave' was coined retroactively to categorize these western movements after the term 'second-wave feminism' began to be used to describe a newer feminist movement that focused as much on fighting social and cultural inequalities as political inequalities. During the late Qing period and reform movements such as the Hundred Days' Reform, Chinese feminists called for women's liberation from traditional roles and Neo-Confucian gender segregation. Later, the Chinese Communist Party created projects aimed at integrating women into the workforce, and claimed that the revolution had successfully achieved women's liberation. In 1899, Qasim Amin, considered the "father" of Arab feminism, wrote *The Liberation of Women*, which argued for legal and social reforms for women. Hoda Shaarawi founded the Egyptian Feminist Union in 1923, and became its president and a symbol of the Arab women's rights movement. Arab feminism was closely connected with Arab nationalism. The Iranian Constitutional Revolution in 1905 triggered the Iranian women's movement, which aimed to achieve women's equality in education, marriage, careers, and legal rights. However, during the Iranian revolution of 1979, many of the rights that women had gained from the women's movement were systematically abolished, such as the Family Protection Law. In France, women obtained the right to vote only with the Provisional Government of the French Republic of 21 April 1944. The Consultative Assembly of Algiers of 1944 proposed on 24 March 1944 to grant eligibility to women but following an amendment by Fernand Grenier, they were given full citizenship, including the right to vote. Grenier's proposition was adopted 51 to 16. In May 1947, following the November 1946 elections, the sociologist Robert Verdier minimized the "gender gap," stating in *Le Populaire* that women had not voted in a consistent way, dividing themselves, as men, according to social classes. During the baby boom period, feminism waned in importance. Wars (both World War I and World War II) had seen the provisional emancipation of some, individual, women, but post-war periods signaled the return to conservative roles.

Feminism During Mid-twentieth Century

French philosopher Simone de Beauvoir provided a Marxist solution and an existentialist standpoint with the publication of *Le Deuxième Sexe* (The Second Sex) in 1949. The book expressed feminists' sense of injustice. Second-wave feminism is a feminist movement beginning in the early 1960s and continuing to the present, and it coexists with third-wave feminism. Second-wave feminism is largely concerned with issues of equality other than suffrage, such as ending discrimination. Second-wave feminists see women's cultural and political inequalities as inextricably linked and encourage women to understand aspects of their personal lives as deeply politicized and as reflecting sexist power structures. The feminist activist and author Carol Hanisch coined the slogan "The Personal is Political", which became synonymous with the second wave. Second and third-wave feminism in China has been characterised by a re-examination of women's roles during the communist revolution and other reform movements, and new discussions about whether women's equality has actually been fully achieved. In 1956, President Nasser of Egypt initiated "state feminism", which outlawed discrimination based on gender and granted women's suffrage, but also blocked political activism by feminist leaders. During Sadat's presidency, his wife, Jehan Sadat, publicly advocated for further women's rights, though Egyptian policy and society began to move away from women's equality with the new Islamist movement and growing conservatism. However, some activists proposed a new feminist movement, Islamic feminism, which argues for women's equality within an Islamic framework. In Latin America, revolutions brought changes in women's status in countries such as Nicaragua, where feminist ideology during the Sandinista Revolution aided women's quality of life but fell short of achieving a social and ideological change.

Feminism During Late Twentieth and Early Twenty-first Centuries

In the early 1990s in the USA, third-wave feminism began as a response to perceived failures of the second-wave and to the backlash against initiatives and movements created by the second wave. Third-wave feminism seeks to challenge or avoid what it deems the second wave's essentialist definitions of femininity, which, they argue, over-emphasise the experiences of upper middle-class white women. Third-wave feminists often focus on "micro-politics" and challenge the second-wave's paradigm as to what is, or is not, good for women, and tend to use a post-structuralist interpretation of gender and sexuality. Feminist leaders rooted in the second-wave, such as Gloria Anzaldua, bell hooks, Chela Sandoval, Cherrie Moraga, Audre Lorde, Maxine Hong Kingston, and many other black feminists, sought to negotiate a space within feminist thought for consideration of race-related subjectivities. Since the 1980s standpoint feminists have argued that the feminist movement should address global issues (such as rape, incest, and prostitution) and culturally specific issues (such as female genital mutilation in some parts of Africa and the Middle East and glass ceiling practices that impede women's advancement in developed economies) in order to understand how gender inequality interacts with racism, homophobia, classism and colonisation in a "matrix of domination." Third-wave feminism also contains internal debates between difference feminists, who believe that there are important differences between the sexes, and those who believe that there are no inherent differences between the sexes and contend that gender roles are due to social conditioning.The term post-feminism is used to describe a range of viewpoints reacting to feminism since the 1980s. While not being "anti-feminist", post-feminists believe that women have achieved second wave goals while being critical of third wave feminist goals. The term was first used to describe a backlash against second-wave feminism, but it is now a label for a wide range of theories that take critical approaches to previous feminist discourses and includes challenges to the second-wave's ideas. Other post-feminists say that feminism is no longer relevant to today's society. Amelia Jones has written that the post-feminist texts which emerged in the 1980s and 1990s portrayed second-wave feminism as a monolithic entity.

Feminism Theory

Feminist theory is the extension of feminism into theoretical or philosophical fields. It encompasses work in a variety of disciplines, including anthropology, sociology, economics, women's studies, literary criticism, art history, psychoanalysis and philosophy. Feminist theory aims to understand gender inequality and focuses on gender politics, power relations, and sexuality. While providing a critique of these social and political relations, much of feminist theory also focuses on the promotion of women's rights and interests. Themes explored in feminist theory include discrimination, stereotyping, objectification (especially sexual objectification), oppression, and patriarchy. In the field of literary criticism, Elaine Showalter describes the development of feminist theory as having three phases. The first she calls "feminist critique", in which the feminist reader examines the ideologies behind literary phenomena. The second Showalter calls "gynocriticism", in which the "woman is producer of textual meaning". The last phase she calls "gender theory", in which the "ideological inscription and the literary effects of the sex/gender system are explored".This was paralled in the 1970s by French feminists, who developed the concept of *écriture féminine* (which translates as female, or feminine writing). Helene Cixous argues that writing and philosophy are *phallocentric* and along with other French feminists such as Luce Irigaray emphasise "writing from the body" as a subversive exercise. The work of the feminist psychoanalyst and philosopher, Julia Kristeva, has influenced feminist theory in general and feminist literary criticism in particular. However, as the scholar Elizabeth Wright points out, "none of these French feminists align themselves with the feminist movement as it appeared in the Anglophone world".

Movements and Ideologies Related to Feminism

For more details on the many feminist movements, see Feminist movements and ideologies. Many overlapping feminist movements and ideologies have developed over the years.

Some branches of feminism closely track the political leanings of the larger society, such as liberalism and conservatism, or focus on the environment. Liberal feminism seeks individualistic equality of men and women through political and legal reform without altering the structure of society. Radical feminism considers the male-controlled capitalist hierarchy as the defining feature of women's oppression and the total uprooting and reconstruction of society as necessary. Conservative feminism is conservative relative to the society in which it resides. Libertarian feminism conceives of people as self-owners and therefore as entitled to freedom from coercive interference. Separatist feminism does not support heterosexual relationships. Lesbian feminism is thus closely related. Other feminists criticise separatist feminism as sexist. Ecofeminists see men's control of land as responsible for the oppression of women and destruction of the natural environment, but a criticism is that ecofeminism focuses too much on a mystical connection between women and nature.

Rosemary Hennessy and Chrys Ingraham say that materialist feminisms grew out of Western Marxist thought and have inspired a number of different (but overlapping) movements, all of which are involved in a critique of capitalism and are focussed on ideology's relationship to women. Marxist feminism argues that capitalism is the root cause of women's oppression, and that discrimination against women in domestic life and employment is an effect of capitalist ideologies. Socialist feminism distinguishes itself from Marxist feminism by arguing that women's liberation can only be achieved by working to end both the economic and cultural sources of women's oppression. Anarcha-feminists believe that class struggle and anarchy against the state require struggling against patriarchy, which comes from involuntary hierarchy.

Sara Ahmed argues that Black and Postcolonial feminisms pose a challenge "to some of the organising premises of Western feminist thought." During much of its history, feminist movements and theoretical developments were led predominantly by middle-class white women from Western Europe and North America. However, women of other races have proposed alternative feminisms. This trend accelerated in the 1960s with the civil rights movement in the United States and the collapse of European colonialism in Africa, the Caribbean, parts of Latin America, and Southeast Asia. Since that time, women in developing nations and former colonies and who are of colour or various ethnicities or living in poverty have proposed additional feminisms. Womanism emerged after early feminist movements were largely white and middle-class. Postcolonial feminists argue that colonial oppression and Western feminism marginalised postcolonial women but did not turn them passive or voiceless. Third-world feminism is closely related to postcolonial feminism. These ideas also correspond with ideas in African feminism, motherism, Stiwanism, negofeminism, femalism, transnational feminism, and Africana womanism.

In the late twentieth century various feminists began to argue that gender roles are socially constructed, and that it is impossible to generalise women's experiences across cultures and histories. Post-structural feminism draws on the philosophies of post-structuralism and deconstruction in order to argue that the concept of gender is created socially and culturally through discourse. Postmodern feminists also emphasise the social construction of gender and the discursive nature of reality, however as Pamela Abbot et al. note, a postmodern approach to feminism highlights "the existence of multiple truths (rather than simply men and women's standpoints)."

Riot grrrl (or riot grrl) is an underground feminist punk movement that started in the 1990s and is often associated with third-wave feminism. It was grounded in the DIY philosophy of punk values. Riot grrls took an anti-corporate stance of self-sufficiency and self-reliance. Riot grrrl's emphasis on universal female identity and separatism often appears more closely allied with second-wave feminism than with the third-wave. The movement encouraged and made "adolescent girls' standpoints central," allowing them to express themselves fully. Lipstick feminism is a cultural feminist movement that attempts to respond to the backlash of second-wave radical feminism of the 1960s and 1970s by reclaiming symbols of "feminine" identity such as make-up, suggestive clothing and having a sexual allure as valid and empowering personal choices.

Societal Impact of Feminism

The feminist movement has effected change in Western society, including women's suffrage; greater access to education; more nearly equitable pay with men; the right to initiate divorce proceedings; the right of women to make individual decisions regarding pregnancy (including access to contraceptives and abortion); and the right to own property.

Civil rights

From the 1960s on, the campaign for women's rights was met with mixed results in the US and the UK Other countries of the EEC agreed to ensure that discriminatory laws would be phased out across the European Community. In the US, the National Organisation for Women (NOW) began in 1966 to seek women's equality, including through the Equal Rights Amendment (ERA), which did not pass, although some states enacted their own. Reproductive rights in the US centered on the court decision in *Roe* v. *Wade* enunciating a woman's right to choose whether to carry a pregnancy to term. Western women gained more reliable birth control, allowing family planning and careers. The movement started in the 1910s in the US under Margaret Sanger and elsewhere under Marie Stopes. In the final three decades of the 20th century, Western women knew a new freedom through birth control, which enabled women to plan their adult lives, often making way for both career and family. The division of labour within households was affected by the increased entry of women into workplaces in the 20th century. Sociologist Arlie Russell Hochschild found that, in two-career couples, men and women, on an average, spend about equal amounts of time working, but women still spend more time on housework, although Cathy Young responded by arguing that women may prevent equal participation by men in housework and parenting.

In International Law, the Convention on the Elimination of All Forms of Discrimination Against Women (CEDAW) is an international convention adopted by the United Nations General Assembly and described as an international bill of rights for women. It came into force in those nations ratifying it.

Language

Gender-neutral language is a description of language usages which are aimed at minimising assumptions regarding the biological sex of human referents. The advocacy of gender-neutral language reflects, at least, two different agendas: one aims to clarify the inclusion of both sexes or genders (gender-inclusive language); the other proposes that gender, as a category, is rarely worth marking in language (gender-neutral language). Gender-neutral language is sometimes described as non-sexist language by advocates and politically-correct language by opponents.

Theology

Feminist theology is a movement that reconsiders the traditions, practices, scriptures, and theologies of religions from a feminist perspective. Some of the goals of feminist theology include increasing the role of women among the clergy and religious authorities, reinterpreting male-dominated imagery and language about God, determining women's place in relation to career and motherhood, and studying images of women in the religion's sacred texts.

Christian feminism is a branch of feminist theology which seeks to interpret and understand Christianity in light of the equality of women and men, and that this interpretation is necessary for a complete understanding of Christianity. While there is no standard set of beliefs among Christian feminists, most agree that God does not discriminate on the basis of sex, and are involved in issues such as the ordination of women, male dominance and the balance of parenting in Christian marriage, claims of moral deficiency and inferiority of women compared to men, and the overall treatment of women in the church.

Islamic feminists advocate women's rights, gender equality, and social justice grounded within an Islamic framework. Advocates seek to highlight the deeply rooted teachings of equality in the Quran and encourage a questioning of the patriarchal interpretation of Islamic teaching through the Quran, *hadith* (sayings of Muhammad), and *sharia* (law) towards the creation of a more equal and just society. Although rooted in Islam, the movement's pioneers have also utilised secular and Western feminist discourses and recognise the role of Islamic feminism as part of an integrated global feminist movement.

Jewish feminism is a movement that seeks to improve the religious, legal, and social status of women within Judaism and to open up new opportunities for religious experience and leadership for Jewish women. The main issues for early Jewish feminists in these movements were the exclusion from the all-male prayer group or *minyan*, the exemption from positive time-bound *mitzvot*, and women's inability to function as witnesses and to initiate divorce.

Secular or atheist feminists have engaged in feminist criticism of religion, arguing that many religions have oppressive rules towards women and misogynistic themes and elements in religious texts.

Relationship between Patriarchy and Feminism

Patriarchy is a social system in which the role of the male as the primary authority figure is central to social Organisation, and where fathers hold authority over women, children, and property. It implies the institutions of male rule and privilege, and is dependent on female subordination. Most forms of feminism characterise patriarchy as an unjust social system that is oppressive to women. As the feminist and political theorist Carole Pateman writes: "The patriarchal construction of the difference between masculinity and femininity is the political difference between freedom and subjection." In feminist theory the concept of patriarchy often includes all the social mechanisms that reproduce and exert male dominance over women. Feminist theory typically characterises patriarchy as a social construction, which can be overcome by revealing and critically analysing its manifestations. Some radical feminists have proposed that because patriarchy is too deeply rooted in society, separatism is the only viable solution. Other feminists have criticised these radical feminist views as being anti-men, though some radical feminists reject this portrayal of their views. Societal tension caused by second-wave feminism gave rise to backlash in the form of anti-feminist men's movements, such as Masculism, though today some see masculism as a complementary movement that does not oppose feminism.

Relevance of Men and Masculinity for Feminism

Feminist theory has explored the social construction of masculinity and its implications for the goal of gender equality. The social construct of masculinity is seen by feminism as problematic because it associates males with aggression and competition, and reinforces patriarchal and unequal gender relations. The patriarchal concept of masculinity is also seen as harmful to men by narrowing their life choices, limiting their sexuality, and blocking full emotional connections with women and other men. Some feminists are engaged with men's issues of activism, such as bringing attention to male rape and spousal battery and addressing negative social expectations for men.

Male participation in feminism is encouraged by feminists and is seen as an important strategy for achieving full societal commitment to gender equality. Many male feminists and pro-feminists are active in both women's rights activism, feminist theory, and masculinity studies. However, some argue that while male engagement with feminism is necessary, it is problematic due to the ingrained social influences of patriarchy in gender relations. The consensus today in feminist and masculinity theories is that both genders can and should cooperate to achieve the larger goals of feminism.

Culture and Feminism

According to the Tate Collection, feminist art can "be defined as art by women artists made consciously in the light of developments in feminist art theory since about 1970."

Architecture

Gender-based inquiries into and conceptualisation of architecture have also come about, leading to feminism in modern architecture. Piyush Mathur coined the term "archigenderic". Claiming that "architectural planning has an inextricable link with the defining and regulation of gender roles, responsibilities, rights, and limitations", Mathur came up with that term "to explore...the meaning of 'architecture' in terms of gender" and "to explore the meaning of 'gender' in terms of architecture".

Literature

The feminist movement produced both feminist fiction and non-fiction, and created new interest in women's writing. It also prompted a general reevaluation of women's historical and academic contributions in response to the belief that women's lives and contributions have been underrepresented as areas of scholarly interest. Much of the early period of feminist literary scholarship was given over to the rediscovery and reclamation of texts written by women. Studies like Dale Spender's *Mothers of the Novel* (1986) and Jane Spencer's *The Rise of the Woman Novelist* (1986) were ground-breaking in their insistence that women have always been writing. Commensurate with this growth in scholarly interest, various presses began the task of reissuing long-out-of-print texts. Virago Press began to publish its large list of 19th and early-20th-century novels in 1975 and became one of the first commercial presses to join in the project of reclamation. In the 1980s Pandora Press, responsible for publishing Spender's study, issued a companion line of 18th-century novels written by women. More recently, Broadview Press continues to issue 18th and 19th-century novels, many hitherto out of print, and the University of Kentucky has a series of re-publications of early women's novels. The widespread interest in women's writing is related to a general reassessment and expansion of the literary canon. Interest in post-colonial literatures, gay and lesbian literature, writing by people of colour, working people's writing, and the cultural productions of other historically marginalised groups has resulted in a whole scale expansion of what is considered "literature," and genres hitherto not regarded as "literary," such as children's writing, journals, letters, travel writing, and many others are now the subjects of scholarly interest. Most genres and sub-genres have undergone a similar analysis, so that one now sees work on the "female gothic" or women's science fiction. According to Elyce Rae Helford "Science fiction and fantasy serve as important vehicles for feminist thought, particularly as bridges between theory and practice." Feminist science fiction is sometimes taught at the university level to explore the role of social constructs in understanding gender. Notable texts of this kind are Ursula K. Le Guin's *The Left Hand of Darkness* (1969), Joanna Russ' *The Female Man* (1970), Octavia Butler's *Kindred* (1979) and Margaret Atwood's *Handmaid's Tale* (1985).

Music

Women's music (or womyn's music or wimmin's music) is the music by women, for women, and about women. The genre emerged as a musical expression of the second-wave feminist movement as well as the labour, civil rights, and peace movements. The movement was started by lesbians such as Cris Williamson, Meg Christian, and Margie Adam, African-American women activists such as Bernice Johnson Reagon and her group Sweet Honey in the Rock, and peace activist Holly Near. Women's music also refers to the wider industry of women's music that goes beyond the performing artists to include studio musicians, producers, sound engineers, technicians, cover artists, distributors, promoters, and festival organisers who are also women. Feminism became a principal concern of musicologists in the 1980s. Prior to this, in the 1970s, musicologists were beginning to discover women composers and performers, and had begun to review concepts of canon, genius, genre and periodisation from a feminist perspective. In other words, the question of how women musicians fit into traditional music history was now being asked. Through the 1980s and 1990s, this trend continued as musicologists like Susan McClary, Marcia Citron and Ruth Solie began to consider the cultural reasons for the marginalising of women from the received body of work. Concepts such as music as gendered discourse; professionalism; reception of women's music; examination of the sites of music production;

relative wealth and education of women; popular music studies in relation to women's identity; patriarchal ideas in music analysis; and notions of gender and difference are among the themes examined during this time.

Visual arts

The feminist art movement refers to the efforts and accomplishments of feminists internationally to make art that reflects women's lives and experiences, as well as to change the foundation for the production and reception of contemporary art. It also sought to bring more visibility to women within art history and art practice. Corresponding with general developments within feminism, and often including such self-organising tactics as the consciousness-raising group, the movement began in the 1960s and flourished throughout the 1970s. Jeremy Strick, director of the Museum of Contemporary Art in Los Angeles, described the feminist art movement as "the most influential international movement of any during the postwar period", and Peggy Phelan says that it "brought about the most far-reaching transformations in both artmaking and art writing over the past four decades". Judy Chicago, who with a team of 129 created *The Dinner Party*, said in 2009 to *ARTnews*, "There is still an institutional lag and an insistence on a male Eurocentric narrative. We are trying to change the future: to get girls and boys to realise that women's art is not an exception—it's a normal part of art history."

Sexuality

In the late 1970s lesbianism and bisexuality were accepted as part of feminism by a significant proportion of feminists, while others considered sexuality irrelevant to the attainment of other goals. Sexuality, sexual representation, sadomasochism, the role of transwomen in the lesbian community, and other sexual issues arose within acrimonious feminist debates known as the feminist sex wars. Opinions on the sex industry are diverse. They are generally either critical of it (seeing it as exploitative, a result of patriarchal social structures and reinforcing sexual and cultural attitudes that are complicit in rape and sexual harassment) or supportive of at least parts of it (arguing that some forms of it can be a medium of feminist expression and a means of women taking control of their sexuality).

Pornography

The "Feminist Sex Wars" is a term for the acrimonious debates within the feminist movement in the late 1970s through the 1980s around the issues of feminism, sexuality, sexual representation, pornography, sadomasochism, the role of transwomen in the lesbian community, and other sexual issues. The debate pitted anti-pornography feminism against sex-positive feminism, and parts of the feminist movement were deeply divided by these debates.

Prostitution and Trafficking

Feminists' views on prostitution vary, but many of these perspectives can be loosely arranged into an overarching standpoint that is generally either critical or supportive of prostitution and sex work. Anti-prostitution feminists are strongly opposed to prostitution, as they see the practice as a form of violence against and exploitation of women, and a sign of male dominance over women. Feminists who hold such views on prostitution include Kathleen Barry, Melissa Farley, Julie Bindel, Sheila Jeffreys, Catharine MacKinnon and Laura Lederer; the European Women's Lobby has also condemned prostitution as "an intolerable form of male violence". Other feminists hold that prostitution and other forms of sex work can be valid choices for women and men who choose to engage in it. In this view, prostitution must be differentiated from forced prostitution, and feminists should support sex worker activism against abuses by both the sex industry and the legal system. The disagreement between these two feminist stances was particularly contentious, and may be comparable to the feminist sex wars of the late twentieth century.

Relationship of Feminism to Political Movements

Feminism had complex interactions with the major political movements of the twentieth century.

Socialism

Since the early twentieth century some feminists have allied with socialism. In 1907 there was an International Conference of Socialist Women in Stuttgart where suffrage was described as a tool of class struggle. Clara Zetkin of the Social Democratic Party of Germany called for women's suffrage to build a "socialist order, the only one that allows for a radical solution to the women's question".

In Britain, the women's movement was allied with the Labour party. In the US, Betty Friedan emerged from a radical background to take leadership. Radical Women is the oldest socialist feminist Organisation in the US and is still active. During the Spanish Civil War, Dolores Ibárruri (*La Pasionaria*) led the Communist Party of Spain. Although she supported equal rights for women, she opposed women fighting on the front and clashed with the anarcha-feminist Mujeres Libres.

Fascism

Cyprian Blamires states that although feminists were among those who opposed the rise of Adolf Hitler, feminism has a complicated relationship with fascism. While fascists glorified traditional notions of patriarchal society and its role for women, they claimed to recognise women's equality in employment. However, both Hitler and Mussolini declared themselves as opposed to feminism, and after the rise of Nazism in Germany in 1933, there was a rapid dissolution of the political rights and economic opportunities that feminists had fought for during the pre-war period and to some extent during the 1920s. Georges Duby et al. note that in practice fascist society was hierarchical and emphasised male virility, with women maintaining a largely subordinate position. Blamires also notes that Neofascism has since the 1960s been hostile towards feminism and advocates that women accept "their traditional roles".

Civil Rights Movement and Anti-racism

The civil rights movement has influenced and informed the feminist movement and vice versa. Many Western feminists adapted the language and theories of black equality activism and drew parallels between women's rights and the rights of non-white people. Despite the connections between the women's and civil rights movements, some tension arose during the late 1960s and early 1970s as non-white women argued that feminism was predominantly white and middle class, and did not understand and was not concerned with race issues. Similarly, some women argued that the civil rights movement had sexist elements and did not adequately address minority women's concerns. These criticisms created new feminist social theories about the intersections of racism, classism, and sexism, and new feminisms, such as black feminism and Chicana feminism.

Science

Sandra Harding says that the "moral and political insights of the women's movement have inspired social scientists and biologists to raise critical questions about the ways traditional researchers have explained gender, sex and relations within and between the social and natural worlds." Some feminists, such as Ruth Hubbard and Evelyn Fox Keller, criticise traditional scientific discourse as being historically biased towards a male perspective. A part of the feminist research agenda is the examination of the ways in which power inequities are created and/or reinforced in scientific and academic institutions. Physicist Lisa Randall, appointed to a task force at Harvard by then-president Lawrence Summers after his controversial discussion of why women may be under represented in science and engineering, said, "I just want to see a whole bunch more women enter the field so these issues don't have to come up anymore."

Lynn Hankinson Nelson notes that feminist empiricists argue that there are fundamental differences between the experiences of men and women, thus they seek to obtain knowledge through the examination of the experiences of women, and attempt to "uncover the consequences of omitting, mis-describing, or devaluing them" for account of human experience. Other feminist scientists eschew objectivity in favour of self-reflexivity and the agenda of helping women. Also, part of the feminist research agenda is the uncovering of ways in which power inequities are created and/or reinforced in society and in scientific and academic institutions.

One criticism of feminist epistemology is that it allows social and political values to influence its findings. Susan Haack also points out that feminist epistemology reinforces traditional stereotypes about women's thinking (as intuitive and emotional, etc.), Meera Nanda further cautions that this may in fact trap women within "traditional gender roles and help justify patriarchy".

Biology and Gender

Modern feminist science challenges the biological essentialist view of gender. However, it is increasingly interested in the study of biological sex differences and their effect on human behaviour. For example, Anne Fausto-Sterling's book, *Myths of Gender*, explores the assumptions embodied in scientific research that purports to support a biologically essentialist view of gender. For example, in *Delusions of Gender,* Cordelia Fine argues that there is currently no scientific evidence for innate biological differences between men and women's minds, and that cultural and societal beliefs contribute to commonly perceived sex differences.

Evolutionary Biology

Sarah Kember—drawing from numerous areas such as evolutionary biology, sociobiology, artificial intelligence, and cybernetics in development with a new evolutionism—discusses the biologisation of technology. She notes how feminists and sociologists have become suspicious of evolutionary psychology, particularly in as much as sociobiology is subjected to complexity in order to strengthen sexual difference as immutable through pre-existing cultural value judgments about human nature and natural selection. Where feminist theory is criticised for its "false beliefs about human nature", Kember then argues in conclusion that "feminism is in the interesting position of needing to do more biology and evolutionary theory in order not to simply oppose their renewed hegemony, but in order to understand the conditions that make this possible, and to have a say in the construction of new ideas and artefacts."

Reactions

Different groups of people have responded to feminism, and both men and women have been among its supporters and critics. Among American university students, for both men and women, support for feminist ideas is more common than self-identification as a feminist. The US media tends to portray feminism negatively and feminists "are less often associated with day-to-day work/leisure activities of regular women."

Pro-feminism

Pro-feminism is the support of feminism without implying that the supporter is a member of the feminist movement. The term is most often used in reference to men who are actively supportive of feminism. The activities of pro-feminist men's groups include anti-violence work with boys and young men in schools, offering sexual harassment workshops in workplaces, running community education campaigns, and counseling male perpetrators of violence. Pro-feminist men also are involved in men's health, activism against pornography including anti-pornography legislation, men's studies, and the development of gender equity curricula in schools. This work is sometimes in collabouration with feminists and women's services, such as domestic violence and rape crisis centers.

Anti-feminism

Anti-feminism is opposition to feminism in some or all of its forms. In the nineteenth century, anti-feminism was mainly focused on opposition to women's suffrage. Later, opponents of women's entry into institutions of higher learning argued that education was too great a physical burden on women. Other anti-feminists opposed women's entry into the labour force, or their right to join unions, to sit on juries, or to obtain birth control and control of their sexuality. Some people have opposed feminism on the grounds that they believe it is contrary to traditional values or religious beliefs. These anti-feminists argue, for example, that social acceptance of divorce and non-married women is wrong and harmful, and that men and women are fundamentally different and thus their different traditional roles in society should be maintained. Other anti-feminists oppose women's entry into the workforce, political office, and the voting process, as well as the lessening of male authority in families.Writers such as Camille Paglia, Christina Hoff Sommers, Jean Bethke Elshtain, Elizabeth Fox-Genovese and Daphne Patai oppose some forms of feminism, though they identify as feminists. They argue, for example, that feminism often promotes misandry and the elevation of women's interests above men's, and criticise radical feminist positions as harmful to both men and women. Daphne Patai and Noretta Koertge argue that the term "anti-feminist" is used to silence academic debate about feminism.

Focus on Separatist Feminism

Separatist feminism is a form of radical feminism that holds that opposition to patriarchy is best done through focusing exclusively on women and girls. Some separatist feminists do not believe that men can make positive contributions to the feminist movement and that even well-intentioned men replicate the dynamics of patriarchy. Author Marilyn Frye describes separatist feminism as "separation of various sorts or modes from men and from institutions, relationships, roles and activities that are male-defined, male-dominated, and operating for the benefit of males and the maintenance of male privilege—this separation being initiated or maintained, at will, by women." In a tract on socialist feminism published in 1972, the Hyde Park Chapter of the Chicago Women's Liberation Union differentiated between Separatism as an "ideological position", and as a "tactical position". In the same document, they further distinguished between separatism as "personal practice" and as "political position".

Heterosexual Separatist Feminism

One of the earliest, and best known examples of heterosexual separatist feminism was Cell 16. Founded in 1968 by Roxanne Dunbar, Cell 16 has been cited as the first Organisation to advance the concept of separatist feminism. Cultural Historian Alice Echols cites Cell 16 as an example of feminist heterosexual separatism, as the group never advocated lesbianism as a political strategy, instead promoting the idea of celibacy or periods of celibacy in heterosexual relationships. Echols credits Cell 16's work for "helping establishing the theoretical foundation for lesbian separatism". In *No More Fun and Games*, the Organisation's radical feminist periodical, Cell Members Roxanne Dunbar and Lisa Leghorn advised women to "separate from men who are not consciously working for female liberation", but advised periods of celibacy, rather than lesbian relationships, which they considered to be "nothing more than a personal solution."

Lesbian Separatism

Lesbian separatism is a form of separatist feminism specific to lesbians. Separatism has been considered by lesbians as both a temporary strategy, and as a lifelong practice. Charlotte Bunch, an early member of The Furies Collective, viewed separatist feminism as a strategy, a "first step" period, or temporary withdrawal from mainstream activism to accomplish specific goals or enhance personal growth. Other lesbians, such as Lambda Award winning author Elana Dykewomon, have chosen separatism as a lifelong practice. In addition to advocating withdrawal from working, personal or casual relationships with men, The Furies recommended that Lesbian Separatists relate "only (with) women who cut their ties to male privilege" and suggest that "as long as women still benefit from heterosexuality, receive its privileges and security, they will at some point have to betray their sisters, especially Lesbian sisters who do not receive those benefits." This was part of a larger idea that Bunch articulated in *Learning from Lesbian Separatism*, that "in a male-supremacist society, heterosexuality is a political institution" and the practice of separatism is a way to escape its domination. In her 1988 book, *Lesbian Ethics: Towards a New Value*, Lesbian Philosopher Sarah Lucia Hoagland alludes to Lesbian Separatism's potential to encourage lesbians to develop healthy community ethics based on shared values. Bette Tallen believes that lesbian separatism, unlike some other separatist movements, is "not about the establishment of an independent state, it is about the development of an autonomous self-identity and the creation of a strong solid lesbian community." Lesbian historian Lillian Faderman describes the separatist impulses of lesbian feminism which created culture and cultural artifacts as "giving love between women greater visibility" in broader culture. Faderman also believes that lesbian feminists who acted to create separatist institutions did so to "bring their ideals about integrity, nurturing the needy, self-determination and equality of labour and rewards into all aspects of institution-building and economics." The practice of Lesbian separatism sometimes incorporates concepts related to queer nationalism and political lesbianism. Some individuals who identify as Lesbian separatists are also associated with the practice of Dianic paganism. The term 'womyn's lands' has been used in America to describe communities of lesbian separatists.

Radical Lesbianism

The radical lesbian movement is a francophone lesbian movement roughly analogous to English-language lesbian separatism. Inspired by the writings of philosopher Monique Wittig, the movement originated in France in the early 1980s, spreading soon after to the Canadian province of Quebec. Wittig, referencing the ideas of Simone de Beauvoir, challenges concepts of biological determinism, arguing that those in power construct sex difference and race difference for the purpose of masking conflicts of interest and maintaining domination. Separatism was, as such, an opportunity for lesbians to diminish the impact of these constructed power differences on their lives.

Controversy

Valerie Solanas' *SCUM Manifesto*, written in 1967, suggested that it was the job for females to rid the planet of men. In a 1982 published conversation about black feminism and lesbian activism with her sister, Beverly Smith, Barbara Smith, co-author of the Combahee River Collective Statement expresses concerns that, "to the extent that lesbians of colour must struggle simultaneously against the racism of white women (as against sexism), separatism impedes the building of alliances with men of colour." Smith writes that race places lesbians of colour in a different relation to men as white lesbians, as "white women with class privilege don't share oppression with white men. They're in a critical and antagonistic position whereas Black women and other women of colour definitely share oppressed situations with men of their race." Smith makes a distinction between the theory of separatism, and the practice of separatism, stating that it is the way separatism has been practiced which has led to "an isolated, single-issued understanding and practice of politics, which ignores the range of oppressions that women experience." In 1983 Anarchist Bob Black wrote that "Separatism may be absurd as a social programme and riddled with inconsistencies (scarcely any separatists separate from patriarchal society to anything like the extent that, say, survivalists do—and nobody intervenes more to mind other people's business than separatists). But semi-isolation makes it easier to indoctrinate neophytes and shut out adverse evidence and argument, an insight radical feminists share with Moonies, Hare Krishna, and other cultists." Feminist Sonia Johnson, while advocating a broadly separatist policy, points out that feminist separatism risks defining itself by what it separates itself from, i.e. men. Lesbian poet Jewelle Gomez refers to her intertwined history with black men and heterosexual women in her essay *Out of the Past*, and explains that "to break away from those who've been part of our survival is a leap that many women of colour could never make." Cultural critic Alice Echols describes the emergence of a lesbian separatist movement as a response to what she sees as homophobic sentiments expressed by feminist Organisations like the National Organisation of Women. Echols argues that "...the introduction of (homo)sex troubled many heterosexual feminists who had found in the women's movement a welcome respite from sexuality." Echols considered separatism as a lesbian strategy to untie lesbianism from sex so heterosexual women in the feminist movement felt more comfortable. Feminist theorist and author Bell Hooks asserts that the beliefs of separatist feminists run counter to many of the original goals of feminism, and instead of seeking to create equality, attempt to establish a female-centric and female-dominated society in which men are subjugated and misandry is brought into the mainstream.

Separatism in Literature and Culture

An important and sustaining aspect of lesbian separatism was the building of alternative community through "creating Organisations, institutions and social spaces ...women's bookstores, restaurants, publishing collectives, and softball leagues fostered a flourishing lesbian culture."

Literature

Lesbian separatism and Separatist Feminism have inspired the creation of art and culture reflective of its visions of female-centered societies, including various works of lesbian science fiction where new technologies in human reproductive strategy have created Lesbian utopias, eliminating the need to have men for human reproduction. *The Wanderground* (Persephone Press,

1978), is a separatist utopian novel written from author Sally Miller Gearhart's personal experience in rural lesbian-separatist collectives.

Periodicals

In the 1970s, lesbians and feminists created a network of publications, presses, magazines, and periodicals designated "for women only" and "for lesbians only", a common sight in the 1970s through the 1990s, (see List of lesbian periodicals) including the London lesbian magazine *Gossip: a journal of lesbian feminist ethics*, *Lesbian Feminist Circle*, a lesbian only journal collectively produced in Wellington, New Zealand, the Australian periodical *Sage: the separatist age*; Canada's Amazones d'Hier, Lesbiennes d'Aujourd'hui, produced for lesbians only in Montreal, Quebec, and the *Killer Dyke* a magazine by the "Flippies" (Feminist Lesbian Intergalactic Party), based in Chicago.

Music

The early 1970s was an active period in Women's music, a genre mostly originated and supported by separatist feminists. Maxine Feldman's *Angry Atthis*, and Alix Dobkin's *Lavender Jane Loves Women*, were two early examples of this phenomenon.

Film

The German vampire film *We Are the Night* explores the idea of separatist feminism. In the film, the female vampire commited a genocide against male vampire somewhere at the end of the 1800's after many of them already had been killed by humans. The female vampires agreed among each other never to turn another man into a vampire.

Community Projects

Separatist feminism provided lesbians opportunities to "live their lives apart from ...mainstream society," and, in the 1970s, "significant numbers of lesbian feminists moved to rural communities. One of these lesbians, Joyce Cheney, interviewed rural separatist feminists and lesbian separatists living in intentional community, land trusts and land co-ops. The result was her book, *Lesbian Land*. Cheney describes the reason for many of these separatists' move to Lesbian Land as a "spatial strategy of distancing ...from mainstream society".

Lipstick Feminism

Lipstick feminism is a variety of Third-wave feminism that philosophically reclaims the sexual power of women, in response to the social and cultural backlash of the ideologically radical varieties of Second-wave feminism of the 1960s and the 1970s. In its course, the ideologic backlash generated negative stereotypes of contemporary Third-wave feminists, including the physical stereotype of the "ugly feminist" and the socio-cultural stereotype of the "anti-sex feminist", which Lipstick-feminist philosophy proposes to correct by reclaiming personal control of female sex appeal. Linguistically, Lipstick feminism proposes to semantically reclaim, for feminist usage, double-standard insult words, such as "slut", in order to eliminate the social stigma applied to a woman whose sexual behaviour was patriarchically interpreted to denote "immoral woman" and to connote the moral corruption of libertinage. Philosophically, Lipstick feminism proposes that a woman is empowered — psychologically, socially, politically — by the wearing of cosmetic make up, sexually suggestive clothes, and the practice of a sexual allure that appeals to men and to women. That such overt sexual practices empower a woman because they are personal social choices, and not coerced acquiescence to societally established gender roles, such as "the good girl", "the decent woman", "the abnegated mother", "the virtuous sister", *et aliæ*. Yet, opponent feminists propose that the empowerment of Lipstick feminism is a philosophic contradiction wherein a woman chooses to sexually objectify herself, and so ceases to be her own woman, in control neither of herself nor of her person. Nonetheless, Lipstick feminism counter-proposes that the practice of sexual allure is a form of power, and that, besides the reproductive power of prettiness, sex appeal is a form of social power in the interpersonal relations between a man and a woman, which occur in the realms of cultural, social, and gender equality. Moreover, Stiletto feminism, a more ideologically radical variety of Lipstick feminism, proposes that there exists no philosophic contradiction in being a feminist and in being female, a woman who is sexually alluring to men and to women. Besides the acceptance of makeup, the adherents of Stiletto feminism accept the existential (philosophic) validity of women practicing occupations specifically predicated upon female physical beauty, such as working as a striptease dancer or as a pole dancer, and the validity of the personal practices of public sexual exposition (flashing) and of lesbian (girl-on-girl) exhibitionism, as not un-feminist because such practices and preferences are personal choices, not external coercion.

Feminist Sociology

Feminist sociology is a conflict theory and theoretical perspective which observes gender in its relation to power, both at the level of face-to-face interaction and reflexivity within a social structure at large. Focuses include sexual orientation, race, economic status, and nationality. At the core of feminist sociology is the idea of the systematic oppression of women and the historical dominance of men within most societies: 'patriarchy'. Feminist thought has a rich history, however, which may be categorised into three 'waves'. The current, 'third wave', emphasises the concepts of globalisation, postcolonialism, post-structuralism and postmodernism. Contemporary feminist thought has frequently tended to do-away with all generalizations regarding sex and gender, closely linked with antihumanism, posthumanism, queer theory and the work of Michel Foucault.

Understanding Heterosexism

Heterosexism is a system of attitudes, bias, and discrimination in favour of male-female sexuality and relationships. At one point, heterosexual marriage was the only lawful union between two people that was recognised and given full benefits in the United States. This clearly put homosexual couples of both sexes at a disadvantage, making their relationships less valid in the eyes of the government than that of a relationship between a man and a woman. However, heterosexism can extend far beyond government validation, as it describes a set of paradigms and institutionalised beliefs that systematically disadvantage anyone other than heterosexual, whether the source of oppression is coming directly from the government or not.

Feminism and Race

Women who suffer from oppression due to race may find themselves in a double bind. The relationship between feminism and race was largely overlooked until the second wave of feminists produced greater literature on the topic of 'black feminism'.

Feminist Critiques of Multiculturalism

Debates within ethnic relations, particularly regarding the opposing perspectives of assimilationism and multiculturalism, have led to the accusation that feminism is incompatible with multiculturalist policy. The remit of multiculturalism is to allow distinct cultures to reside in Western societies, or separate societies in general, and one possible consequence is that certain religious or traditional practices may negate Western feminist ideals. Central debates include the topics of arranged marriage and female genital mutilation. Others have argued that these debates stem from Western orientalism and general political reluctance to accept foreign migrants.

Types of Feminism

- Liberal feminism
- Cultural feminism
- Feminist existentialism
- Radical feminism
- Marxist feminism
- Erotic feminism
- Psychoanalytic feminism
- Postmodern feminism.

5

Gender Sociology, Gender Role and Gender Equality: Focus on Sexism and Gender Apartheid or Gap

Understanding the Sociology of Gender

Sociology of gender is a prominent subfield of sociology. Since 1950 an increasing part of the academic literature, and of the public discourse uses gender for the perceived or projected (self-identified) masculinity or femininity of a person. The term was introduced by Money (1955):

> "The term gender role is used to signify all those things that a person says or does to disclose himself/herself as having the status of boy or man, girl or woman, respectively. It includes, but is not restricted to, sexuality in the sense of eroticism."

A person's gender is complex, encompassing countless characteristics of appearance, speech, movement and other factors not solely limited to biological sex. Societies tend to have binary gender systems in which everyone is categorised as male or female. Some societies include a third gender role; for instance, the Native American Two-Spirit people and the hijras of India. There is debate over the extent to which gender is a social construct or a biological construct.

Feminist Theory

During the 1970s, there was no consensus about how the terms were to be applied. In the 1974 edition of *Masculine/Feminine or Human*, the author uses "innate gender" and "learned sex roles", but in the 1978 edition, the use of sex and gender is reversed. By 1980, most feminist writings had agreed on using gender only for socio-culturally adapted traits.

Other Languages

In English, both sex and gender are used in contexts where they could not be substituted (sexual intercourse; anal sex; safe sex; sex worker; sex slave). Other languages, like German, use the same word *Geschlecht* to refer both to grammatical gender and to biological sex, making the distinction between sex and gender advocated by some anthropologists difficult. In some contexts, German has adopted the English loan-word gender to achieve this distinction. Sometimes 'Geschlechtsidentitaet' is used as gender (although it literally means gender identity) and 'Geschlecht' as sex (translation of Judith Butler's *Gender Trouble*). More common is the use of modifiers: *iologisches Geschlecht* for *sex*, *Geschlechtsidentität* for gender identity and *Geschlechterrolle* for gender role etc.

US Media

Media criticism is a reflection of the gender inequality in society through print, advertisements, television and music. Media influences and reinforces the idea of The Beauty Myth as discussed in Naomi Wolf's book, *The Beauty Myth*: How images of beauty are used against women, which refers to unrealistic standards of beauty for women. The media perpetuates the idea of heteromasculinity by portraying men as dominant. Men and women in the United States are influenced by the media which objectifies and oppresses women, and men who don't fall into the heteronormative category.

Oppression

Both men and women are oppressed in the media. Women are oppressed in the media through musical lyrics that discuss violence, distrust, and overall inferiority to men. Through the media, men are taught to be ultra-masculine by being desensitised, violent, and physically strong. Other forms of media that often portray the ultra-masculine figure are advertisements, specifically beer commercials. These forms encourage men to oppress other men if they do not fit the ideals of heteromasculinity.

Objectification of Women

Women are often objectified and portrayed as objects. This is shown through advertisements where women become the objects. There are many repercussions, such as low self-esteem and eating disorders, this encourages the idea of women being subordinate to men in the sense that women are disposable and controllable.

Gender in the Workplace

Women and men experience different types of mobility within the workplace. Women tend to experience a glass ceiling, an invisible barrier that prevents them from moving up the corporate ladder. Men in jobs traditionally held by women, such as nursing, elementary school teaching, and social work, experience a "glass escalator" effect in which they are able to quickly ascend the job hierarchy to become managers and principals. Also there tends to be a gender pay gap between men and women, with women only earning 77 per cent as much as men. One cause of the gender pay gap may be due to occupational segregation, which pushes men and women towards gender-specific forms of employment, rather than pay discrimination. Another cause is the double burden, a phenomenon in which women perform most of the unpaid childcare and household work despite being otherwise employed for pay. A third cause is occupational sexism, one part of which favours men for promotions due to their traditional breadwinner status. The 2001 class action lawsuit, *Dukes* v. *Wal-Mart Stores, Inc.*, charged Wal-Mart with sexist hiring and promotion practices. Another issue in the workplace is parental leave. The United States is currently one of only four countries that do not mandate paid paternal leave for new parents. However, among countries that do offer paid parental leave, almost all of them offer few or no benefits for fathers. In addition, the emergence of transgender individuals in the workplace have begun to disrupt the gender binary of male and female. By creating a hybrid gender identity, the transgender community suggests notions of movement toward postgenderism.

Understanding Intersectionality

Intersectionality suggests that forms of inequality, oppression, and privilege shaped by interconnected axes of identity are mutually reinforced by social interactions and by social, political, and economic structures, such as capitalism, patriarchy, and institutionalised heternormativity. Intersectionality emphasizes that race, class, gender, and other markers of identity are social constructions. This theory disassembles the assumption that systems of power relations are normative and can hold individuals accountable for their own character and efforts. West and Fenstermaker in their 1995 article Doing Difference offer that models that conceive gender, race and class as distinct axes are highly limiting in their understanding of the whole experience or identity of an individual. For example, they critique the additive model, in which the whole will never be greater (or lesser) than the sum of its parts. By analysing each identity marker as an individual characteristic, we ignore the effect of the interconnection of these markers. Additional sociologists have written about the intersectionality of class, race, and gender. Joan Acker outlines four gendered processes of intersectionality. The first includes procedures that create hierarchies based on gender and race. Another is the process in which social images and ideas condone gendered institutions. The third is a process of interaction between individuals and groups that, through communication, creates gender. The fourth is the internal labeling of the self and others to gendered personas. Evelyn Nakano Glenn critiques both the patriarchy model of gender, which ignores racial differences among oppressed women, and the internal colonialism model, which focuses on minority populations in general, ignoring gender differences.

Embodiment

Embodiment may be defined as the ways in which cultural ideals of gender in a given society create expectations for and influence the form of our bodies. There is a bidirectional relationship between biology and culture; by embodying societally determined gender roles we reinforce cultural ideals and simultaneously shape, both temporarily and permanently, our bodies, which then perpetuates the cultural ideal. While there is actually more variation in body type within the male and female sexes than there is between the two sexes, embodiment exaggerates the perceived bodily differences between gender categories. Social embodiment, for both men and women, is variable across cultures and over time. Examples of women embodying gender norms across cultures include foot binding practices in Chinese culture, neck rings in African and Asian cultures, and corsets in Western cultures. Another interesting phenomenon has been the practice of wearing high heels, which shifted from a masculine fashion to a feminine fashion over time. In the United States, the ideal body image and dimensions have changed for both women and men, with the body ideal female body shape becoming progressively slimmer and the body ideal for men becoming progressively larger. These differences are epitomized in the example of children's toys; G.I. Joe dolls depict the physical ideals for boys and Barbie dolls embody the ideals for girls. The Beauty Myth, as discussed in Naomi Wolf's books *The Beauty Myth and How Images of Beauty Are Used Against Women*, refers to the unattainable standard of beauty for women, which sustains consumer culture. In contrast, men's bodies are also "dictated" by cultural ideals of gender, as is evident in consumer culture—especially beer commercials—in which men are portrayed as outgoing, tough, strong, and "manly."

Sexuality

Sexuality is related to a variety of factors, including an individual's Sex, Gender identity and expression, and Sexual orientation. Sexuality encompasses both sexual behaviour and sexual desire. however, heteronormativity structures social life so that heterosexuality is always assumed, expected, ordinary and privileged. Its pervasiveness makes it difficult for people to imagine other ways of life. Mass media works to glorify heterosexuality, which in turn lends to its pervasiveness and to its power. Both ordinary and exceptional constructions of heterosexuality work to normalise heterosexuality; thus, it becomes difficult to imagine anything other than this form of social relationship or anyone outside of these bonds. There is a common perception of heterosexuality as the "natural" emotional and sensual inclination for Human sexuality. Furthermore, marital heterosexuality occupies the largely invisible core of normative and desirable sexuality, while all other sexualities are marginalized and considered perverse and unnatural. Alfred Kinsey created a Heterosexual-Homosexual Rating Scale called the Kinsey Scale, which challenges the common perception of human sexuality as strictly binary and directly linked to gender. Drag queens are an example of "troubling" gender, complicating the understanding of sexuality in our society by causing people to think outside the binary of male/female.

Masculinity

Masculinity is a performed gender identity. Contrary to popular perception, it is not the same as sex or sexual orientation. The contents and practices of masculinity are socially constructed and reproduced through daily interaction, especially on a more micro scale. Theorists West and Zimmerman emphasized that gender is maintained through accountability. Men are expected to perform masculinity to the point that it is naturalized. Thus, a man's status depends on his performance. It is important to note, however, that masculinity can be performed by any sex. The dominant form of masculinity in a society is known as hegemonic masculinity. Men are constantly performing this to prove their status as men. It is not really possible to reach it, especially as peers are in constant surveillance of each other, looking for flaws in their performance. Hegemonic masculinity is constructed in opposition to femininity and is dominant to all other gender identities including alternative masculinities. Men are socialized from birth to perform it, especially through behaviour and symbolism. One of the prominent behaviours is aggression in order to protect one's reputation. An example of symbols used would be clothing. Sociologist Michael Kimmel describes three cultures that support masculinity (especially in young men) in his 2008 book, *Guyland*:

- *The Culture of Entitlement*: Men are raised to feel they deserve something. They feel entitled to power, sex and women.
- *The Culture of Silence*: Men are not to talk to outsiders (those not embedded in the cultures of masculinity) about drinking, bullying, rape, or any performance of masculinity by their peers that they may get in trouble for. If they do talk, they will be seen as unmanly traitors.
- *The Culture of Protection*: Communities do not hold men responsible for questionable and illegal actions. Many turn a blind eye, assuming their boys would never do that. Others write off dangerous acts as "boys will be boys".

Some of the prominent attitudes and behaviours of western hegemonic masculinity are: power, sexual dominance and activity, wealth, aggression, independence, and lack of emotion. Rape and murder are extreme forms of masculinity. However, even in mainstream masculinity, women's bodies become a "currency" with which to demonstrate one's sexual prowess. Less extreme sexual harassment is often seen as normal behaviour. Exemplifying control theory, the norms of masculinity are so rigidly ingrained that men find little room to escape and end up constantly reproducing them. Hegemonic masculinity is often reproduced and reinforced through media and culture. "Media representations of men...often glorify men's use of physical force, a daring demeanor, virility, and emotional distance." Contemporary rap music is a striking example of masculinity on display. Rappers boast about their sexual conquests of women emphasizing heterosexuality as well as, wealth, power and violence.

Gender and Violence

Gender-based violence is the physical, sexual or emotional harm or suffering enacted upon an individual as contextualised by societal gender norms. Violence affects the lives of millions worldwide, in all socio-economic and educational classes. It cuts across cultural and religious barriers, impeding the right of many to participate fully in society. Violence is about power, control, and domination. Systems of inequality and oppression interact positioning certain groups as particularly vulnerable to violence. Gendered violence takes place within a socially constructed power dynamic in which one ideology (masculinity) dominates another (femininity). What it means to be a woman in society is influenced and ascribed by the media, which acts a "powerful educational force". The media glamorises violence against women cultivating a "toxic cultural environment" in which women are institutionally positioned as inferior and worthy objects of violence. Men are disproportionally the offenders, and women disproportionally the victims. Those that commit violent crimes are overwhelmingly male—rape (98 per cent), armed robbery (92 per cent), drunk driving (90 per cent), murder (88 per cent), aggregated assault (87 per cent), arson (86 per cent), and family violence (83 per cent). According to Michael Kimmel, hegemonic masculinity creates a culture of entitlement, silence, and protection, which effectively normalises violence against women and silences victims of violence. The Declaration on the Elimination of Violence defines three social arenas in which violence commonly takes place (1) in the family—including domestic violence, infanticide, and traditional practices such as female genital mutilation, foot binding, and bride burning; (2) in the community—including rape, sexual assault, sexual harassment, and commercialised violence such as sexual slavery, labour exploitation, female migrant workers;

and (3) by the State—including violence against women in detention, and in situations of armed conflict such as systematic war rape. In order to address and end gendered violence, solutions must address both the root causes and interpersonal manifestations of gender roles and power relations in order to ensure a balance of power at all levels of society.

Globalisation and Gender

Globalisation refers to the increasingly global relationships of culture, people and economic activity. It impacts female equality on a large and international scale, both negatively and positively. With continuous changes in international relations, the perception of feminism in Western and Nonwestern societies is frequently revised. It is important to be wary of Western bias in sociological accounts of global feminism. As *Modern Western Society is not always due credit for feminist reform* in other cultures and countries Feminist sentiments – or a push for gender equality – emerge as a result of the nation-specific circumstances, not according to the exported beliefs of Western society. Advances in female equality and status are often the result of individuals and small groups, not national groups or corporations. One of the results of globalisation is the increased use of female factory workers in nonwestern countries. In Mexico, the female worker is ideal because she is seen as docile and inexpensive labour. Stereotypical feminine traits such as beauty, domesticity, and docility are exaggerated and exploited for the production of goods. These gender traits then frame the behaviour of the women beyond the occupational realm. Despite increasing feminism, the lack of economic and social mobility prevents women in many nations from having equal status in society. One of the solutions to erasing gender inequalities globally, is to provide resources and funds to impoverished women who will in turn use them for education as well as business ventures. The global economy could benefit drastically from incorporating educated women into the workforce, *New York Times*.

Gender Role

Gender roles refer to the set of social and behavioural norms that are considered to be socially appropriate for individuals of a specific sex in the context of a specific culture, which differ widely between cultures and over time. There are differences of opinion as to whether observed gender differences in behaviour and personality characteristics are, at least in part, due to cultural or social factors, and therefore, the product of socialisation experiences, or to what extent gender differences are due to biological and physiological differences. Views on gender-based differentiation in the workplace and in interpersonal relationships have often undergone profound changes as a result of feminist and/or economic influences, but there are still considerable differences in gender roles in almost all societies. It is also true that in times of necessity, such as during a war or other emergency, women are permitted to perform functions which in "normal" times would be considered a male role, or *vice versa.* Gender has several definitions. It usually refers to a set of characteristics that are considered to distinguish between male and female, reflect one's biological sex, or reflect one's gender identity. Gender identity is the gender(s), or lack thereof, a person self-identifies as; it is not necessarily based on biological sex, either real or perceived, and it is distinct from sexual orientation? It is one's internal, personal sense of being a man or a woman (or a boy or girl). There are two main genders: masculine (male), or feminine (female), although some cultures acknowledge more genders. Androgyny, for example, has been proposed as a third gender. Some societies have more than five genders, and some non-Western societies have three genders – man, woman and third gender. Gender expression refers to the external manifestation of one's gender identity, through "masculine," "feminine," or gender-variant or gender neutral behaviour, clothing, hairstyles, or body characteristics.

Understanding the Gender Role Theory

Gender role theory posits that boys and girls learn the appropriate behaviour and attitudes from the family and overall culture they grow up with, and so non-physical gender differences are a product of socialisation. Social role theory proposes that the social structure is the underlying force for the gender differences. Social role theory proposes that the sex-differentiated behaviour is driven by the division of labour between two sexes within a society. Division of labour creates gender roles, which in turn, lead to gendered social behaviour. The physical specialisation of the sexes (Eagly *et al.*, 2004) is considered to be the distal cause of gender roles. Men's unique physical advantages in terms of body size and upper body strength provided them an edge over women in those social activities that demanded such physical attributes such as hunting, herding and warfare. On the other hand, women's biological capacity for reproduction and child-bearing is proposed to explain their limited involvement in other social activities. Such divided activity arrangement for the purpose of achieving activity- efficiency led to the division of labour between sexes. Social role theorists have explicitly stressed that the labour division is not narrowly defined as that between paid employment and domestic activities, rather, is conceptualised to include all activities performed within a society that are necessary for its existence and sustainability. The characteristics of the activities performed by men and women became people's perceptions and beliefs of the dispositional attributes of men or women themselves. Through the process of correspondent inference (Gilbert, 1998), division of labour led to gender roles, or gender stereotype. Ultimately, people expect men and women who occupy certain position to behave according to these attributes. These socially constructed gender roles are considered to be hierarchical and characterised as a male-advantaged gender hierarchy (Wood and Eagly, 2002). The activities men were involved in were often those that provided them with more access to or control of resources and decision making power, rendering men not only superior dispositional attributes via correspondence bias (Gilbert, 1998), but also higher status and authority as society progressed. The particular pattern of the labour division within a certain society is a dynamic process and determined by its specific economical and cultural characteristics. For instance, in an industrial economy, the emphasis on physical strength in social activities becomes less compared with that in a less advanced economy.

In a low birth rate society, women will be less confined to reproductive activities and thus more likely to be involved in a wide range of social activities. The beliefs that people hold about the sexes are derived from observations of the role performances of men and women and thus reflect the sexual division of labour and gender hierarchy of the society (Eagly *et al.*, 2000). The consequences of gender roles and stereotypes are sex-typed social behaviour (Eagly *et al.*, 2004) because roles and stereotypes are both socially shared descriptive norms and prescriptive norms. Gender roles provide guides to normative behaviours that are typical, ought-to-be and thus "likely effective" for each sex within certain social context. Gender roles also depict ideal, should-be, and thus desirable behaviours for men and women who are occupying a particular position or involving in certain social activities. Put it another way, men and women, as social beings, strive to belong and seek for approval by complying and conforming to the social and cultural norms within their society. The conformity to social norms not only shapes the pattern, but also maintains the very existence of sex-typed social behaviour (Eagly *et al.*, 2004). In summary, social role theory "treats these differing distributions of women and men into roles as the primary origin of sex-differentiated social behaviour, their impact on behaviour is mediated by psychological and social processes" (Eagly, 1997), including "developmental and socialisation processes, as well as by processes involved in social interaction (e.g., expectancy confirmation) and self-regulation" (Eagly *et al.*, 2004).

Social Construction of Gender Difference

This perspective proposes that gender difference is socially constructed (see Social construction of gender difference). Social constructionism of gender moves away from socialisation as the origin of gender differences; people do not merely internalise gender roles as they grow up but they respond to changing norms in society. Children learn to categorise themselves by gender very early on in life. A part of this is learning how to display and perform gendered identities as masculine or feminine. Boys learn to manipulate their physical and social environment through physical strength or other skills, while girls learn to present themselves as objects to be viewed. Children monitor their own and others' gendered behaviour. Gender-segregated children's activities creates the appearance that gender differences in behaviour reflect an essential nature of male and female behaviour. Judith Butler, in works such as *Gender Trouble* and *Undoing Gender*, contends that being female is not "natural" and that it appears natural only through repeated performances of gender; these performances in turn, reproduce and define the traditional categories of sex and/or gender. A social constructionist view looks beyond categories and examines the intersections of multiple identities, the blurring of the boundaries of essentialist categories. This is especially true with regards to categories of male and female that are typically viewed by others as binary and opposites of each other. By deconstructing categories of gender, the value placed on masculine traits and behaviours disappears. However, the elimination of categories makes it difficult to make any comparisons between the genders or to argue and fight against male domination.

Talcott Parsons' View

Working in the United States, Talcott Parsons developed a model of the nuclear family in 1955, which at that place and time was the prevalent family structure. It compared a strictly traditional view of gender roles (from an industrial-age American perspective) to a more liberal view. The Parsons model was used to contrast and illustrate extreme positions on gender roles. Model A describes total separation of male and female roles, while Model B describes the complete dissolution of gender roles. (The examples are based on the context of the culture and infrastructure of the United States.)

	Model A – Total role segregation	*Model B – Total integration of roles*
Education	Gender-specific education; high professional qualification is important only for the man.	Co-educative schools, same content of classes for girls and boys, same qualification for men and women.
Profession	The workplace is not the primary area of women; career and professional advancement is deemed unimportant for women.	For women, career is just as important as for men; equal professional opportunities for men and women are necessary.
Housework	Housekeeping and child care are the primary functions of the woman; participation of the man in these functions is only partially wanted.	All housework is done by both parties to the marriage in equal shares.
Decision making	In case of conflict, man has the last say, for example in choosing the place to live, choice of school for children, buying decisions.	Neither partner dominates; solutions do not always follow the principle of finding a concerted decision; status quo is maintained if disagreement occurs.
Child care and education	Woman takes care of the largest part of these functions; she educates children and cares for them in every way	Man and woman share these functions equally.

However, these extreme positions are rarely found in reality; actual behaviour of individuals is usually somewhere between these poles. The most common 'model' followed in real life in the United States and Britain is the 'model of double burden'. According to the interactionist approach, roles (including gender roles) are not fixed, but are constantly negotiated between individuals. In North America and southern South America, this is the most common approach among families whose business is agriculture. Gender roles can influence all kinds of behaviours, such as choice of clothing, choice of work and personal relationships, e.g., parental status (See also *Sociology of Fatherhood*).

Socialisation

The process through which the individual learns and accepts roles is called socialisation. Socialisation works by encouraging wanted and discouraging unwanted behaviour. These sanctions by agents of socialisation such as the family, schools, and the media make it clear to the child what is expected of the child by society. Mostly, accepted behaviour is not produced by outright reforming coercion from an accepted social system. In some other cases, Various forms of coercion have been used to acquire a desired response or function.

Homogenisation vs. Ethnoconvergence Difference

It is claimed that even in monolingual, industrial societies like much of urban North America, some individuals do cling to a "modernised" primordial identity, apart from others and with this a more diverse gender role is recognised or developed. Some intellectuals, such as Michael Ignatieff, argue that convergence of a general culture does not directly entail a similar convergence in ethnic, social and self identities. This can become evident in social situations, where people divide into separate groups by gender roles and cultural alignments, despite being of an identical "super-ethnicity", such as nationality.

Within each smaller ethnicity, individuals may tend to see it perfectly justified to assimilate with other cultures including sexuality and some others view assimilation as wrong and incorrect for their culture or institution. This common theme, representing dualist opinions of ethnoconvergence itself, within a single ethnic or common values groups is often manifested in issues of sexual partners and matrimony, employment preferences, etc. These varied opinions of ethnoconvergence represent themselves in a spectrum; assimilation, homogenisation, acculturation, gender identities and cultural compromise which are commonly used terms for ethnoconvergence which flavour the issues to a bias. Often it is in a secular, multi-ethnic environment that cultural concerns are both minimalised and exacerbated; Ethnic prides are boasted, hierarchy is created ("center" culture versus "periphery") but on the other hand, they will still share a common "culture", and common language and behaviours. Often the elderly, more conservative-in-association of a clan, tend to reject cross-cultural associations, and participate in ethnically similar community-oriented activities.

Anthropology and Evolution

The idea that differences in gender roles originate in differences in biology has found support in parts of the scientific community. 19th-century anthropology sometimes used descriptions of the imagined life of paleolithic hunter-gatherer societies for evolutionary explanations for gender differences. For example, those accounts maintain that the need to take care of offspring may have limited the females' freedom to hunt and assume positions of power. More recently, sociobiology and evolutionary psychology have explained those differences in social roles by treating them as adaptations. This approach, too, is considered controversial. Due to the influence of (among others) Simone de Beauvoir's feminist works and Michel Foucault's reflections on sexuality, the idea that gender was unrelated to sex gained ground during the 1980s, especially in sociology and cultural anthropology. This view claims that a person could therefore be born with male genitals but still be of feminine gender. In 1987, R.W. Connell did extensive research on whether there are any connections between biology and gender role and concluded that there were none. However, there continues to be debate on the subject. Simon Baron-Cohen, a Cambridge University. professor of psychology and psychiatry, claims that "the female brain is predominantly hard-wired for empathy, while the male brain is predominantly hard-wired for understanding and building systems." Dr. Sandra Lipsitz Bem is a psychologist who developed the gender schema theory to explain how individuals come to use gender as an organising category in all aspects of their life. It is based on the combination of aspects of the social learning theory and the cognitive-development theory of sex role acquisition. In 1971, she created the Bem Sex Role Inventory to measure how well you fit into your traditional gender role by characterising your personality as masculine, feminine, androgynous, or undifferentiated. She believed that through gender-schematic processing, a person spontaneously sorts attributes and behaviours into masculine and feminine categories. Therefore, an individual processes information and regulate their behaviour based on whatever definitions of femininity and masculinity their culture provides. The current trend in Western societies toward men and women sharing similar occupations, responsibilities and jobs suggests that the sex one is born with does not directly determine one's abilities. While there are differences in average capabilities of various kinds (E.g. physical strength) between the sexes, the capabilities of some members of one sex will fall within the range of capabilities needed for tasks conventionally assigned to the other sex. In addition, research at the Yerkes National Primate Research Center has also shown that gender roles may be biological among primates. Yerkes researchers studied the interactions of 11 male and 23 female Rhesus monkeys with human toys, both wheeled and plush. The males played mostly with the wheeled toys while the females played with both types equally. Psychologist Kim Wallen has, however, warned against overinterpeting the results as the colour and size of the toys may also be factors in the monkey's behaviour.

Changing Roles

A person's gender role is composed of several elements and can be expressed through clothing, behaviour, choice of work, personal relationships and other factors. These elements are not concrete and have evolved through time (for example women's trousers). Traditionally only feminine and masculine gender roles existed, however, over time many different acceptable male or female gender roles have emerged. An individual can either identify themselves with a subculture or social group which results in them having diverse gender roles. Historically, for example, eunuchs had a different gender role because their biology was changed.

Androgyny, a term denoting the display of both male and female behaviour, also exists. Many terms have been developed to portray sets of behaviours arising in this context. The masculine gender role in the West has become more malleable since the 1950s. One example is the "sensitive new age guy", which could be described as a traditional male gender role with a more typically "female" empathy and associated emotional responses. Another is the metrosexual, a male who adopts or claims to be born with similarly "female" grooming habits. Some have argued that such new roles are merely rebelling against tradition more so than forming a distinct role. However, traditions regarding male and female appearance have never been concrete, and men in other eras have been equally interested with their appearance. The popular conceptualisation of homosexual men, which has become more accepted in recent decades, has traditionally been more androgynous or effeminate, though in actuality homosexual men can also be masculine and even exhibit machismo characteristics. One could argue that since many homosexual men and women fall into one gender role or another or are androgynous, that gender roles are not strictly determined by a person's physical sex. Whether or not this phenomenon is due to social or biological reasons is debated. Many homosexual people find the traditional gender roles to be very restrictive, especially during childhood. Also, the phenomenon of intersex people, which has become more publicly accepted, has caused much debate on the subject of gender roles. Many intersexual people identify with the opposite sex, while others are more androgynous. Some see this as a threat to traditional gender roles, while others see it as a sign that these roles are a social construct, and that a change in gender roles will be liberating.

According to sociology research, traditional feminine gender roles have become less relevant in Western society since industrialisation started. For example, the cliché that women do not follow a career is obsolete in many Western societies. On the other hand, the media sometimes portrays women who adopt an extremely classical role as a subculture. Women take on many roles that were traditionally reserved for men, as well as behaviours and fashions, which may cause pressure on many men to be more masculine and thus confined within an even smaller gender role, while other men react against this pressure. For example, men's fashions have become more restrictive than in other eras, while women's fashions have become more broad. One consequence of social unrest during the Vietnam War era was that men began to let their hair grow to a length that had previously (within recent history) been considered appropriate only for women. Somewhat earlier, women had begun to cut their hair to lengths previously considered appropriate only to men. Some famous people known for their androgynous appearances in the 20th century include Brett Anderson, Gladys Bentley, David Bowie, Pete Burns, Boy George, Norman Iceberg, k.d. lang, Annie Lennox, Jaye Davidson, Marilyn Manson, Freddie Mercury, Marlene Dietrich, Mylène Farmer, Gackt, Mana (musician), Michael Jackson, Grace Jones, Marc Bolan, Brian Molko, Julia Sweeney (as Pat), Genesis P-Orridge, Prince and Kristen McMenamy.

Culture

Ideas of appropriate behaviour according to gender vary among cultures and era, although some aspects receive more widespread attention than others. R.W. Connell in *Men, Masculinities and Feminism* claims:

"There are cultures where it has been normal, not exceptional, for men to have homosexual relations. There have been periods in 'Western' history when the modern convention that men suppress displays of emotion did not apply at all, when men were demonstrative about their feeling for their friends. Mateship in the Australian outback last century is a case in point."

Other aspects, however, may differ markedly with time and place. In the Middle Ages, women were commonly associated with roles related to medicine and healing. Due to the rise of witch-hunts across Europe and the institutionalisation of medicine, these roles eventually came to be monopolised by men. In the last few decades, however, these roles have become largely gender-neutral in Western society. The elements of convention or tradition seem to play a dominant role in deciding which occupations fit in with which gender roles. In the United States, physicians have traditionally been men, and the few people who defied that expectation received a special job description: "woman doctor". Similarly, there were special terms like "male nurse", "woman lawyer", "lady barber", "male secretary," etc. But in the former Soviet Union countries, medical doctors are predominantly women, and in Germany and Taiwan it is very common for all of the barbers in a barber shop to be women. Also, throughout history, some jobs that have been typically male or female have switched genders. For example, clerical jobs used to be considered a men's jobs, but when several women began filling men's job positions due to World War II, clerical jobs quickly became dominated by women. It became more feminised, and women workers became known as "typewriters" or "secretaries". There are many other jobs that have switched gender roles. Many jobs are continually evolving as far as being dominated by women or men. In Western society, people whose gender appears masculine are sometimes ridiculed for exhibiting what the society regards as a woman's gender role. For instance, someone with a masculine voice, a five o'clock shadow (or a fuller beard), an Adam's apple, etc., wearing a woman's dress and high heels, carrying a purse, etc., would most likely draw ridicule or other unfriendly attention in ordinary social contexts (the stage and screen excepted). It is seen by some in that society that such a gender role for a man is not acceptable. The traditions of a particular culture often direct that certain career choices and lifestyles are appropriate to men, and other career choices and lifestyles are appropriate to women. In recent years, many people have strongly challenged the social forces that would prevent people from taking on non-traditional gender roles, such as women becoming fighter pilots or men becoming stay-at-home fathers. Men who defy or fail to fulfill their expected gender role are often called effeminate. In modern western societies, women who fail to fulfill their expected gender roles frequently receive only minor criticism for doing so.

Religion

Some Conservative Christian congregations enforce the rule set forth in 1 Corinthians 11:4 and 5 that, in praying or prophesying, no man should cover his head, but that every woman should cover hers.

I Corinthians, 11:14 and 15 indicates that it is inappropriate for a man to wear his hair long, and good for a woman to wear her hair long.

Marriage

In the USA, single men are greatly outnumbered by single women at a ratio of 100 single women to every 86 single men, though never-married men over age 15 outnumber women by a 5:4 ratio (33.9 per cent to 27.3 per cent) according to the 2006 US Census American Community Survey. This very much depends on age group, with 118 single men per 100 single women in their 20s, versus 33 single men to 100 single women over 65.

The numbers are different in other countries. For example, China has many more young men than young women, and this disparity is expected to increase. In regions with recent conflict such as Chechnya, women may greatly outnumber men. In a cross-cultural study by David Buss, men and women were asked to rank certain traits in order of importance in a long-term partner. Both men and women ranked "kindness" and "intelligence" as the two most important factors. Men valued beauty and youth more highly than women, while women valued financial and social status more highly than men.

Communication

Masculine and feminine cultures and individuals generally differ in how they communicate with others. For example, feminine people tend to self-disclose more often than masculine people, and in more intimate details. Likewise, feminine people tend to communicate more affection, and with greater intimacy and confidence than masculine people. Generally speaking, feminine people communicate more and prioritise communication more than masculine. Traditionally, masculine people and feminine people communicate with people of their own gender in different ways. Masculine people form friendships with other masculine people based on common interests, while feminine people build friendships with other feminine people based on mutual support. However, both genders initiate opposite-gender friendships based on the same factors. These factors include proximity, acceptance, effort, communication, common interests, affection and novelty. Context is very important when determining how we communicate with others. It is important to understand what script it is appropriate to use in each respective relationship. Specifically, understanding how affection is communicated in a given context is extremely important. For example, masculine people expect competition in their friendships. They avoid communicating weakness and vulnerability. They avoid communicating personal and emotional concerns. Masculine people tend to communicate affection by including their friends in activities and exchanging favours. Masculine people tend to communicate with each other shoulder-to-shoulder (e.g. watching sports on a television). In contrast, feminine people do not mind communicating weakness and vulnerability. In fact, they seek out friendships more in these times. For this reason, feminine people often feel closer to their friends than masculine people do. Feminine people tend to value their friends for listening and communicating non-critically, communicating support, communicating feelings of enhances self-esteem, communicating validation, offering comfort and contributing to personal growth. Feminine people tend to communicate with each other face-to-face (e.g. meeting together to talk over lunch). Communicating with a friend of the opposite gender is often difficult because of the fundamentally different scripts that masculine people and feminine people use in their friendships. Another challenge in these relationships is that masculine people associate physical contact with communicating sexual desire more than feminine people. Masculine people also desire sex in their opposite-gender relationships more than feminine people. This presents serious challenges in cross-gender friendship communication. In order to overcome these challenges, the two parties must communicate openly about the boundaries of the relationship.

Communication and Gender Cultures

A communication culture is a group of people with an existing set of norms regarding how they communicate with each other. These cultures can be categorised as masculine or feminine. Other communication cultures include African Americans, older people, Indian Native Americans, gay men, lesbians, and people with disabilities. Gender cultures are primarily created and sustained by interaction with others. Through communication we learn about what qualities and activities our culture prescribes to our sex. While it is commonly believed that our sex is the root source of differences and how we relate and communicate to others, it is actually gender that plays a larger role. Whole cultures can be broken down into masculine and feminine, each differing in how they get along with others through different styles of communication. Julia T. Wood's studies explain that "communication produces and reproduces cultural definitions of masculinity and femininity." Masculine and feminine cultures differ dramatically in when, how and why they use communication

Communication Styles

Deborah Tannen's studies found these gender differences in communication styles (where men more generally refers to masculine people, and women correspondingly refers to feminine people):

- Men tend to talk more than women in public situations, but women tend to talk more than men at home.
- Women are more inclined to face each other and make eye contact when talking, while men are more likely to look away from each other.
- Men tend to jump from topic to topic, but women tend to talk at length about one topic.
- When listening, women make more noises such as "mm-hmm" and "uh-huh", while men are more likely to listen silently.

- Women are inclined to express agreement and support, while men are more inclined to debate.

The studies also reported that in general both genders communicated in similar ways. Critics, including Suzette Haden Elgin, have suggested that Tannen's findings may apply more to women of certain specific cultural and economic groups than to women in general. Although it is widely believed that women speak far more words than men, this is actually not the case. Julia T. Wood describes how "differences between gender cultures infuse communication." These differences begin at childhood. Maltz and Broker's research showed that the games children play contribute to socialising children into masculine and feminine cultures. For example, girls playing house promotes personal relationships, and playing house does not necessarily have fixed rules or objectives. Boys, however, tended to play more competitive team sports with different goals and strategies. These differences as children make women operate from assumptions about communication and use rules for communication that differ significantly from those endorsed by most men. Wood produced the following theories regarding gender communication:

- Misunderstandings stem from differing interaction styles.
- Men and women have different ways of showing support, interest and caring.
- Men and women often perceive the same message in different ways.
- Women tend to see communication more as a way to connect and enhance the sense of closeness in the relationship.
- Men see communication more as a way to accomplish objectives.
- Women give more response cues and nonverbal cues to indicate interest and build a relationship.
- Men use feedback to signal actual agreement and disagreement.
- For women, "ums" "uh-huhs" and "yeses" simply mean they are showing interest and being responsive.
- For men, these same responses indicate is agreement or disagreement with what is being communicated.
- For women, talking is the primary way to become closer to another person.
- For men, shared goals and accomplishing tasks is the primary way to become close to another person.
- Men are more likely to express caring by doing something concrete for or doing something together with another person.
- Women can avoid being hurt by men by realising how men communicate caring.
- Men can avoid being hurt by women by realising how women communicate caring.

- Women who want to express caring to men can do so more effectively by doing something for them or doing something with them.
- Men who want to express caring to women can do so more effectively by verbally communicating that they care.
- Men emphasise independence and are therefore less likely to ask for help in accomplishing an objective.
- Men are much less likely to ask for directions when they are lost than women.
- Men desire to maintain autonomy and to not appear weak or incompetent.
- Women develop identity within relationships more than men.
- Women seek out and welcome relationships with others more than men.
- Men tend to think that relationships jeopardize their independence.
- For women, relationships are a constant source of interest, attention and communication.
- For men, relationships are not as central.
- The term "Talking about us" means very different things to men and women.
- Men feel that there is no need to talk about a relationship that is going well.
- Women feel that a relationship is going well as long as they are talking about it.
- Women can avoid being hurt by realising that men don't necessarily feel the need to talk about a relationship that is going well.
- Men can help improve communication in a relationship by applying the rules of feminine communication.
- Women can help improve communication in a relationship by applying the rules of masculine communication.
- Just as Western communication rules wouldn't necessarily apply in an Asian culture, masculine rules wouldn't necessarily apply in a feminine culture, and vice versa.

Suggestions for Effective Cross-Gender Communication

Finally, Wood describes how different genders can communicate to one another and provides six suggestions to do so.

1. Individuals should suspend judgment. When a person finds his or herself confused in a cross-gender conversation, he or she should resist the tendency to judge and instead explore what is happening and how that person and their partner might better understand each other.

opportunity to women were warned in a 2008 United Nations-sponsored report that this disempowerment is a critical factor crippling these nations' return to the first rank of global leaders in commerce, learning and culture. In 2010, the European Union opened the European Institute for Gender Equality (EIGE) in Vilnius, Lithuania to promote gender equality and to fight sex discrimination.

Sexism

Sexism, also known as gender discrimination or sex discrimination, is the application of the false belief that there are characteristics implicit to one's gender that indirectly affect one's abilities in unrelated areas. It is a form of discrimination or devaluation based on a person's sex, with such attitudes being based on beliefs in traditional stereotypes of gender roles. The term *sexism* is most often used in relation with discrimination against women, in the context of patriarchy. Sexism involves hatred of, or prejudice towards a gender as a whole or the blind application of gender stereotypes. Sexism is often associated with gender-supremacy arguments.

Generalisation and Partition

In philosophy, a sexist attitude is one which suggests human beings can be understood or judged on the basis of the essential characteristics of the group to which an individual belongs—in this case, their sexual group, as men or women. This assumes that all individuals fit into the category of male or female and does not take into account people who identify as neither or both.

Gender Stereotypes

Gender stereotypes are widely held and often inaccurate beliefs about the characteristics and behaviour of women and men. Gender stereotypes are not only descriptive, but also prescriptive beliefs about "how men and women should be and behave". Members of either sex who deviate from prescriptive gender stereotypes are punished; assertive women, for example, are called "bitches" whereas men who lack physical strength are seen as "wimps". Emperical studies have found widely shared cultural beliefs that men are more socially valued and more competent than women at most things, as well as specific assumptions that men are better at some particular tasks (e.g., mechanical tasks) while women are better at others (e.g., nurturing tasks). For example, Fiske and colleagues surveyed nine diverse samples, from different regions of the United States, and found that members of these samples, regardless of age, consistently rated the category "men" higher than the category "women" on a multidimensional scale of competence. Gender stereotypes can facilitate and impede intellectual performance. For instance, stereotype threat can lower women's performance on mathematics tests due to the stereotype that women have inferior quantitative skills compared with men. Stereotypes can also affect the assessments people make of their own competence. Studies found that specific stereotypes (e.g., women have lower mathematical ability) affect women's and men's perceptions of their abilities (e.g., in math and science) such that men assess their own task ability higher than women performing at the same level. These "biased self-assessments" have far-reaching effects because they can shape men and women's educational and career decisions. Gender stereotypes are sometimes applied at an early age. Various interventions were reviewed including the use of fiction in challenging gender stereotypes. For example, in a study by A. Wing, children were read *Bill's New Frock* by Anne Fine. The content of the book was discussed with them. Children were able to articulate, and reflect on, their stereotypical constructions of gender and those in the world at large. There was evidence of children considering 'the different treatment that boys and girls receive', and of classroom discussion enabling stereotypes to be challenged.

Sexist and Gender-neutral Language

Research has found that the use of *he* as a generic masculine pronoun evokes a disproportionate number of male images and excludes thoughts of women in non-sex specific instances. Results also suggest that while the plural *they* functions as a generic pronoun for both males and females, males may comprehend *he/she* in a manner similar to *he.*

Nearing the end of the 20th century, there is a rise in the use of gender-neutral language in Western worlds. This is often attributed to the rise of feminism. Gender-neutral language is the avoidance of gender-specific job titles, non-parallel usage, and other usage that is felt by some to be sexist. Supporters feel that having gender-specific titles and gender-specific pronouns either implies a system bias to exclude individuals based on their gender, or else is as unnecessary in most cases as race-specific pronouns, religion-specific pronouns, or persons-height-specific pronouns. Some of those who support gender-specific pronouns assert that promoting gender-neutral language is a kind of "semantics injection" itself.

Anthropological Linguistics and Gender-specific Language

Unlike the Indo-European languages in the West, for many other languages around the world, gender-specific pronouns are a recent phenomenon that occur around the early-20th century. As a result of colonialism, cultural revolution occurred in many parts of the world with attempts to "modernise" and "westernise" by adding gender-specific pronouns and animate-inanimate pronouns to local languages. This resulted in the situation of what was gender-neutral pronouns a century ago suddenly becoming gender-specific.

(See for example Gender-neutrality in languages without grammatical gender: Turkish.)

Gender-specific Pejorative Terms

Gender-specific pejorative terms intimidate or harm another person because of their gender. Sexism can be expressed in a pseudo-subtle manner through the attachment of terms which have negative gender-oriented implications, such as through condescension. Many examples are swear words and will not be enumerated here. A mildly vulgar example is the uninformative attribution of the term 'hag' for a woman or 'fairy' for a man. Although hag and fairy both have non-sexist interpretations, when they are used in the context of a gender-specific pejorative term these words become representations of sexist attitudes, to wit, sexism.

The Relationship between Rape and Misogyny

Research into the factors which motivate perpetrators of rape against women frequently reveals patterns of hatred of women and pleasure in inflicting psychological and/or physical trauma, rather than sexual interest. Researchers have argued that rape is not the result of pathological individuals, but rather of systems of male dominance and from cultural practices and beliefs that objectify and degrade women. Mary Odem and Jody Clay-Warner, along with Susan Brownwiller, consider sexist attitudes to be propagated by a series of myths about rape and rapists. They state that contrary to these myths, rapists often plan a rape before they choose a victim, and that acquaintance rape is the most common form of rape rather than assault by a stranger. Odem also states that these rape myths propagate sexist attitudes about men by perpetuating a myth that men cannot control their sexuality.

To counteract this dangerous imbalance, the "Men Can Stop Rape" movement has been implemented. The success of the MCSR campaign has inspired a similar movement in the military with the tagline "My strength is for defending."

Occupational Sexism

Occupational sexism refers to any discriminatory practices, statements, actions, etc., based on a person's sex that are present or occur in a place of employment. One form of occupational sexism is wage discrimination. In 2008, the Organisation for Economic Co-operation and Development (OECD) found that while female employment rates have expanded considerably and the gender employment and wage gaps have narrowed virtually everywhere, women still have 20 per cent less chance to have a job than men, on average, and they are paid 17 per cent less than their male counterparts. Moreover, the report stated:

[In] many countries, labour market discrimination – i.e. the unequal treatment of equally productive individuals only because they belong to a specific group – is still a crucial factor inflating disparities in employment and the quality of job opportunities [...] Evidence presented in this edition of the *Employment Outlook* suggests that about 8 per cent of the variation in gender employment gaps and 30 per cent of the variation in gender wage gaps across OECD countries can be explained by discriminatory practices in the labour market."

The OECD report also found that despite the fact that almost all OECD countries, including the United States, have established anti-discrimination laws, these laws are difficult to enforce.

Gender-role Stereotypes

According to the OECD women's labour market behaviour "is influenced by learned cultural and social values that may be thought to discriminate against women (and sometimes against men) by stereotyping certain work and life styles as "male" or "female"." Further, the OECD argues that women's educational choices "may be dictated, at least in part, by their expectations that [certain] types of employment opportunities are not available to them, as well as by gender stereotypes that are prevalent in society." There is a long record of women being excluded from participation in many professions. Often, women have gained entry into a previously male profession only to be faced by many additional obstacles. Elisabeth Blackwell, the first woman to receive an M.D. in the United States and Myra Bradwell, the first female lawyer in the state of Illinois, are examples. Professional discrimination continues today, according to studies done by Cornell University and others. It has been hypothesized that gender bias has been influencing which scientific research gets published. This hypothesis coincides with a test conducted at the University of Toronto led by Amber Budden. Based on the results of this study, almost 10 per cent of female authors get their papers published when their gender is hidden. In addition, women frequently earn significantly lower wages than their male counterparts who perform the same job. In the United States, for example, women earn an average of 23.5 per cent less than men. In 1833, women working in factories earned only one-quarter of men's wages and in 2007, women's median annual paychecks reflected only 78 cents for every $1.00 earned by men. Women make up most of the "less meaningful, less skillful jobs" such as working in daycares. A study showed women comprised 87 per cent of workers in the child care industry and 86 per cent of the health aide industry. Some experts believe that parents play an important role in the creation of values and perceptions of their children. The fact that many girls are asked to help their mothers do housework, while many boys do technical tasks with their fathers, seems to influence their behaviour and can sometimes discourage girls from performing such tasks. Girls will then think that each gender should have a specific role and behaviour. A 2009 study found that being overweight harms women's career advancement but it presents no barrier for men. Overweight or obese women were significantly under-represented among company bosses whereas a significant proportion of male executives were overweight or obese. The author of the study stated that the results suggest that "the 'glass ceiling effect' on women's advancement may reflect not only general negative stereotypes about the competencies of women, but also weight bias that results in the application of stricter appearance standards to women. Overweight women are evaluated more negatively than overweight men. There is a tendency to hold women to harsher weight standards." At other times, there are accusations that some traditionally female professions have been or are being eliminated by its roles being subsumed by a male dominated profession. The assumption of baby delivery roles by doctors and subsequent decline of midwifery is sometimes claimed to be an example.

Wage Gap

Eurostat found a persisting gender pay gap of 17.5 per cent on average in the 27 EU Member States in 2008. Similarly, the OECD found that female full-time employees earned 17 per cent less than their male counterparts across OECD countries in 2009. In the United States, the female-to-male earnings ratio was 0.77 in 2009, meaning that, in 2009, female full-time, year round (FTYR) workers earned 77 per cent as much as male FYTR workers. Women's earnings relative to men's fell from 1960 to 1980 (from 60.7 per cent to 60.2 per cent) and then rose rapidly from 1980 to 1990 (from 60.2 per cent to 71.6 per cent), and less rapidly from 1990 to 2000 (from 71.6 per cent to 73.7 per cent) and from 2000 to 2009 (from 73.7 per cent to 77.0 per cent). At the time when the first Equal Pay Act was passed in 1963, female full-time workers earned 58.9 per cent as much as male full-time workers. The gender pay gap has been attributed to differences in personal and workplace characteristics between women and men (education, hours worked, occupation etc.) as well as direct and indirect discrimination in the labour market (gender stereotypes, customer and employer bias etc.). Studies always find that some portion of the gender pay gap remains unexplained even after controlling for factors that are assumed to influence earnings. The unexplained portion of the wage gap is attributed to gender discrimination. The estimates for the discriminatory component of the gender pay gap vary widely. The OECD estimated that approximately 30 per cent of the gender pay gaps across OECD countries is due to discrimination. Australian research shows that discrimination accounts for approximately 60 per cent of the wage differentials between women and men. Studies examining the gender pay gap in the United States show that large parts of the wage differential remain unexplained even after controlling for factors that affect pay. One study examined college graduates and found that the portion of the pay gap that remains unexplained after all other factors are taken into account is 5 per cent one year after graduating college and 12 per cent ten years after graduation. One study found that women are less likely to negotiate raises, while another study found that women do not negotiate less than men. Research done at Cornell University and elsewhere indicates that mothers are less likely to get hired than equally qualified fathers and if hired would be paid a lower salary than male applicants with children. The OECD found that "a significant impact of children on women's pay is generally found in the United Kingdom and the United States." Fathers, on the other hand, earn $7,500 more on average than men without children.

Glass Ceiling

The term "glass ceiling" is used to describe a perceived barrier to advancement based on discrimination, particularly gender discrimination. In academic achievement, great improvements have been made. However, as of 1995 in the United States, women received about half of all Master's degrees but 95 to 97 per cent of the senior managers of Fortune 1000 Industrial and Fortune 500 companies were male and in the Fortune 2000 industrial and service companies, only 5 per cent of senior managers were women. The United Nations asserts "progress in bringing women into leadership and decision-making positions around the world remains far too slow."

Objectification

It is argued that sexual objectification is a form of sexism. Some countries, such as Norway and Denmark, have laws against sexual objectification in advertising. Nudity itself is not banned, and nude people can be used to advertise a product, but only if they are relevant to what is being advertised. Sol Olving, head of Norway's Kreativt Forum, an association of the country's top advertising agencies explained: "You could have a naked person advertising shower gel or a cream, but not a woman in a bikini draped across a car."

Pornography

It is sometimes asserted that pornography, as a form of objectifying a gender, contributes to sexism. Some researchers suggest that pornography depicting women contributes to violence against women by eroticizing scenes in which women are dominated, coerced, humiliated, or even sexually assaulted. Anti-pornography feminists, notably Catherine MacKinnon, charge that the production of pornography entails physical, psychological, and/or economic coercion of the women who perform and model in it. Opponents of pornography charge that pornography presents a severely distorted image of sexual relations, and reinforces sex myths; that it always shows women as readily available and desiring to engage in sex at any time, with any men, on men's terms, always responding positive to any advance men make. Catherine MacKinnon states that:

Pornography affects people's belief in rape myths. So for example if a woman says 'I didn't consent' and people have been viewing pornography, they believe rape myths and believe the woman did consent no matter what she said. That when she said no, she meant yes. When she said she didn't want to, that meant more beer. When she said she would prefer to go home, that means she's a lesbian who needs to be given a good corrective experience. Pornography promotes these rape myths and desensitises people to violence against women so that you need more violence to become sexually aroused if you're a pornography consumer. This is very well documented.

Historical Examples of Gender Discrimination

Certain forms of sex discrimination are illegal in some countries, while in other countries sex discrimination may be legally sanctioned under various circumstances.

Coverture

U.S. and English law subscribed until the 20th century to the system of coverture, where "by marriage, the husband and wife are one person in law; that is the very being or legal existence of the woman is suspended during the marriage." Not until 1875 were women in the U.S. legally defined as persons (*Minor v Happersett*, 88 U.S. 162). In many countries, women still lose significant legal rights during marriage. For example, in Chile "the marital partnership is to be headed by the husband, who shall administer the spouses' joint property as well as the property owned by his wife."

Gender Discrimination in Voting and Political Candidacy

Suffrage is the civil right to vote. Gender is sometimes used as a criterion for the right to vote. Women's suffrage in the United States was achieved gradually, at state and local levels, during the 19th and early 20th centuries, culminating in 1920 with the passage of the Nineteenth Amendment to the United States Constitution, which provided: "The right of citizens of the United States to vote shall not be denied or abridged by the United States or by any State on account of sex." Since women have gained the right to vote through the Nineteenth Amendment, females have emerged in the field of politics whether in local/state politics or as presidential candidates. Although women certainly have the capability to successfully gain political power, gender stereotypes are evident in politics/candidacy. Data from the

2006 American National Election Studies Pilot Study measured "perceptions of women's and men's issue competency. For example, a question that was asked was "who would do a better job in the U.S. Congress handling crime - a democrat who is a man, a democrat who is a woman or would they equally do a good or bad job?". The same question was rephrased to say "a republican..." The data shows that voters hold gender stereotypes for both democrats and republicans. Specifically, when asked the previous question, voters stated that the male would do a better job in handling crime. Meanwhile, when "handling crime" was changed to "handling education," voters said that women would do a better job. The reason why the voters responded in such a manner is because "women politicians are perceived to possess typically feminine traits such as being warm and sensitive and are believed to be expert on so called woman issues such as education... Meanwhile, men politicians are perceived to possess typically masculine traits, such as being assertive and tough." The data specifically shows that about 2 per cent of the voters (average: 1.9 per cent Democrats in Congress, 2.3 per cent Republicans in Congress) believed that men would do a better job handling education while about 6.4 per cent of voters (average 6.8 per cent Democrats in Congress, 6.2 per cent Republicans in Congress) said that women would do a better job handling education. While voters may believe that women do a better job in areas than men and vice versa, the survey then limits the analysis to respondents that associate with a specific political party. When Republicans were asked the same questions regarding issue competency in education and crime, the results show that about 26 per cent of democratic women state that female democratic politicians would do a better job handling education while just under 20 per cent of Republican women held the same belief. Meanwhile more Republicans believed that republican men are better able to handle crime. (36 per cent of voters) while democrats believed that democratic men were not as able (14 per cent of voters). The scientists conclude that "although it is often argued that any gender effect will disappear in the presence of the party cue, [they] find that gender stereotypes transcend party. Both Democratic and Republican politicians are believed to differ by gender in perceived issue competency and issue positions. Democrats are more likely to hold gender stereotypes that benefit women in politics. Democrats are more likely than Republicans to see an advantage for women on the issue of education and are less likely than Republicans to see men at advantage on the issue of crime." Therefore, while Democrats are more likely to believe that women are better able to handle education, Republicans believe that men are better able to handle crime. "Overall, gender stereotypes appear to be more detrimental to the electoral chances of Republican women than Democratic women. In the end, this research offers support for the notion that women and men who run for office are viewed through multiple lenses by a public employing a range of stereotypes to the degree that people continue to see women and men as possessing different issue competencies." This is clearly sexist because in a politically and socially correct world, women would be considered just as capable of handling crime than men but, unfortunately, citizens view issue competencies based on gender. This is also split by political parties because, based on the data and conclusions, Democrats believe that women are better able to handle education while Republicans believe that men are better fit to handle crime.

Examples

Domestic Violence

Domestic violence takes on many different forms which include verbal, physical and psychological abuse. Domestic violence occurs in unequal proportion in men and women and is often considered related to sexism. Domestic violence is more likely to occur in a relationship where there is perceived to be a natural imbalance of power. The types of violence (physical, psychological, sexual) also differ in proportion across the gender spectrum.

Hate-motivated Sexual Assault

Rape and sexual assault are considered to be acts of hate. Their relationship to sexism is that there is often a desire for the perpetrator to feel power over the other due to the sex.

Marital Relationships

There is a high rate of pop culture references to restricted gender roles in marriage. In divorce, wife selling is a sexist custom.

Education

Women in the past have generally been disadvantaged from higher education. When women were admitted to higher education, they were encouraged to major in subjects that were considered less intellectual; the study of English literature in American and British colleges and universities was in fact instituted as a field of study considered suitable to women's "lesser intellects". Since 1991, however, the proportion of young women enrolled in college in the United States has exceeded the enrollment rate for young men, and the gap has widened over time. Women now make up the majority—54 per cent—of the 10.8 million young adults enrolled in college in the United States. Research studies have found that discrimination continues today: boys receive more attention and praise in the classroom in grade school along with more blame and punishment, and "this pattern of more active teacher attention directed at male students continues at the postsecondary level". Over time, female students speak less and less in classroom settings.

Girls earn higher grades than boys until the end of high school. Girls in some districts achieve higher marks despite scoring the same or lower than boys on standardised tests.

Military Service

Military service is an area where gender roles have often been considered paramount. However, some countries, like Israel, have mandatory military service regardless of gender. In the United States, women are prohibited from serving in active ground combat. However, in the current wars in Afghanistan and Iraq, "the unpredictable nature of the attacks in this war blurs the distinction between front-line and rear areas ... (women) find themselves in the thick of the battle." Initially, women deployed in support roles were not trained in active service. This created an imbalanced dangerous situation for women and now all soldiers receive the same combat training. Some experts purport that women's perceived role as a sub-class of soldier encourages sexual violence against women in the military. In the USA, the Department of Defense's new Sexual Assault Prevention and Response office is addressing these concerns.

Transphobia

Transphobia refers to prejudice against transsexuality and transsexual or transgender people, based on their personal gender identification (see Phobia - terms indicating prejudice or class discrimination). Whether intentional or not, transphobia can have severe consequences for the person the object of the negative attitude. The LGBT movement has campaigned against sexism against transsexuals. One form of sexism against transsexuals is how many "women-only" and "men-only" events and organisations have been criticized for rejecting trans women and trans men, respectively.

Antisexism Movements

In Ecuador, the Pink Helmets (or Cascos Rosas), created in May, 2011, by Freddy Caleron and Damian Valencia, both 18, seek to unite young men against machismo. The Pink Helmets published a manual suggesting 30 actions aimed at putting an end to violence in society, in relationships, within families, and among friends. The Pink Helmets' creators and participating members, who call themselves "neomasculinos" and are 15–20 years old, visit schools and streets to give talks and take part in festivals, such as the Quito Fest, in collabouration with UN Women, to raise awareness on violence and on the movement against it. Chauvinism and violence are common in Ecuador, with 40 per cent of children under age 15 saying that they have witnessed acts of violence at home. According to the *National Plan for the Eradication of Gender Violence of the Government of Ecuador*, 80 per cent of women have been victims of violence at least once and 21 per cent of children and adolescents have been sexually abused. However, no official data provide a concrete number of women who have been killed or injured by men. The overall movement aims to promote gender equality, eliminate gender violence against women, and encourage "dialogue of respect between men and women from adolescence without hesitation to criticise sexist concepts that live in their culture".

Occupational Sexism

Occupational sexism (also called sexism in the work place and employment sexism) refers to any discriminatory practices, statements, actions, etc. based on a person's sex that are present or occur in a place of employment.

Select Markers of Occupational Sexism

- Wage discrimination
- Systematic sex-based hiring and promotional practices (when employers do not hire or promote a person who is "otherwise apparently qualified for a job" solely on the grounds that they are a woman or man)
- Sexual harassment
- The belief (or tendency toward such a belief) that certain occupational fields or types of jobs, particularly those that are degrading and/or low-paying, are "women's work" or those that are dangerous and/or hazardous are "men's work".

Wage Discrimination

The differences that exist in pay between men and women performing the same or similar jobs (also known as the gender gap or the gender wage gap) constitute a well-documented, but highly disputed phenomenon. Though there is little debate as to whether or not women earn less than men do, the exact amount of women's earnings in comparison to men's is debated. Currently, this figure is usually estimated at about 76 per cent, meaning that women earn 76 per cent of what men doing the same job earn. According to Ellen Bravo of the *Miami Herald,* overall, as of 2003, women in the US indeed made 76 cents for every dollar earned by men doing the same job. She states that this figure is even more disparate in the context of race with Black women making 67 cents for every dollar earned by US males and Latino women making 54 cents. The US Census Bureau, however, estimated that as of 2003, women were only earning 75.5 cents for every dollar that their male counterparts earned. These and other such figures have been challenged by a number of critics for being too low including Howard J. Wall, a senior economist with the Federal Reserve Bank of St. Louis. Wall purports that these estimates only look at annual wages as opposed to weekly or hourly wages and that they are artificially deflated by certain institutions such as the US Department of Labour. He asserts that as of 1999, women earned an hourly income that was equal to 83.8 per cent of what men earned.

Causes of Wage Discrimination

There is great disagreement over what causes and perpetuates the gender gap with myriad theories having been supplied by sociologists, economists, politicians, etc. For example, scholars from varying disciplines assert that the differences in women's earnings are the result, at least in part, of women consistently choosing to concentrate themselves in certain types of low-paying jobs, namely those in the administrative, clerical, and service fields (see also Pink-collar worker). This is said to be particularly true in the cases of the many women who select these careers because of how easily they can continue working in or quit them if they have a family or choose to start one. Others blame the wage gap on antiquated perspectives of female employment and the financial needs of women, citing that women in the US have historically been seen as requiring less money than men because it was the job of their parents and/or husbands to subsidise their needs.

Challenging Occupational Sexism

Historically, in the US, occupationally sexist practices have often been so permissible and encouraged that they have become institutionalized. For example, when women were originally "allowed" to join the workforce by men (primarily in the 20th Century), they were paid one-half to two-thirds of what their male counterparts earned. Since they could perform many jobs at the same level as men, it became economical and considered "good business" to hire women at lesser wages. Several groups such as the American Civil Liberties Union (ACLU) and the National Organization for Women (NOW) have since formed to fight against such practices, leading to the creation of groundbreaking laws such as the Equal Pay Act of 1963. However, identifying and challenging sex discrimination in the workplace (on legal grounds) has been argued as being too difficult for the average person to attempt and even harder to prove in court. For example, in a 2007 Supreme Court case, Lilly Ledbetter, a former employee of the Goodyear Tire and Rubber Company, recently had a judgment in her favour overturned that had awarded her back pay and damages for several years of receiving disproportionately low pay in comparison to her male counterparts because she waited too long to file suit. After a 5-4 decision delivered by Justice Samuel Alito, the court issued a statement saying that "Federal law states that 'employees must file their discrimination complaints within 180 days of the incident,'" a task that dissenting Justice Ruth Bader Ginsburg claimed was unreasonable considering that quite often women have no reason to suspect discrimination until certain unfair patterns develop and they are made aware of them. Despite the Equal Pay Act of 1963, women have continued to receive less than equal pay of their male counterparts. In 2001, six women brought suit against Wal-Mart, claiming they received less pay and promotion opportunities than their fellow male coworkers. One woman claimed that she was paid $23,000 less a year than a man doing the same job. In 2004, the case of *Dukes* v. *Wal-Mart* became the largest class action lawsuit in history, with approximately 1.5 million women claiming to have suffered similar discrimination at Wal-Mart. Wal-Mart is the largest private employer in the world, and the women suing the company hope to set an example for other large businesses around the world to treat their female employees equally.

Understanding Gender Pay Gap

The gender pay gap (also known as gender wage gap) is the difference between male and female earnings expressed as a percentage of male earnings, according to the OECD. The European Commission defines it as the average difference between men's and women's hourly earnings. There is a debate to what extent this is the result of gender differences, lifestyle choices (e.g., number of hours worked), or because of discrimination.

Adjusted and Unadjusted Gender Pay Gap

It is important to differentiate between the unadjusted (also known as raw) wage gap and the adjusted (also known as discriminatory or unexplained) wage gap. The unadjusted or raw pay gap does not take into account differences in personal (e.g., age, education, the number of children, job tenure and occupation) and workplace characteristics (e.g., the economic sector and place of employment) between men and women. Parts of the raw pay gap can be attributed to the fact that women, for instance, tend to engage more often in part-time work and tend to work in lower paid industries. The remaining part of the raw wage gap that cannot be explained by variables that are thought to influence pay is then referred to as the adjusted gender pay gap and is interpreted as being discriminatory. However, a 2010 report by the European Foundation for the Improvement of Living and Working Conditions, for example, pointed out that "interpreting the adjusted gap as being the only discriminatory component falls short of the reality." The report found that the part of the pay gap which is attributed to observed differences in characteristics (such as age, education, hours worked etc.) may still reflect the outcome of discriminatory social processes. Eurofond found that "the major reasons for this gap are very often related to both horizontal and vertical segregation

– or the fact that women tend to choose lower-paid professions, reach a 'glass ceiling' in their careers, or have their jobs valued less favourably. The origins of these factors could be judged as being discriminatory in themselves – that is, when they are rooted in gender stereotypes of male and female occupations."

Gender Pay Gap Among OECD Nations

The 2008 edition of the *Employment Outlook* report by the Organisation for Economic Co-operation and Development (OECD) found that while female employment rates have expanded considerably and the gender employment and wage gaps have narrowed virtually everywhere, women still have 20 per cent less chance to have a job than men, on average, and they are paid 17 per cent less than their male counterparts. Moreover, the report stated:

"[In] many countries, labour market discrimination – i.e. the unequal treatment of equally productive individuals only because they belong to a specific group – is still a crucial factor inflating disparities in employment and the quality of job opportunities [...] Evidence presented in this edition of the *Employment Outlook* suggests that about [...] 30 per cent of the variation in gender wage gaps across OECD countries can be explained by discriminatory practices in the labour market."

Gender Pay Gap in European Union

At EU level, the gender pay gap is defined as the relative difference in the average gross hourly earnings of women and men within the economy as a whole. Eurostat found a persisting gender pay gap of 17.5 per cent on average in the 27 EU Member States in 2008. There were considerable differences between the Member States, with the pay gap ranging from less than 10 per cent in Italy, Malta, Poland, Slovenia and Belgium to more than 20 per cent in Slovakia, the Netherlands, Czech Republic, Cyprus, Germany, United Kingdom and Greece and more than 25 per cent in Estonia and Austria.

Gender Pay Gap over Time

Looking at the gender pay gap over time, the United States Congress Joint Economic Committee showed that as explained inequities decrease, the unexplained pay gap remains unchanged. Similarly, according to economists Francine Blau and Lawrence Kahn and their research into the gender pay gap in the United States, a steady convergence between the wages of women and men is not automatic. They argue that after a considerable rise in women's wages during the 1980s, the gain decreased in the 1990s. The 2000s are characterised by a mixed picture of increase and decline. Thus, Blau and Kahn assume:

"With the evidence suggesting that convergence has slowed in recent years, the possibility arises that the narrowing of the gender pay gap will not continue into the future. Moreover, there is evidence that although discrimination against women in the labour market has declined, some discrimination does still continue to exist."

A wide ranging meta-analysis by Doris Weichselbaumer and Rudolf Winter-Ebmer (2005) of more than 260 published adjusted pay gap studies for over 60 countries has found that, from the 1960s to the 1990s, raw wage differentials worldwide have fallen substantially from around 65 to 30 per cent. The bulk of this decline, however, was due to better labour market endowments of women. The 260 published estimates show that the unexplained or discriminatory component of the gap has not declined over time. Using their own specifications, Weichselbaumer and Winter-Ebmer found that the yearly overall decline of the gender pay gap would amount to a slow 0.17 log points, implying a slow level of convergence between the wages of men and women. According to economist Alan Manning of the London School of Economics, the process of closing the gender pay gap has slowed substantially and women could earn less than men for the next 150 years because of discrimination and ineffective government policies. A 2011 study by the British CMI revealed that if pay growth continues for female executives at current rates, the gap between the earnings of female and male executives would not be closed until 2109.

Gender Pay Gap by Country

United States

In the United States, the gender pay gap is measured as the ratio of female to male median yearly earnings among full-time, year-round (FTYR) workers. The female-to-male earnings ratio was 0.77 in 2009, meaning that, in 2009, female FTYR workers earned 77 per cent as much as male FTYR workers. Women's median yearly earnings relative to men's rose rapidly from 1980 to 1990 (from 60.2 per cent to 71.6 per cent), and less rapidly from 1990 to 2000 (from 71.6 per cent to 73.7 per cent) and from 2000 to 2009 (from 73.7 per cent to 77.0 per cent). The gender pay gap has been attributed to differences in personal and workplace characteristics between women and men (education, hours worked, occupation etc.) as well as direct and indirect discrimination in the labour market (gender stereotypes, customer and employer bias etc.). The estimates for the discriminatory component of the gender pay gap vary widely although studies always find that some portion of the gender pay gap remains unexplained even after controlling for factors that are assumed to influence earnings.

Australia

In Australia, the gender pay gap is calculated on the average weekly ordinary time earnings for full time employees published by the Australian Bureau of Statistics. The gender pay gap excludes part time, casual earnings and overtime payments.

Australia has a persistent gender pay gap. Between 1990 and 2009, the gender pay gap remained within a narrow range of between 15 and 17 per cent. In August 2010, the Australian gender pay gap was 16.9 per cent.

I an Watson of Macquarie University examined the gender pay gap among full-time managers in Australia over the period 2001-2008, and found that between 65 and 90 per cent of this earnings differential could not be explained by a large range of demographic and labour market variables. In fact, a "major part of the earnings gap is simply due to women managers being female." Watson also notes that despite the "characteristics of male and female managers being remarkably similar, their earnings are very different, suggesting that discrimination plays an important role in this outcome." A 2009 report to the Department of Families, Housing, Community Services and Indigenous Affairs also found that "simply being a woman is the major contributing factor to the gap in Australia, accounting for 60 per cent of the difference between women's and men's earnings, a finding which reflects other Australian research in this area." The second most important factor in explaining the pay gap was industrial segregation.

Impacts of Gender Pay Gap

Pensions

The European Commission argues that the gender pay gap has far-reaching effects, especially in regard to pensions. Since women's earnings over a lifetime are on average 17.5 per cent (as of 2008) lower than men's, these lower earnings result in lower pensions. As a result, elderly women are more likely to face poverty: 22 per cent of women aged 65 and over are at risk of poverty compared to 16 per cent of men.

Economy

A 2009 report for the Australian Department of Families, Housing, Community Services and Indigenous Affairs argued that in addition to fairness and equity there are also strong economic imperatives for addressing the gender wage gap. The report found that the gender pay gap has a substantial effect on Australia's economic performance, measured in terms of GDP per capita, and that the value of reducing the gap is substantial. For example, the researchers estimated that a decrease in the gender wage gap of 1 percentage point from 17 per cent to 16 per cent would increase GDP per capita by approximately $260. This equates to around $5,497 million or 0.5 per cent of total GDP, assuming that the Australian population is held constant. The results also indicate that eliminating the whole gender wage gap from 17 per cent (in February 2009) to zero, could be worth around $93 billion or 8.5 per cent of GDP. The researchers also estimate that removing the negative effects associated with the prime determinant of the gap, that is being a woman, could add around $56 billion or 5.1 per cent to total annual GDP.

Role of Anti-discrimination Legislation

According to the 2008 edition of the *Employment Outlook* report by the OECD, almost all OECD countries have established laws to combat discrimination on grounds of gender. Legal prohibition of discriminatory behaviour, however, can only be effective if it is enforced. The OECD points out that:

> "herein lies a major problem: in all OECD countries, enforcement essentially relies on the victims' willingness to assert their claims. But many people are not even aware of their legal rights regarding discrimination in the workplace. And even if they are, proving a discrimination claim is intrinsically difficult for the claimant and legal action in courts is a costly process, whose benefits down the road are often small and uncertain. All this discourages victims from lodging complaints."

Moreover, although many OECD countries have put in place specialized anti-discrimination agencies, only in a few of them are these agencies effectively empowered, in the absence of individual complaints, to investigate companies, take actions against employers suspected of operating discriminatory practices, and sanction them when they find evidence of discrimination.

In 2003, the U.S. Government Accountability Office (GAO) found that women in the United States, on average, earned 80 per cent of what men earned in 2000 and workplace discrimination may be one contributing factor. In light of these findings, GAO examined the enforcement of anti-discrimination laws in the private and public sectors. In a 2008 report, GAO focused on the enforcement and outreach efforts of the Equal Employment Opportunity Commission (EEOC) and the Department of Labor (Labor). GAO found that EEOC does not fully monitor gender pay enforcement efforts and that Labor does not monitor enforcement trends and performance outcomes regarding gender pay or other specific areas of discrimination. GAO came to the conclusion that "federal agencies should better monitor their performance in enforcing anti-discrimination laws."

Understanding Gender Apartheid

The term gender apartheid, like sex apartheid, is a term used to describe economic and social sexual discrimination against women, including strict sex segregation, as well as an "absence of justice for women in much of the non-Western world." It is used especially to describe treatment of women in Muslim societies. However, fundamentalist strains of Christianity, Judaism and Buddhism also have been described as practicing "gender apartheid."

In Context of South African Apartheid

The word "apartheid" - for "apart" - originated in South Africa under racial apartheid. Among other things, the government forbade African women from living with their husbands who worked in the mines, which Ali Mazrui describes as "gender apartheid." Some human rights advocates have argued for sanctions against states practicing gender apartheid, similar to those imposed on South Africa under apartheid.

Gender Segregation in Islam

Women's rights activist Mahnaz Afkhami writes that the fundamentalist world view "singles out women's status and her relations to society as the supreme test of the authenticity of the Islamic order." This is symbolized by the institutions of Purdah (physical separation of the sexes) and Awrah (concealing the body with clothing). As in much of the world, institutions suppressing women were becoming less powerful until the resurgence of Islamic fundamentalism at the end of the 20th century. Walid Phares writes that Marxism in the Soviet Union nations and China and "secular anticlericalism" in Turkey forced women to "integrate themselves into an antireligious society" resulting in a backlash of "gender apartheid" by Islamic fundamentalists. He notes that other religions also have "witnessed similar historical struggles." Phyllis Chesler describes Islamic gender apartheid as being "characterised by normalised daughter- and wife-battering, forced veiling, female genital mutilation, polygamy, purdah, (the segregation or sequestration of women), arranged marriage, child marriage, first cousin marriage" and punishment for not complying with these. Several Muslim nations have been criticised for practicing "gender apartheid": Afghanistan, under Taliban religious leadership, has been characterised by feminist groups and others as a "gender apartheid" system where women are segregated from men in public and do not enjoy legal equality or equal access to employment or education. The Feminist Majority Foundation launched a "Campaign for Afghan Women and Girls" denouncing gender apartheid. According to the Women's Human Rights Resource Programme of the University of Toronto Bora Laskin Law Library "Throughout the duration of Taliban rule in Afghanistan, the term "Gender Apartheid" was used by a number of women's rights advocates to convey the message that the rights violations experience by Afghan women were in substance no different than those experienced by blacks in Apartheid South Africa." In 2006 Marina Mahathir, the daughter of Malaysia's former Prime Minister, and a campaigner for women's rights, described the status of Muslim women in Malaysia as similar to that of Black South Africans under apartheid. She stated "In our country, there is an insidious growing form of apartheid among Malaysian women, that between Muslim and non-Muslim women." The Malaysian Muslim Professionals Forum criticised her comments stating "Her prejudiced views and assumptions smack of ignorance of the objectives and methodology of the Sharia, and a slavish capitulation to western feminism's notions of women's rights, gender equality and sexuality." Dr Harlina Halizah Siraj, women's chief of the reform group Jamaah Islah Malaysia said "Women in Malaysia are given unlimited opportunities to obtain high education level, we are free to choose our profession and career besides enjoying high standard of living with our families."Saudi Arabia's practices with respect women have been referred to as "gender apartheid". Women's rights activist Wajiha Al-Huwaidar describes Saudi Arabia as the 'gender apartheid kingdom.' Azar Majedi, of the Centre for Women and Socialism, attributes sexual apartheid in Saudi Arabia to political Islam: "Women are the first victims of political Islam and Islamic terrorist gangs. Sexual apartheid, stoning, compulsory Islamic veil and covering and stripping women of all rights are the fruits of this reactionary and fascistic movement." According to *The Guardian*, "[i]n the kingdom of Saudi Arabia, sexual apartheid rules": "The kingdom's sexual apartheid is enforced, in a crude fashion, by the religious police, the mutawa. Thuggish, bigoted and with little real training in Islamic law, they are much feared in some areas but also increasingly ridiculed. In Jeddah - a more laid-back city than Riyadh - they are rarely seen nowadays.

Christian Churches

The terms gender apartheid and sexual apartheid have also been used to describe differential treatment of women in institutions such as the Church of England or the Roman Catholic Church. See, for example, Patricia Budd Kepler in her 1978 *Theology Today* article "Women Clergy and the Cultural Order". Courtney W. Howland describes the patriarchal family structure of evangelical Christian churches in America as maintaining gender apartheid.

Other Uses

Nora Ephron, who worked as a journalist in Japan, described it as a "society of 'gender apartheid.'" Peter Gran writes that the treatment of prostitutes in many societies is gender apartheid upheld by the state. Attorney Gloria Allred called the Boy Scouts of America refusal to admit girls "gender apartheid."

6

Women, Gender Role, Gender Equality and Religion

Relationship between Gender and Religion

Gender and religion encompasses a range of topics related to gender and religion. Some gender and religion issues can be classified as either "internal" or "external". Internal religious issues are studied from the perspective of a given religion, and might include religious beliefs and practices about the roles and rights of men and women in government, education and worship; beliefs about the sex or gender of deities and religious figures; and beliefs about the origin and meaning of human gender. External religious issues can be broadly defined as an examination of a given religion from an outsider's perspective, including possible clashes between religious leaders and laity; and the influence of, and differences between, religious perspectives on social issues. For example, various religious perspectives have either endorsed or condemned alternative family structures, homosexual relationships, and abortion. External religious issues can also be examined from the "lens of gender" perspective embraced by some in feminism and/or critical theory and its offshoots.

Gender of Deities

The earliest documented religions, and some contemporary animist religions, involve deification of characteristics of the natural world. These spirits are typically, but not always, gendered. It has been proposed, since the 19th century, that polytheism arose out of animism, as religious epic provided personalities to autochthonous animist spirits in various parts of the world, notably in the development of ancient near eastern and Indo-European literature. Polytheistic gods are also typically gendered. The earliest evidence of monotheism is the worship of the goddess Eurynome, Aten in Egypt, the teaching of Moses in the Hebrew Bible and Zoroastrianism in Persia. Aten, Yahweh and Ahura Mazda are all masculine deities, embodied only in metaphor, so masculine rather than reproductively male. Some scholars suggest that ancient religious Goddesses have been reinterpreted to follow specific gender roles. For example, the Nordic goddess Freya first represented war and love, but after centuries, she was transformed into only representing love and a sexual behaviour. The Hindu goddess Kali is interesting because she breaks the typical gendered role of women representing love, sex, fertility and beauty because she is simultaneously the goddess of the life cycle as well as destructive war. An example of the typical female goddess is Aphrodite, who is shown as vain, simple, and beautiful. Various 19th century scholars of comparative religion proposed that prehistoric animism worshipped nature viewed predominantly as matriarchal religion, a feature notable also within neopaganism. However, anthropological research of the early 20th century, among many pre-literate cultures, established a consensus against this theory. In Christianity, one entity of the Trinity, the Son, is believed to have become incarnate as a human male. Christians believe that the other two entities in the Trinity, the Father and the Holy Spirit, have never been incarnated, hence having masculine gender rather than male sex. Islam, on the other hand, has a tradition that the name Allah, like its referent, can be allocated neither grammatical nor natural gender. Masculine pronouns for Allah in the Qur'an are interpreted as generic. The gender or genderlessness of God is a controversial issue in monotheistic and some henotheistic religions. While God has traditionally been portrayed as a masculine figure, this deity is also called Mother and there has been an increasing view that God is synominous for mother nature and more feminine.

Creation Myths about Human Gender

The creation myths of many religions contain stories about how humans came to have gender. In many stories, man and woman are created at the same time, with equal standing. Some scholars suggest that one such example is the creation story in Genesis 1: "And God created the man in his image. In the image of God he created him. Male and female he created them.". Some commentators interpret the parallelism to be deliberately stressing that mankind is, in some sense, a "unity in diversity" from a divine perspective (compare *e pluribus unum*), and that women as well as men are included in God's image. The first man, Adam, has been viewed as a spiritual being or an ideal who can be distinguished as both male and female; an androgynous being with no sex. Some argue that Genesis' gender-inclusive conception of humanity contrasts sharply with the views of gender found in older literature from surrounding cultures. Some go so far as to suggest a higher status of women in western society due to Judæo-Christian influence, and based on this verse. Some scholars, such as Philo, argue that the "sexes" were developed through an accidental division of the "true self" which existed prior to being assigned with gender. In other accounts, man is created first, followed by woman. This is the case in the creation account of Genesis 2, where the first woman (Eve) is created from the rib of the first man (Adam), as a companion and helper. This version is normally cited by Jewish authorities in support of patriarchy, and likewise by Christian interpreters. A similar story appears in the Qur'an. There is an interesting correlation between the two gender creation stories, both stories imagine the ideal of the unitary self. However, the unitary self is either androgynous or physically male; both of which are masculine in configuration. Thus, male and female are to become one; meaning that she is to become male. The second creation story of Adam and Eve became influential in regards to how women were viewed in Victorian society by means of the "Eva/Ave Palidrome" where Eva was woman in her weak and evil state, based on Eve in the Garden of Eden and Ave was Mary (as in Ave Maria), the new holy and pure ideal that was impossible for women to mimic. Historically, women have been placed into two categories; women and virgins. Women who become intimate with men are marked women, whereas those who do not participate in such acts and who are divinely inspired are considered virgins. Thus, women can escape from being gendered as women if they participate in celibacy. In Plato's *Symposium*, Aristophanes provides an account to explain gender and romantic attraction. There were originally three sexes: the all male, the all female, and the "androgynous," who was half man, half woman. As punishment for attacking the gods, each was split in half. The halves of the androgynous being became heterosexual men and women, while the halves of the all male and all female became gays and lesbians, respectively.

Leadership Roles

Some religions restrict leadership to men. The ordination of women has been a controversial issue in some religions where either the rite of ordination, or the role that an ordained person fulfills, has traditionally been restricted to men because of cultural or theological prohibitions. Beginning in the 19th century, some Christian denominations have ordained women. Among those who do not, many believe it is forbidden by 1 Timothy 2. Some of those denominations ordain women to the diaconate, believing this is encouraged by 1 Timothy 3-4. Some Islamic communities (mainly outside the Middle East) have recently appointed women as imams, normally with ministries restricted to leading women in prayer and other charitable ministries.

Indian Religions

Both masculine and feminine deities feature prominently in Hinduism. The identity of the Vedic writers is not known, but the first hymn of the Rigveda is addressed to the masculine deity Agni, and the pantheon of the Vedas is dominated by masculine gods. The most prominent Avatars of Vishnu are men. The traditional religious leaders of Jainism are all men. Siddhartha Gautama (the Buddha) was a man, but the female Buddha Vajrayogini is very important in Buddhism. Buddha stated that men and women are equally capable of attaining Nirvana, but some prominent Buddhist thinkers have expressed contrary opinions.

Abrahamic Religions

In Abrahamic religions, Abraham himself, Moses, David and Elijah are among the most significant leaders documented according to the traditions of the Hebrew Bible. John the Baptist, Jesus and his apostles, and Saul of Tarsus again give the New Testament an impression of the founders and key figures of Christianity being male dominated. They were followed by a millennium of theologians known as the Church Fathers. Islam was founded by Muhammad, and his successor, Abu Bakr, was also a man. On the other hand, The Virgin Mary, the mother of Jesus of Nazareth, is not associated with leadership or teaching, but is nonetheless a key figure in Catholicism. Fatimah, daughter of Muhammad is regarded by Muslims as an exemplar for men and women. The Bahá'í Faith teaches that men and women are equal, and there have been a large number of prominent female teachers celebrated in Bahá'í history such as Bahiyyih Khánum who was acting head of the faith for a period following the passing of `Abdu'l-Bahá. Nakayama Miki was the founder of Tenrikyo, which may be the largest religion to have a woman founder. Ellen G. White was instrumental to the founding of the Seventh-day Adventist Church and is officially considered a prophet by Seventh-day Adventists. In particular, White's biblical commentaries and other writings are often considered inspired or even infallible. Mary Baker Eddy was the founder of the Christian Science movement.

Segregation

Many religions have traditionally practiced sex segregation. In traditional Jewish synagogues, the women's section is separated from the men's' section by a wall or curtain called a *mechitza*. Men are not permitted to pray in the presence of women, to prevent distraction. The *mechitza* shown in the picture on the right is one in a synagogue affiliated with the 'left wing' (more modern side) of Modern Orthodox Judaism, which requires the *mechitza* to be of the height shown in the picture. More traditional or 'right wing' Modern Orthodox Judaism, and all forms of Haredi Judaism, requires the *mechitza* to be of a type which absolutely prevents the men from seeing the women.

Enclosed religious orders are usually segregated by gender. Sex segregation in Islam includes restrictions on interaction between men and women. Men and women also worship separately in mosques.

Roles in Marriage

Nearly all religions recognize marriage, and many religions also promote views on appropriate gender roles within marriage. Two notable views are Complementarianism and Christian Egalitarianism.

In Genesis 3, Adam names his wife Eve ("life") because she "was the mother of all living." (Genesis 3:20)

Islam

In Islam, a woman's primary responsibility is usually interpreted as fulfilling her role as a wife and mother, whereas women still have the right and are free to work. A man's role is to work and be able to protect and financially support his wife and family.

Abortion

In some religions abortion is considered to be immoral, the taking of God's gift of life to a child, for the sake of self-interest. The rationale for this view often also involves appeals to mothering responsibilities and privileges considered to be divine gifts exclusively given to women.

Homosexuality

Homosexuality is expressly forbidden in many religions, but typically in casuistic rather than apodictic laws. As such, the rationale for such proscriptions is not clearly evident, though avoidance of procreation and contribution to society via establishing families are sometimes offered as pragmatic considerations.

Christianity

The feminist study of gender and religion began in the 1960s and '70s, when some scholars and women (e.g., Mary Daly) began to feel increasingly dissatisfied with the position of women in religion. There were two main aspects of traditional religious institutions that were problems for feminists in Christianity:

1. Christianity was typically androcentric. The texts, leaders, experiences, and rituals were focused on men, and women were seen as the deviants from the cultural normality.
2. It was patriarchal. All of the leaders were men and assumed to be strong and assertive, whereas women were seen as subservient, passive and weak and thus unfit to be in a high position within religion. In support of these claims, feminists have noted that

some religious leaders considered women as morally inferior to men, and many have considered women the source of temptations, especially sexual temptations, for men. In traditions where God is considered male, there is sometimes a view that men are more like God than women. For example, in 1 Corinthians 11:7, Paul asserts that man "is the image and glory of God: but the woman is the glory of the man". In some cases leading to a view of male superiority and female inferiority.

Feminism has engaged with Christians in three main ways:

- From outside religions as, often critically or as "Rejectionists", feminist scholars have cited religious texts and practice as evidence of patriarchal institutions within humans societies, antithetical to feminist aims;
- From within religions as "Traditionalists," some members, scholars and leaders sympathetic to feminism have attempted reforms to harmonize contemporary religious thought and practice to be more in line with feminism; and
- Independently of established religion, also as Rejectionists, some feminist thinkers have attempted to construct a theology or range of religious practices based on feminist principles, notably but not restricted to Wicca, neopaganism and various New Age religions.

In contrast, Christian writer and speaker Paul Coughlin argues that male influence in Christianity is overstated, and moreover that a substantial misandric undercurrent has existed in American Protestantism for many decades:

Here are some of the messages Christian men have been told [by religious leaders], some for decades:

- If there is a major problem in a couple's marriage, whether or not it leads to divorce, it is ultimately the husband's fault.
- Women are more moral and spiritual than men.
- Women are more sensitive to the Holy Spirit than men. [...]

...beating up on Christian men in church is good business in Christian media [and husbands] have been told that a "good Christian man" does not confront his wife about her [abusive, self-absorbed or unreasonable] behaviour. His spiritual training has told him that accepting abuse is synonymous with sacrifice, so he sits there and takes it.

Feminist Theology

Feminist theology is a movement, generally in Christianity and Judaism, to reconsider the traditions, practices, scriptures, and theologies of their religion from a feminist perspective. Likewise, those who practice feminist spirituality may adhere to a feminist re-interpretation of Western monotheistic traditions.

In these cases, the notion of God as having a male gender is rejected, and God is not referred to using male pronouns.

Religious Support for Gender Equality

Some religions and religious scholars have argued that "gender inequality" exists either generally or in certain instances, and have supported a variety of remedies. Pierre Chaunu has argued that the influence of Christianity is the main factor leading to equality for women. Priyamvada Gopal argues that increased gender equality is indeed a product of Judeo-Christian doctrine, but not exclusive to it. She expresses concern that gender equality is used by western countries as a rationale for "neocolonialism". Jamaine Abidogun argues another interesting perspective: that Judeo-Christian influence has indeed shaped gender roles in Nigeria (a strongly Christianised country), however, she doesn't consider feminism to be a product of Judeo-Christian doctrine, but rather a preferable form of "neocolonialism".

Understanding Women in Islam

The study of women in Islam investigates the role of women within the religion of Islam. The complex relationship between women and Islam is defined by Islamic texts, the history and culture of the Muslim world. The Qur'an states that both men and women are equal, but also, as in 4:34, that "Men are the protectors and maintainers of women, because Allah has made one of them to excel the other, and because they spend from their means. Therefore the righteous women are devoutly obedient and guard in the husband's absence what Allah orders them to guard." Although the Quran does say this, the superiority of men is interpreted in terms of strength by the context - men maintain women. *Sharia* (Islamic law) provides for complementarianism, differences between women's and men's roles, rights, and obligations. However neither the Quran nor Hadith mention women have to be housewives. Majority Muslim countries give women varying degrees of rights with regards to marriage, divorce, civil rights, legal status, dress code, and education based on different interpretations. Scholars and other commentators vary as to whether they are just and whether they are a correct interpretation of religious imperatives.

Gender Roles

The Quran expresses two main views on the role of women. It both stresses the equality of women and men before God in terms of their religious duties (i.e. belief in God and his messenger, praying, fasting, paying zakat (charity), making hajj (pilgrimage to Mecca/ Medina)) and places them "under" the care of men (i.e. men are financially responsible for their wives). In one place it states: "Men are the maintainers and protectors of women, because Allah hath made the one of them to excel the other, and because they spend from their property (for the support of women)." The Quran explains that men and women are equal in creation and in the afterlife, but not identical. Surah an-Nisa' 4:1 states that men and women are created from a single soul (*nafs wahidah*). One person does not come before the other, one is not superior to the other, and one is not the derivative of the other. A woman is not created for the purpose of a man. Rather, they are both created for the mutual benefit of each other.

Female Education

Historically, women played an important role in the foundation of many Islamic educational institutions, such as Fatima al-Fihri's founding of the University of Al Karaouine in 859 CE. This continued through to the Ayyubid dynasty in the 12th and 13th centuries, when 160 mosques and madrasahs were established in Damascus, 26 of which were funded by women through the Waqf (charitable trust or trust law) system. Half of all the royal patrons for these institutions were also women.

According to the Sunni scholar Ibn Asakir in the 12th century, there were various opportunities for female education in what is known as the medieval Islamic world. He writes that women could study, earn *ijazahs* (academic degrees), and qualify as scholars *(ulama')* and teachers. This was especially the case for learned and scholarly families, who wanted to ensure the highest possible education for both their sons and daughters. Ibn Asakir had himself studied under 80 different female teachers in his time. In nineteenth-century West Africa, Nana Asma'u was a leading Islamic scholar, poet, teacher and an exceptionally prolific Muslim female writer who wrote more than 60 works. Female education in the Islamic world was inspired by Muhammad's wives: Khadijah, a successful business woman, and Aisha, a renowned hadith scholar and military leader. The education allowed was often restricted to religious instruction. According to a hadith attributed to Muhammad, he praised the women of Medina because of their desire for religious knowledge:

> "How splendid were the women of the *ansar*; shame did not prevent them from becoming learned in the faith."

While it was not common for women to enroll as students in formal classes, it was common for women to attend informal lectures and study sessions at mosques, madrassas and other public places. For example, the attendance of women at the Fatimid "sessions of wisdom" (*majālis al-hikma*) was noted by various historians including Ibn al-Tuwayr and al-Musabbihi. Similarly, although unusual in 15th-century Iran, both women and men were in attendance at the intellectual gatherings of the Ismailis where women were addressed directly by the Imam.

While women accounted for no more than one percent of Islamic scholars prior to the 12th century, there was a large increase of female scholars after this. In the 15th century, Al-Sakhawi devotes an entire volume of his 12-volume biographical dictionary *Daw al-lami* to female scholars, giving information on 1,075 of them. Recently there have been several female Muslim scholars including Sebeca Zahra Hussain who is a prominent female scholar from the Sunni sect.

Female Employment

The labour force in the Caliphate were employed from diverse ethnic and religious backgrounds, while both men and women were involved in diverse occupations and economic activities. Women were employed in a wide range of commercial activities and diverse occupations in the primary sector (as farmers, for example), secondary sector (as construction workers, dyers, spinners, etc.) and tertiary sector (as investors, doctors, nurses, presidents of guilds, brokers, peddlers, lenders, scholars, etc.). Muslim women also held a monopoly over certain branches of the textile industry, the largest and most specialized and market-oriented industry at the time, in occupations such as spinning, dyeing, and embroidery. In comparison, female property rights and wage labour were relatively uncommon in Europe until the Industrial Revolution in the 18th and 19th centuries.

In the 12th century, the famous Islamic philosopher and qadi (judge) Ibn Rushd, known to the West as *Averroes*, claimed that women were equal to men in all respects and possessed equal capacities to shine in peace and in war, citing examples of female warriors among the Arabs, Greeks and Africans to support his case. In early Muslim history, examples of notable female Muslims who fought during the Muslim conquests and Fitna (civil wars) as soldiers or generals included Nusaybah Bint k'ab Al Maziniyyah a.k.a. Umm Amarah, Aisha, Kahula and Wafeira.

A unique feature of medieval Muslim hospitals was the role of female staff, who were rarely employed in hospitals elsewhere in the world. Medieval Muslim hospitals commonly employed female nurses. Muslim hospitals were also the first to employ female physicians, the most famous being two female physicians from the Banu Zuhr family who served the Almohad ruler Abu Yusuf Ya'qub al-Mansur in the 12th century. This was necessary due to the segregation between male and female patients in Islamic hospitals. Later in the 15th century, female surgeons were illustrated for the first time in Serafeddin Sabuncuo lu's *Cerrahiyyetu'l-Haniyye* (*Imperial Surgery*).

Employment Patterns Today

Patterns of women's employment vary throughout the Muslim world: as of 2005, 16 per cent of Pakistani women were "economically active" (either employed, or unemployed but available to furnish labour), whereas 52 per cent of Indonesian women were.

Women are allowed to work in Islam, subject to certain conditions, such as if a woman is in financial need and her employment does not cause her to neglect her role as a mother and wife. It has been claimed that it is the responsibility of the Muslim community to organise work for women, so that she can do so in a Muslim cultural atmosphere, where her rights (as set out in the Qur'an) are respected. Islamic law however, permits women to work in Islamic conditions.

- The work should not require the man or the woman to violate Islamic law (e.g., serving alcohol), and be mindful of the woman's safety.
- If the work requires the woman to leave her home, she must maintain her 'modesty' just as with men.

Due to cultural and not religious beliefs, in some cases, when women have the right to work and are educated, women's job opportunities may in practice be unequal to those of men. In Egypt for example, women have limited opportunities to work in the private sector because women are still expected to put their role in the family first, which causes men to be seen as more reliable in the long term.

An indicator of the attitude of the Qur'an to women in the workplace can be seen in the quotes regarding working women. These are the examples of two female shepherds Qur'an 28:23, and Khadijah (prophet Muhammad's wife), who was an eminent businesswoman. Khadijah is called up as a role model for females in the Qur'an.

Sharia Law

The cumulative doctrines contained within the Qur'an, *hadith* and *fiqh* are codified by Sharia law, which attempts to set down rules for collective conduct, even including behaviour and attitudes of individuals within society. In some Muslim countries, Sharia has become the sole legal prescription on which judges base their rulings. In Saudi Arabia, for example, practises such as severing the hand of a thief or the tongue of a liar persist as they are set in Sharia law. Similarly, the death penalty is codified for offences such as murder, rape, apostasy, drug trafficking, and homosexuality. In some theocratic states, it is in practise impossible for legal officials to question the articles of the Sharia. In orthodox countries such as Saudi Arabia, Sudan, Iran, Afghanistan under the Taliban regime, and Pakistan, perceived moral weakness by individuals is punished as aggressively as desecrating a tomb or a mosque.

This legal framework has resulted in human rights and women's rights groups worldwide condemning and protesting convictions and sentences of women under Sharia law, as in the case of Amina Lawal. Lawal is a Nigerian woman who was sentenced to be stoned to death in 2002 for bearing a child outside of marriage. Her sentence was based on a *fetwa*, issued by an imam, a recognised religious authority, citing ancient rules, a right promulgated in the name of Sharia.

The status of women's testimony in Islam is disputed. Some Islamic jurists have held that certain types of testimony by women may not be accepted. In other cases, the testimony of two women can equal that of one man (although the Qur'an says two women and two male are needed but if a male cannot find another male he may carry this testimony out himself). The reasons put forward for such attitudes include: women's temperament, women's lack of interest in legal matters, and also the need to spare women from the "burden of testifying". In other areas, women's testimony may be accepted on an equal basis with men's. The verse itself however relates to finances only.

Controversial tribal customs such as *diyyat* or blood money remain an integral part of Islamic jurisprudence. By implementation this also discriminate against women. Diyya existed in Arabia since pre-Islamic times. While the practice of diyya was affirmed by Muhammed, Islam does not prescribe any specific amount for *diyyat* nor does it require discrimination between men and women. The Qur'an has left open to debate, its quantity, nature, and other related affairs to be defined by social custom and tradition. However, in practice, the killing of a woman will generally invoke a lesser *diyyat* than the killing of a man. Commentators on the status of women in Islam have often focused on disparities. In *diyyat*, the fines paid by killers to victims' next of kin after either intentional or unintentional homicide, between men and women.

Financial Matters

Historically, many scholars maintain that women in Muslim societies had more property rights than in many other parts of the world. However, as the world has modernised, women's rights in many Muslim dominated countries are comparatively restricted. As Valentine M. Moghadam argues, "much of the economic modernisation [of women] was based on income from oil, and some came from foreign investment and capital inflows. Economic development alters the status of women in different ways across nations and classes."

Women's rights in the Qur'an are based around the marriage contract. A woman, according to Islamic tradition, does not have to give her pre-marriage possessions to her husband and receives a *mahr* (dowry) which she is allowed to keep. Furthermore, any earnings that a woman receives through employment or business is hers to keep and need not be contributed towards family expenses. This is because the financial responsibility for reasonable housing, food and other household expenses for the family, including the spouse, falls entirely on the husband. In traditional Islamic law, a woman is also not responsible for the upkeep of the home and may demand payment for any work she does in the domestic sphere.

In Islam, women are entitled to the right of inheritance, Qur'an 4:7. In general, Islam allows females half the inheritance share available to males who have the same degree of relation to the deceased. Qur'an 4:11. This difference derives from men's obligations to financially support their families.

The Qur'an contains specific and detailed guidance regarding the division of inherited wealth, such as Surah Baqarah, chapter 2 verse 180, chapter 2 verse 240; Surah Nisa, chapter 4 verse 7-9, chapter 4 verse 19, chapter 4 verse 33; and Surah Maidah, chapter 5 verse 106-108. Three verses in the Qur'an describe the share of close relatives, Surah Nisah chapter 4 verses 11, 12 and 176. However, many Islamic majority countries have allowed inherently unfair (towards women) inheritance laws and/or customs to dominate.

Rape

According to the Sunnah, a woman should not be punished for having been coerced into having sex. This is made clear by the following hadith: During the time of the Prophet (saw) punishment was inflicted on the rapist on the solitary evidence of the woman who was raped by him. Wa'il ibn Hujr reports of an incident when a woman was raped. Later, when some people came by, she identified and accused the man of raping her. They seized him and brought him to Allah's messenger, who said to the woman, "Go away, for Allâh has forgiven you," but of the man who had raped her, he said, "Stone him to death." (Tirmidhi and Abu Dawud)

According to a Sunni *hadith*, the punishment for committing rape is death, there is no blame attached to the victim.

Muslim Marriage Customs

Marriage customs vary in Muslim dominated countries. Cultural customs are sometimes implemented under the cover of Islam. However, Islamic law allows limited polygyny under strict conditions. According to Islamic law (*sharia*), marriage cannot be forced. Islamic jurists have traditionally held that Muslim women may only enter into marriage with Muslim men, on the other hand, the Qur'an allows Muslim men to marry women of the People of the Book, a term which includes Jews and Christians, but they must be chaste. However, *fiqh* law has held that it is *makruh* (reprehensible, though not outright forbidden) for a Muslim man to marry a non-Muslim woman in a non-Muslim country. Notable scholar Bilal Philips has said the verse that permits Muslim men to marry non-Muslim women is not valid anymore today due to several reasons including its misunderstood interpretation. One explanation for marriage restrictions is that they are pursuant to the principle that Muslims may not place themselves in a position inferior to that of the followers of other religions.Marriage within some predominantly Muslim countries still retains practises from pre-Islamic times. Endogamy, virilocality and polygyny are practiced in some Islamic countries. In some countries, however, polygamy is outlawed or restricted by new family codes; for example the *Moudawwana* in Morocco. Polygamy is permitted under restricted conditions, but it is not widespread. However, it is strongly discouraged in the

Qur'an, which says, 'do justice to them all, but you won't be able to, so don't fall for one totally while ignoring other wife(wives)'. This also must be taken in historical context, as this was actually a restriction on the number of wives men of the Arabian tribes can take. Sometimes Pre-Islamic men had up to eight wives. Women are not allowed to engage in polyandry, whereas men are allowed to engage in polygyny.

A marriage of pleasure, where a man pays a sum of money to a woman or her family in exchange for a temporary spousal relationship, is an ancient practise that has been revived in Iraq in recent years. Its practitioners cite sharia law as permitting the practise. Women's rights groups have condemned it as a form of legalised prostitution.

Behaviour within Marriage

The Qur'an considers the love between men and women to be a Sign of God. Husbands are asked to be kind to their wives and wives are asked to be kind to their husbands. The Qur'an also encourages discussion and mutual agreement in family decisions. Muslim scholars have adopted differing interpretations of An-Nisa, 34, a Sura of the Qur'an. In the event where a woman rebels against her husband, Muslim scholars disagree on what is prescribed by the Sura. According to some interpretations, it is permissible for the man to then lightly beat his spouse. However, this is disputed by many scholars who contend that the expression used alludes to temporary physical separation.

Sexuality

Some hold that Islam enjoins sexual pleasure within marriage; see Asra Nomani's polemic "Islamic Bill of Rights for Women in the Bedroom". Some examples of this influence are set out below:

> Also (prohibited are) women already married, except those whom your right hands possess: Thus, hath Allah ordained (Prohibitions) against you: Except for these, all others are lawful, provided ye seek (them in marriage) with gifts from your property,- desiring chastity, not lust, seeing that ye derive benefit from them, give them their dowers (at least) as prescribed; but if, after a dower is prescribed, agree Mutually (to vary it), there is no blame on you, and Allah is All-knowing, All-wise. (Qur'an 4:24)
>
> The Believers must (eventually) win through—those who humble themselves in their prayers; who avoid vain talk; who are active in deeds of charity; who abstain from sex; except with those joined to them in the marriage bond, or (the captives) whom their right hands possess—for (in their case) they are free from blame. (Qur'an 23:1-6)
>
> Prophet! We have made lawful to thee thy wives to whom thou hast paid their dowers; and those whom thy right hand possesses out of

> the prisoners of war whom Allah has assigned to thee . . . (Qur'an 33:50—O)
>
> Not so those devoted to Prayer—those who remain steadfast to their prayer; and those in whose wealth is a recognized right for the (needy) who asks and him who is prevented (for some reason from asking); and those who hold to the truth of the Day of Judgement; and those who fear the displeasure of their Lord—for their Lord's displeasure is the opposite of Peace and Tranquillity—and those who guard their chastity, except with their wives and the (captives) whom their right hands possess—for (then) they are not to be blamed. (Qur'an 70:22-30)

A high value is placed on female chastity (not to be confused with celibacy). To protect women from accusations of unchaste behaviour, the scripture lays down severe punishments towards those who make false allegations about a woman's chastity. However, in some societies, an accusation is rarely questioned and the woman who is accused rarely has a chance to defend herself in a fair and just manner. This is always due to the local cultural customs and not a result of Islamic teachings.

Female genital mutilation has been erroneously associated with Islam. In fact it is practiced predominantly in Africa, where in certain areas it has acquired a religious dimension due to the justification that the practise is used to ensure female chastity. A UNICEF study of fourteen African countries found no correlation between religion and prevalence of female genital mutilation. In Mauritania, where "health campaigners estimate that more than 70 percent of Mauritanian girls undergo the partial or total removal of their external genitalia for non-medical reasons", Thirty four Islamic scholars signed a fatwa banning the practice in January 2010. Their aim was to prevent people from citing religion as a justification for genital mutilation. The authors cited the work of Islamic legal expert Ibn al-Hajj as support for their assertion that "[s]uch practices were not present in the Maghreb countries over the past centuries". FGM is "not an instinctive habit, according to the Malkis; therefore, it was abandoned in northern and western regions of the country," added the authors.

Birth Control

Islam, as the pre-Islamic Arabic culture before it, is natalist, and promotes the birth of as many children as a Muslim couple can produce. However, under certain circumstances, it is permissible according to Islamic doctrine to limit (*tahdid an-nasl*) or at least control (*'azl*) reproduction, without suffering the fate of a penalty for the gesture. Limiting the number of children is recommended when a family lacks the resources to provide for them. General opinions among Muslims can sometimes be lenient with women who, being weakened, seek to end an unwanted pregnancy, particularly if her health is endangered or if she has given birth many times. These conditions were supplemented in the writings of Al-Ghazzali (1058-1111), with the clause, "if the woman fears for her beauty" ("ida khafat al-mar'a 'ala jamâliha"). However, these permissive attitudes are contrary to some teaching of current Islamic theologians. Abortion (*isqât al-ham* or *ijhadh*) is not outlawed in itself, on the condition that the embryo is less than 120 days in gestation, the point at which Muslim teaching considers the pregnancy to have progressed too far for an abortion to be permissible.

Divorce

In Islam, a woman can initiate a divorce. According to Sharia Law, a woman can file a case in the courts for a divorce in a process called *Khul'a*, meaning "release from". To prevent irrational decisions and for the sake of the family's stability, Islam enjoins that both parties observe a waiting period (of roughly three months) before the divorce is finalized.

Sharia Law states that divorce has to be confirmed on three separate occasions and not, as is commonly believed, simply three times at once. The first two instances the woman and the man are still in legal marriage. The third occasion of pronouncing divorce in the presence of the woman, the man is no longer legally the husband and therefore has to leave the house. The purpose of this procedure of divorce in Islam is to encourage reconciliation where possible. Even after divorce, the woman should wait three monthly cycles during which her husband remains responsible for her and her children's welfare and maintenance. He is not permitted to drive her out of the house. This process may leave the woman destitute should her family not take her back or the ex-husband fail to support her and possibly his children.

After the third pronouncement they are not allowed to get back together as husband and wife, unless first the wife is divorced in another lawful and fully consummated marriage. This rule was made to discourage men from easily using the verbal declaration of divorce by knowing that after the third time there would be no way to return to the wife and thus encourage men's tolerance and patience.

Usually, assuming her husband demands a divorce, the divorced wife keeps her *mahr* (dowry), both the original gift and any supplementary property specified in the marriage contract. She is also given child support until the age of weaning, at which point the child's custody will be settled by the couple or by the courts.

In actual practice and outside of Islamic judicial theory, a woman's right to divorce is often extremely limited compared with that of men in the Middle East. While men can divorce their wives easily, women face many legal and financial obstacles. In practice in most of the Muslim world today divorce can be quite involved as there may be separate secular procedures to follow as well.

In some instances, a Sharia court may pronounce a marriage dissolved as a punitive measure against a woman who they have deemed to be *haram*, or sinful. In a 2005 case in India, a Muslim woman named Imrana turned to a Sharia court to complain of being raped by her father-in-law, Ali Mohammed. Her marriage was dissolved by the court on these grounds. Although India is a secular country, Muslim communities in rural India generally make use of the Sharia judicial system rather than the secular one. The Sharia verdict was upheld by the Indian Muslim seminary Darul ul Uloom Madrasa, which issued a *fetwah* in support of it. The All India Muslim Personal Law Board, consisting of 41 Muslim scholars, also upheld the verdict. In this instance, Imrana refused to accept the verdict of the Sharia court. Her case was heard in a secular court, which resulted in Ali Mohammed receiving an eight year sentence and a fine.

This contentious area of religious practice and tradition is being increasingly challenged by those promoting more liberal interpretations of Islam.

In contrast to the Western world where divorce was relatively uncommon until modern times, and in contrast to the low rates of divorce in the modern Middle East, divorce was a more common occurrence in certain states of the late medieval Muslim world. In the Mamluk Sultanate and Ottoman Empire, the rate of divorce was higher than it is today in the modern Middle East. The Qur'an is explicit in addressing *zawaj al-hall*, or a disrupted marriage, where a man intends to remarry a former wife for a second time; (2:230) indicates that for the second marriage to be lawful for the former husband, the former wife must have been remarried during the intervening time to a second man since the renunciation of the previous marriage. The intention behind this Qur'an passage was to end abuses of the right to marital renunciation dating from ancient customs.

In medieval Egypt, Al-Sakhawi recorded the marital history of 500 women, the largest sample of married women in the Middle Ages, and found that at least a third of all women in the Mamluk Sultanate of Egypt and Syria married more than once, with many marrying three or more times. According to Al-Sakhawi, as many as three out of ten marriages in 15th century Cairo ended in divorce. In the early 20th century, some villages in western Java and the Malay peninsula had divorce rates as high as 70 per cent.

Movement and Travel

Although no limitation or prohibition against women's travelling alone is mentioned in the Qur'an, there is a debate in some Islamic sects, especially Salafis, regarding whether women may travel without a *mahram* (unmarriageable relative). Some scholars state that a woman may not travel by herself on a journey that takes longer than three days (equivalent to 48 miles in medieval Islam). According to the European Council for Fatwa and

Research, this prohibition arose from fears for women's safety when travel was more dangerous. Some scholars relax this prohibition for journeys likely to be safe, such as travel with a trustworthy group of men or men and women, or travel via a modern train or plane when the woman will be met upon arrival.

Sheikh Ayed Al-Qarni, a Saudi Islamic scholar, has said that neither the Qur'an nor the sunnah prohibits women from driving and that it is better for a woman to drive herself than to be driven by a stranger without a legal escort. (He also stated, however, that he "personally will not allow [his] wife or daughters or sisters to drive.") Women are forbidden to drive in Saudi Arabia per a 1990 *fatwa* (religious ruling); Saudi Arabia is currently the only Muslim country that bans women from driving. When the Taliban ruled Afghanistan, they issued a 2001 decree that also banned women from driving. John Esposito, professor of International Affairs and Islamic Studies at Georgetown University, has argued that these restrictions originate from cultural customs and not Islam.

Dress Code

Hijab is the Qur'anic requirement that Muslims, both male and female, dress and behave modestly. The most important Qur'anic verse relating to *hijab* is *sura* 24:31, which says, "And tell the believing women to lower their gaze and guard their private parts and not to display their adornment except that which ordinarily appears thereof and to draw their headcovers over their chests and not to display their adornment except to their [maharim]..."

There are regional and sectarian variations of the veil associated with *hijab*. Depending upon local views regarding female modesty, they may or may not cover the face or the eyes, or the entire body. These variations include:

- *Hijab* - A scarf covering the hair.
- *Chador* - A cloak covering the head and body, but leaving the face uncovered; worn by many women in Iran when outside the home.
- *Shayla* - A long rectangular scarf, pinned or tucked at the shoulder, leaving the face uncovered; worn by many women in the Persian Gulf region.
- *Khimar* - A long rectangular scarf, covering the head, neck and shoulders, but leaving the face uncovered.
- *Burka* - Covers the entire head and body, including the eyes; the wearer sees through a cloth mesh eye veil sewn into the burka.
- *Al-Amira* - A two-piece veil that includes a close-fitting cap and a tube-shaped scarf covering the head and neck, but leaving the face uncovered.
- *Niqab* - A veil that leaves the eye clear (although it may be worn with an eye veil), and worn with a headscarf.

The *hijab*, and the veil in particular, have often been viewed by many as a sign of oppression of Muslim women. The wearing of the *hijab* has become controversial in countries where Muslims are a minority, and where majority secular opinions regard the *hijab* as violating women's freedom, especially in Europe amid increasing immigration of Muslims. The 2006 United Kingdom debate over veils and the 2004 French law on secularity and conspicuous religious symbols in schools are two notable examples. However, it is argued that if it is acceptable for a Christian Nun to cover her head and body for religious reasons, then why is it not for a Muslim woman? In France, the law banning the wearing of a face veil in public is being enforced. Sentencing includes a 150 euro fine and a citizenship course. Two women were detained in April 2011 when the law came into force.

In some countries where Muslims are a minority, there is much less public opposition to the practise, although concerns about it are discussed. Canadian media, for example, have covered controversies where concerns have been raised over the veil being a possible security risk, as in cases where Muslim women have refused to remove their *niqab* or *burka* veil for voter identification at polls. In 2007, the federal government of Canada introduced a bill to ban face coverings for voter identification, but this bill was dropped as not required:

> It was pointed out that thousands of Canadians have no photo ID. Requiring them to show their faces would be meaningless without photo identification against which to verify their identities. The Elections Act gives voters three ways to prove their identification in order to cast a ballot: provide a government photo ID; provide two pieces of approved ID, at least one of which must state their address (but neither of which must contain a photo); or have another voter registered in the same district vouch for them.

Women in Religious Life

In Islam, there is no difference between men and women's relationship to God; they receive identical rewards and punishments for their conduct. According to a saying attributed to Muhammad, women are allowed to go to mosques. However, as Islam spread, it became unusual for women to worship in mosques because of fears of unchastity caused by interaction between sexes; this condition persisted until the late 1960s. Since then, women have become increasingly involved in the mosque, though men and women generally worship separately. (Muslims explain this by citing the need to avoid distraction during prayer prostrations that raise the buttocks while the forehead touches the ground.) Separation between sexes ranges from men and women on opposite sides of an aisle, to men in front of women (as was the case in the time of Muhammad), to women in second-floor balconies or separate rooms accessible by a door for women only.

In Islam's earlier history, female religious scholars were relatively common. Mohammad Akram Nadwi, a Sunni religious scholar, has compiled biographies of 8,000 female jurists, and orientalist Ignaz Goldziher earlier estimated that 15 per cent of medieval hadith scholars were women. After the 16th century, however, female scholars became fewer, and today — while female activists and writers are relatively common — there has not been a significant female jurist in over 200 years. Opportunities for women's religious education exist, but cultural barriers often keep women from pursuing such a vocation.

Women's right to become imams, however, is disputed by many. A fundamental role of an *imam* (religious leader) in a mosque is to lead the *salah* (congregational prayers). Generally, women are not allowed to lead mixed prayers, because certain positions of the prayer would likely prove distracting for her and those praying behind her. However, some argue that Muhammad gave permission to Ume Warqa to lead a mixed prayer at the mosque of Dar.

Hui women are self aware of their relative freedom as Chinese women in contrast to the status of Arab women in countries like Saudi Arabia where Arab women are restricted and forced to wear encompassing clothing. Hui women point out these restrictions as "low status", and feel better to be Chinese than to be Arab, claiming that it is Chinese women's advanced knowledge of the Qur'an which enables them to have equality between men and women.

Sufi Female Mystics

The Islamic mystic movement known as Sufism is believed to have been created by a female holy woman, Rabiah al-Basri (d. 801). She created the doctrine of "disinterested love of God".

Sufi Islam teaches the doctrine of *tariqa*, meaning following a spiritual path in daily living habits. To support followers of this concept, separate institutions for men (*ta'ifa, hizb, rabita*) and women (*khanqa, rabita, derga*) were created. Initiates to these groups pursued a progression of seven stages of spiritual discipline, called *makamat* (stations) or *ahwal* (spiritual states).

Current Female Religious Scholars

There are a number of prominent female Islamic scholars. They generally focus on questioning gender-based interpretations of the Qur'an, the traditions of the Prophet and early Islamic history. Some notable Muslim women scholars are: Azizah al-Hibri, Amina Wadud, Fatima Mernissi, Asma Barlas, Riffat Hassan, Leila Ahmed, Aisha Abdul-Rahman, and Merryl Wyn Davies.

Women and Politics

The only *hadith* relating to female political leadership is Sahih al-Bukhari, 5:59:709, in which Muhammad is recorded as saying that people with a female ruler will never be successful. (Muhammed was referring to the Persian people. He said, "Such people as ruled by a lady will never be successful." (The al-Bukhari collection is generally regarded as authentic, though one Muslim feminist has questioned the reliability of the recorder of this particular hadith.) However, many classical Islamic scholars, such as al-Tabari, supported female leadership. In early Islamic history, women including Aisha, Ume Warqa, and Samra Binte Wahaib took part in political activities. Other historical Muslim female leaders include Razia Sultana, who ruled the Sultanate of Delhi from 1236 to 1239, and Shajarat ad-Durr, who ruled Egypt from 1250 to 1257.

In the past several decades, many countries in which Muslims are a majority, including Indonesia, Pakistan, Bangladesh, Turkey, and Kyrgyzstan have been led by women. Nearly one-third of the Parliament of Egypt also consists of women.

According to Sheikh Zoubir Bouchikhi, Imam of the Islamic Society of Greater Houston's Southeast Mosque, nothing in Islam specifically allows or disallows voting by women. Until recently most Muslim nations were non-democratic, but most today allow their citizens to have some level of voting and control over their government. The disparate times at which women's suffrage was granted in Muslim-majority countries is indicative of the varied traditions and values present within the Muslim world. Azerbaijan has had women's suffrage since 1918.

Since 2002, Afghanistan is one of the Muslim states with the highest number of female politicians. Saudi women have been allowed to vote in some elections.

Modern Debate on the Status of Women in Islam

Within the Muslim community, conservatives and Islamic feminists have used Islamic doctrine as the basis for discussion of women's rights, drawing on the Quran, the *hadith*, and the lives of prominent women in the early period of Muslim history as evidence. Where conservatives have seen evidence that existing gender asymmetries are divinely ordained, feminists have seen more egalitarian ideals in early Islam. Still others have argued that this discourse is essentialist and ahistorical, and have urged that Islamic doctrine not be the only framework within which discussion occurs.

Conservatives and the Islamic Movement

Conservatives reject the assertion that different laws prescribed for men and women imply that men are more valuable than women. Ali ibn Musa

Al-reza reasoned that at the time of marriage a man has to pay something to his prospective bride, and that men are responsible for both their wives' and their own expenses but women have no such responsibility.

The nebulous revivalist movement termed Islamism is one of the most dynamic movements within Islam in the 20th and 21st centuries. The experience of women in Islamist states has been varied. Women in Taliban-controlled Afghanistan faced treatment condemned by the international community. Women were forced to wear the *burqa* in public, not allowed to work, not allowed to be educated after the age of eight, and faced public flogging and execution for violations of the Taliban's laws. The position of women in Iran, which has been a theocracy since its 1979 revolution, is more complex. Iranian Islamists are ideologically in favour of allowing female legislators in Iran's parliament and 60% of university students are women.

Liberal Islam, Islamic Feminism, and other Progressive Criticism

Liberal Muslims have urged that *ijtihad*, a form of critical thinking, be used to develop a more progressive form of Islam with respect to the status of women. In addition, Islamic feminists have advocated for women's rights, gender equality, and social justice grounded in an Islamic framework. Although rooted in Islam, pioneers of Islamic feminism have also used secular and western feminist discourses and have sought to include Islamic feminism in the larger global feminist movement. Islamic feminists seek to highlight the teachings of equality in Islam to question patriarchal interpretations of Islamic teachings. Others point out the incredible amount of flexibility of shariah law, which can offer greater protections for women if the political will to do is present.

After the September 11, 2001, attacks, international attention was focused on the condition of women in the Muslim world. Critics asserted that women are not treated as equal members of Muslim societies and criticized Muslim societies for condoning this treatment. Some critics have gone so far as to make allegations of gender apartheid due to women's status. At least one critic has alleged that Western academics, especially feminists, have ignored the plight of Muslim women in order to be considered "politically correct."

The Indonesian Islamic professor Nasaruddin Umar is at the forefront of a reform movement from within Islam that aims at giving women equal status. Among his works is a book *The Qur'an for Women*", which provides a new feminist interpretation.

Some Muslim women exposed to the growth in civil rights accessible to secular or non-Muslim women have protested to strengthen their own rights within Islamic communities. One example is Malaysia, where 60 per cent of the population is Muslim, and where there are separate parallel legal systems for secular law and sharia law. In 2006, Marina Mahathir, the daughter of Malaysia's former Prime Minister, Mahathir Mohamad, published an editorial in the Malaysia *Star* newspaper to denounce what she termed "a growing form of apartheid" for Malaysia's Muslim women:

> Non-Muslim Malaysian women have benefited from more progressive laws over the years while the opposite has happened for Muslim women.

She pointed out that polygamy was illegal in Malaysia for non-Muslims but not for Muslims, and that child custody arrangements for Muslims were biased towards fathers as opposed to the shared-custody arrangements of non-Muslim parents. Women's groups in Malaysia began campaigning in the 1990s to have female sharia judges appointed to the sharia legal system in the country, and in 2010 two female judges were appointed.

Understanding the Gender Roles in Christianity

Gender roles in Christianity vary considerably today as they have during the last two millennia. This is especially true with regards to marriage and ministry. Christianity traditionally has given men the position of authority in marriage, society and government. This position places women in submissive roles, and usually excludes women from church leadership, especially from formal positions requiring any form of ordination. The Catholic and Eastern Orthodox Churches, and many conservative Protestant denominations assert today that only men can be ordained—as clergy and as deacons. Many progressive Christians disagree with the traditional male-authority and female-submission paradigm. They take a Christian egalitarian or Christian feminist view, holding that the overarching message of Christianity provides positional equality for women in marriage and in ministry. Accordingly, some Protestant churches now ordain women to positions of ecclesiastical leadership. Despite these emerging theological differences, the majority of Christians regard women with dignity and respect as having been created alongside men in the Image of God. The Bible is seen by many as elevating and honouring women, especially as compared with certain other religions or societies. Women have filled prominent roles in the Church historically, and continue to do so today in spite of significant limitations imposed by ordination restrictions.

Women in the New Testament Church

Beyond generally accepted social standards which are continually shifting, Christianity sets a moral standard, regarding attitudes toward and treatment of women, as was personally exemplified by Jesus.

Jesus and Women

Jesus always showed the greatest esteem and the greatest respect for woman, for every woman, and in particular He was sensitive to female suffering. Going beyond the social and religious barriers of the time, Jesus reestablished woman in her full dignity as a human person before God and before men ... Christ's way of acting, the Gospel of his words and deeds, is a consistent protest against whatever offends the dignity of women.

— *John Paul II, "Thoughts on Women Address to Italian Maids,"* April 1979

From the beginning of the early Christian church, starting with Jesus, women were important members of the movement. The examples of the manner of Jesus reveal his attitudes toward women and show repeatedly how he liberated and affirmed women. Both complementarians and egalitarians see Jesus as treating women with compassion, grace and dignity. The gospels of the New Testament, especially Luke, often mention Jesus speaking to or helping women publicly and openly, contrary to the social norms of the time. He reached out to the marginalized in his society and thus, his appeal was great. Martha's sister Mary sat at Jesus' feet being taught, a privilege reserved for men in Judaism. Jesus had female followers who were his sponsors, and he stopped to express concern for the women of Jerusalem on his way to be crucified, while Mary Magdalene is recorded to be the first person to have the privilege of seeing Jesus after resurrection, having been charged by Jesus to tell others of what she had seen even though the testimony of a woman was at that time not considered valid. As time went on and the disciples continued to spread Jesus' message by word of mouth, groups of Christians organised within the homes of believers. Those who could offer their home for meetings were considered important within the movement and assumed leadership roles.

Paul of Tarsus

The letters of Paul—dated to the middle of the 1st century CE—and his casual greetings to acquaintances offer information about Jewish and Gentile women who were prominent in the movement. His letters provide clues about the kind of activities in which women engaged more generally.

- He commends with great affection to the Roman community Phoebe, a servant of the church at Cenchreae, for she had been the patron of many, including himself.
- He greets Priscilla (Prisca), Junia, Julia, and Nereus' sister.
- Paul writes that Priscilla and her husband risked their lives to save his life.
- He praises Junia (or Junias) as "prominent among the apostles" (NRSV) or "well known to the apostles" (ESV), who had been imprisoned for their labour. Some theologians understand the name to be that of a woman, suggesting that Paul recognised female apostles in the Church.
- Mary and Persis are commended for their hard work.
- Euodia and Syntyche are called his fellow-workers in the gospel.

Some theologians believe that these biblical reports provide evidence of women leaders active in the earliest work of spreading the Christian message, while others reject that understanding. The evidence also indicates that these women "ministered" in supporting roles of the church much as the women who followed Christ supported his ministry.

Women in Church History

Apostolic Age

From the very beginning of the early Christian church, women were important members of the movement, although some complain that much of the information in the New Testament on the work of women has been overlooked. Some also argue that many assumed that it had been a "man's church" because sources of information stemming from the New Testament church were written and interpreted by men. Recently, scholars have begun looking in mosaics, frescoes, and inscriptions of that period for information about women's roles in the early church.

Patristic Age

From the early patristic age, the offices of teacher and sacramental minister were reserved for men throughout most of the church in the East and West. Tertullian, the 2nd century Latin father, wrote that "It is not permitted to a woman to speak in church. Neither may she teach, baptize, offer, nor claim for herself any function proper to a man, least of all the sacerdotal office" ("On the Veiling of Virgins").

Origen (AD 185-254) stated that,

> Even if it is granted to a woman to show the sign of prophecy, she is nevertheless not permitted to speak in an assembly. When Miriam the prophetess spoke, she was leading a choir of women ... For [as Paul declares] "I do not permit a woman to teach," and even less "to tell a man what to do."

Christian historian Philip Schaff records early church fathers of the 3rd and 4th centuries as teaching regarding 1 Cor. 14:34-35:

> From the early patristic age, the offices of teacher and sacramental minister were reserved for men throughout most of the church in the East and West. Tertullian, second century Latin prelate, wrote that "It is not permitted to a woman to speak in church. Neither may she teach, baptize, offer, nor claim for herself any function proper to a man, least of all the sacerdotal office." "On the Veiling of Virgins"

In early centuries, the Eastern church allowed women to participate to a limited extent in ecclesiastical office by ordaining deaconesses.

Middle Ages

In the Catholic and Eastern Orthodox Church, the priesthood and the ministries dependent upon it such as Bishop, Patriarch and Pope, were restricted to men. The first Council of Orange (441) forbade the ordination of women to the diaconate.

With the establishment of Christian monasticism, other influential roles became available to women. From the 5th century onward, Christian convents provided opportunities for some women to escape the path of marriage and child-rearing, acquire literacy and learning, and play a more active religious role. In the later Middle Ages women such as Saint Catherine of Siena and Saint Teresa of Avila, played significant roles in the development of theological ideas and discussion within the church, and were later declared Doctors of the Roman Catholic Church.

Post Reformation

The Protestant Reformation ended female convents, which had existed within Roman Catholicism, and which the Reformers saw as bondage. By shutting down female convents within the movement, Protestantism effectively closed off the option of a full-time religious role for Protestant women, as well as one which had provided some women a life in academic study. Among the many nuns who abandoned the monastic life was the wife of Martin Luther, Katherine von Bora.

The majority of Protestant churches upheld the traditional position, and restricted ruling and preaching roles within the Church to men until the 20th century, although there were early exceptions among some groups such as the Quakers and within some Pentecostal holiness movements.

John Knox (1510–1572) also denied women the right to rule in the civic sphere, as he asserted in his famous *First Blast of the Trumpet Against the Monstrous Regimen of Women.*

Baptist theologian Dr. John Gill (1690–1771) comments on 1 Corinthians 14:34,35, stating

> In Gen_3:16, "thy desire shall be to thy husband, and he shall rule over thee". By this the apostle would signify, that the reason why women are not to speak in the church, or to preach and teach publicly, or be concerned in the ministerial function, is, because this is an act of power, and authority; of rule and government, and so contrary to that subjection which God in his law requires of women unto men. The extraordinary instances of Deborah, Huldah, and Anna, must not be drawn into a rule or example in such cases.

Methodist founder John Wesley (1703–1791) and Methodist theologian Adam Clarke (1762–1832) both upheld male headship, but allowed that spiritual Christian women could publicly speak in church meetings if they "are under an extraordinary impulse of the Spirit" (Wesley), and that such were to obey that influence, and that "the apostle lays down directions in chap. 11 for regulating her personal appearance when thus employed." (Clarke) Puritan theologian Matthew Poole (1624–1679) concurred with Wesley, adding,

> But setting aside that extraordinary case of a special afflatus, [strong Divine influence] it was, doubtless, unlawful for a woman to speak in the church.

Matthew Henry (1662–1714) in his commentary, entertains allowing "praying, and uttering hymns inspired" by women, as such "were not teaching".

Modern Views

Some 19th-century Christian authors began codifying challenges to traditional views toward women both in the church and in society. Only since the 1970s have more diverse views become formalized.

There are four main viewpoints in the modern debate. They are known respectively as Christian feminism, Christian Egalitarianism, Complementarianism, and Biblical patriarchy.

Christian Feminism

Christian Feminists take an actively feminist position from a Christian perspective. Recent generations have experienced the rise of what has been labeled by some as "Christian feminism" —a movement that has had a profound impact on all of life, challenging some traditional basic Christian interpretations of Scripture with respect to roles for women.

However, Christian feminism represents the views of the more theologically liberal end of the spectrum within Christianity. In contrast to the more socially conservative Christian egalitarians, Christian feminists tend to support homosexual rights and a pro-choice stance on abortion. The Evangelical and Ecumenical Women's Caucus, a major international Christian feminist organisation, values "inclusive images and language for God."

Egalitarian View

Christian Egalitarians' interpretation of Scripture brings them to the conclusion that the manner and teachings of Jesus, affirmed by the Apostle Paul, abolished gender-specific roles in both the church and in marriage.

Official Statement

Men, Women and Biblical Equality was prepared in 1989 by several evangelical leaders to become the official statement of Christians for Biblical Equality (CBE). The statement lays out their biblical rationale for equality as well as its application in the community of believers and in the family. They advocate ability-based, rather than gender-based, ministry of

Christians of all ages, ethnicities and socio-economic classes. Egalitarians support the ordination of women and equal roles in marriage, and are more conservative both theologically and morally than Christian feminists.

Some key Christian Egalitarian beliefs

- Both women and men were created equal by God.
- Neither man nor woman was cursed by God at The Fall of Man but were warned by God in a prophetic sense what would be the natural consequences of sin having entered the human race.
- Jesus' radical "new Covenant" view was correctly articulated by Paul of Tarsus when he wrote that "...there is no male nor female, for you are all one in Christ."

A Scripture passage they consider key to the advocacy of full equality of responsibility and authority for both women and men is contained in a Pauline polemic containing three antitheses:

> There is neither Jew nor Greek, slave nor free, male nor female, for you are all one in Christ Jesus.
>
> — *Galatians 3:28*

Christian Egalitarians interpret this passage as expressing that the overarching teaching of the New Testament is that all are "one in Christ." The three distinctions, important for Jewish life, are declared by Paul to be invalid in Christ. Therefore, among those "in Christ" there must be no discrimination based on race or national origin, social level, or gender. They respect the natural biological uniqueness of each gender, not seeing it as requiring any dominant/submissive applications of gender to either marriage or church leadership.

David Scholer, prominent New Testament scholar at Fuller Theological Seminary, affirms this view. He believes that Galatians 3:28 is "the fundamental Pauline theological basis for the inclusion of women and men as equal and mutual partners in all of the ministries of the church." Galatians 3:28 represents "the summation of Paul's theological vision," according to Pamela Eisenbaum, professor at Iliff School of Theology, who is one of four Jewish New Testament scholars teaching in Christian theological schools.

Christian Egalitarianism holds that the submission of the woman in marriage and womanly restrictions in Christian ministry are inconsistent with the true picture of biblical equality. The equal-yet-different doctrine taught by Complementarians is considered by them to be a contradiction in terms.

Conservative theologian Roger Nicole, a Baptist considered an expert in Calvinism and regarded as one of the preeminent theologians in America, is a Christian Egalitarian and also a Biblical Inerrantist. He recognizes that biblical egalitarianism is still viewed by many as inconsistent with biblical inerrancy, although he disagrees. He writes that "the matter of the place of women in the home, in society, and in the church is not an issue that can be conclusively determined by a few apparently restrictive passages that are often advanced by those who think that subordination represents God's will for women."

> I believe that most, if not all, of the restrictions on women in society have no basis in Scripture, and that those maintained in the Church are based on an inadequate interpretation of a few restrictive passages, which put them in contradiction with the manifest special concern and love of God for women articulated from Genesis to Revelation.
>
> — *Roger Nicole, 2006*

A limited notion of gender complementarity is held and is known as "complementarity without hierarchy."

Complementarian View

Complementarians believe that God made men and women to be equal in personhood and value but different in roles. They understand the Bible as teaching that God created men and women to serve different roles in the church and the home. In the 1991 book *Recovering Biblical Manhood and Womanhood*, leading Complementarian theologians outlined what they consider to be biblically sanctioned definitions of masculinity and femininity:

> "At the heart of mature masculinity is a sense of benevolent responsibility to lead, provide for and protect women in ways appropriate to a man's differing relationships.
>
> "At the heart of mature femininity is a freeing disposition to affirm, receive and nurture strength and leadership from worthy men in ways appropriate to a woman's differing relationships."

Official Statement

The *Danvers Statement on Biblical Manhood and Womanhood* was prepared by several evangelical leaders at a Council on Biblical Manhood and Womanhood (CBMW) meeting in Danvers, Massachusetts, in December 1987. The statement lays out their biblical rationale for male priority and female submission in the community of believers and in the family. Additionally it cites a set of concerns shared by complementarians over other contemporary philosophies about gender:

- Cultural uncertainty and confusion over complementary differences between masculinity and femininity.
- Unraveling marriages.
- Increasing attention given what they termed to be feminist egalitarianism.
- Ambivalence about motherhood and homemaking.
- Claims of legitimacy for illicit sexual relationships and pornography.
- Upsurge of physical and emotional abuse in the family.

- Emergence of roles for men and women in church leadership seen as nonconforming to Biblical teaching.
- Nontraditional reinterpretation of apparently plain meanings of Biblical texts.
- A growing threat to Biblical authority.

They attribute these ills to the "apparent accommodation of some within the church to the spirit of the age at the expense of winsome, radical Biblical authenticity which...may reform rather than reflect our ailing culture."

Interpretation of Scripture

Complementarians tend to be biblical inerrantists who take a more literal view of biblical interpretation. They disagree with Christian Egalitarians on theological positions related to gender, such as in holding that:

- Man was created with "headship" over the woman by being created first.
- Female exclusion from leadership over men is also justified due to her deception by the devil, which resulted in The Fall, for which Adam is also, or primarily, culpable.
- Both Old and New Testaments set a pattern of male leadership; for instance the priestly and kingly offices of the Old Testament were restricted to males; the Apostles of Jesus were all male; and Paul's instructions regarding church eldership in the epistles 1 Timothy and Titus appear to restrict this position to men.

Primary texts in the New Testament which are understood to support male headship include 1 Corinthians 11:3, 1 Timothy 2:12 and Ephesians 5:22ff:

> But I would have you know, that the head of every man is Christ; and the head of the woman is the man; and the head of Christ is God. (KJV)
>
> But I permit not a woman to teach, nor to have dominion over a man, but to be in quietness. (ASV)
>
> Wives, submit yourselves to your own husbands as you do to the Lord. For the husband is the head of the wife as Christ is the head of the church, his body, of which he is the Savior. Now as the church submits to Christ, so also wives should submit to their husbands in everything. (TNIV)

In Galatians 3:28, complementarians believe that the Apostle Paul is establishing that all believers, no matter what their racial, social, or gender status, share the same spiritual status in their union with Christ. However, they do not believe that or any other scriptures put an end to positional and functional distinctions based on gender, which they see as being clearly stated and upheld in the New Testament, as a matter of Christian principle.

Complementarians' understanding is that both Old and New Testaments do prescribe a male-priority based hierarchy and gender roles in the church and in marriage, where women have equal dignity with men but subordinate roles.

Biblical Patriarchy View

Biblical patriarchy as expressed by the Vision Forum is similar to Complementarianism in that it affirms the equality of men and women, but goes further in its expression of the different gender roles. It asserts that "a husband and father is the head of his household, a family leader, provider, and protector" and that the "God-ordained and proper sphere of dominion for a wife is the household and that which is connected with the home".

Biblical patriarchy maintains that women do not have authority over men in the church and in the home, but also deny that women should rule in the civic sphere. Thus, William Einwechter calls the Complementarian view referred to above, "two point complementarianism", and regards the biblical patriarchy view as "three-point" or "full" complementarianism.

Although much of the contemporary literature settles on the terms *Complementarianism* and *Christian Egalitarianism*, a number of other more pejorative terms are frequently encountered.

- In complementarian literature, the term "Christian feminism" is sometimes incorrectly used synonymously with "egalitarianism." For examples, see books by Wayne Grudem on the topic. Christian egalitarians generally object to being labeled "feminist" or "evangelical feminist." Their belief in biblical equality is said to be grounded in the biblical teaching that all believers have been given authority in Christ. Conversely, feminist ideology is derived from cultural factors and philosophies. Christian egalitarian author Rebecca Groothuis writes, "Like most cultural systems of thought, feminist ideology is partly true and partly false—almost entirely false at this point in history."
- In egalitarian literature, the terms "gender traditionalist," "patriarchalist" and "hierarchicalist" are sometimes used with reference to complementarians. The use of these terms in egalitarian literature is defended in Rebecca Merrill Groothuis and Ronald W. Pierce, *Discovering Biblical Equality: Complementarity without Hierarchy*, IVP 2004, p. 17. "...it is probably most fitting to refer to those who believe in restricting leadership to men as simply advocates of male leadership, or patriarchalists... traditionalists... or hierarchicalists."

William J. Webb describes himself as a "complementary egalitarian." He defines, this as "full interdependence and 'mutual submission' within marriage, and the only differences in roles are 'based upon biological differences between men and women'." He uses "Complementarianism" to describe what he calls "a milder form of the historical hierarchical view."

Complementarian scholar Wayne A. Grudem objects to Webb's use of "complementary" and "egalitarian" together to describe a thoroughly egalitarian position. Calling the terminology "offensive and confusing," he reasons that doing so simply confuses the issues by using the term "complementary" for a position totally antithetical to what complementarians hold. Grudem finds Webb's use of the term "patriarchy" to be especially pejorative because of its connotations in modern society. He also rejects the term "hierarchicalist" because he says it overemphasizes structured authority while giving no suggestion of equality or the beauty of mutual interdependence.

Theological Issues

Biblical Authority

In general, all evangelicals involved in the gender debate claim to adhere to the authority of the Bible. Egalitarians typically argue that the dispute has arisen because of differences in interpretation of specific passages. Nevertheless, Wayne Grudem and other complementarians have accused egalitarians of adopting positions which deny the authority, sufficiency and inerrancy of Scripture.

> ...I believe that ultimately the effective authority of Scripture to govern our lives is at stake in this controversy. The issue is not whether we *say* we believe the Bible is the Word of God or that we believe it is without error, but the issue is whether we actually obey *it* when its teachings are unpopular and conflict with the dominant viewpoints in our culture. If we do not obey it, then the effective authority of God to govern His people and His church through His Word has been eroded.
>
> — *Wayne Grudem (emphases original), Evangelical Feminism and Biblical Truth*

Biblical Hermeneutics

The egalitarian and complementarian positions differ significantly in their approach to hermeneutics, and specifically in their interpretation of biblical history. Christian egalitarians believe that male and female were created equally without any hierarchy of roles. God created *both* woman and man in His own image and likeness. God made the first couple equal partners in leadership over the earth. Both were jointly commissioned to "be fruitful and multiply...to fill the earth...subdue the earth...and rule over it." At the Fall, God prophesied to Eve that one result of sin entering the human race would be that her husband would "rule over" her. Conservative Christian theologian Gilbert Bilezikian points out that throughout the Old Testament era and beyond, just as God had prophesied, men continued to rule over women in a patriarchal system which he sees as being a "compromise" or "accommodation" between sinful reality and the divine ideal. The coming of Jesus is understood as moving forward from Old Testament patriarchy, re-instituting full equality of gender roles, as succinctly articulated in Galatians 3:28. New Testament passages such as Ephesians 5:22-24 which teach submission of wives to husbands are typically understood by egalitarians as a temporary accommodation to a harsh 1st century culture.

The Christian egalitarian hermeneutic has received a highly systematic treatment from William J. Webb, professor of New Testament at Heritage Theological Seminary, Ontario, Canada. Webb argues that a major challenge is determining which biblical commands are "transcultural" and therefore applicable today, versus those which are "cultural" and therefore only applicable to the original (1st century) recipients of the text. His "redemptive movement" hermeneutic is justified using the example of slavery, which Webb sees as analogous to the subordination of women. Christians today largely perceive that slavery was "cultural" in biblical times and not something that should be re-introduced or justified, although slavery was (*a*) found in the Bible and (*b*) not explicitly banned there. Webb recommends that biblical commands be examined in light of the cultural context in which they were originally written. According to the "redemptive approach", slavery and women's subordination are found in the Bible; however, the same Scriptures also contain ideas and principles which, if developed and taken to their logical conclusion, would bring about the abolition of these institutions. According to that ideal, biblical patriarchy should be replaced by the "all one in Christ Jesus" proclamation of Galatians 3:28 which says "There is no Jew nor Greek, slave nor free, male nor female. For you are all one in Christ Jesus."

Some other New Testament instructions that are almost universally considered "cultural" and therefore only applicable to the original (1st century) recipients of the text are for women to wear veils when praying or prophesying, Christians to wash each other's feet (a direct command from Jesus in the Upper Room discourse, the instruction, appearing five times in the New Testament, to greet one another with a holy kiss—among others.

In contrast to egalitarian teaching, complementarians teach that male priority and headship (positional leadership) were instituted prior to the Fall and that the decree in Genesis 3:16 merely distorted this leadership by introducing "ungodly domination." Complementarians teach that the male leadership seen throughout the Old Testament (i.e., the patriarchs, priesthood and monarchy) was an expression of the creation ideal, as was Jesus' selection of 12 male apostles and New Testament restrictions on church leadership to men only.

Complementarians criticize Webb's hermeneutic. Grudem argues that Webb expects Christians to pursue a "superior ethic" to that found in the New Testament, therefore undermining the authority and sufficiency of Scripture. He claims that Webb and some other evangelicals misconstrue the biblical teaching about both slavery and women, and inappropriately confuse the two. He writes that slavery is tolerated in Scripture but never commanded but in some cases is criticized, whereas wives are explicitly commanded to submit to their husbands and male leadership is never criticized. Additionally, Grudem believes that Webb's "redemptive-movement" hermeneutic (itself a variation of the "trajectory" hermeneutic commonly employed by egalitarians) ultimately relies on subjective judgments that are incapable of producing certainty about ethical views.

Gender and the Image of God

Complementarians have traditionally held that Christian ministers ought to be men, because of the need to represent Jesus Christ, who was the "Son" of God, and incarnate as a male human being. A related position is that while both male and female were made in the image of God, the woman shares in the divine image through the man because she was created out of him, and is his "glory."

> To us a priest is primarily a representative, a double representative, who represents us to God and God to us... We have no objection to a woman doing the first: the whole difficulty is with the second. But why? ... Suppose the reformer stops saying that a good woman may be like God and begins saying that God is like a good woman. Suppose he says that we might just as well pray to 'Our Mother which art in Heaven' as to 'Our Father'. Suppose he says that the Incarnation might just as well have taken a female as a male form, and the Second Person of the Trinity be as well called the Daughter as the Son. Suppose, finally, that the mystical marriage were reversed, that the Church were the Bridegroom and Christ the Bride. All this, as it seems to me, is involved in the claim that a woman can represent God as a priest does.
>
> — *C. S. Lewis, Priestesses in the Church? 1948*

Christian egalitarians respond by arguing that God is not gendered, and that males and females image God equally and without any differences. In addition, terms such as "Father" and "Son", used in reference to God, should be understood as analogies or metaphors used by the biblical authors to communicate attributes about God in a culture where men had social privilege. Similarly, Christ became a male not because it was theologically necessary, but because 1st century Jewish culture would not have accepted a female Messiah. Wayne Grudem takes exception to these egalitarian arguments, insisting that Christ's maleness was theologically necessary; he also alleges that egalitarians are increasingly advocating that God should be thought of as "Mother" as well as "Father", a move which he sees as theologically liberal.

The Christian doctrine of the Trinity has become a major focus of the contemporary gender debate, specifically in relation to 1 Cor. 11:3. In 1977, George W. Knight III argued in a book about gender roles that the subordination of women to men is theologically analogous to the subordination of the Son to the Father in the Trinity. Australian theologian Kevin Giles has more recently responded that complementarians have "reinvented" the doctrine of the Trinity to support their views of men and women, suggesting that some complementarians have adopted a heretical view of the Trinity similar to Arianism. A vigorous debate has ensued, with some egalitarians moving towards the idea that there is "mutual dependence" within the Trinity, including "subordination of the Father to the Son", which must be reflected in gender role relations. Wayne Grudem has countered this by asserting that mutual submission in the Trinity cannot be supported by scripture and church history.

Relationship between Ontology and Roles

Modern complementarians argue that Genesis 1:26-28 and Galatians 3:28 establish the full equality of males and females in terms of status, worth and dignity. Complementary roles in marriage and church leadership, including the primary authority of men and the submission of wives, are not thought to contradict this principle of ontological equality. The equation of role or functional subordination and ontological inferiority is considered to be a category confusion.

Egalitarian author Rebecca Merrill Groothuis has objected to this position. She argues that "woman's spiritual and ontological equality with man rules out the sort of subordination prescribed by gender traditionalists.... It is not logically possible for woman to be essentially equal to man, yet universally subordinate to man on the basis of an essential attribute (i.e., femaleness)."

Women and Mormonism

The status of women in Mormonism has been a source of public debate since before the death of Joseph Smith, Jr. in 1844. Various denominations within the Latter Day Saint movement have taken different paths on the subject of women and their role in the church and in society. Views range from the full equal status and ordination of women to the priesthood as practiced by the Community of Christ, to the Catholic-like patriarchal system practiced by The Church of Jesus Christ of Latter-day Saints, to the ultra-patriarchal plural marriage system practiced by the Fundamentalist Church of Jesus Christ of Latter-Day Saints and other Mormon fundamentalist groups.

Women in early Mormonism

For its time, early Mormonism had a relatively liberating stance toward women. Joseph Smith, Jr., the founder of the Latter Day Saint movement, lived in and abided by a male-centered world; most of the early founding events of Mormonism involved only men. However, a number of women had significant supporting roles; for example, Smith's wife Emma Hale Smith served as a scribe in the translation of the *Book of Mormon*, and later as head of the Relief Society, originally a self-governing women's organisation within the church, which is one of the oldest women's organisations in the world.

In addition, early Mormon doctrine was comparatively women-friendly. Notably, early Mormonism rejected the Augustinian doctrine of original sin, which held that humanity inherits the sin of Adam and Eve in which they ate the forbidden fruit. This sin was historically blamed on Eve, and was thought to be the source of women's submissive and dependent state. Mormonism rejects the doctrine of original sin. The second Article of Faith states "We believe that men will be punished for their own sins, and not for Adam's transgression."

Other issues included the beginning of plural marriage, the Gifts of the spirit as exercised by women, like prophecy and speaking in tongues, performing ordinances, "Priestesses" in the temple, and priesthood blessings of women by women (Hanks, 2002). For example, while en route to the Salt Lake Valley, the diary of midwife Patty Bartlett Sessions describes women giving each other blessings:

> "...we had a feast in the afternoon at sister Millers...there we blessed and got blessed and I blesed [*sic*] sister Christeen by laying my hands upon her head and the Lord spoke through me to her great and marvelous things." (Sessions, 1996)

Women participated in the Anointed Quorum and founded the Relief Society, among other projects in the early Church.

Women in The Church of Jesus Christ of Latter-day Saints

The status of women in The Church of Jesus Christ of Latter-day Saints] has been a source of public debate beginning in the 19th century, when the church clashed with the federal government over its practice of polygamy. Despite the legal and cultural issues related to the LDS practice known as plural marriage, 19th century women played a significant public leadership role in Latter-day Saint culture, politics, and even doctrine. Indeed, some critics view the role of women in the 19th century Church as the zenith of women's institutional and leadership participation in the church hierarchy. (Cornwall, 1994, at 239-264; Iannaccone & Miles, 1994, at 265-86; Jorgensen, 2000, at 105.)

In the mainstream of the church today, women continue to have a significant public role, mostly in non-ecclesiastical areas such as art and culture. Ecclesiastically, the church is firmly committed to patriarchy and gender role.

Women also have retained a certain degree of authority in some areas, including a number of leadership positions, which include authority over children or other women, although these women leaders are subject to supervision and guidance by priesthood-holding leaders. Women are "endowed" with priesthood power, but are not ordained as clergy. Though not considered clergy, women play a significant part in the operation of local congregations. Women teach classes to adults, teenagers, and children. Women also organise social, educational, and humanitarian activities. Women may also serve as missionaries, and a select few may perform certain ordinances such as washing and anointing on behalf of women in Latter-day Saint temples. Unofficially, wives of male clergy also often play an indirect leadership role by influencing and counseling their husbands. (Hanks, 2002)

Within and outside the church mainstream, there is a minority of influential Latter-day Saint women who attempt to influence Church policy and doctrine. However, women who are viewed as publicly oppositional toward the church's patriarchal structure are often subject to ecclesiastical discipline, including excommunication for apostasy.

Frontier Women in 19th Century Utah

In common with a number of other frontier areas, women took a more prominent role than they would have in the East. President Brigham Young taught: "As I have often told my sisters in the Female Relief Societies, we have sisters here who, if they had the privilege of studying, would make just as good mathematicians or accountants as any man; and we think they ought to have the privilege to study these branches of knowledge that they may develop the powers with which they are endowed. We believe that women are useful not only to sweep houses, wash dishes, make beds, and raise babies, but that they should stand behind the counter, study law or physic [medicine], or become good book-keepers and be able to do the business in any counting house, and this to enlarge their sphere of usefulness for the benefit of society at large."

Along with the promotion of women's rights in the secular sphere, women in Utah, like renowned poet Eliza R. Snow, worked toward equality in sacred matters. This included the development of a Heavenly Mother theology. Snow in particular spoke of equal rights:

> "Is it necessary for sisters to be set apart to officiate in the sacred ordinances of washing, anointing, and laying on of hands in administering to the sick? It certainly is not. Any and all sisters who honor their holy endowments, not only have right, but should feel it a duty, whenever called upon to administer to our sisters in these ordinances, which God

> has graciously committed to His daughters as well as to His sons; and we testify that when administered and received in faith and humility they are accompanied with almighty power." (Snow, 1884)

Snow also spoke of the need for women to stick together. She counseled that women confide personal issues to the Relief Society president and her counselors, rather than the bishops. (Snow, 1884).

In the secular sphere, Utah was at the forefront of women's suffrage, becoming one of the first states in the Union to grant women the vote. Education and scholarship was also a primary concern for Mormon women.

The Relief Society was also a forum for women. Religious missions, like Bathsheba W. Smith's mission to southern Utah to preach "woman's rights", were launched. The *Woman's Exponent* publication (the R.S. official newspaper) published a 1920 editorial in favour of "Equal rights before the law, equal pay for equal work, equal political rights", stating that a women's place is not just "in the nursery" but "in the library, the laboratory, the observatory."

> Relief Society president Emmeline B. Wells (1875) said
> "Let woman speak for herself; she has the right of freedom of speech. Women are too slow in moving forward, afraid of criticism, of being called unwomanly, of being thought masculine. What of it? If men are so much superior to women, the nearer we come up to the manly standard the higher we elevate ourselves."

Women in 20th and 21st Century Mormonism

In 1977, N. Eldon Tanner told the Church Coordinating Council that the Relief Society Presidency should be considered a partner with the Melchizedek Priesthood.

Other developments during the presidency of Spencer W. Kimball included having women granted their young women advancements in sacrament meeting. In 1978 the First Presidency and Twelve issued a policy allowing women to pray in Sacrament Meeting In 1980 the general presidents of the Relief Society, Young Women and Primary were invited to sit on the stand during general conference and in 1984 women spoke in general conference for the first time since 1930. Since then women have spoken in every general conference. In 1978 a conference session specifically for women was added, initially two weeks before the October General Conference, and later one week beforehand.

Brigham Young University, the LDS Church's flagship educational institution, has made several changes in its policy towards women. In 1975 the four-year, full tuition and boarding expenses presidential scholarship was changed from only being available to men to being available to an equal number of men and women. BYU established a Women's Research Institute in 1978. Among its directors over its 21 years of existence was Marie Cornwall. At the end of 2009 BYU restructured its Women's Studies Programmes, freeing more money for research on women's issues by ending an institute staff, placing the Women's Studies Minor in the Sociology Department and thus putting all the money that previously was split between research and staff directly into research expenditures.

Women in 'Mormon Fundamentalist' Groups

Mormon fundamentalists are groups or individuals who break from the dominant form of Mormonism practiced by The Church of Jesus Christ of Latter-day Saints. Since the mid-19th century, numerous fundamentalist sects have been established, many of which are located in small, cohesive, and isolated communities in areas of the Western United States, western Canada and Mexico. Mormon fundamentalists advocate a return to Mormon doctrines and practices which adherents believe the LDS Church has wrongly abandoned, such as plural marriage, the Law of Consecration, the Adam-God theory, the Patriarchal Priesthood, elements of the Mormon Endowment ritual, and often the exclusion of Blacks from the priesthood.

Plural marriage is generally considered the most central and significant doctrine separating fundamentalists from the mainstream Latter Day Saint movement. In Mormon fundamentalist groups, women are typically expected or encouraged to adhere to a strongly patriarchal perspective on women's roles and activities and, in many cases, participate in plural marriage.

Women in the Community of Christ

The Community of Christ, who are a part of the Latter Day Saint movement, but not commonly considered part of Mormonism, now ordains women to the priesthood.

Women in Hinduism

The role of women in Hinduism is often disputed, and positions range from equal status with men to restrictive. Hinduism is based on numerous texts, some of which date back to 2000 BCE or earlier. They are varied in authority, authenticity, content and theme, with the most authoritative being the Vedas. The position of women in Hinduism is widely dependent on the specific text and the context. Positive references are made to the ideal woman in texts such as the *Ramayana* and the *Mahabharata*, while some texts such as the *Manu Smriti* advocate a restriction of women's rights. In modern times the Hindu wife has traditionally been regarded as someone who must at all costs remain chaste or pure. This is in contrast with the very different traditions that have prevailed at earlier times in 'Hindu' kingdoms, which included highly respected professional courtesans (such as Amrapali of Vesali), sacred devadasis, mathematicians and female magicians (the *basavis*, the Tantric *kulikas*). Some European scholars observed in the nineteenth century Hindu women were "naturally chaste" and "more virtuous" than other women, although what exactly they meant by that is open to dispute. In any case, as male foreigners they would have been denied access to the secret and sacred spaces that women often inhabited. *Mahabharata* and *Manusmriti* asserts that gods are delighted only when women are worshipped or honoured, otherwise all spiritual actions become futile.

Gender of God

There is a wide variety of viewpoints within the different schools and sects of Hinduism concerning the exact nature and gender (where applicable) of the Supreme person or being; there are even sects that are skeptical about the existence of such a being. Shaktism, for example, focuses worship on the goddess Devi as the supreme embodiment of power, or Shakti (feminine strength; a female form of God). Vaishnavism and Shaivism both worship Lakshmi with Vishnu and Parvati with Shiva respectively as beings on an equal level of magnitude (the male and female aspects of God). In some instances such as with Gaudiya Vaishnavism, specific emphasis is placed on the worship of God's female aspect (Radharani) even above that of her paramour Krishna. Thus it could be said that Hinduism considers God to have both male and female aspects, as the original source of both.

Male deities (such as Shiva and Indra) are believed, in some traditions, to themselves offer worship to the Goddess, Durga:

> "*O Parameshwari, (The supreme Goddess) who is praised by the husband of the daughter of Himalayas (Shri Shiva)...*"
> "*O Parameshwari, who is worshipped with true feelings by the husband of Indrani (Indra) please give us the spiritual personality, the victory, the glory and destroy our enemies.*"

Elsewhere Shiva and Vishnu are also described as possessing feminine qualities represented through their Ardhanarishvara and Mohini forms respectively. There have also been male devotees who have claimed to be incarnations of goddesses, such as Narayani Peedam and Bangaru Adigalar of Melmaruvathur, Tamil Nadu who claim to be forms or avatars of the goddess Narayani.

Hindu feminists such as Phoolan Devi have also used the goddess Durga as their icon. Traditions which follow the advaita philosophy consider that ultimately the supreme being is formless without any particular gender, or is transcendental to such considerations.

Women in Rig Vedic hymns

In the marriage hymn (RV 10.85.26), the wife "should address the assembly as a commander."

A Rig Veda hymn says:

Rig Veda, Book 10. HYMN CLIX. Saci Paulomi.

—I am the banner and the head, a mighty arbitress am I: I am victorious, and my Lord shall be submissive to my will.

There are also verses which demean women.

Rig Veda, Book 8. HYMN XXXIII. Verse 17. Saci Paulomi.

—Indra himself hath said, The mind of woman brooks not discipline, Her intellect hath little weight.

These are probably the earliest references to the position of women in Hindu society.

Status of Mothers in Hindu Scripture

"A son must always serve his mother even if she has been an outcast."

"The professor is equivalent of ten teachers, the father is equal to hundred professors, the mother exceeds a thousand fathers."

"All other sins are expiable but he who is cursed the mother never liberated."

"An outcast father may be forsaken, but not the mother, she is never an outcast to the son".

"One conquers this world through respect for the mother, the middle religion (the firmament) through respect for the father, and through service to the preceptor one gains the region of Brahman."

"Janani Janmabhumischa Svargadapi Gariasi" i.e. *The mother and the motherland are superior to heaven.*

Property Rights

Arthashastra and *Manusmriti* are sources about the woman's right to property or 'Stridhan', (literally meaning, property of wife). It is of two types: maintenance (in money or land given by the husband), and anything else like ornaments given to her by her family, husband, in-laws and the friends of her husband. Manu further subdivides this into six types - the property given by parents at marriage, given by the parental family when she is going to her husband's house, given by her husband out of affection (not maintenance which he is bound to give), and property given separately by brother, mother and father [Manu IX 194]. Pre-nuptial contracts are also mentioned where the groom would agree to give a set amount of brideprice to both parents and the bride. Such property belonged to the wife alone and was not to be touched by the groom or her parents except in emergencies (in sickness, in famine, threatened by robbers, or for performing holy deeds). At the same time, the

Manu Smriti contradicts itself by declaring that a wife has no property and the wealth earned is for the husband [Manu VIII.416].

Daughters and sons equally inherited their mother's property; but some scriptures insist that a mother's property belongs solely to the daughters [Manu IX 131], in order of preference: unmarried daughters, married but poor daughters, married and rich daughters. When a father died, unmarried daughters had to be given a share in their father's property, equal to one-fourth from every brother's share [since it is assumed that the married daughter had been given her share at marriage] [Manu IX. 118]. If the family has no sons, the (appointed) daughter is the sole inheritor of the property [Manu IX 127].

Study of Scriptures

Several women sages and seers are mentioned in the *Upanishads*, the philosophical part of the *Vedas*, notable among them being Gargi and Maitreyi. The Sanskrit word for female teachers as Achary (as opposed to Acharya for teacher and Acharyini for teacher's wife) reveal that women were also given a place as Gurus.

The *Harita Dharmasutra* (of the Maitrayaniya school of Yayurveda) declares that there are two kind of women: Sadhyavadhu who marry, and the Brahmavaadini who are inclined to religion, they can wear the sacred thread, perform rituals like the agnihotra and read the *Vedas*. Bhavabhuti's *Uttararamacharita* 2.3 says that Atreyi went to Southern India where she studied the *Vedas* and Indian philosophy. Shankara debated with the female philosopher Ubhaya Bharati, and Madhava's *Shankaradigvijaya* (9.63) mentions that she was well versed in the *Vedas*. Tirukkoneri Dasyai (15th century) wrote a commentary on Nammalvar's *Tiruvaayamoli*, with reference to Vedic texts like the *Taittiriya Yajurveda*.

The *Bhagavata Purana* states that the *Mahabharata* was written specifically for women and also men who were not in the priestly Brahmin caste :

"Out of compassion, the great sage thought it wise that this would enable men to achieve the ultimate goal of life. Thus, he compiled the great historical narration called the *Mahabharata* for women, labourers and friends of the twice-born."

In several schools for Vedic priests, many graduates are women.

Education

Katyayana's *Varttika* 125, 2477 mentions that there were female teachers of grammar. Patanjali wrote in his comments to *Ashtadhyayi* 3.3.21 and 4.1.14, that women undergo the thread ceremony before beginning their education, and says that women studied grammar.

Marriage

The most sacred part of the Hindu wedding ceremony involves circumambulating the sacred fire in seven steps to a Vedic mantra where the groom addresses his wife.

In the *Manu Smriti*, on the other hand, 8 types of marriage are specified: two involve bedecking the bride with costly garments and ornaments before giving her away, two involve the groom's family giving a gift to the family of the bride, and the other four do not involve an exchange of gifts. According to *Manusmriti* there are eight different types of Hindu marriages. Among the eight types all didn't have religious sanction. The last four were not religiously defined and were condemned. These are: Brahma Marriage, Daiva Marriage, Arsha Marriage, Prajapatya Marriage, Gandharva Marriage, Asura Marriage, Rakshasa Marriage, Paishacha Marriage. In Brahma marriage, once the boy completes his Brahmacharya Ashram (religious student-hood), he is eligible to get married. His parents then approach the parents or guardian of a girl belonging to a good family and ask them for the hand of their daughter-for their son. The father of the girl also carefully chooses the bridegroom who is well versed in Vedas and of a noble character. This is how a Brahma marriage was arranged. The bride came with only two garments and few ornaments. According to Dharmashastras "Brahma Vivah" is the best marriage among all. "The son born of the Brahma marriage sanctifies 21 GENERATION.-(that of the Daiva marriage 14 generations; that of Arsha marriage and Kayah marriage six each.")

The *Manusmriti* enjoins, "Let mutual fidelity continue until death.' This may be considered the summation of the highest" law for husband and wife. *(Manu Smriti IX 101)*

Rigvedic verses suggest that the women married at a mature age and were probably free to select their husband. The wedding hymn in the *Rigveda* (RV 10.85.37-38) speaks of "husbands" (plural) for a single wife, but this may have a mythological character.

Dowry

The practice of dowry is not endorsed by orthodox Hinduism and "may be a perversion of Sanskritic marriage prescriptions." Dowries are linked to caste status: among higher castes a dowry is expected from the girl's family; among lower caste families the dowry is paid to the girl's family. As a result, the prevalence of dowry increases with the processes known as "Sanskritisation" and urbanisation; abuse of the practice has thus increased in recent years.

The modern Hindi word for *dowry* is *dahej*, which comes from the Arabic loanword *jihayz* (variously spelled *jiha-z*, *jihez*, etc.), which literally means furnishings or equipment (i.e. brought by the wife for her new family).

Polygamy

Thus, certain mantras in Vedas describe demerits of Polygamy.

- Rig Veda 10.105.8 compares existence of multiple wives with multiple worldly miseries.
- Rig Veda 10.101.11 states that a man with two wives is pressed from both sides and weeps like a horse that neighs when pressed from both sides by spokes while driving a chariot.
- Rig Veda 10.101.11 state that two wives make life aimless.
- Atharva Veda 3.18.2 prays that may a woman never face threat of another co-wife.
- However, other mantras in the Vedas seem to support polygamy.
- Rig Veda 1.62.11 states that "As yearning wives cleave to their yearning husband, so cleave our hymns to thee, O Lord most potent."

Divorce

Hinduism in general disapproves of divorce. A divorced woman is generally forced to live as a widow. However in theological terms, both the *Manusamhita* and the *Arthashastra* state that if a husband is impotent, a traitor, an ascetic or an outcast, or missing for a prescribed number of years, the wife may leave him without blame and marry again. The *Arthashastra* also declares that in other circumstances, divorce can take place only by mutual consent. Manu discusses situations where the wife wishes to return to her first husband, whether she has simply deserted him or married another.

Widowhood and Remarriage

In traditional families, widows were, and in some cases still are, required to wear white sarees, and to give up their ornaments, including the bindi, which signifies auspiciousness. The presence of widows at religious rites in such families is considered inauspicious. Widows are expected to devote their lives to an austere pursuit of religion. These restrictions are traditionally strongest in the highest castes, in which the head is frequently shaved as well. The highest castes also have severe restrictions on remarriage. Such restrictions are now strictly observed only by a small minority of widows, though some degree of ritual inauspiciousness lingers.

In *NAsmR* 12.45-48, there are three types of *punarbhu*, or a remarried widow: The virgin widow, the woman who abandons her husband to take up with another man and then returns to her husband, and the woman who has no brothers-in-law whom can give her offspring. Although this list is not exhaustive, it makes it clear that a *punarbhu* is not just any widow. Indeed, she may not have been a widow at all (as in the second case). In the other two cases, she is a childless widow, which is an important distinction. Although many texts do seem to address the remarriage of widows and sometimes permit it, it is not considered an ideal situation. A *punarbhu* is often not given the same rights as a woman who was married only once. The son of a *punarbhu*, a *punarbhava*, is often listed as one who is unfit to invite to a sacrifice, as is the husband of a remarried woman. The *punarbhu* also does not inherit as would a 'natural son'.

As of 2007, 3 per cent of the population of India consists of widows. Most widows are abandoned to survive on charity, and many are reduced to begging on the streets. Some surveys show that as they are steeped in their religious beliefs and fearful of violating social customs, many widows do not wish to remarry.

Sati

Sati (as verb) is the act of immolation of a woman on her husband's funeral pyre. *Sati* (as noun) refers to one who either immolated herself willingly or through societal inducement and compulsion.

Sati was *ideally* performed as an act of immortal love, and was believed to purge the couple of all accumulated sin. (*Sati* was practiced by the ancient peoples of Scythia, Egypt, Scandinavia and China).

Though no scripture mandates *sati*, the *Puranas*, part of the Hindu *Smriti*, mention *sati* as highly meritorious in several instances. A few examples of *sati* are recorded in the Hindu epics, which are otherwise replete with influential widows. Some examples from the *Mahabharata* include:

- Several of Vasudeva's wives (Rohini, Devaki, Bhadraa and Madira) [M.Bh. *Mausalaparvan* 7.18].
- Madri, second wife of Pandu, who held herself responsible for his death, performed *sati*. His first wife Kunti did not. [M.Bh. *Adiparvan* 95.65]

Moreover, Kunti in the *Mahabharata* even had a son before marriage (Karna, given as boon by Sun God), but went on to become a queen by marrying another man (king Pandu). This tale shows that society valued women more for their qualities of intelligence, determination, loyalty and leadership over personal and private issues like pre-marital virginity. Needless to say, Kunti, in spite of her pre-marital indiscretion, not only married a king, but also remained highly respected and loved by all (family and others) throughout her entire long life, and did not choose to commit *sati* at the time of her husband's death.

Female Gurus and Saints

- Gargi Vachaknavi - A female Rishi who challenged Yajnavalkya on questions relating to the human soul.
- Lopamudra - Wife of Sage Agastya.
- Andal - A 8th century Tamil saint-poet and one of the twelve Alvars.

- Karaikkal Ammeiyar - A 6th century Tamil saint-poet, one of the sixty three Nayanmars.
- Mangayarkkarasiyar - A Pandya Queen, wife of King Nedumaranan, one of the sixty three Nayanmars.
- Isaignaniyaar - A Tamil saint-poet, one of sixty three Nayanmars.
- Avvaiyar - A Sangam period Tamil saint-poet, ethicist, social reformer.
- Akka Mahadevi - A prominent figure and Kannada poet of the 12th century Veerashaiva Bhakti movement.
- Mirabai – Hindu mystical poet and a devotee of Krishna whose bhajans are sung all over India.
- Lalleshwari – Hindu saint-poetess, and a mystic of the Kashmiri Shaivites.
- Bahinabai and Kanhopatra: Hindu poetess-saints of the Varkari sect of Maharashtra. Kanhopatra was a courtesan and dancing-girl by profession.
- Sarada Devi – Wife of the saint Ramakrishna and revered as an embodiment of the Divine Mother.

Understanding Women in Buddhism

Women in Buddhism is a topic that can be approached from varied perspectives including those of theology, history, anthropology and feminism. Topical interests include the theological status of women, the treatment of women in Buddhist societies at home and in public, the history of women in Buddhism, and a comparison of the experiences of women across different forms of Buddhism. As in other religions, the experiences of Buddhist women have varied considerably.

Statements on the Topic

Scholars such as Faure and Miranda Shaw are in agreement that Buddhist Studies is in its infancy in terms of addressing gender issues. Shaw gave an overview of the situation in 1994:

> In the case of Indo-Tibetan Buddhism, some progress has been made in the areas of women in early Buddhism, monasticism, and Māhayā na Buddhism. Two articles have seriously broached the topic of women in Indian Tantric Buddhism, while somewhat more attention has been devoted to Tibetan nuns and lay yoginis.

Khandro Rinpoche, a female lama in Tibetan Buddhism, downplays the significance of growing attention to the topic:

> When there is a talk about women and Buddhism, I have noticed that people often regard the topic as something new and different. They believe that women in Buddhism has become an important topic

> because we live in modern times and so many women are practicing the Dharma now. However, this is not the case. The female sangha has been here for centuries. We are not bringing something new into a twenty-five hundred-year-old tradition. The roots are there, and we are simply re-energizing them.

Women in Early Buddhism

The founder of Buddhism, Gautama Buddha, permitted women to join his monastic community and fully participate in it, although there were certain provisos or *garudhammas*. As Susan Murcott comments, "The nun's sangha was a radical experiment for its time." Dr. Mettanando Bhikkhu says of the First Buddhist council:

> Perhaps Mahakassappa and the bhikkhus of that time were jealous of the bhikkhunis being more popular and doing more teaching and social work than the bhikkhus. Their anti-women prejudice became institutionalised at that time with the eight garudhammas, the eight weighty restrictions. We must discontinue that prejudice. There is no anti-women prejudice in Jainism and they survived in India; whereas Buddhism had prejudice and did not survive in India.

This is factually incorrect, because Digambara Jains believe that women are capable of spiritual progress but must be reborn male in order to attain final spiritual liberation. They are prohibited from becoming full monastics, unlike the Svetambara school.

According to Ajahn Sujato, the early texts state that the most severe of the *garudhammas*, which states that every nun must bow to every monk, was instituted by the Buddha because of the customs of the time, and modern scholars doubt that the rule even goes back to the Buddha at all. Furthermore, an identical rule is found in Jainism.

According to Diana Paul, the traditional view of women in Early Buddhism is that they are inferior. Rita Gross agrees that "a misogynist strain is found in early Indian Buddhism. But the presence of some clearly misogynist doctrines does not mean that the whole of ancient Indian Buddhism was misogynist". The mix of positive attitudes to femininity with blatantly negative sentiment has led many writers to characterise early Buddhism's attitude to women as deeply ambivalent.

Some commentators on the *Aganna-Sutta* from the Pāli Canon, a record of the teachings of Gautama Buddha, interpret it as showing women as responsible for the downfall of the human race. However, Buddhist interpretation is generally that it shows lust in general, rather than women, as causing the downfall.

However, despite some less positive images of women in Early Buddhism, there are also examples in the Pali Canon which suggest that the very concept of gender differentiation can serve as a hinderance to attaining nirvana, or enlightenment. For example, in the *Bhikkhuni-samyutta*, found in the *Sagatha-vagga* of the Samyutta Nikaya, gender discrimination is stated to be the work of Mara, a personification of temptation from the Buddhist spiritual path. In the Soma Sutta, the Bhikkhuni Soma states: "Anyone who thinks 'I'm a woman' or 'a man' or 'Am I anything at all?' — that's who Mara's fit to address", linking gender neutrality to the Buddhist concept of *anatta*, or "not-self", a strategy the Buddha taught for release from suffering. In a sutta titled "Bondage", the Buddha states that when either a man or a woman clings to gender identity, that person is in bondage.

Women's Spiritual Attainment

The various schools and traditions within Buddhism hold different views as to the possibilities of women's spiritual attainments. Feminist scholars have also noted than even when a woman's potential for spiritual attainment is acknowledged, records of such achievements may not be kept - or may be obscured by gender-neutral language or mis-translation of original sources by Western scholars.

Limitations on Women's Attainments in Buddhism

According to Bernard Faure, "Like most clerical discourses, Buddhism is indeed relentlessly misogynist, but as far as misogynist discourses go, it is one of the most flexible and open to multiplicity and contradiction."

In the Buddhist tradition, positions of apparently worldly power are often a reflection of the spiritual achievements of the individual. For example, any gods are living in higher realms than a human being and therefore have a certain level of spiritual attainment. Cakravartins and Buddhas are also more spiritual advanced than an ordinary human being. However, as Zen nun Heng-Ching Shih states, women in Buddhism are said to have five obstacles, namely being incapable of becoming a Brahma King, 'Sakra', King `Mara` Cakravartin or Buddha. This is based on the statement of Gautama Buddha in the Bahudh tuka-sutta of the Majjhima Nikaya in the Pali Canon that it is impossible that a woman should be "the perfectly rightfully Enlightened One", "the Universal Monarch", "the King of Gods", "the King of Death" or "Brahmaa."

Women and Buddhahood

Although early Buddhist texts such as the Cullavagga section of the Vinaya Pitaka of the Pali Canon contain statements from Gautama Buddha, the founder of Buddhism, speaking to the fact that a woman can attain enlightenment, it is also clearly stated in the *Bahudhātuka-sutta* that there could never be a female Buddha. As Prof. Heng-Ching Shih states, women in Buddhism are said to have five obstacles, namely being incapability of becoming a Brahma King, 'Sakra' , King 'Mara' , Cakravartin or Buddha. This is based on the statement of Gautama Buddha in the *Bahudhātuka-sutta* of the Majjhima Nikaya in the Pali Canon that it is impossible that a woman could be "the perfectly rightfully Enlightened One'", "the Universal Monarch", "the King of Gods", "the King of Death" or "Brahmā".

In Theravada Buddhism, the modern school based on the Buddhist philosophy of the earliest dated texts, Buddhahood is a rare event. The focus of practice is primarily on attaining Arhatship and the Pali Canon has examples of both male and female Arhats who attained nirvana. Yashodhara, the former wife of Buddha Shakyamuni, mother of his son Rahula, is said to have become an arhat after having joined the Bhikkhuni order of Buddhist nuns. In Mahayana schools, Buddhahood is the universal goal for Mahayana practitioners. The Mahayana sutras, like the Pali Canon literature, maintain that a woman can become enlightened, only not in female form. For example, the *Bodhisattvabhūmi*, dated to the 4th Century, states that a woman about to attain enlightenment will be reborn in the male form. According to Miranda Shaw, "this belief had negative implications for women insofar as it communicated the insufficiency of the female body as a locus of enlightenment".

However, in the tantric iconography of the Vajrayana practice path of Buddhism, female Buddhas do appear. Sometimes they are the consorts of the main *yidam* of a meditation mandala but Buddhas such as Vajrayogini, Tara and Simhamukha appear as the central figures of tantric sadhana in their own right. Vajrayana Buddhism also recognizes many female yogini practitioners as achieving the full enlightenment of a Buddha, Miranda Shaw as an example cites sources referring to "Among the students of the adept Naropa, reportedly two hundred men and one thousand women attained complete enlightenment". Yeshe Tsogyal, one of the five tantric consorts of Padmasambhava is an example of a woman (Yogini) recognised as a female Buddha in the Vajrayana tradition. According to Karmapa lineage however Tsogyel has attained Buddhahood in that very life. On the website of the Karmapa, the head of the Karma Kagyu school of Tibetan Buddhism, it is stated that Yeshe Tsogyal - some thirty years before transcending worldly existence - finally emerged from an isolated meditation retreat, (c.796-805 AD), as "a fully enlightened Buddha" (samyak-sambuddha).

There are predictions from Sakyamuni Buddha to be found in the thirteenth chapter of the Mahayana Lotus Sutra, referring to future attainments of Mahapajapati and Yasodhara.

In the 20th Century Tenzin Palmo, a Tibetan Buddhist nun in the Drukpa Lineage of the Kagyu school, stated "I have made a vow to attain Enlightenment in the female form - no matter how many lifetimes it takes".

Female Tulku Lineages

In the fifteenth century CE, Princess Chokyi-dronme (Wylie:*Chos-kyi sgron-me*) was recognised as the embodiment of the meditation deity and female Buddha in the Vajrayana tradition, Vajravarahi. Chokyi-dronme became known as Samding Dorje Pagmo (Wylie: *bSam-lding rDo-rje phag-mo*) and began a line of female *tulkus*, reincarnate lamas. At present, the twelfth of this line lives in Tibet.

Another female tulku lineage, that of Shugseb Jetsun Rinpoche (Wylie: *Shug-gseb rJe-btsun Rin-po-che*) (c. 1865–1951), began in the late nineteenth century CE. While she received teachings of all the Tibetan schools, Shugseb Jetsun Rinpoche was particularly known for holding a lineage of Chöd, the meditation practice of offering one's own body for the benefit of others. At the start of the twentieth century, Shugsheb Jetsun Rinpoche - also called Ani Lochen Chönyi Zangmo - founded the Shuksep or Shugsep (Wylie:*shug gseb*) nunnery located thirty miles from Lhasa on the slopes of Mount Gangri Thökar. It became one of the largest and most famous nunneries in Tibet. Shugsep Nunnery, part of the Nyingma school of Tibetan Buddhism, has been re-established in Gambhir Ganj, India. In exile in India, the nuns of Shugsep are now determined to maintain the identity and traditions of their nunnery, and they continue the practices for which they were famous, particularly those of Longchen Nyingtig and Chöd.

Buddhist Ordination of Women

Gautama Buddha first ordained women as nuns five years after his enlightenment and five years after first ordaining men into the sangha. The first Buddhist nun was his aunt and foster mother Mahapajapati Gotami. Bhikkhunis have to follow the eight rules of respect, which are vows called The Eight Garudhammas. According to Peter Harvey "The Buddha's apparent hesitation on this matter is reminiscent of his hesitation on whether to teach at all", something he only does after persuasion from various devas.

Family Life in Buddhism

According to Diana Paul, Buddhism inherited a view of women whereby if they are not represented as mothers then they are portrayed as either lustful temptresses or as evil incarnate.

Motherhood

The status of motherhood in Buddhism has also traditionally reflected the Buddhist perspective that *dukkha*, or suffering, is a major characteristic of human existence. In her book on the Therigatha collection of stories of women arhats from the Pali Canon, Susan Murcott states: "Though this chapter is about motherhood, all of the stories and poems share another theme - grief. The mothers of this chapter were motivated to become Buddhist nuns by grief over the death of their children."

However, motherhood in Early Buddhism could also be a valued activity in its own right. Queen Maya, the mother of Gautama Buddha, the founder of Buddhism, had a certain following, especially in Lumbini, where she gave birth to him. Since Maya died some days after his birth, Gautama Buddha was brought up by a fostermother, his mother's sister Mahapajapati, who also had two children of her own. She become the first Buddhist nun. Both of her children, her son Nanda and her daughter Sundari Nanda joined the Buddhist sangha of monastics. The wife of Gautama Buddha, Yasodhara, was the mother of one son named Rahula, meaning "fetter", who became a Buddhist monk at the age of seven and Yasodhara also eventually became a nun.

One of the attractions for women in Vajrayana Buddhism of following the path of a *yogini* rather than that of a *bhikkhuni* nun was the opportunity to practice amidst family life with a husband or spiritual consort and possibly have children. Also Yoginis - unlike nuns - were not obliged to shave their hair. Machig Labdrön followed such a path, living in a monastery for a while but later leaving to unite with Topabhadra as her consort. According to Machig's *namthar* he cared for the children whilst she practiced and taught. Some of Machig's children followed her on the spiritual path, becoming accomplished yogins themselves. Tsultrim Allione, a recognised emanation of Machig Labdron, herself was a nun for four years but left to marry and have children. She has spoken of the contribution motherhood has made to her practice:

...in Buddhism the image of the mother as the embodiment of compassion is used a lot. She'll do anything for the children. As a mother I felt that depth of love and commitment and having somebody who I really would give my own life for - it was very powerful to have that kind of relationship. I also felt that I didn't really grow up until I had my children. There were ways that maturity was demanded of me and having children brought forth that maturity. So I wouldn't say my children were an inspiration in the sense of what I thought would have been a spiritual inspiration before I had children. More so I think meeting the challenges of motherhood with what I had learned made my practice very rich.

Love, Sexual Conduct and Marriage

In general, "While Buddhism regards the celibate monastic life as the higher ideal, it also recognises the importance of marriage as a social institution". Some guidelines for marriage are offered. Although Buddhist practice varies considerably amongst its various schools, marriage is one of the few concepts specifically mentioned in the context of Sila, the Buddhist formulation of core facets of spiritual discipline. The fundamental code of Buddhist ethics, The Five Precepts contains an admonishment against sexual misconduct, although what constitutes misconduct from the perspective of a particular school of Buddhism varies widely depending on the local culture.

In early Buddhism, the Sigalovada Sutta of the Digha Nikaya in the Pali Canon describes the respect that one is expected to give to one's spouse. However, since the ideal of early Buddhism is renunciation, it can be seen from examples such as the story of the monk Nanda and his wife Janapada Kalyāni that striving for the bliss of Nirvana is valued above love and marriage. Despite having married her just that day, encouraged by his cousin Gautama Buddha, Nanda left his wife to become a bhikkhu in the Buddhist Sangha. In stories like this from the Pali Canon, love is generally perceived as part of attachment to samsara, the endless cycle of rebirth. Susan Murcott has pointed out that early Buddhist attitudes to love and marriage generally reflect the Brahmanic ideals of India at the time... including the recent rise of the renunciate ideal and the associated decline in the status of love and marriage.

In Vajrayana Buddhism, a sexual relationship with a consort is seen in a technical way as being a spiritual practice in anuttarayoga tantra intended to allow the practitioners to attain realisations and attain enlightenment. The union of tantric consorts is depicted in the yab-yum iconography of meditation deities.

In Buddhism the concept of love or metta is connected to the Buddha to come Maitreya.

Words

June Campbell writes in her book *Traveller in space* that Chandra Das in his *Tibetan English Dictionary* describes twenty synonyms for *woman*. The words used most often are *kyemen* (tibetan: skye.dman) meaning inferior birth and *pumo* (tibetan: bu.mo.) meaning female human being. There are others like *tsamdenma* (tibetan: mtshams.ldan.ma.), *chingchema* (tibetan: bching.byed.ma.), *dodenma* (tibetan: bdod.ldan.ma.), *gaweshi* (tibetan: dgah.wabi.gshi.) and *tobmema* (tibetan: stobs.med.ma.).

Throughout the Mahāyāna world, Avalokiteśvara, who takes on both male and female form e.g., Guan Yin, and Tara, a female Vajrayana yidam, are bodhisattvas who embody karuā, and Prajnaparamita is a female buddha who embodies wisdom.

The Dalai Lama

The Dalai Lama spoke at a conference on Women in Buddhism at the University of Hamburg in 2007:

"Warfare has traditionally been carried out primarily by men, since they seem better physically equipped for aggressive behaviour. Women, on the other hand, tend to be more caring and more sensitive to others' discomfort and pain. Although men and women have the same potentials for aggression and warm-heartedness, they differ in which of the two more easily manifests. Thus, if the majority of world leaders were women, perhaps there would be less danger of war and more cooperation on the basis of global concern – although, of course, some women can be difficult! I sympathise with feminists, but they must not merely shout. They must exert efforts to make positive contributions to society."

Well-known Female Buddhists

Celebrities

Tina Turner

Tibetan Buddhist Tulkus and Emanations

- Dorje Pakmo
- Khandro Rinpoche
- Tsultrim Allione
- Jetsunma Ahkon Lhamo - western woman

Notable Buddhist Nuns

- Master Cheng Yen is a Taiwanese Buddhist nun (bhikkhuni), teacher, and philanthropist. Cheng Yen founded the Buddhist Compassion Relief Tzu Chi Foundation, commonly known as Tzu Chi.
- Jetsunma Tenzin Palmo is a Tibetan Buddhist nun, author, teacher and founder of the Dongyu Gatsal Ling Nunnery in Himachal Pradesh, India. She spent twelve years living in a remote cave in the Himalayas, three of those years in strict meditation retreat.
- Pema Chödrön is an ordained Tibetan Buddhist nun, author, and teacher. She has conducted workshops, seminars, and meditation retreats in Europe, Australia, and throughout North America. She is resident and teacher of Gampo Abbey, a monastery in rural Cape Breton, Nova Scotia, Canada.
- Thubten Chodron is an American Tibetan Buddhist nun and a central figure in reinstating the Tibetan Bhikshuni (Gelongma) ordination of women. She is a student of H. H. XIVth Dalai Lama, Tsenzhap Serkong Rinpoche, Thubten Zopa Rinpoche and other Tibetan masters.

Women in Sikhism

The role of women in Sikhism is outlined in the Sikh scriptures, which state that the Sikh woman is to be regarded as equal to the Sikh man. In Sikhism, women are considered to have the same souls as men and an equal right to grow spiritually. They are allowed to lead religious congregations, take part in the Akhand Path (the continuous recitation of the Holy Scriptures), perform *Kirtan* (congregational singing of hymns), work as a Granthi, and participate in all religious, cultural, social, and secular activities. As such, Sikhism was the first major world religion to state that women were equal in every single respect. Sikh history has prominently recorded the role of women, portraying them as equal in service, devotion, sacrifice, and bravery to men. Examples of various women's moral dignity, service, and self-sacrifice are a source of inspiration to the Sikhs. According to Sikhism, men and women are two sides of the same coin of the human race, a system of inter-relation and inter-dependence in which man takes birth from a woman, and woman is born of a man. According to Sikhism a man can never feel secure and complete during his life without a woman, and a man's success depends upon the love and support of the woman who shares her life with him, and vice-versa. The founder of Sikhism, Guru Nanak, reportedly said in 1499 that "[it] is a woman who keeps the race going" and that we should not "consider woman cursed and condemned, [when] from woman are born leaders and rulers."

Sikhs, therefore, have had an obligation to treat women as equals, and gender discrimination in Sikh society has not been allowed. However, gender equality has been difficult to achieve.

Women who were used to having the same privileges as men in Vedic India were reduced to a position of subordination during the time of the Lawgivers.

Purdah and Sati

Sikhism was a liberating force for women in Indian society. Affirmation of the dignity of humans, both men and women, was central to Guru Nanak's teaching. He said that all creatures were equal before God, so to make distinctions among them on the grounds of birth or sex was sinful. He was also bold, at least for his time, in his praise of women. In the *Asa di Var*, a long composition sung in *sangat* in the morning service, he expresses extreme respect and admiration for women, "of whom great men are born".

Sutak and Celibacy

In another stanza in the *Asa di Var*, Guru Nanak Dev Ji rejects the prevalent superstition of *sutak*, the belief that a woman giving birth to a child is unclean for a given number of days depending upon the caste to which she belongs:

"The impurity of the mind is greed, and the impurity of the tongue is falsehood. The impurity of the eyes is to gaze upon the beauty of another man's wife, and his wealth. The impurity of the ears is to listen to the slander of others. O Nanak, the mortal's soul goes, bound and gagged, to the city of Death. All impurity comes from doubt and attachment to duality. Birth and death are subject to the Command of the Lord's Will; through His Will we come and go." (GG, 472)

Instead of celibacy and renunciation, Guru Nanak recommended *grhastha* — the life of a householder. Husband and wife were seen as equal partners and fidelity was enjoined upon both. In sacred verse, domestic happiness was presented as a cherished ideal and marriage provided a running metaphor for the expression of love for the Divine. Bhai Gurdas Ji, poet of early Sikhism and authoritative interpreter of Sikh doctrine, pays high tribute to women. He says:

"A woman, is the favourite in her parental home, loved dearly by her father and mother. In the home of her in-laws, she is the pillar of the family, the guarantee of its good fortune... Sharing in spiritual wisdom and enlightenment and with noble qualities endowed, a woman, the other half of man, escorts him to the door of liberation." (Varan, V.16)

Equal Status for Women

To ensure equal status for women, the Gurus made no distinction between the sexes in matters of initiation, instruction or participation in *sangat* (holy fellowship) and *pangat* (eating together). According to Sarup Das Bhalla, Mahima Prakash, Guru Amar Das disfavoured the use of the veil by women. He assigned women to supervise some communities of disciples and preached against the custom of *sati.* Sikh history records the names of several women, such as Mata Gujri, Mai Bhago, Mata Sundari, Rani Sahib Kaur, Rani Sada Kaur and Maharani Jind Kaur, who played an important role in the events of their time.

Women's displays of steadfastness during the eighteenth century when Sikhs were fiercely persecuted have had a strong impact on modern day Sikhs, who recount these stories in their *ardas*:

"Our mothers and sisters they repeat every time in their prayer, who plied handmills in the jails of Mannu [the Mughal governor of Lahore (1748-53)], grinding daily a maund-and-a-quarter of corn each, who saw their children being hacked to pieces in front of their eyes, but who uttered not a moan from their lips and remained steadfast in their Sikh faith—recall their spirit of fortitude and sacrifice, and say, Vahiguru, Glory be to God!"

Praised Treatment of Enemy Women

Even in times of severe trial and suffering, Sikhs were guided in their treatment of the women prisoners of war by the highest standards of chivalry. In 1763, for instance, one of Ahmad Shah Durrani's generals, Jahan Khan, was defeated by the Sikhs at Sialkot and a number of his female relations and dependants fell into their hands. Ali ud-Din writes in his *Ibratnamah*, "as the Sikhs of old would not lay their hands on women, they had them escorted safely to Jammu."

Another Muslim chronicler, Ghulam Muhaiy ud-Din, vituperates against the Sikhs in his *Fatuhat Namah-i-Samadi*, but notices the esteem they had for women. He writes, "[The Sikhs] look upon all women in the light of mothers." This had been how a Sikh was defined by Bhai Gurdas a century earlier, "A Sikh casting his eyes upon the beautiful womenfolk of families other than his own regards them as his mothers, sisters and daughters."

Monogamy and Banning of Infanticide and Widow Burning

Such being the respect for womanhood among the Sikhs, monogamy has been the rule for them, and polygamy is exceptionally rare. Female infanticide is prohibited. The Rahitnamas (codes of conduct) prohibit Sikhs from having any contact or relationship with those who indulge in this practice. As for *sati* (widow-burning), Scripture itself rejects it.

In a *shabad* (hymn) Guru Amar Das says, "Satis are not those that burn themselves on the husband's funeral pyre; satis are they, O Nanak, who die of the pangs of separation (GG, 787)"

"They, too must be reckoned satis who live virtuously and contentedly in the service of the Lord, ever cherishing Him in their hearts... Some burn themselves along with their dead husbands: but they need not, for if they really loved them they would endure the pain alive."

As a practical step towards discouraging the practice of sati, Sikhism permitted remarriage of widows.

Current Status

In the present-day democratic politics of India, women as a whole have been rid of many of their disadvantages. They enjoy political franchise and many new opportunities for advancement have opened up for them. Sikh women have shown enterprise in several fields and are among the most progressive in education and in the professions such as teaching and medicine. Within the Sikh system, they are the equals of men in all respects. They can lead congregational services and participate in akhand paths, uninterrupted readings of scripture to be accomplished within forty-eight hours. They vote with men to elect Sikhs' central religious body, the Shiromani Gurdwara Parbandhak Committee, which administers their places of worship.

Famous Women in Sikhism

The first woman to be remembered in Sikhism is Mata Tripta Ji, the mother of the first and founding *guru*, Guru Nanak. She is said to have meditated while carrying the child Nanak in her womb, and to have brought him up with love and tender care, while attempting to protect him from his father Mehta Kalu's undue wrath.

Another famous woman is Bebe Nanaki Ji, the elder and only sister of Guru Nanak. She is a highly intelligent, spiritually awake, and pious lady who recognised the divine light in her brother and envisaged his mission of life before anyone else could perceive it; she did not treat him just as a brother but also respected him as she would a Guru, supporting him throughout her life.

Women in Judaism

The role of women in Judaism is determined by the Hebrew Bible, the Oral Law (the corpus of rabbinic literature), by custom, and by non-religious cultural factors. Although the Hebrew Bible and rabbinic literature mention various female role models, religious law treats women differently in various circumstances.

Biblical Times

Relatively few women are mentioned in the Bible by name and role, suggesting that they were rarely in the forefront of public life. There are a number of exceptions to this rule, including the Matriarchs Sarah, Rebecca, Rachel, and Leah, Miriam the prophetess, Deborah the Judge, Huldah the prophetess, Abigail who married David, and Esther. In the Biblical account these women did not meet with opposition for the relatively public presence they had. According to Jewish tradition, a covenant was formed between the Israelites and the God of Abraham at Mount Sinai. The Torah relates that both Israelite men and Israelite women were present at Sinai, however, the covenant was worded in such a way that it bound men to act upon its requirements and to ensure that the members of their household (wives, children, and slaves) met these requirements as well. In this sense, the covenant bound women as well, though indirectly. Marriage and family law in biblical times favoured men over women. For example, a husband could divorce a wife if he chose to, but a wife could not divorce a husband without his consent. The practice of levirate marriage applied to widows of childless deceased husbands, but not to widowers of childless deceased wives. Laws concerning the loss of female virginity have no male equivalent. These and other gender inequalities found in the Torah suggest that women were subordinate to men during biblical times, however, they also suggest that biblical society viewed continuity, property, and family unity as paramount. However, men had specific obligations they were required to perform for their wives. These included the provision of clothing, food, and sexual relations to their wives.

Women also had a role in ritual life. Women (as well as men) were required to make a pilgrimage to the Temple in Jerusalem once a year and offer the Passover sacrifice. They would also do so on special occasions in their lives such as giving a *todah* ("thanksgiving") offering after childbirth. Hence, they participated in many of the major public religious roles that non-levitical men could, albeit less often and on a somewhat smaller and generally more discreet scale. Women depended on men economically. Women generally did not own property except in the rare case of inheriting land from a father who didn't bear sons. Even "in such cases, women would be required to remarry within the tribe so as not to reduce its land holdings."

Talmudic Times

Classical Jewish rabbinical literature contains quotes that may be seen as both laudatory and derogatory of women. The Talmud states that:

- Greater is the reward to be given by the All-Mighty to the (righteous) women than to (righteous) men.

- Ten measures of speech descended to the world; women took nine.
- Women are light on raw knowledge — i.e. they possess more intuition.
- A man without a wife lives without joy, blessing, and good; a man should love his wife as himself and respect her more than himself.
- When Rav Joseph heard his mother's footsteps he would say: Let me arise before the approach of the divine presence.
- Israel was redeemed from Egypt by virtue of its (Israel's) righteous women.
- A man must be careful never to speak slightingly to his wife because women are prone to tears and sensitive to wrong.
- Women have greater faith than men.
- Women have greater powers of discernment.
- Women are especially tenderhearted.

While few women are mentioned by name in rabbinic literature, and none are known to have authored a rabbinic work, those who are mentioned are portrayed as having a strong influence on their husbands, and occasionally having a public persona. Examples are Bruriah, the wife of the Tanna Rabbi Meir; Rachel, the wife of Rabbi Akiva; and Yalta, the wife of Rabbi Nachman. Rabbi Eliezer's wife (of Mishnaic times) counselled her husband in assuming leadership over the Sanhedrin.

Middle Ages

Like most women in Europe, Jewish women in the Middle Ages had exclusively household roles and arranged marriages; child brides were common. Jewish women were generally prohibited from holding formal leadership roles with authority over men. Regarding European Jewry, Avraham Grossman wrote, "Throughout the Middle Ages, which continued for about a thousand years, we do not find so much as a single women of importance among the sages of Israel... Moreover, over a period of a thousand years, not a single Jewish woman wrote a halakhic, literary, theoretical, mystical, or poetic work, with the exception of a handful of poems written by Jewish women in Spain." Middle Eastern Jewry, on the other hand, had an abundance of female literates. The Cairo Geniza is filled with correspondences written (sometimes dictated) between family members and spouses. Many of these letters are pious and poetic and express a desire to be in closer or more frequent contact with a loved one that is far enough away to only be reached by written correspondence. There are also records of wills and other personal legal documents as well as written petitions to officials in cases of spouse abuse or other conflicts between family members written or dictated by women.

After the expulsion of the Jews from Spain in 1492, women became virtually the only source of Jewish ritual and tradition in the Catholic world in a phenomenon known as crypto-Judaism. Crypto-Jewish women would slaughter their own animals and made sure to keep as many of the Jewish dietary laws and life cycle rituals as possible without raising suspicion. Occasionally, these women were prosecuted by Inquisition officials for suspicious behaviour such as lighting candles to honour the Sabbath or refusing to eat pork when it was offered to them. The Inquisition targeted crypto-Jewish women at least as much as it targeted crypto-Jewish men because women were accused of perpetuating Jewish tradition while men were merely permitting their wives and daughters to organise the household in this manner.

Domestic Law

Rabbeinu Gershom instituted a rabbinic decree (*takhanah*) prohibiting polygamy among Ashkenazic Jews. The rabbis instituted legal methods to enable women to petition a rabbinical court to compel a divorce. Maimonides ruled that a woman who found her husband "repugnant" could compel a divorce, "because she is not like a captive, to be subjected to intercourse with one who is hateful to her."

The rabbis also instituted and tightened prohibitions on domestic violence. Rabbi Peretz ben Elijah ruled, "The cry of the daughters of our people has been heard concerning the sons of Israel who raise their hands to strike their wives. Yet who has given a husband the authority to beat his wife?" Rabbi Rothberg ruled that "For it is the way of the Gentiles to behave thus, but Heaven forbid that any Jew should do so. And one who beats his wife is to be excommunicated and banned and beaten." Rabbi Rothenberg also ruled that a battered wife could petition a rabbinical court to compel a husband to grant a divorce, with a monetary fine owed her on top of the regular *ketubah* money. These rulings occurred in the midst of societies where wife-beating was legally sanctioned and routine.

Religious Developments

Religious developments included relaxation on prohibitions against teaching women Torah, and the rise of women's prayer groups in France and Germany. These changes were accompanied by increased pietistic strictures, including greater requirements for modest dress, and greater strictures during the period of menstruation. At the same time, there was a rise in philosophical and midrashic interpretations depicting women in a negative light, emphasising a duality between matter and spirit in which femininity was associated, negatively, with earth and matter.

The rise and increasing popularity of Kabbalah, which emphasised the *shechinah* and female aspects of the divine presence and human-divine relationship, and which saw marriage as a holy covenant between partners rather than a civil contract, had great influence. Kabbalists explained the phenomenon of menstruation as expressions of the demonic or sinful character of the menstruant. Mystical understandings of what occurs to men's souls in the afterlife and on Shabbat differed significantly from what was understood about what occurs to women's souls.

Present Day

Orthodox Judaism

Orthodox Judaism sometimes prescribes different roles and religious obligations for men and women. There are different opinions among Orthodox Jews concerning these differences. Most claim that men and women have complementary, yet different roles in religious life, resulting in different religious obligations. A minority within the Orthodox tradition believe that some of these differences are not a reflection of religious law, but rather of cultural, social, and historical causes. In the area of education, women were historically exempted from any study beyond an understanding of the practical aspects of Torah, and the rules necessary in running a Jewish household – both of which they have an obligation to learn. Until the twentieth century, women were often discouraged from learning Talmud and other advanced Jewish texts. In the past 100 years, Orthodox Jewish education for women has advanced tremendously.

Some Orthodox rabbis view contemporary efforts at change as motivated by sociological reasons and not by true religious motivation. They also view these suggested changes as a break with the accepted norms of observance, and do not allow women to engaging in activities traditionally reserved for men. For example, Orthodox, Haredi, and Hasidic rabbis discourage women from wearing a *yarmulke*, *tallit* or *tefillin*.

In most Orthodox synagogues women do no to give *ad'var Torah* (brief discourse, generally on the weekly Torah portion) after or between services. Furthermore, a few Modern Orthodox synagogues have *mechitzot* dividing the left and right sides of the synagogue (rather than the usual division between the front and back of the synagogue, with women sitting in the back), with the women's section on one side and the men's section on the other. This is often seen as more equal since the women are not farther away from the service than the men.

Rules of Modesty

The importance of modesty in dress and conduct is particularly stressed among girls and women in Orthodox society. Many Orthodox women only wear skirts and avoid wearing trousers, and some married Orthodox women cover their hair with a wig, hat, or scarf. Judaism prescribes modesty for both men and women.

Rules of Family Purity

In accordance with Jewish Law, Orthodox Jewish women refrain from contact with their husbands while they are menstruating, and for a period of 7 clean days after menstruating, and after the birth of a child. The Israeli

Rabbinate has recently approved women acting as *yoatzot, halakhic* advisers on sensitive personal matters such as family purity.

Modern Orthodox Judaism

Rabbi Joseph B. Soloveitchik, a leader of profound influence in modern Orthodoxy in the United States, forbade women from serving as presidents of synagogues or any other official positions of leadership, and from performing other *mitzvot* (commandments) traditionally performed by males exclusively, such as wearing a tallit or tefillin. Soloveitchik wrote that while women do not lack the capability to perform such acts, there is no *mesorah* (Jewish tradition) that permits it. In making his decision, he relied upon Jewish oral law, including a mishnah in Chulin 2a and a Beit Yoseph in the Tur Yoreh Deah stating that a woman can perform a specific official communal service for her own needs but not those of others.

Women's issues garnered more interest with the advent of feminism. Many Modern Orthodox Jewish women and Modern Orthodox rabbis sought to provide greater and more advanced Jewish education for women. Since most Modern Orthodox women attend college, and many receive advanced degrees in a variety of fields, Modern Orthodoxy generally believes that their Jewish education should equal their secular education. An entire genre of Orthodox feminist literature now exists, and has caused changes within some Orthodox synagogues and communities (*The Status of Women in Halakhic Judaism,* Berman, Tradition, 14:2, 1973.). Orthodox girls' and women's Jewish education has expanded tremendously in the past 30 years. Of some controversy are the questions of whether girls and women should or may learn Talmud. While all segments of Modern Orthodoxy strongly support women's education, the permissibility of Talmud study for women is still not accepted among most of Modern Orthodoxy.

Women's Prayer Groups

Separate Jewish women's prayer groups were a sanctioned custom among German Jews in the Middle Ages. The *Kol Bo* provides, in the laws for Tisha B'Av:

> And they recite dirges there for about a quarter of the night, the men in their synagogue and the women in their synagogue. And likewise during the day the men recite dirges by themselves and the women by themselves, until about a third of the day has passed.

In Germany, in the 12th and 13th centuries, women's prayer groups were led by female cantors. Rabbi Eliezar of Worms, in his elegy for his wife Dulca, praised her for teaching the other women how to pray and embellishing the prayer with music. The gravestone of Urania of Worms, who died in 1275, contains the inscription "who sang *piyyutim* for the women with musical voice." In the Nurnberg Memorial Book, one Richenza was inscribed with the title "prayer leader of the women."

Orthodox women more recently began holding organised women's *tefila* (prayer) groups beginning in the 1970s. While no Orthodox legal authorities agree that women can form a *minyan* (prayer quorum) for the purpose of regular services, women in these groups read the prayers and study Torah. A number of leaders from all segments of Orthodox Judaism have commented on this issue, but it has had little impact on Haredi and Sephardi Judaism. However, the emergence of this phenomenon has enmeshed Modern Orthodox Judaism in a debate which still continues today. There are two schools of thought on this issue:

- The most common view, held by some Modern Orthodox authorities, and most Haredi Rabbis, rules that all women's prayer groups are absolutely forbidden by *halakha* (Jewish law).
- A second view maintains that women's prayer groups can be compatible with halakha, but only if they do not carry out a full prayer service (i.e. do not include certain parts of the service known as *devarim she-bi-kdusha*), and only if services are spiritually and sincerely motivated; they cannot be sanctioned if they are inspired by a desire to rebel against *halakha*. People in this group include Rabbi Avraham Elkana Shapiro, former British Chief Rabbi Immanuel Jakobovits, and Rabbi Avi Weiss.
- A third view argues in favour of the acceptability of calling women to the Torah in mixed services, and leading certain parts of the service which do not require a minyan, under certain conditions.

Women as Witnesses

Traditionally, women are not generally permitted to serve as witnesses in an Orthodox Beit Din (rabbinical court), although they have recently been permitted to serve as *toanot* (advocates) in those courts. This limitation has exceptions which have required exploration under rabbinic law as the role of women in society, and the obligations of religious groups under external civil law, have been subject to increasing recent scrutiny.

The recent case of Rabbi Mordecai Tendler, the first rabbi to be expelled from the Rabbinical Council of America following allegations of sexual harassment, illustrated the importance of clarification of Orthodox halakha in this area. Rabbi Tendler claimed that the tradition of exclusion of women's testimony should compel the RCA to disregard the allegations. He argued that since the testimony of a woman could not be admitted in Rabbinical court, there were no valid witnesses against him, and hence the case for his expulsion had to be thrown out for lack of evidence. In a ruling of importance for Orthodox women's capacity for legal self-protection under Jewish law, Haredi Rabbi Benzion Wosner, writing on behalf of the *Shevet Levi* Beit Din (Rabbinical court) of Monsey, New York, identified sexual harassment cases as coming under a class of exceptions to the traditional exclusion, under which "even children or women" have not only a right but an obligation to testify, and can be relied upon by a rabbinical court as valid witnesses:

> The Ramah in Choshen Mishpat (Siman 35, 14) rules that in a case where only women congregate or in a case where only women could possibly testify, (in this case the alleged harassment occurred behind closed doors) they can and should certainly testify. (Terumas Hadeshen Siman 353 and Agudah Perek 10, Yochasin)
>
> This is also the ruling of the Maharik, Radvaz, and the Mahar"i of Minz. Even those "Poskim" that would normally not rely on women witnesses, they would certainly agree that in our case ... where there is ample evidence that this Rabbi violated Torah precepts, then even children or women can certainly be kosher as witnesses, as the Chasam Sofer pointed out in his *sefer* (monograph) (Orach Chaim T'shuvah 11)[4]

The Rabbinical Council of America, while initially relying on its own investigation, chose to rely on the Halakhic ruling of the Haredi Rabbinical body as authoritative in the situation.

Orthodox Approaches to Change

Leaders of the Haredi community have been steadfast in their opposition to a change in the role of women, arguing that the religious and social constraints on women, as dictated by traditional Jewish texts, are timeless and are not affected by contemporary social change. Many also argue that giving traditionally male roles to women will only detract from both women's and men's ability to lead truly fulfilling lives. Haredim have also sometimes perceived arguments for liberalisation as in reality stemming from antagonism to Jewish law and beliefs generally, arguing that preserving faith requires resisting secular and "un-Jewish" ideas.

Modern Orthodox Judaism, particularly in its more liberal variants, has tended to look at proposed changes in the role of women on a specific, case-by-case basis, focusing on arguments regarding the religious and legal role of specific prayers, rituals, and activities individually. Such arguments have tended to focus on cases where the Talmud and other traditional sources express multiple or more liberal viewpoints, particularly where the role of women in the past was arguably broader than in more recent times. Feminist advocates within Orthodoxy have tended to stay within the traditional legal process of argumentation, seeking a gradualist approach, and avoiding wholesale arguments against the religious tradition as such.

Conservative Judaism

Although the position of Conservative Judaism toward women originally differed little from the Orthodox position, it has in recent years minimised legal and ritual differences between men and women. The Committee on

Jewish Law and Standards (CJLS) of the Rabbinical Assembly has approved a number of decisions and responses on this topic. These provide for women's active participation in areas such as:

- Publicly reading the Torah (*ba'al kriah*)
- Being counted as part of a *minyan*
- Being called for an *aliyah* to read the Torah
- Serving as a cantor (*shalich tzibbur*)
- Serving as rabbi and halakhic decisor (*posek* - an arbiter in matters of religious law)
- Wearing a *tallit* and *tefillin*

A rabbi may or may not decide to adopt particular rulings for the congregation; thus, some Conservative congregations will be more or less egalitarian than others. However, there are other areas where legal differences remain between men and women, including:

- *Matrilineal descent.* The child of a Jewish mother is born Jewish; the child of a Jewish father is born Jewish if and only if the mother is Jewish.
- Pidyon Ha-Bat, a proposed ceremony based on the biblical redemption of the eldest newborn son (Pidyon Ha-Ben). The CJLS has stated that this particular ceremony should not be performed. Other ceremonies, such as a *Simchat Bat* (welcoming a newborn daughter), should instead be used to mark the special status of a new born daughter. [CJLS teshuvah by Rabbi Gerald C. Skolnik, 1993]

The CJLS recently reaffirmed the obligation of Conservative women to observe *niddah* (sexual abstinence during and after menstruation) and *mikvah* (ritual immersion) following menstruation, although somewhat liberalising certain details. Such practices, while requirements of Conservative Judaism, are not to be widely observed among Conservative laity.

Changes in the Conservative Position

Prior to 1973, Conservative Judaism had more limited roles for women and was more similar to current Modern Orthodoxy, with changes on issues including mixed seating, synagogue corporate leadership, and permitting women to be called to the Torah. In 1973, the CJLS of the Rabbinical Assembly voted, without issuing an opinion, that women could count in a *minyan*, although it continued to hold that women could not serve as rabbis or cantors. In 1983, the Jewish Theological Seminary of America (JTSA) faculty voted, also without accompanying opinion, to ordain women as rabbis and as cantors.

In 2002, the CJLS adapted a responsum by Rabbi David Fine, *Women and the Minyan*, which provides an official religious-law foundation for these actions and explains the current Conservative approach to the role of women in prayer.

In 2006, the CJLS adopted three responsa on the subject of *niddah*, which reaffirmed an obligation of Conservative women to abstain from sexual relations during and following menstruation and to immerse in a *mikvah* prior to resumption, while liberalising observance requirements including shortening the length of the niddah period; lifting restrictions on non-sexual contact during niddah, and reducing the circumstances under which spotting and similar conditions would mandate abstinence.

In all cases continuing the Orthodox approach was also upheld as an option. Individual Conservative rabbis and synagogues are not required to adopt any of these changes, and a small number have adopted none of them.

Conservative Approaches to Change

Prior to 1973, Conservative approaches to change were generally on an individual, case-by-case basis. Between 1973 and 2002, the Conservative movement adapted changes through its official organisations, but without issuing explanatory opinions. Since 2002, the Conservative movement has coalesced around a single across-the board approach to the role of women in Jewish law.

In 1973, 1983, and 1993, individual rabbis and professors issued six major opinions which influenced change in the Conservative approach, the first and second Sigal, Blumenthal, Rabinowitz, and Roth responsa, and the Hauptman article. These opinions sought to provide for a wholesale shift in women's public roles through a single, comprehensive legal justification. Most such opinions based their positions on an argument that Jewish women always were, or have become, legally obligated to perform the same *mitzvot* as men and to do so in the same manner.

The first Sigal and the Blumenthal responsa were considered by the CJLS as part of its decision on prayer roles in 1973. They argued that women have always had the same obligations as men. The first Sigal responsum used the Talmud's general prayer obligation and examples of cases in which women were traditionally obligated to say specific prayers and inferred from them a public prayer obligation identical to that of men. The Blumenthal responsum extrapolated from a minority authority that a *minyan* could be formed with nine men and one woman in an emergency. The Committee on Jewish Law and Standards (CJLS) declined to adopt either responsum. Rabbi Siegel reported to the Rabbinical Assembly membership that many on the CJLS, while agreeing with the result, found the arguments unconvincing.

The Rabinowitz, Roth, and second Sigal responsa were considered by the JTSA faculty as part of its decision to ordain women as rabbis in 1983. The Rabbinowitz responsum sidestepped the issue of obligation, arguing that there is no longer a religious need for a community representative in prayer and hence there is no need to decide whether a woman can *halakhically* serve as one. The CJLS felt that an argument potentially undermining the value of community and clergy was unconvincing: "We should not be afraid to recognise that the function of clergy is to help our people connect with the holy." The Roth and second Sigal responsa accepted that time-bound *mitzvot* were traditionally optional for women, but argued that women in modern times could change their traditional roles. The Roth responsum argued that women could individually voluntarily assume the same obligations as men, and that women who do so (e.g. pray three times a day regularly) could count in a *minyan* and serve as agents. The JTSA accordingly required female rabbinical students wishing to train as rabbis to personally obligate themselves, but synagogue rabbis, unwilling to inquire into individual religiosity, found it impractical. The second Sigal responsum called for a *takkanah*, or rabbinical edict, "that would serve as a *halakhic* ERA," overruling all non-egalitarian provisions in law or, in the alternative, a new approach to *halakhic* interpretation independent of legal precedents. The CJLS, unwilling to use either an intrusive approach or a repudiation of the traditional legal process as bases for action, did not adopt either and let the JTS faculty vote stand unexplained.

In 1993, Professor Judith Hauptman of JTS issued an influential paper [9] arguing that women had historically always been obligated in prayer, using more detailed arguments than the Blumenthal and first Sigal responsa. The paper suggested that women who followed traditional practices were failing to meet their obligations. Rabbi Roth argued that Conservative Judaism should think twice before adopting a viewpoint labeling its most traditional and often most committed members as sinners. The issue was again dropped.

In 2002, the CJLS returned to the issue of justifying its actions regarding women's status, and adopted a single authoritative approach, the Fine responsum, as the definitive Conservative halakha on role-of-women issues. This responsum holds that although Jewish women do not traditionally have the same obligations as men, Conservative women have, as a collective whole, voluntarily undertaken them. Because of this collective undertaking, the Fine responsum holds that Conservative women are eligible to serve as agents and decision-makers for others. The Responsum also held that traditionally-minded communities and individual women could opt out without being regarded by the Conservative movement as sinning. By adopting this Responsum, the CJLS found itself in a position to provide a considered Jewish-law justification for its egalitarian practices, without having to rely on potentially unconvincing arguments, undermine the religious importance of community and clergy, ask individual women intrusive questions, repudiate the halakhic tradition, or label women following traditional practices as sinners.

Reform Judaism

Reform Judaism believes in the equality of men and women. The Reform movement rejects the idea that halakha (Jewish law) is the sole legitimate form of Jewish decision making, and holds that Jews can and must consider their conscience and ethical principles inherent in the Jewish tradition when deciding upon a right course of action. There is widespread consensus among Reform Jews that traditional distinctions between the role of men and women are antithetical to the deeper ethical principles of Judaism. This has enabled Reform communities to allow women to perform many rituals traditionally reserved for men, such as:

- Publicly reading the Torah (*ba'al kriah*)
- Being part of the *minyan*
- Being called for an *aliyah* to read the Torah
- Serving as a cantor (*shalich tzibbur*)
- Serving as rabbi and halakhic decisor (*posek*)
- Wearing a *tallit* and *tefillin*

Concerns about intermarriage have also influenced the Reform Jewish position on gender. In 1983, the Central Conference of American Rabbis passed a resolution waiving the need for formal conversion for anyone with at least one Jewish parent who has made affirmative acts of Jewish identity. This departed from the traditional position requiring formal conversion to Judaism for children without a Jewish mother.

The 1983 resolution of the American Reform movement has had a mixed reception to Reform Jewish communities outside of the United States. Most notably, the Israel Movement for Progressive Judaism has rejected patrilineal descent and requires formal conversion for anyone without a Jewish mother.

Reform Approaches to Change

Reform Judaism generally holds that the various differences between the roles of men and women in traditional Jewish law are not relevant to modern conditions and not applicable today. Accordingly, there has been no need to develop legal arguments analogous to those made within the Orthodox and Conservative movements.

Reconstructionist Judaism

The equality of women is a central tenet and hallmark of Reconstructionist Judaism. From the beginning, Reconstructionist Jewish ritual allowed men and women to pray together — a decision based on egalitarian philosophy. The halakhah had to be changed to rid Judaism of these inequities. It was on this basis that Rabbi Mordecai Kaplan called for the full equality of women, despite the obvious difficulties reconciling this stance with norms of traditional

Jewish practice. The Reconstructionist Movement ordained women Rabbi from the start. In 1968, women were accepted into the Reconstructionist Rabbinical College, under the leadership of Ira Eisenstein. The first ordained female Reconstructionist rabbi, Sandy Eisenberg Sasso, served as rabbi of the Manhattan Reconstructionist Congregation in 1976 and gained a pulpit in 1977 at Beth El Zedeck congregation in Indianapolis. Sandy Eisenberg Sasso was accepted without debate or subsequent controversy. In 2005, 24 out of the movement's 106 synagogues in the US had women as senior or assistant rabbis.

The Reconstructionist Community began including women in the minyan and allowing them to come up to the Torah for *aliyot.* They also continued the practice of *bat mitzvah.* But other changes in the role of women, such as serving as witnesses, leading services, public Torah reading, and wearing ritual prayer garments like kippot and tallitot. Reconstructionist women rabbis have been instrumental in the creation of rituals, stories, music, that have begun to give women's experience a voice in Judaism. Most of the focus has been on rituals for life-cycle events. New ceremonies have been created for births, weddings, divorces, conversions, weaning, and the onset of menarche and menopause. The Recontructionist movement as a whole has been committed to creating liturgy that is in consonance with equality ideas and practices and that reflects a new role for women's celebration. Another major step: The Federation of Reconstructionist Congregations has also developed educational Programmes that lead toward the full acceptance of lesbians, as well as rituals that affirm lesbian relationships. In Canada, the reconstructionist Rabbis does officiate at same-sex wedding.

The reconstructionist Judaism will be of big importance for the community implication of her members. Several members of the Reconstructionist community have focused on issues like domestic violence. Others have devoted energy to helping women gain the right of divorce in traditional communities. Many have spoken out for the right of Jewish women to pray aloud and read from the Torah at the Western Wall in Jerusalem, the Women of the Wall group.

When the roles of women in religion change, there may also be changed roles for men. With their advocacy of patrilineal descent in the 1970s, the Reconstructionist Rabbinical Association supported the principle that a man who takes responsibility for raising a Jewish child can pass Judaism on to the next generation as well as a woman. The children who receive a Jewish education are allowed whatever is the sex of their Jewish parent.

Bahá'í Faith and Gender Equality

One of the fundamental teachings of the Bahá'í Faith is that men and women are equal, and that the equality of the sexes is a spiritual and moral standard that is essential for the unification of the planet and the unfoldment of peace.

The Bahá'í teachings note the importance of implementing the principle in individual, family, and community life. While the Bahá'í teachings assert the full spiritual and social equality of women to men, the notion of equality does not imply sameness and there are some aspects of gender distinctiveness or gender differentiation in certain areas of life.

Equality

The equality of men and women is a fundamental Bahá'í principle, that is explicit in the writings of Bahá'u'lláh, the founder of the Bahá'í Faith, and particularly in the writings and discourses of 'Abdu'l-Bahá, his son and chosen interpreter. The teaching and its vision of the community is central to Bahá'í community life as is implemented as a practical level. The Bahá'í teachings state that women are not inferior to men, and should not be subordinate to men in aspects of social life. In the Bahá'í view, women have always been equal to men, and the reason why women have so far not achieved this equality is due to the lack of adequate educational and social opportunities, and because men have used their greater physical strength to prevent women from developing their true potential.

Spiritual Station

Bahá'u'lláh noted that there was no distinction in the spiritual stations of men and women, and that women and men were equal in the sight of God. Bahá'u'lláh wrote:

> Exalted, immensely exalted is He Who hath removed differences and established harmony...[T]he Pen of the Most High hath lifted distinctions from between His servants and handmaidens and ... hath conferred upon all a station and rank on the same plane.

Instead of their gender, Bahá'u'lláh wrote that the spiritual station of each person depends on their recognition and devotion to God. `Abdu'l-Bahá stated that God did not differentiate between people based on gender and that all were made in the image of God. He further stated that both women and men have the same potential for intelligence, virtue and prowess.

Advancement of Humanity and Perquisite to Peace

'Abdu'l-Bahá stated that gender equality was not simply righting historical social injustices against women, but would serve as a key factor in wide-ranging societal changes that would help develop a new civilisation in which more 'feminine' qualities such as tender-heartedness and receptivity would balance previously dominant 'masculine' forces. The Bahá'í writings state that until women are provided equal status to men, humanity cannot advance or progress. 'Abdu'l-Bahá in a series of analogies has compared men and women to the two wings of a bird and the two hands of a human body and stated that both need to be strong to allow for advancement. 'Abdu'l-Baha wrote:

The world of humanity is possessed of two wings: the male and the female. So long as these two wings are not equivalent in strength, the bird will not fly. Until womankind reaches the same degree as man, until she enjoys the same arena of activity, extraordinary attainment for humanity will not be realized; humanity cannot wing its way to heights of real attainment. When the two wings or parts become equivalent in strength, enjoying the same prerogatives, the flight of man will be exceedingly lofty and extraordinary.

Both Bahá'u'lláh and 'Abdu'l-Bahá wrote that an important aspect of world unity will be a greater balance between feminine and masculine influences on society, and stated that because of the greater feminine influence that wars will cease and a permanent peace attained. 'Abdu'l-Bahá wrote that women, as mothers, would be a force in establishing peace as they would oppose sending their children to war. 'Abdu'l-Bahá wrote:

War and its ravages have blighted the world; the education of woman will be a mighty step toward its abolition and ending, for she will use her whole influence against war. Woman rears the child and educates the youth to maturity. She will refuse to give her sons for sacrifice upon the field of battle. In truth, she will be the greatest factor in establishing universal peace and international arbitration. Assuredly, woman will abolish warfare among mankind.

Moojan Momen writes that the goal of achieving equality of women and men in the Bahá'í Faith does not amount to bringing women into power in masculine roles, but instead a more radical change to the very nature of society, to make feminine qualities more valued.

Education of Women

In the Bahá'í view, women have always been equal to men, and the reason why women have as of yet not achieved this equality is because of the lack of adequate educational and social opportunities. Thus, Bahá'í teachings stress the need for women's education, not only as a means to increase opportunity for women to help achieve equality, but also since the education of mothers is essential to the proper upbringing of children. Because of the importance of the education of women, the education of daughters takes precedence over that of sons when financial resources do not exist to educate all of their children. Despite the linkage between motherhood and education, 'Abdu'l-Bahá encouraged women to excel in arts and sciences, and stated that women's participation in the political sphere would be a prerequisite for peace.

Historical Women Figures in Bahá'í History

There have been a large number of women heroines who are celebrated in the history of the Bahá'í Faith including Táhirih, Navváb, Queen Marie, Bahíyyih Khánum, Martha Root, Lidia Zamenhof, and many others.

Táhirih

Táhirih was an influential poet and follower of the Bábí faith, the predecessor to the Bahá'í Faith, and often mentioned in Bahá'í literature as an example of couragc in the struggle for women's rights. While the writings of Táhirih do not address the issue of women's rights precisely, Tahirih experienced the Báb's revelation as liberating, and broke with Islamic practices that were expected of women, such as appearing in public without a veil. Her actions which were out of norm caused controversy in the community and some saw her as scandalous or unchaste. To combat the attitudes of the community against Táhirih, the Báb gave her the title Táhirih, meaning the "pure." One of her most notable quotes is her final utterance in 1852, "You can kill me as soon as you like, but you cannot stop the emancipation of women."

Bahíyyih Khánum

Bahíyyih Khánum was born in 1846 and was the eldest daughter of Bahá'u'lláh and Ásíyih Khánum. She was entitled *the Greatest holy Leaf.* Ṣhe was particularly dear to her father and is seen within the Bahá'í Faith as one of the greatest women to have lived. During World War I, she distributed food, clothing and medical aid to the local population suffering from starvation. After the death of `Abdu'l-Bahá, Shoghi Effendi, was named the head of the religion, but he was distraught with the passing of his grandfather and so went into meditation for a period of time. During that time Bahíyyih Khánum assumed the role of acting leader of the Bahá'í Faith, which was a rare position for a woman to be in at that time. She was entrusted as head of the religion when Shoghi Effendi was absent from the Bahá'í World Centre in Haifa. She died on 15 July 1932 was buried in the Bahá'í gardens below the Bahá'í Arc on Mount Carmel; the Monument of the Greatest Holy Leaf was built in her memory at the Bahá'í World Centre.

Serving in Administration

In terms of Bahá'í administration, all positions except for membership on the Universal House of Justice are open to men and women. No specific reason has been given for this exception, but 'Abdu'l-Bahá has stated that there is a wisdom for it, which would eventually become clear. The only other field where `Abdu'l-Baha did not extend full and equal participation to women was in military endeavours, since he regarded the taking of human life incompatible with women's role as mothers.

There are two branches of Bahá'í administration - appointed and elected.

Appointed

Hands of the Cause

Hands of the Cause were a select group of Bahá'ís, appointed for life, whose main function was to propagate and protect the Bahá'í Faith. Unlike the members of the elected institutions and other appointed institutions in the Bahá'í Faith, who serve in those offices, these are considered to have demonstrated sincerity and praiseworthy morals and qualities and achieved a distinguished rank in service to the religion and an overall station above a National Spiritual Assembly. as well as individual members of the Universal House of Justice - indeed it is the highest station that could be achieved open to anyone in the religion. The title is no longer given out. The work of the Hands of the Cause is now carried out by the Continental Counsellors and the Auxiliary Boards.

Eight out of the fifty known Hands of the Cause were women (in order of appointment):

- Keith Ransom-Kehler (1876-1933) (singled out as the first woman Hand of the Cause and first American martyr).
- Martha Root (1872-1939) (singled out as the foremost Hand of the Cause of the first Bahá'í century and the "first finest fruit" of the Formative Age.)
- Dorothy Beecher Baker (1898–1954)
- Amelia Engelder Collins (1873–1962)
- Clara Dunn (1869–1960)
- Corinne Knight True (1861–1961)
- Rúhíyyih Khánum (1910–2000)
- Agnes Baldwin Alexander (1875–1971)

During the period between the death of Shoghi Effendi and the election of the Universal House of Justice the Hands of the Cause held a convocation from which they constituted a body of nine from among their number to serve in the Holy Land and to act as Custodians of the Bahá'í Faith, a body which functioned without officers and with a quorum of five, whose duties included taking care of Bahá'í World Center properties and other assets; corresponding with and advising National and Regional Spiritual Assemblies; acting on behalf of the Bahá'í Faith for its protection; and maintaining close contact with the rest of the Hands, who would henceforth devote their time to the successful completion of the goals of the Ten Year Crusade. The Hands of the Cause maintained the number of Custodians, replacing those who died or were unable, for health or personal reasons, to remain at the Bahá'í World Center permanently. Of these nine, two women served as Custodians: Amelia Collins and Rúhíyyih Khánum.

International Bahá'í Council

The International Bahá'í Council was a precursor to the Universal House of Justice, which replaced it in 1963. In March 1951 Shoghi Effendi began appointing its membership and in 1961 elections were held (and once elections were the rule, Hands of the Cause were exempted from being members.) The women members of the International Bahá'í Council, and their dates of their service were:

- Rúhíyyih Khanum (1951–61) Liaison with Shoghi Effendi; Hands of the Cause of God.
- Amelia Collins (1951–61) Vice president; Hands of the Cause.
- Jessie Revell (1951–63) Treasurer.
- Ethel Revell (1951–63) Western Assistant Secretary.
- Gladys Weeden (1951–52).
- Sylvia Ioas (1955–61).
- Mildred Mottahedeh (1961–63).

Continental Councellors

After the election of the Universal House of Justice, Boards of Counsellors were created in 1973 by appointment who outrank the national assemblies, though individually Counsellors ranked lower than that of the Hands of the Cause. There are 90 counsellors - 81 serving on continental boards and 9 serving at the International Teaching Center. From a picture of a gathering of all Counsellors in 2005 a number of them are clearly women. The number of members of the International Teaching Center have varied. Initially, excluding the Hands of the Cause (all of whom were initial members), there were three, in 1979 they were four, seven in 1983, and nine in 1988 with a quorum of five present at the Baha'i World Center. Not counting the Hands of the Cause, the women and their years of service are:

- Florence Mayberry (1973–1983)
- Anneliese Bopp (1979–1988)
- Dr. Magdalene Carney (1983–1991)
- Isobel Sabri (1983–1992)
- Lauretta King (1988–2003)
- Joy Stevenson (1988–1998)
- Joan Lincoln (1993–)
- Kimiko Schwerin (1993–1998)
- Violette Haake (1998-2008)
- Dr. Penny Walker (1998-)
- Zenaida Ramirez (2000-)
- Rachel Ndegwa (2003-)
- Uransaikhan Baatar (2008-)

Elected

Women serve on National Assemblies. Bahá'í elections are secret ballots and electees are chosen without running for office on plurality up to the number of members of the institution. That women could be elected was in development by 1909 when the Baha'i temple unity executive board was elected in the United States. Of the nine members chosen, three were women, with Corinne True (later appointed as a Hand of the Cause) serving as an officer. The all-male administrative bodies finally were completely dissolved by 'Abdu'l-Bahá in his visit to America in 1912. By 1925 the executive board evolved into the National Spiritual Assembly of the Baha'is of the United States and Canada. There were specific developments in the eastern Bahá'í communities in 1951. At this time women were allowed to be and were elected according to the rules of Bahá'í administration to local assemblies of the Bahá'í Faith in Egypt. (indeed some were elected officers in 1952.) However, as late as the 1970s one observer could only count two women delegates out of the more than one hundred attending the national Baha'i convention in Teheran. Yet when the members of the National Spiritual Assembly of the Baha'is of Iran were arrested and executed in 1981, the chairperson was a woman, Zhinus Mahmudi. However a statistical review across continents and for the Baha'is world population shows a general upward track of women being elected to national assemblies:

For one comparison note that in 1989 Mikhail Gorbachev abandoned the quota for female representation in the Supreme Soviet and the proportion of women immediately fell from 1/3 to 15 per cent. And more women than ever before served in US Congress in 2009 - 74 women out of 435 (17 per cent) in the House and 17 out of 100 in the Senate. In Canada women in parliament in 2004 were 24.7 per cent of the members. In 2010 the world average for members of parliaments was 19 per cent though regional averages varied from 23 per cent to 9 per cent.

Social or Professionally Notable Bahá'í Women

Some more recent socially or professionally notable women Bahá'ís include:

- Zhang Xin
- Dorothy Wright Nelson
- Zia Mody
- Mona Mahmudnizhad
- Helen Elsie Austin
- Patricia Locke

Social Initiatives

The Bahá'í Faith's emphasis is on male-female equality and thus the Bahá'í Faith actively promotes a number of Programmes with the aim of the advancement of women with greater access for women to health, education, child-care, and business opportunities. In the early 1900s Bahá'í women became active in seeking advancement and were encouraged by 'Abdu'l-Baha and were thus able to gain a position of equality in Bahá'í administration. In Iran, education for girls was started by a Bahá'ís leading to the eventual establishment in 1910 of the *Tarbiyat School for Girls* which helped train the first generation of Iranian professional women. By the 1970s, while the majority of Iranian women were illiterate, most Bahá'í women could read and write.

Since the International Women's Year in 1975, the Universal House of Justice, the governing body of the Bahá'ís, has repeatedly called national Bahá'í communities to promote the equal participation of women in Bahá'í activities. In 1993, the Bahá'í International Community established the *Office of the Advancement of Women* in New York at the United Nations, and various national communities have also created their own offices. Activities in these programmes include the promotion of girls' education, literacy, rural health care, and income-generating skills.

The Bahá'í-inspired Tahirih Justice Center and the Barli Vocational Institute for Rural Women in Indore in India are projects that have received particular attention. Layli Miller-Muro founded the Tahirih Justice Center in 1997 following a well-publicized asylum case in which she was involved as a student attorney. Miller-Muro later co-wrote a book with the client she had aided and used her portion of the proceeds for the initial funding of Tahirih. As of 2003, the organisation had assisted more than 4,000 women and children fleeing from a wide variety of abuses. The Barli Vocational Institute for Rural Women was founded in 1985 in India and offers a six-month programme for tribal women at its facilities in the Indian state of Madhya Pradesh. Through June 1996, a total of 769 rural tribal women have been trained at the Institute; the women came from 119 villages, and after returning home to their cities or villages 45 per cent of them established small businesses, 62 per cent are functionally literate or semi-literate (which has motivated people to send their children to school), 42 per cent have started growing vegetables, 97 per cent are using safe drinking water, all the former trainees and many of their male relatives have given up drinking alcohol, and caste prejudices have been eliminated.

Distinction

While the Bahá'í teachings assert the full spiritual and social equality of women to men, there are some aspects of gender distinctiveness or gender differentiation in certain areas of life. One of these aspects relate to biological fact of potential motherhood for women, and thus the Bahá'í teaching that girls should be given priority in education as they potentially would be the children's first educator. In the same sense, the Bahá'í view of family life gives the right to the mother to be supported by the husband if needed. Similarly, the differences in the provisions of the *Kitáb-i-Aqdas*, Bahá'u'lláh's book of laws, where in the case of intestacy it provides slightly more inheritance to men than women, can be seen in the same light.

While most of the teachings and laws of the Bahá'í Faith between a man and a woman apply *mutatis mutandis* as between a woman and a man, there are some Bahá'í teachings or laws that provide preference to women or men. Menstruating women are exempt from saying the obligatory prayer and from fasting due to biological differences; these exemptions are not compulsory and do not reflect any concepts of ritual impurity. Women also do not have the obligation of making pilgrimage, although they can if they choose; men who are financially able to do so are obliged to make the pilgrimage. In terms of Bahá'í administration, all positions except for membership on the Universal House of Justice are open to men and women. No specific reason has been given for this exception, but 'Abdu'l-Bahá has stated that there is a wisdom for it, which would eventually become clear.

'Abdu'l-Bahá implies that women will become equal in "sciences and arts, in virtues and perfections", and are actually superior in "tenderness of heart and the abundance of mercy and sympathy" - virtues identified as gaining ascendancy as the world becomes more permeated with feminine ideals to balance the masculine ideals that now dominate.

7

Language and Gender Neutrality: An Analysis

Gender-neutral Language

Gender-neutral language, gender-inclusive language, inclusive language, or gender neutrality is linguistic prescriptivism that aims to eliminate (or neutralise) reference to gender in terms that describe people. For example, the words chairman, fireman, lesbian, and stewardess are gender-specific; the corresponding gender-neutral terms are chairperson (or chair), firefighter, homosexual, and flight attendant. The pronoun he may be replaced with he or she or s/he when the gender of the person referred to is unknown. Other gender-specific terms, such as actor and actress may be replaced by the originally male term (actor used for either gender). "Gender-neutral language" should not be confused with genderless language, which refers to languages without grammatical gender. Advocates of gender-neutral language believe it promotes inclusion of all sexes or genders (gender-inclusive language), and that traditional terms are sexist. Opponents may consider the traditional terms to be non-sexist (e.g., "steward" and "stewardess" as distinct but equal terms) or may accept the pronoun "he" as a generic for both genders. Various forms of gender-neutral language became a common feature in written and spoken versions of many languages in the late twentieth century. Feminists argue that previously the practice of assigning masculine gender to generic antecedents stemmed from language reflecting "the prejudices of the society in which it evolved, and English evolved through most of its history in a male-centered, patriarchal society. Various languages employ different means to achieve gender neutrality. See the following articles for specific discussions:

- Gender neutrality in English
- Gender-neutrality in languages with grammatical gender
- Gender-neutrality in genderless languages

A distinct issue arises in Japanese – the Japanese language does not have grammatical gender, but the speech of men and women differ – see gender differences in spoken Japanese. In this context, gender-neutrality refers to eliminating these differences from the language – for men and women to speak the same. This characteristic of Japanese is unusual among major languages – while intonation differs between men and women in many languages, use of distinctly different grammar and vocabulary is unusual.

Genderless Language

A genderless language is a natural or constructed human language that has no category of grammatical gender. Some linguists use the term "noun class" to be a broader categorisation which includes the categorisation by gender as a special case. The notion of "genderless language" must not be confused with that of gender-neutral language. Also, a discourse in a genderless language is not necessarily gender-neutral, although genderless languages exclude many possibilities to gender-related stereotypes, such as using masculine pronouns when referring to persons by their occupations. Genderless languages do have various means to recognise gender, such as gender-specific words, ("she", "mother", "son", etc.), as well as gender-specific context, both biological and cultural. Genderless languages are listed in Noun class: languages without noun classes or grammatical genders.

Gender-neutrality in Genderless Languages

Gender neutrality in genderless languages is typically achieved by using gender-inclusive words ("human being", "person", "businessperson", and so on) instead of gender-specific ones ("man", "he", "businessman", etc.) when one speaks of people whose gender is unknown, ambiguous, or unimportant. When only a gender-specific word happens to be available, a gender-inclusive neologism may be coined to replace it.

Finno-Ugric Languages

Estonian

Estonian word *ta* (or *tema*) is gender-neutral and means both "she" and "he". The suffix *-tar* or *-nna* can be added to the end of some words (mostly professions) to make them feminine, although these nouns are in their basic form gender-neutral: *laulja* (singer), *lauljatar* (female singer) or *lauljanna* (female singer); *näitleja* (actor) - *näitlejanna* (actress) or *näitlejatar* (actress).

This is rather common. Also, for instance, there are separate words for chairman: *esimees* (chairman) and *esinaine* (chairwoman), although the first form is used a lot more often. Most of the professions are gender-neutral: *politseinik* (policeman or woman), *arst* (doctor), *müüja* (salesman or woman), *õpetaja* (teacher), *sõdur* (soldier), *ehitaja* (builder), even *lüpsja* (milkmaid, male or female). A well-known exception is *med. õde* (nurse, literally "med[ical] sister"). Some words are clearly masculine or feminine. For example, in Estonian there is no "Motherland", there is only a "Fatherland" (*isamaa*) and a "Homeland" (*kodumaa*). There is also only a "mother" (native) tongue (*emakeel*). A very popular Estonian saying is *"Kes ees, see mees"* — "The first one is the man".

Finnish

Finnish has only gender-neutral pronouns and completely lacks grammatical gender. The word *hän* is gender-neutral and means both "she" and "he". The suffix *-tar* or *-tär* can be added to some words (mostly professions) to make them feminine if required, for example *näyttelijä* (actor), *näyttelijätär* (actress), but these forms are not commonly used any more; using the basic word for both genders (*näyttelijä* for male and female actors) is the norm. There are also some professions or expressions of which the word *mies* (man) is an integral part, for example, *puhemies*, meaning chairman; *palomies*, fireman, etc. These are mostly retained in their traditional forms, unless a suitable gender-free word is easily available. As a special case the chairperson of the Finnish Parliament is referred as *puhemies* irrespective of the actual gender — either *herra puhemies* (Mr. Chairman) or *rouva puhemies* (Mrs. or Madame Chairman). Despite having gender-neutral pronouns, Finnish is similar to most other Western languages in favoring gender-biased adjectives due to social values. As an example, in the first few years after women were permitted to serve as volunteers in the Finnish armed forces, they were required to swear to defend the country in a manly way (*miehuullisesti*).

Hungarian

Hungarian does not have gender-specific pronouns and lacks grammatical gender: referring to a gender needs explicit statement of "the man" (he) or "the woman" (she). The third person singular pronoun ö means "he/she" and *ök* means "they". Hungarian does distinguish persons from things, as the latter are referred to as *az* (it) or *azok* (those).

However there is a way to distinguish between male and female persons having a certain profession by adding *-nö* "woman" to the end of the word: *színész-színésznö* (actor-actress, lit. "actorwoman") or *rendör-rendörnö* (lit. policeman-policewoman). This though does not work with all the professions as quite many would sound very awkward, like *postás* meaning "letter carrier", lit. "someone associated with the post", so that there is no such thing as *postásnö* (mailwoman). This usage has been criticised by Hungarian feminists, as it implies that the normal word or profession is masculine in nature and must only be qualified if a woman is performing it.

Indo-Iranian Languages

Persian

Among all Iranians languages only Kurdish and Zazaki have got feminine/masculine/neutral genders. All other Iranians languages like Persian, Afganian, Darian... are genderless. Persian is a genderless language. For both males and females, the same nouns, pronouns, and adjectives are used. For example,

- *oo* is used for both "he" and "she";
- *aan* is used for "it" as in English.

In Persian, the same nouns are used for male and female professionals. For example: *baazigar* means both actor and actress. *Pish khedmat* might mean waiter or waitress. The noun suffix *-ash* serves either as a possessive adjective or an object pronoun for both males and females as well as things, situations, etc. For example,

ketaabash means "her/his book";

paayash means "its/her/his leg";

Oo labash raa boosid means "He kissed her lips" or "she kissed his lips" or "he kissed his lips" or "she kissed her lips" or if we consider *-ash* as an object pronoun we can translate the sentence as "he/she kissed her/him on the lips".

Bengali

In Bengali, although there are different nouns for professions, but they are not commonly used, so the language has consequently become gender-neutral. In addition, objects, pronouns and almost all adjectives are gender-neutral.

Other Natural Languages

Basque

The Basque language is largely gender-free. Most nouns have no gender, though there are different words for males and females in some cases (*ama*, "mother"; *aita*, "father"; *aita-ama*, "father and mother"; *guraso*, "parent"). Some words take suffixes according to gender (*aktore*, "actor"; *aktoresa*, "actress"), but they are rare, and both purists who avoid Romance influences and the Basque Institute of the Woman recommend against it. For animals, there are particles (*oilo*, "hen"; *oilar*, "cock"; *hartz eme*, "female bear"; *hartz arra*, "male bear") or different words (*behi*, "cow"; *zezen*, "bull").

While there are no gender-specific pronouns, Basque verbs can agree allocutively with the gender in the intimate singular second person (this provides no information since the listener already knows his or her gender): *hik duk*, "you (male) have it"; *hik dun*, "you (female) have it". The verb is marked for addressee's gender, if they are intimate singular, whether or not they are referred to in the clause. Non-sexism supporters propose substituting those forms by the more formal ones: *zuk duzu* "you have it". In earlier stages, the relation between *hik* and *zuk* was like that of *you* and *thou* in early modern English. Some Basque dialects already avoid *hik* as too disrespectful.

Chinese

The Chinese language or languages/topolects are largely gender-neutral, and possess few linguistic gender markers, even though the Chinese society has historically been shown to have significant degree of male dominance in the social structure as well as education and literature.

Comprehension of written and spoken Chinese is almost wholly dependent on word order, as it has no inflections for gender, tense, or case. There are also very few derivational inflection; instead, the language relies heavily on compounding to create new words. A Chinese word is thus inherently gender-neutral, but any given word can be preceded by an adjective/ root indicating masculinity or femininity. For example, the word for "doctor" is *yīshēng* and can only be made gender-specific by adding the root for "male" or "female" to the front of it; thus to specify a male doctor, one would need to prefix *nán* (male), as in *nányīshēng*. Under normal circumstances both male and female doctors would simply be referred to as *yīshēng*.

Spoken Mandarin Chinese also has only one third-person pronoun, *tā* for all referents (though *-men* can be added as a plural suffix). *Tā* can mean "he", "she", or "it". However, the different meanings of *tā* are written with different characters: containing the human radical, from meaning person, for he or a person of undetermined gender; containing the feminine radical, for "she"; and for "it".

The character for "she", containing the "woman" radical (glyphic element of a character's composition), was invented in the late nineteenth or early twentieth century due to western influence; prior to this, the character indicating "he" today was used for both genders — it contains the "person" radical, which, as noted above, is not gender-specific (likewise there exists a written feminine form for "you", which is almost never used).

In written Cantonese, the third-person singular pronoun is *keui*, written as ; it may be used to refer to people of either gender. The practice of replacing the radical with (forming the character) to specifically indicate the female gender may also be seen occasionally in informal writing; however, this is neither widely accepted nor grammatically or semantically required, and the character has a separate meaning in standard Chinese.

Japanese

Japanese has no grammatical gender or number. Thus, *isha* can mean one or many male doctors, one or many female doctors, or many male and female doctors. Another example of the lack of European-style gender in this language is the using of compound characters. The *sha* in *geisha* (art person) and the *ja* in *ninja* (sneaking person) are the same character. Pronouns are generally avoided unless the meaning is unclear.

The plural of *kare*, *karera*, may also refer to groups of females, and is preferable to the rather demeaning *kanojo-tachi* (those women). Gender neutral language modification advocates suggest avoiding *karera* by instead using "those people" (*ano hito-tachi*), which they praise as gender neutral, grammatical and natural-sounding. However, until the Meiji Restoration in the 19th century, *kare* was used for both genders; *kanojo* meant "girlfriend", as it still does.

In general, Japanese, unlike most European languages, has no grammatical gender, although certain words and expressions *semantically* refer specifically to males or specifically to females (such as *haha* "mother", *bijin* "beautiful woman"). However, the language spoken by Japanese women is markedly different from the speech of Japanese men in terms of vocabulary, use of grammar and idioms, pronunciation, etc.

An increasing number of Japanese avoid the traditional common terms for "[your] wife" (*okusan*) and "[your] husband" (*goshujin*), which literally mean "the person inside" and "the master". Japanese custom has also dictated that women be expected to use a polite form of language (*keigo*) in more situations than men. This expectation has diminished more among urban young female Japanese in the past decade.

The major issues with regard to gendered language in Japanese are overall speech patterns. There exists a "woman's language" (*onna kotoba*). Women's speech has different sentence endings than that of men, especially in non-polite speech. (Polite speech tends to be less differentiated, with male speech becoming more similar to female). A good example is the gender-neutral use of *watashi* or *watakushi* for "I" in polite speech. In informal speech, women are still more likely to use *watashi* or *atashi*, while men use *boku*, *ore* or *washi*. Women's speech is characterized by sentences ending with *wa* (rising intonation) and by dropping the verbs *da* or *desu* (meaning "is"). Male speech never drops the word *da* in a sentence. The differences are quite intricate, but very persistent, and there is little or no movement in Japan to change male/female speech patterns, since changes can sound awkward or confusing. However, some historians note that over time Japanese usage as a whole is shifting toward the feminine forms. Before recent times, men never used words like *kane* ("money") with the honorific prefix *o*-. Today *okane* is standard Japanese and is used by men in non-polite situations, something unthinkable a hundred years ago.

Korean

Korean, like a few other East Asian languages such as Japanese, does not use pronouns in everyday language, relying on context to clarify the intended meaning. In case of confusion, there are pronouns to clarify the position, but normally the actual subject (person) is named rather than the pronoun. As for job titles, these are not gender-specific. Again, the meaning is normally clear in the context.

Malay

As an Austronesian language, Malay is fundamentally gender-neutral. The third-person singular pronoun *dia* can 'he', 'she' or sometimes 'it', and the object/possessive suffix *-nya* can mean 'him/his', 'her' or 'it/its'. For example, *dia mencintainya* means 'he/she loves him/her/it'.

Most nouns that refer to people are also gender-neutral, and need to be qualified when gender is to be expressed. For example, *budak* means 'child', and is used far more frequently than the gender-specific phrases *budak perempuan*, 'female child' and so 'girl' and *budak lelaki*, 'male child' and so 'boy'. Likewise, the words *doktor* ('doctor'), *pelayan* ('waiter') and most other nouns that are attributable to people are gender-neutral, and need to be modified by the adjectives *perempuan* or *lelaki* to become engendered (for animals, the adjectives *betina* and *jantan* are used instead; a *harimau betina* is a 'tigress'). However, Malay vocabulary has many nouns borrowed from Arabic and Sanskrit that do indicate gender. For example, an Islamic religious teacher is either an *ustaz* (male) or an *ustazah* (female), and a noble person is either a *puteri* ('princess') or a *putera* ('prince'), as used in the legal ethnic classification Bumiputera.

Quechuan

Quechuan languages, spoken in the central Andes, are agglutinative using only suffixes, but have no gender suffix.

With the exception of *mama* and *tata*, and *wallpa* and *k'anka* (hen and rooster), no nouns are gender-specific. In Southern Quechuan, *qhari* (man) and *warmi* (woman) are very seldom used along with a noun referring to a person, as in *warmi wawa* and *qhari wawa* for daughter and son. For animals *urqu* and *china* serve the same purpose, as in *urqu khuchi* and *china khuchi* for pig and sow.

No pronouns distinguish gender, the third singular *pay* being he/she/it.

Tagalog

Tagalog, like other Austronesian languages, is gender-neutral; pronouns do not even have specific genders.

However, because Tagalog has had over three centuries of Spanish influence, gender is usually differentiated in certain Spanish loanwords by way of the suffixes *-o* (masculine) and *-a* (feminine). These words mostly refer to ethnicities, occupations, and family. Some examples are: *Pilipino/Pilipina* (Filipino/a), *Pinoy/Pinay* (nickname for a Filipino person), *tindero/tindera* (vendor), *inhinyero/inhinyera* (engineer), *tito/tita* (uncle/aunt), *manong/manang* (elder brother/sister), and *lolo/lola* (grandfather/grandmother).

Dravidian Languages

Dravidian languages have a gender-neutral form for the third-person plural, which is also used for the third-person singular in all formal communication. Most job titles are derived from this form as they are mostly used in a formal context. They are thus gender-free. It is commonly used to address also, people of higher status, age or stature.

Turkish

Turkish is a gender neutral language, like most other Turkic languages. Nouns have a generic form and this generic form is used for both males and females. For example, *doktor* (doctor), *eczacı* (pharmacist), *mühendis* (engineer) etc. Very few words for person reference contain a clue to the gender of the referred person, such as *anne/baba* "mother/father", *kız/oğlan* "girl/boy", *hanım/bey* "lady/sir".

The Turkish equivalent to "he", "she", and "it" is *o*. For example:

O, gece yürümeyi çok seviyor — *He/she/it likes to walk at night.*

Onu çok seviyorum — *I love him/her/it so much.*

There are a few exceptions, where it is mandatory to provide gender (because of a word's foreign origin):

iş + adam + ı = işadamı — *business + man = businessman.*

iş + kadın + ı = işkadını — *business + woman = businesswoman.*

Very minor exceptions were constructed from native Turkish words after the 1900s:

bilim + adam + ı = bilim adamı — *science + man = male scientist.*

bilim + kadın + ı = bilim kadını — *science + woman = female scientist.*

However, there is an alternative gender neutral use for words like these, which has become more popular in the 2000s:

bilim + insan + ı = bilim insanı — *science + person = scientist.*

At the same time research has shown a significant presence of semantically-implied genderness (covert gender) in Turkish. In addition to the absence of semantic gender neutrality it was also noted that the usage of gender markings in Turkish is asymmetrical. In translations of sentences from English texts where the gender is evident (e.g., usage of he/she or male vs. female context, such as police job vs. pregnancy, etc.) it was noticed that feminine gender was marked in 50 per cent of cases, while masculine was marked only in 5 per cent of cases. While translations is not a typical representative of linguistic data, similar asymmetry was also observed in Turkish literary and newspaper texts.

Constructed Languages

Ido

In Ido, only two couples of nouns are gender-specific: *viro-muliero* (man-woman) and *patro-matro* (father-mother). Other nouns referring to people, and all nouns referring to animals can equally be used to refer to a male or female: *doktoro* (a doctor), *frato* (a brother or a sister, i.e.: a sibling), *hundo* (a dog). And even the two pairs of words above have related nouns that are ambiguous about gender: *homo* (a human being), *adulto* (an adult person), *genitoro* (a parent).

When it is necessary to specify the gender, the suffixes *-in* for females, and *-ul* for males is inserted right before the final *-o* of any noun referring to either human beings or animals. Thus, from *frato* (sibling) the words *fratino* (a sister) and *fratulo* (a brother) can be obtained. However these forms are to be used only if the gender is relevant for the context, as in the following examples:

- *El esas mea sola fratino.* (She is my only sister, implying I may have brothers)
- *El esas mea sola frato.* (She is my only sibling)
- *Me ne prizas doktorini.* (I don't like female doctors, implying I prefer male doctors)
- *Me ne prizas doktori.* (I don't like doctors, male or female)

As for pronouns, they are not gender-specific in the first or second persons, singular and plural. In the third person singular, there are four pronouns (the U between brackets can be used or left out, mostly according to personal choice): *il*(*u*) (he), *el*(*u*) (she), *ol*(*u*) (it, when it refers back to an actual inanimate noun, and not in sentences as "It's raining"), and additionally *lu*, which can be used instead of any of the other three pronouns, whether it be for stylistic purposes, personal choice, or to refer to an indefinite being (usually human or animal) that can be thought of indifferently as male or female. For example:

Mea kapo doloras. Me advokos doktoro e lu decidez quon me agos (My head aches. I'll call a doctor, so he/she decides what I'll do)

Since I don't know whether a male or female doctor will come, I cannot use here *il*(*u*) or *el*(*u*). And I definitely cannot use *ol*(*u*) since I know for a fact that the doctor who comes is going to be a human being.

Now if instead of "a" doctor, I decided to call "my" doctor (therefore, knowing whether it will be a man or a woman), I could use any of the following:

1. **Mea kapo doloras. Me advokos mea doktoro ed il decidez quon me agos** (My head aches. I'll call my doctor, so he decides what I'll do)
2. **Mea kapo doloras. Me advokos mea doktoro ed el decidez quon me agos** (My head aches. I'll call my doctor, so she decides what I'll do)
3. **Mea kapo doloras. Me advokos mea doktoro e lu decidez quon me agos** (My head aches. I'll call my doctor, so he/she decides what I'll do)

In sentence number 1, the doctor is a man, so the masculine pronoun is used. In sentence number 2, the doctor is a woman, so the noun is referred back with a feminine pronoun. But in sentence number 3, even though I know if the doctor is a man or a woman, it is perfectly possible to still dodge the definition by using the always available gender-neutral pronoun *lu*. Notice however that **doktoro** is never marked for gender in these sentences, since the doctor will be called in his/her professional capacity, and not for being a man or a woman. Actually, saying *Me advokos mea doktorino* (or *mea doktorulo*) implies I have a choice between a male and a female doctor, and I have decided on either of them.

In the third person plural, all of these pronouns have a correlative: *ili*, *eli*, and *oli* (only if a group of men, women or inanimate things or concepts respectively is referred). And *li* if no gender-specificity is required or even possible (for example, if the pronoun refers to a group including both men and women). In practice, the first three pronouns are usually avoided unless a point wants to be made as to the gender of the people referred, or in complex sentences, where gender information is given to clarify the meaning. For example:

La matri e sua filii recevis la premio quan ***eli*** *decidis*. ("The mothers and their children received the prize they -i.e.: the mothers, not the children-decided", provided that the children are not all girls).

Me pruntis ta libri de mea amiki, e nun me ne povas trovar ***oli*** ("I borrowed those books from my friends, and now I can't find them *-i.e.:* the books, not the friends who are not inanimate beings that can be referred back with oli").

Lingua Franca Nova

Lingua Franca Nova completely lacks grammatical gender. The word *el* means "she", "he", and "it". If gender is significant, one may use words such as *la fem, la om, la xica, la xico,* etc. (the woman, the man, the girl, the boy).

In place of "it", one can use words such as *la cosa, la idea, esta, acel,* etc. (the thing, the idea, this, that).

Terms for various professions are gender neutral, as are terms for animals. If need be, *mas* o *fema* can be used as adjectives for "male" and "female", respectively. Certain traditional roles have *-esa* for the female, such as *prinsesa, contesa,* etc. Most family terms distinguish male and female by varying the final vowel, such as *tia/tio, fia/fio, ava/avo* etc. (aunt/uncle, daughter/son, grandmother/grandfather). Only *madre/padre* and *sore/frate* (mother/father, sister/brother) use distinct terms.

Gender-neutrality in Languages with Grammatical Gender

Gender neutrality in languages with grammatical gender implies promoting language usage which is balanced in its treatment of the genders. For example, advocates of gender-neutral language challenge the traditional use of masculine nouns and pronouns ("man", "businessman", "he", and so on) when referring to both genders or to a person or people of an unknown gender in most Indo-European and Afro-Asiatic languages.

Overview

The situation of gender neutral language modification in languages that have masculine and feminine grammatical genders, such as French, German, and Spanish, is very different from that of English, because it is often impossible to construct a gender-neutral sentence as can be done in English. For example, in French, the masculine gender supersedes the feminine; the phrase la femme et l'homme (the woman and the man) is replaced by the pronoun ils (they [masculine]). Accordingly, language modification advocates have focused much of their attention on issues such as job titles. Due to the presence of grammatical gender, their immediate goal in this case is often the exact opposite of that in English: creating feminine job titles rather than eliminating them. As such, "gender-inclusiveness" does not necessarily mean eliminating gender, but rather a use of language which they feel is balanced in its treatment of the two genders. For example, they feel that it is insulting to use the masculine gender for a female professional, for example calling a woman le médecin (the [male] doctor). They feel this would imply that women change gender or became somehow more manly when they went to work. The creation of new job titles for women is often less controversial than language modifications proposed by advocates of gender-neutral language for English, as it is often seen simply as a natural evolution as women have entered more professions. At the same time, the newer feminine forms in most such languages are usually derived from the primary masculine term by adding or changing a suffix (such as the German Ingenieurin from Ingenieur, engineer), so some feminists hold that these words are not equivalent to the masculine words because they are secondary forms. Others object to the perceived clumsiness of such neologisms. Citing German as an example, almost all the names for female professionals end in -in, and because of the suffix none can consist of a single syllable as many masculine job titles do (such as Arzt, doctor). A further complication is that the creation of distinctly different job titles for men and women means that in writing about hypothetical people of undetermined sex, both words must be mentioned each time, which can become quite cumbersome. In languages where the gender of a noun also affects the formation of other words in a sentence, such as gender-marked adjectives, pronouns, or verbs, this can lead to repetitive or complicated sentences if both terms are used, as the sentence must essentially be repeated twice. But in some languages, for example in Spanish, there have also been campaigns against the traditional use of the masculine gender to refer to mixed gender groups. Advocates of these changes feel that they are necessary in order for the language to not further the subordination of women. These modification efforts have been much more controversial. In addition to the sorts of conflict seen in the English-speaking world, some opponents of these changes see them as examples of cultural imperialism, or the exporting of Anglo-Saxon ideas and standards. English had already naturally lost most of its gender well before the beginning of the feminist movement, making a gender-neutral modification of the language much more feasible.

Hebrew

In Hebrew, which has a high degree of grammatical gender, virtually every noun (as well as most verbs and pronouns of the second and third person) is either grammatically masculine or feminine. As a result of campaigns by advocates for employment equality or gender neutral language modification, laws have been passed in Israel that require job ads to be written in a form which explicitly proclaims that the job is offered for both males and females. The separator "/" is often used, for example *dru'shim/ot, maz'kir/a.*

Note that certain feminine plural verb forms of earlier Hebrew have become archaic in modern Israeli Hebrew, so that the old masculine plural forms are now used for both masculine and feminine.

Germanic Languages

German

German has four third-person nominative singular pronouns: *er* (male), *sie* (female), *es* (neuter) and *man* (impersonal). *Man* is frequently used in general statements such as *Man kann hier nicht parken* (One cannot park here). The pronoun *man* is distinguished from the noun *Mann* (capitalized and with double "n"), which means "male adult human". However, *man* cannot easily be used to refer to a specific person of indeterminate sex. In modern times, *frau* (distinguished from *Frau*) is also used to emphasize that the person referred to is female. However, this is done as a comic effect (in advertisement for products aimed at women, e.g.) or by radical feminists.

Gender-neutral language-modification advocates feel that the traditional phraseology of the language reflects a domination of the masculine over the feminine, as they feel it does in many other languages. They object to certain set phrases where the masculine form usually comes first, such as "man and woman" (*Mann und Frau*), and to the differential use of words like *Fräulein* (although this has dropped out of common use).

Grammatical gender is a primary topic of contention among gender-neutral language advocates. *Der Mensch* is a grammatically masculine word which means "human being" or "person", and is the traditional Germanic word used to mean this. Alternatives are, however, fairly widespread. *Die Person* means the same thing, is not considered awkward or overly politically correct, and is grammatically feminine.

Feminine job titles are usually created by adding *-in* to the masculine word in question. For example, the general masculine term for computer scientist is *Informatiker* (singular or plural). This yields the feminine form *Informatikerin* (plural: *Informatikerinnen*). As in other languages, the use of a suffix to mark the feminine form implies that the unmarked masculine form is the main form of the word.

There is no universally accepted solution to the trade-off between inclusiveness and wordiness. As a result of campaigns by advocates of gender-neutral language modification, many job advertisements are now formulated so as to explicitly address both sexes (*Informatiker oder Informatikerin*). The option of repeating all terms in both gender forms is considered clumsy, and in the singular requires adjectives, articles, and pronouns to be stated twice. The use of slashes or parenthesis is commonplace, too, as in *Informatiker/in*, but this is considered visually ungainly and there is no consensus on how it is read.

A common tactic is to use a phrase such as *Kolleginnen und Kollegen* in an introductory paragraph, but use only the simpler masculine form in the rest of the document, often with a disclaimer.

Sometimes a form of contraction with capitalisation inside the word is used (*InformatikerIn*; *InformatikerInnen*). In some circles this is especially used to formulate written openings, such as *Liebe KollegInnen* (Dear colleagues). One obstacle to this form is that you cannot audibly distinguish between terms (*InformatikerIn* sounds the same as *Informatikerin*). Opponents of such modification consider the capitalized *I* in the middle of a word to be a corruption of the language. It is also not clear which gender declension the *-In* form is to be used with; sometimes all adjectival endings are likewise capitalized, such as *jedeR* for "each person" instead of *jede* (each woman) or *jeder* (each man). This form also tends to be associated with the political left, as it is often used by left-leaning newspapers, notably *Die Tageszeitung* and the Swiss weekly *Die Wochenzeitung*.

"We need an experienced computer scientist" could thus be expressed in several ways, among which:

Stated twice (hendiadys):
Wir brauchen eine erfahrene Informatikerin oder einen erfahrenen Informatiker.
Using slashes:
Wir brauchen eine/n erfahrene/n Informatiker/in.
By highlighting the suffix -in*:*
Wir brauchen eine erfahrene InformatikerIn;
sometimes Wir brauchen eineN erfahreneN InformatikerIn. This is considered bad style, although frequently used.
Masculine form, with indication that both genders are implied:
Wir brauchen einen erfahrenen Informatiker (m/w).
Frequently, too, job ads will use a pseudo-English term to avoid the issue:
Computer-Scientist (m/w) gesucht! *"Computer scientist (m/f) sought!"*

In some cases, neologisms may be formed: some university communities are replacing *Student* (male college student) and *Studentin* (female college student) with the participle *Studierende(r)*, meaning "the studying/college-going person", which does not face quite as many problems with declension. Terms like *Lehrer* (teacher) are increasingly being replaced by collective nouns such as *Lehrkraft* (teaching force; faculty). *Kellner* (waiter) and *Kellnerin* (waitress) are often transformed into *Bedienung* (service), which can be interpreted as having the effect of dehumanising the referent: *"Fragen Sie bitte die Bedienung, falls Sie einen Wunsch haben"* ("If you need anything, ask the service/help").

Swedish

Like other Germanic languages, Swedish used to have three genders, masculine, feminine, and neuter. Today, it only has two, *neutrum* (neuter), which uses the pronoun *det*, and another formed from the merger of the masculine with the feminine, known as *utrum* (common gender), which uses the pronoun *den*. A few fossilized uses of the original genders linger on. For instance, the clock as an object is a common gender word, but when used to ask or tell the time, it is treated as feminine: *"Vad är klockan?" "Hon är sex"* ("What time is it?" lit. "*She* is six o'clock"). Dialectically, the three gender system nouns survive to some extent.

Customarily, feminine pronouns are used when referring to both genders or to a person or people of an unknown gender. For example, a correct phrase is: *Den tidiga människan och hennes verktyg* (Early Man and *her* tools). The anglicization of Swedish in the late 20th century has made the usage of masculine pronouns to refer to unspecified genders more habitual, but it is still not the rule.

Swedish adjectives are always inflected according to number, and they used to be inflected for gender as well. Gender inflection of adjectives — *den sure chefen* (m), *den sura mamman* (f) — , has not yet fallen completely into disuse and the extent of its use is dialectual. Some still use it for occupational and kinship words, but the fact remains that it no longer serves any purpose for any other nouns. This has caused some debate as to which gender inflection should be the standard one for all nouns. The feminine inflection has become the one most widely used over the country, more likely because it is more distinct before nouns that begin with a vowel than due to any wide sense of gender equality.

Until the 1970s, it was rare that women would have professions other than secretary, teacher or nurse. A *majorska* was the wife of a major, a *biskopinna* the wife of a bishop. As nearly all Swedish women are in the work force today, this usage is deprecated. The word *sekreterare* (secretary) now mirrors its English counterpart in usage. A woman in a profession is now usually referred to by the same title as a man, save for *lärarinna*, which is often still used for a female teacher, and *sjuksköterska* which means male or female nurse (although it is now supplemented by the neologism *sjukskötare*). The typical Swedish way of making occupational titles more neutral is by coining euphemisms. What for instance used to be a *städare* (male janitor) or *städerska* (female janitor) is now uniformly, at least in formal language, a *lokalvårdare* (custodian).

None of this changes the fact that many Swedish women still occupy traditional women's jobs - a caretaker in a kindergarten, while formally referred to in the collective as *daghemspersonal* (day care staff), is still in common language a *dagisfröken* (kindergarten maid/female teacher), regardless of gender, because nearly all of them are women.

Yet another concern among the champions of a gender-neutral Swedish is the complete abandon of gendered personal and possessive pronouns. The most well-known attempt to replace the gendered Swedish pronouns that are currently in use is the proposal to drop *han* (him) and *hon* (her) for the neologism *hen* (which is said to be inspired by the Finnish gender-neutral third-person pronoun *hän*). The origin of the pronoun is contested, but it is reported to have been in use, albeit at an extremely small scale, already in the 1960's. Drawing on *hen* advocates of new pronouns usually form corresponding new pronouns such as *henom* (objective form of *hen*) and *hens* (third-person, gender-neutral possessive pronoun). These pronouns are not in wide usage and might even be unknown by Swedish-speakers not familiar with terms and discourse of third-wave feminism and Queer theory.

A subtler strategy of gender-neutralising pronouns is the replacement of *man* (which means either *man* or *one*, as in: One ought to gender-neutralise pronouns) with *en* (which, literally translated, means *one*). Fact is that *en* is already used in some dialects and contexts as a replacement for *man* and some native speakers of Swedish would thus consider the word as belonging to regional or low-prestige language.

Icelandic

The policy of gender neutrality in the Icelandic language is that the speaker uses the normal grammatical gender of the word of a public office or another office, even if a woman is the holder. The words president and minister (*forseti* and *ráðherra*) are thus used in these cases, for example when Vigdís Finnbogadóttir was president of Iceland.

Romance Languages

Historical note

Ancient Greek and Classical Latin had generic words for "human"/"humanity in general" or "human being", *anthropos* and *homo* respectively, which are the etyma of such modern terms as "anthropology" or *Homo sapiens*. For "male human as opposed to female human", there existed the separate words *aner* (*andros-*) and *vir* (the etyma of English "androgen" and "virile", respectively).

Most modern derivatives of the Latin noun *homo*, however, such as French *homme*, Italian *uomo*, Portuguese *homem*, and Spanish *hombre*, have acquired a predominantly male denotation, although they are sometimes still used generically in high registers. For example, French *Musée de l'homme* for an anthropology museum exhibiting human culture, not specifically "male culture". This semantic shift was parallel to the evolution of the word *man* in English. These languages therefore lack a third, neutral option aside from the gender-specific words for "man" and "woman". In Romanian, however, the cognate *om* retains its original meaning of "any human person", as opposed to the gender-specific words for "man" and "woman" (*bărbat* and *femeie*, respectively). In Romansh the word *um* only refers to a male, whereas "human being" is expressed in different ways in the different dialects: *carstgaun* or *uman*.

French

The use of non-sexist job titles in French is common and generally standard practice among the francophones in Belgium and in Canada. By law in Quebec, the use of gender-inclusive job titles is obligatory if the writer has not opted for gender-free terms. In France, however, the practice of using exclusively masculine job titles is still widespread in educated use and has been upheld by the Académie Française.

The most common way of feminizing job titles in French is by adding a feminine suffix to the masculine version of the noun, most commonly *-e* (*l'avocat, l'avocate*), *-eure* (*le docteur, la docteure*), *-euse* (*le travailleur, la travailleuse*), *-esse* (*le maire, la mairesse*), *-trice* (*le directeur, la directrice*). For job titles ending in epicene suffixes such as *-iste* (*le/la dentiste*) or *-logue* (*le/la psychologue*), the only change is in the article (*le/la*) and any associate adjectives. Abbreviated professions only change the article as well (le/la prof).

In some cases, words already had a feminine form which was rarely used, and a new one was created. For instance "docteur" had the feminine "doctoresse" but "docteure" was still created. "Chasseur" had the feminine "chasseresse" (typically used only of the goddess Artemis) but "chasseuse" was still created. Nowadays both feminine forms can be encountered, with the old ones being generally more prevalent in Europe and the new ones in Québec.

To make words or phrases gender-inclusive, French-speakers use two methods:

1. Hyphens, brackets or capital letters to insert feminine endings: *étudiant-e-s*, *étudiant(e)s* or *étudiantEs*; most writers avoid this practice in official titles such as Governor General and favour the next process;
2. Hendiadys containing a feminine word and a masculine word: *toutes et tous, citoyennes et citoyens.*

Words that formerly referred solely to a dignitary's wife (*l'ambassadrice*) are now used to refer to a woman holding the same dignitary position. Although marriage titles have mainly dropped out of use, many cite the possible confusion as a reason for continuing to use those such as *Madame le Président* or *Madame l'ambassadeur*. For this reason, the traditional use remains the most frequent in France. Nonetheless, in France, the husband of a female ambassador would never be known as *Monsieur l'ambassadrice*. Instead, he would be called literally "the ambassador's husband", *le mari de l'ambassadeur*.

Although some long-established positions of high prestige, such as Governor General of Canada exist in both masculine and feminine variants, honorary titles remain masculine throughout the Francophonie even when the award or honour is bestowed unto a woman. Examples are titles such as *Grand Officier*, *Commandeur*, *Officier*, *Chevalier*, *Compagnon*, *Immortel* used in the Order of Canada, the National Order of Quebec, France's Legion of Honor and the Académie Française, or Belgium's and Monaco's Order of the Crown.

Italian

In Italian, female job titles are easily formed with *-a*, *-essa* and other feminine suffixes, but they are often perceived as ridiculous neologisms. A female doctor is a *dottoressa*, while a female lawyer can be called both *avvocato* (masculine) or *avvocatessa* (a feminine neologism, sometimes perceived as ridiculous or even offensive, as it seems to overemphasize the gender). Italian job announcements often use a specific expected gender (*segretaria, meccanico*) or they address both genders with a slash (*candidato/a*). Many adjectives have identical feminine and masculine forms, so they are effectively gender-neutral when used without articles as job titles (*dirigente, responsabile di...*) and in many other contexts; slashes are often applied to articles (*il/la cliente*, the customer). There are full sets of masculine and feminine pronouns and articles (with some coincidences) and some traces of neuter; adjectives are declined, even if many remain the same, and adjective declension is also used in the many verbal tenses involving the past participle. The masculine gender is the default, and most correct form, for isolated adjectives and pronouns, for mixed-gender groups and for generic usage.

Spanish and Portuguese

In Spanish, similarly, the feminine is usually marked with the suffix *-a*, and it is generally easy to make a feminine noun from a masculine one by changing the ending *-o* to *-a*: *cirujano, cirujana* (surgeon; m./f.); *escribano, escribana* (notary; m./f.); *maestro, maestra* (teacher; m./f.) If the masculine version ends with a consonant, the feminine is typically formed by adding an *-a* to it as well: *el doctor, la doctora*. However, not all nouns ending in *-o* are masculine, and not all nouns ending in *-a* are feminine:

- Singular nouns ending in *-o* or *-a* are invariable in some cases: *testigo* (witness; either male or female). *La persona* (the person), *las personas* (the people), *la población* (the population) and *la víctima* (the victim).
- Nouns with the epicene ending *-ista*, such as *dentista, ciclista, turista, especialista* (dentist, cyclist, tourist, specialist; either male or female) are almost always invariable. One exception is *modisto* (male fashion designer), which was created as a counterpart to *modista* (fashion designer, or clothes maker).
- Some nouns ending in *-a* refer only to men: *cura*, that is "priest", a word which ends in *-a* but is grammatically masculine, for a profession held only by men.

Invariable words in Spanish are often derived from the Latin agent participles *-antem* and *-entem* (accusative case): *representante, comerciante, estudiante*. But a female *cliente* is a *clienta*, and a female *jefe* is a *jefa*.

A few problematic cases remain:

- *Presidenta* used to be "the president's wife", but there have been several women presidents in Latin American republics, and in modern usage the word means mainly a female president, with the meaning of "the president's wife" being replaced by the phrase *primera dama* (first lady). Some feel that *presidente* can be treated as invariable, given that it ends in *-ente*, but others prefer to use a different feminine form.

- *El policía* (the policeman). Since *la policía* means "the police force", the only useful feminine counterpart is *la mujer policía* (the police woman).
- *Juez* (judge). Many new judges in Spain are women. Since the ending of *juez* is uncommon in Spanish, some prefer being called *la juez* while others have created the neologism *jueza*. Common nouns ending in *-z* are usually feminine, as in the cases of *vez* and *paz*.

Activists against perceived sexism in language are also concerned about words where the feminine form has a different (usually less prestigious) meaning:

- An ambiguous case is "secretary": a *secretaria* is an attendant for her boss or a typist, usually female, while a *secretario* is a high-rank position (as in *secretario general del partido comunista*), usually held by males. With the access of women to positions labelled as "secretary general" or similar, some have chosen to use the masculine gendered *la secretario* and others have to clarify that *secretaria* is a decision position, not a subordinate one.
- An offensive example is *hombre público* ("public man", a politician) and *mujer pública* ("public woman", a prostitute).

As in other Romance languages, it is traditional to use the masculine form of nouns and pronouns when referring to both males and females. Advocates of gender neutral languages modification consider this to be sexist and favour new ways of writing and speaking. Two methods have begun to come into use. One of them, seen most often in Spain and Mexico, is to use the at-sign (@) or the anarchist circled A (Ⓐ) to replace *-o* or *-a*, especially in radical political writing (*¡Ciudadan@s!*), but use of the slash (/) as in (*el/ la candidato/a*) is more common. The ligature æ can be used in the same way (*escritoræs* for writers of both sexes, although *escritores/as* is more common). Opponents of such language modification feel that they are degrading to the language. Many also raise the question of how these new words are to be pronounced. See also Alternative political spellings.

Some politicians have begun to avoid perceived sexism in their speeches; the Mexican president Vicente Fox Quesada, for example, was famous for repeating gendered nouns in their masculine and feminine versions (*ciudadanos y ciudadanas*). This way of speaking is subject to parodies where new words with the opposite ending are created for the sole purpose of contrasting with the gendered word traditionally used for the common case (like **felizas* and **especialistos* in **felices y felizas* or **las y los especialistas y especialistos*).

Being very similar to Spanish, all considerations and almost all the examples above apply also to Portuguese. Minoritarian languages of this group can probably use expressions with at-sign (*biólog@* in Galician), ligature æ (*outoræs* in Mirandese language and *autor/a* in Aragonese language).

Slavic languages

Serbian

Like most other Slavic languages, Serbian has more obstacles to gender-neutral language modification than English. The Serbian language has different forms for masculine and feminine past tense: *on je radio* (he was working), *ona je radila* (she was working). Only the rare aorist (in Serbian the aorist is a tense, not an aspect) makes no distinction between genders. Also, all nouns in Serbian have grammatical gender: masculine, feminine or neuter. Almost all nouns which end with a consonant are masculine, almost all which end with *a* are feminine and almost all that end with *o* or *e* are neuter. Adjectives and verb aspects (but not in all tenses) inflect for gender, too.

Gender-neutral language advocates are also unhappy with Serbian's use of noun gender. Some masculine nouns signify an occupation, while the corresponding feminine nouns refer to objects: the masculine noun *govornik* means "male speaker", while the cognate feminine noun *govornica* means "female speaker", but also "podium", or a "speaker's platform"; masculine *trener* means "male coach", while the feminine word *trenerka* means "female coach", but also "warm-up suit".

Many feminists argue that in the Serbian language it is natural to differentiate the gender of job titles, as opposed to just using the masculine grammatical gender. Some of the language which they consider sexist includes: *ministar* for (male) minister and *ministarka* for the wife of a minister, and *profesorka* for the wife of professor instead of a female professor, etc. For example, they favor using *učiteljica* for "female teacher" (*učitelj* is "male teacher") and *profesorka* for "female professor" (*profesor* is "male professor").

But many more traditional linguists, including women, argue that feminine names for occupations are not natural for the Serbian language. They feel that the masculine gender variants should be used, even when the professional in question is female.

Advocates of gender-neutral language find it difficult to avoid specifying gender in Serbian, since it is so built into the language. But one area where they have a bit more flexibility is the word "person," in its various forms: a person can be referred to as *čovek* ("human"; masculine gender), *osoba* ("person"; feminine gender) or *ljudsko biće* ("human being"; neuter gender).

Only plural forms have clear general meaning: *profesori* means both "male professors" and "female and male professors", but *profesorke* means only "female professors". Many feminists prefer to say *profesori i profesorke* (male professors and female professors) and to write *profesori/ke*.

Russian

Russian intrinsically shares many of the same non-gender-neutral characteristics with other European languages. Certain words are understood to refer to either men or women regardless of their grammatical gender. For example, ("human"; grammatically masculine), as opposed to ("man"; masculine with respect to agreement, but morphologically feminine) and ("woman"; feminine), and are in fact traditionally used in cases where gender-specific terms would be used in English. Several terms that roughly mean "person" are grammatically neuter or feminine, and can similarly be used to refer to either men or women: (neuter, lit. "face"), (feminine), (feminine). All such terms have a bureaucratic connotation and are seldom used colloquially. Note also that as a general rule Russian does not use neuter terms for people, just as English does not use "it" as gender-neutral pronoun.

Job titles have a masculine and a feminine version in Russian, though in most cases the feminine version is only used in colloquial speech. The masculine form is typically treated as "unmarked", i.e. it does not necessarily imply that the person is male, while the feminine form is "marked" and can only be used when referring to a woman. In some cases, the feminine title is derogatory or connotes a suboptimal performance and is only used as slang, e.g. (female doctor), or sometimes (female director). In other cases, this is not the case: (actress), (poetess; e.g. Anna Akhmatova insisted to be called instead). Even in cases where the feminine term is not seen as derogatory, however, there is a growing tendency to use masculine term in more formal contexts that stress the individual's membership in a profession: "B 15" ("At age 15 she became a piano teacher", formal register). The feminine form may be used in less formal context to stress a personal description of the individual: ("Nastia became a teacher", informal register).

For this reason, use of the masculine occupation terms when referring to women, is in fact seen as more politically correct and constitutes a growing trend. The actual gender of the person can still be indicated through the verb: for example, in the phrase (the doctor/m advised/f), the gender of the verb shows that the doctor was female, even as the masculine (more respectful) occupation term is used. Note, however, that there are also some grammatically feminine terms with positive connotations that are routinely used for both men and women, for example, (celebrity).

Russian adjectives are inflected for grammatical gender and so are verbs in the past tense. When a masculine term is used to refer to a woman, the verb usually remains in the feminine, while adjectives and possessive pronouns may take either masculine or feminine form: (our/m new/m doctor/m recommended/f) or (our/f new/f doctor/m recommended/f). The former usage is more formal, while the latter is more colloquial.

The third-person pronoun typically reflects the actual gender of the person when this is known, ... (the doctor/m said/f that *she*...), but typically agrees with the grammatical gender of its antecedent when an abstract person is discussed: ... (Every/m doctor/m must/m remember that *he*...)

International Auxiliary Languages

Esperanto

Esperanto follows the pattern of more natural languages, in assigning the male genders to specific roles (family member, aristocracy, etc.), and further deriving the female term from that. The generic form of nouns is the same as the male form and different from the female form — for example, *doktoro(j)* means "doctor(s)" (male or unspecified sex), while *doktorino(j)* means "female doctor". Some words, like *patro* (father), are intrinsically masculine, but there is no root word to express "a parent".

The prefix *ge-* may be used for groups of mixed sex, for example, *gedoktoroj* (male and female doctors). Reformers have used *ge-* to create explicitly sex-neutral singulars such as *gepatro*, "a parent". Though not generally adopted, this usage has appeared in some authoritative reference works.

Explicitly marked feminine forms such as *doktorino* may be used to emphasise the noun's female character, but unmarked forms are also commonly used for females. Reformers have proposed morphologically well-formed but rarely used forms like *virdoktoro* (literally "man-doctor") and neologisms like *-iĉ-* (*doktoriĉo*) to emphasize maleness. The first form is somewhat insufficient because *viro* traditionally means "man, male", but does not really show any male lexeme or morpheme, *virino* meaning "woman". This is discussed about, some people prefer *viriĉo* for "man, male" as opposed to *virino*.

Concerning pronouns there is much discussion: *ŝi* is clearly female, like English *she*. For male persons *li* is used and for (not personified) animals as well as for inanimate objects *ĝi*. It is not clear however what form to use when a person of unknown sex is spoken of. It is officially accepted, though very rarely practiced, to use *ĝi* in this case. Also *li* is officially accepted to refer to both sexes, what of course causes some opposition. There are some suggestions for neologisms like *ŝli* or *ri*. On the other hand, some people consider *li* to be clearly sex-neutral, what requires a new only-male pronoun, e.g. *hi*.

Arguments about the character and implications of "gendered" or "sexist" features in Esperanto closely parallel those raised for other, particularly European languages.

Ido

Ido, a constructed language that is heavily based on Esperanto but seeks to avoid what some see as Esperanto's shortcomings, does not have this asymmetric sex-marking system. For example, *frato* means "brother" in Esperanto, but "sibling" in Ido. Ido nouns for kinds of people are sex-neutral in their ordinary form, but may be made either female- or male-specific by use of the suffixes *-ino* ("female", used as in Esperanto) and *-ulo* ("male", not to be confused with the same Esperanto suffix which means "person"). Examples: *sekretario*, secretary — *sekretariulo*, man secretary — *sekretariino*, woman secretary; *doktoro*, doctor — *doktorulo*, man doctor — *doktorino*, woman doctor. Thus, "sister" is *fratino* (the same as Esperanto), but brother is *fratulo*. Some communities use three separate words: *patro* ("father"), *matro* (mother) and *genitoro* (parent). Compare this with Esperanto *patro*, *patrino* and *gepatroj* respectively.

It also has an epicene pronoun *lu*, which, somewhat ambiguously, can refer to beings of any (or no) gender as well as inanimate objects. (The words "man", "woman", "baby", "goat", and "table" are all referred to by *lu*.)

Interlingua

Interlingua is an auxiliary language that was developed to have a widely international vocabulary and a very simple grammar. In Interlingua, nouns have no gender except to reflect natural sex. For example, the words *homine* (man) and *femina* (woman) are masculine and feminine, respectively, but *persona* (person) has no gender. Adjectives are invariable and so never have to agree in gender with the nouns they modify. There is a separate nongender pronoun (*illo*, "it") and the possessive pronoun *su* ("his", "her" or "its") is gender-neutral.

Nouns such as *professor* and *conductor* denote both men and women, but specifically feminine forms such as *professora conductora* have been used occasionally over time. Interlingua has largely escaped charges of sexism, perhaps because the language changes easily as social values change.

Gender Neutrality in English

Gender neutrality in English is a form of linguistic prescriptivism that aims at using a form of English that minimizes assumptions about the gender or biological sex of people referred to in speech.

Rationale

Proponents of gender-neutral language argue that the use of gender-specific language often implies male superiority or reflects an unequal state of society. According to *The handbook of English linguistics*, generic masculine pronouns and gender-specific job titles are instances "where English linguistic convention has historically treated men as prototypical of the human species." Words that refer to women often devolve in meaning, frequently taking on sexual overtones.

These differences in usage are criticised on two grounds: one, that they reflect a biased state of society, and two, that they help to uphold that state. Studies of children, for instance, indicate that the words children hear affect their perceptions of the gender-appropriateness of certain careers. Other research has demonstrated that men and women apply for jobs in more equal proportions when gender-neutral language is used in the advertisement, as opposed to the generic "he" or "man". Some critics make the further claim that these differences in usage are not accidental, but have been deliberately created for the purpose of upholding a patriarchal society. Proponents of gender-neutral language give many examples of usages that they find problematic.

Words for Humans

Proponents of gender-neutral language often point to the history of the word "man" to argue that, although the word once referred to both males and females, it no longer does so unambiguously. In Old English, "wer" referred to males only and "wif" to females only; "man" referred to both, although in practice "man" was sometimes also used in Old English to refer only to males. In time, "wer" fell out of use, and "man" came to refer sometimes to both sexes and sometimes to males only; "[a]s long as most generalisations about men were made by men about men, the ambiguity nestling in this dual usage was either not noticed or thought not to matter." By the eighteenth century, "man" had come to refer primarily to males; some writers who wished to use the term in the older sense deemed it necessary to spell out their meaning: Anthony Trollope, for example, writes of "the infinite simplicity and silliness of mankind and womankind" and when "Edmund Burke, writing of the French Revolution, used men in the old, inclusive way, he took pains to spell out his meaning: 'Such a deplorable havoc is made in the minds of men (both sexes) in France....'"

Proponents of gender-neutral language argue that seemingly generic uses of the word "man" are often not in fact generic:

> One author, ostensibly generalizing about all human beings, wrote: *"As for man, he is no different from the rest. His back aches, he ruptures easily, his women have difficulties in childbirth...."* If *man* and *he* were truly generic, the parallel phrase would have been *he has difficulties in childbirth.*

Other commentators have suggested that truly generic uses of the word "man" would be perceived as "false, funny, or insulting", citing as an example the phrase "Some men are female."

Further, some commentators point out that, in the past, the ostensibly gender-neutral use of "man" has in fact been used to exclude women:

> Thomas Jefferson did not make the same distinction in declaring that "all men are created equal" and "governments are instituted among men, deriving their just powers from the consent of the governed." In a time when women, having no vote, could neither give nor withhold consent, Jefferson had to be using the word men in its principal sense of "males", and it probably never occurred to him that anyone would think otherwise.

For these reasons, proponents of gender-neutral language claim that linguistic clarity as well as equality would be better served by having "man" refer unambiguously to males, and "human" to all persons.

Pronouns

The use of masculine pronouns to refer to antecedents of mixed or indeterminate gender, while traditional, is a target of frequent criticism by proponents of gender-neutral language. Critics of the use of the generic "he" argue that this usage was invented and propagated by men, such as Thomas Wilson and Joshua Poole, whose explicit goal was the linguistic representation of men's superiority. The use of the generic "he" was in fact enforced by an Act of Parliament and, despite its putative inclusiveness, has been used to deny women's entry into professions and schools.

Proposed alternatives to the generic "he" include "he or she" (or "she or he"), "s/he", or the use of "they" in the singular; each of these alternatives has met with objections. Some feel the use of the singular "they" sounds like a grammatical error, but according to some references, "they", "their", and "them" have long been grammatically acceptable as gender-neutral singular pronouns in English:

Proponents of the singular "they" argue that the word has been used in the singular continuously since the Middle Ages, and cite its use by a number of prominent authors, including Geoffrey Chaucer, William Shakespeare, and Jane Austen. Linguist Steven Pinker goes further and argues that traditional grammar prescriptions regarding the use of singular "they" are themselves grammatically incorrect:

> The next time you get corrected for this sin [of using "they" in the singular], ask Mr. Smartypants how you should fix the following: *Mary saw everyone before John noticed them.*
>
> Now watch him squirm as he mulls over the downright unintelligible "improvement", *Mary saw everyone before John noticed him.* The logical point that you, Holden Caulfield, and everyone but the language mavens intuitively grasp is that everyone and they are not an "antecedent" and a "pronoun" referring to the same person in the world, which would force them to agree in number. They are a

"quantifier" and a "bound variable", a different logical relationship. Everyone returned to their seats means "For all X, X returned to X's seat." The "X" does not refer to any particular person or group of people; it is simply a placeholder that keeps track of the roles that players play across different relationships. In this case, the X that comes back to a seat is the same X that owns the seat that X comes back to. The their there does not, in fact, have plural number, because it refers neither to one thing nor to many things; it does not refer at all. The same goes for the hypothetical caller: there may be one, there may be none, or the phone might ring off the hook with would-be suitors; all that matters is that every time there is a caller, if there is a caller, that caller, and not someone else, should be put off.

Most style guides agree with these arguments, and generally accept the singular "they" as grammatically correct, while others continue to reject it. Some, such as *The Chicago Manual of Style*, hold a neutral position on the issue, and contend any approach used is likely to displease some readers.

Research has found that the use of generic masculine pronouns creates "male bias" by evoking a disproportionate number of male images and excluding thoughts of women in non-sex specific instances. Moreover, a study by John Gastil found that while the plural they functions as a generic pronoun for both males and females, males may comprehend he/she in a manner similar to he.

Naming Practices

Some critics oppose the practice of women changing their names upon marriage, on the grounds that it makes women historically invisible: "In our society 'only men have real names' in that their names are permanent and they have 'accepted the permanency of their names as one of the rights of being male.'... Essentially this practice means that womens' family names do not count and that there is one more device for making women invisible." Historically, as women have been granted greater access to the professions they have been less likely to change their names, either professionally or legally; names are tied to reputations and women have been less likely to change their names when they have higher reputations.

Honorifics

Proponents of gender-neutral language point out that while Mr is used for men regardless of marital status, the titles Miss and Mrs indicate a woman's marital status, and thus signal her sexual availability in a way that men's titles do not. The honorific "Mx", full form Mixter, can be used in place of traditional honorifics in order to provide gender-neutrality.

The practice of referring to married women by their husband's first and last names has also been criticised, beginning in the nineteenth century: when the Reverend Samuel May "moved that Mrs Stephen Smith be placed on a Committee" of the National Women's Rights Convention in Seneca Falls, Lucretia Mott "quickly replied: Woman's Rights' women do not like to be called by their husbands' names, but by their own". Elizabeth Cady Stanton refused to be addressed as "Mrs Henry B. Stanton". The practice was developed in the mid-eighteenth century and was tied to the idea of coverture, the idea that "By marriage, the husband and wife are one person in law; that is, the very being or legal existence of the woman is suspended during the marriage."

Feasibility

Advocates of gender-neutral language argue that language is rich in alternatives that speakers and writers, sensitive to attitudes and beliefs of audiences, can use without impinging on the effectiveness of their communication. They are also able to be true to their notions of grammatical propriety. In some cases, gender-neutral language may be achieved through the use of gender-inclusive, gender-neutral or epicene words ("human being", "person", "individual", and so on) instead of gender-specific ones ("man", "woman", "he", "she", "businessman", "mother", etc.), when speaking of people whose gender is unknown, ambiguous, or unimportant. If no gender-inclusive terms exist, new ones may be coined (e.g., "businessperson"). There may also be parallel usage of existing gender-specific terms - for example, "men and women" rather than "men and ladies", or "husband and wife" instead of "man and wife".

Further, proponents of gender-neutral language argue that making language less biased is not only laudable, but achievable. Many people find non-neutral language to be offensive.

> There is a growing awareness that language does not merely reflect the way we think: it also shapes our thinking. If words and expressions that imply that women or men are inferior are constantly used, that assumption of inferiority tends to become part of our mindset.... Language is a powerful tool: poets and propagandists know this — as, indeed, do victims of discrimination.

However, the use of the word "man" as a generic word referring to all humans has been declining, particularly among female speakers and writers. Other potentially male-centric terms such as woman are generally acceptable. Many editing houses, corporations, and government bodies have official policies in favour of in-house use of gender-neutral language. In some cases, laws exist regarding the use of gender-neutral language in certain situations, such as job advertisements. The majority of advocates for gender-neutral language, however, generally prefer persuasion rather than enforcement.

One method for such persuasion is creating guidelines that indicate how they believe language should be used, or providing an example through their own use of gender-neutral language.

Different authorities have presented guidelines on whether and how to use gender-neutral, or "non-sexist" language. Several are listed below:

- The "Publication Manual" of the American Psychological Association has an oft-cited section on "Guidelines to Reduce Bias in Language". ISBN 1-55798-791-2.
- American Philosophical Association — published 1986.
- The Guardian — see section "gender issues."
- Avoiding Heterosexual Bias in Language, published by the Committee on Lesbian and Gay Concerns, American Psychological Association.

In addition, gender-neutral language has gained support from some major textbook publishers, and from professional and academic groups such as the American Psychological Association and the Associated Press. Newspapers such as the *New York Times* and the *Wall Street Journal* use gender-neutral language. Many law journals, psychology journals, and literature journals will only print articles or papers that use gender-inclusive language.

Employee policy manuals have recently started to include strongly worded statements prescribing avoidance of language that potentially could be considered discriminatory. The wording of this statement from a policy manual is typical: "All documents, publications or presentations developed by all constituencies...*shall be written* in gender neutral and/or gender inclusive language." Employees are told that they need to be aware of their responsibilities to avoid discriminatory language, and that they must implement the enterprise's commitment to treat stakeholders equally and with courtesy. Institutional members are instructed, as a matter of corporate policy, to avoid using language that may even appear to be discriminatory, or that may gratuitously give offense in verbal or written communication. Manuals sometimes provide guidance about how to reflect the concept of valuing diversity in language usage.

Standards advocated by supporters of the gender-neutral modification in English have been applied differently and to differing degrees among English speakers worldwide. This reflects differences in culture and language structure, for example American English in contrast to British English. They are also affected by other factors, such as whether a person uses English as a first language or as a second language, regional variants or whether a particular form of English is based on grammatical structures inherited from another language (for example, Hiberno-English) or owes its linguistic structure to earlier Old English or Elizabethan English. In these cases, language structure from the native tongue or linguistic inheritance may be engaged.

Arguments Against

Various criticisms have been leveled against the use of gender-neutral language, most focusing on specific usages, such as the use of "human" for "man" and "he or she" for "he". The use of the singular "they" is called "grammatical nonsense", as are such little-used neologisms as "her story". Any other alternatives to gender-specific language are claimed to "lead one into using awkward or grating constructions" or neologisms that are so ugly as to be "abominations".

Some argue that gender-neutral language is unnecessary because no bias exists, finding the endeavour to be "useless, for we all know that the masculine pronoun refers to female and male people". A common argument is that historically terms such as "man" have been uniformly used as gender-neutral, and opponents of gender-neutral language often point to the fact that "man" in Old English referred to either men or women; feminists are claimed to be engaged in an attempt to "blot out" this fact and "re-write history".

Others argue that the linguistic differentiation of women actually reflects women being "more" valued than men, not less. Opponents of gender-neutral language often argue that proponents of gender-neutral language are impinging on the right of free expression and promoting censorship. A few commentators do not disagree with the usage of gender-neutral language *per se*, but they do question the effectiveness of gender-neutral language in overcoming sexism.

Bibliography

- King, Toni C. and Ferguson, S. Alease. *Black Womanist Leadership: Tracing the Motherline*, State University of New York Press, 2011.
- Gillman, Laura. *Unassimilable Feminisms: Reappraising Feminist, Womanist, and Mestiza Identity Politics (Breaking Feminist Waves)*, Palgrave Macmillan, 2010.
- Eaton, Kalenda C. *Womanism, Literature, and the Transformation of the Black Community, 1965, 1980 (Studies in African American History and Culture)*, Routledge, 2007.
- Phillips, Layli. *The Womanist Reader: The First Quarter Century of Womanist Thought*, Routledge, 2006.
- Floyd-Thomas, Stacey. *Deeper Shades of Purple: Womanism in Religion and Society (Religion, Race, and Ethnicity)*, NYU Press, 2006.
- Silva-Wayne, Susan. *Feminisms and Womanisms: A Women's Studies Reader*, Women's Press, Ltd., 2003.
- Walker, Alice. *In Search of Our Mothers' Gardens: Womanist Prose*, Mariner Books, 2003.
- Douglas, Kelly Brown. *Sexuality and the Black Church: A Womanist Perspective*, Orbis Books, 1999.
- Cannon, Katie Geneva. *Katie's Canon: Womanism and the Soul of the Black Community*, Continuum, 1998.
- Cannon, Katie G. *Black Womanist Ethics (Aar Academy Series)*, An American Academy of Religion Book, 1988.
- (English) Maria Jaschok: "Religious Women in a Chinese City: Ordering the past, recovering the future - Notes from fieldwork in the central Chinese province of Henan". February 2005. *QEH Working Paper Series - QEHWPS125* (Working Paper Number 124).

- (English) Maria Jaschok, Jingjun Shui: *The History of Women's Mosques in Chinese Islam.* Richmond, Surrey: Curzon Press, 2000 (die chinesische Ausgabe erschien unter dem Titel: *Zhongguo Qingzhen nüsi shi*, ISBN: 9787108016997; vgl. Vorschau)
- (English) Ping-Chun Hsiung, Maria Jaschok, Cecilia Nathansen Milwertz: *Chinese women organizing: cadres, feminists, Muslims, queers.*
- (English) Jaschok, Maria & Shui Jingjun, 'Restoring history to women, restoring women to history: reconstructing the evolution of Qingzhen Nüsi (women's mosques) in China's Islam', Pakistan *Journal of Women's Studies: Alam-e-Niswan* 10 (2003) 2, 153-173.
- (French) Elisabeth Allés: "Des oulémas femmes : le cas des mosquées féminines en Chine", *Revue du monde musulman et de la Méditerranée*, Année 1999, Volume 85, Numéro 85-86, pp. 215-236.
- (French) icampus.ucl.ac.be "Les minorités musulmanes en Chine" ("Les mosquées féminines").

Further Reading

- Chafe, William H., *"The American Woman: Her Changing Social, Economic, and Political Roles, 1920–1970"*, Oxford University Press, 1972. ISBN 0-19-501785-4.
- *Roget's II: The New Thesaurus*, (Boston: Houghton Mifflin, 2003 3rd edition) ISBN 0-618-25414-5.
- McWhorter, John. 'The Uses of Ugliness', *The New Republic Online*, January 31, 2002. Retrieved May 11, 2005 ["bitch" as an affectionate term].
- McWhorter, John. *Authentically Black: Essays for the Black Silent Majority* (New York: Gotham, 2003) ISBN 1-59240-001-9 [casual use of "bitch" in ebonics].
- *Routledge International Encyclopaedia of Women*, 4 Vols., ed. by Cheris Kramarae and Dale Spender, Routledge 2000.
- *Women in World History : A Biographical Encyclopedia*, 17 Vols., ed. by Anne Commire, Waterford, Conn. [etc.] : Yorkin Publ. [etc.], 1999–2002.
- Lucia-Hoagland, Sarah and Penelope, Julia. *For Lesbians Only: A Separatist Anthology*. Onlywomen Press, Ltd. (1988) ISBN 978-0906500286.
- Abbott, Pamela and Claire Wallace (1990). *An Introduction to Sociology: Feminist Perspectives.* London, UK; New York, NY: Routledge. ISBN 0415010365. OCLC 19887117.
- Chafetz, Janet Saltzman (1990). *Gender Equity: An Integrated Theory of Stability and Change.* Newbury Park, CA: Sage Publications. ISBN 0803934017. OCLC 20131005.
- Chambers, Clare (2008). *Sex, Culture, and Justice: The Limits of Choice.* University Park, PA: Pennsylvania State University Press. ISBN 9780271033013. OCLC 153772741.

- Cudworth, Erika (2005). *Developing Ecofeminist Theory: The Complexity of Difference*. Basingstoke, England; New York, NY: Palgrave Macmillan. ISBN 1403941157. OCLC 59098859.
- Enns, Carolyn Zerbe and Ada L. Sinacore (2005). *Teaching and Social Justice: Integrating Multicultural and Feminist Theories in the Classroom*. Washington, DC: American Psychological Association. ISBN 1591471672. OCLC 55625673.
- Frye, Marilyn (1983). *The Politics of Reality: Essays in Feminist Theory*. Trumansburg, NY: Crossing Press. ISBN 0895941007. OCLC 9323470.
- Gottfried, Heidi (1996). *Feminism and Social Change: Bridging Theory and Practice*. Urbana, IL: University of Illinois Press. ISBN 0252021983. OCLC 32049514.
- Kail, R., & Cavanaugh, J. (2010). *Human Growth and Development* (5 ed.). Belmont, Ca: Wadworth Learning.

References

- Douglas, Mary (1982). "Cultural Bias," in: Douglas, M.: *In the Active Voice*, London: Routledge & Kegan Paul; 183-254.
- Seidner, Stanley S.(1982). *Ethnicity, Language, and Power from a Psycholinguistic Perspective.* Bruxelles: Centre de recherche sur le pluralinguisme.
- Collins, P. H. (1996, Winter/Summer). What's in a Name? Womanism, Black Feminsim, and Beyond. *The Black Scholar*, 26(1), 9.
- Dove, N. (1998) "Africana Womanism: An Afrocentric Theory". *Journal of Black Studies*, 28(5), 535.
- Hudson-Weems, C. (2008). *Africana Womanism and Race and Gender in the Presidential Candidacy of Barack Obama.* Authorhouse, ISBN 1-4389-0906-3, Amazon.com.
- Hudson-Weems, C. (1998). *Africana Womanism: Reclaiming Ourselves.* Troy, MI: Bedford Publishing, ISBN 0-911557-14-8.
- Ntiri, D. W. (2001). "Reassessing Africana Womanism: Continuity and Change." *The Western Journal of Black Studies*, 25(3).
- "Africana Womanism: The Flip Side of a Coin," in *The Western Journal of Black Studies* (2001).
- "Africana Womanism: An Overview," in *Out of the Revolution: The Development of Africana Studies,* Delores Aldridge and Carlene Young, Editors, Lexington Books, 2000, pp. 205–217.
- "Africana Womanism: An Historical, Global Perspective for Women of African Descent," *Call and Response: The Riverside Anthology of the African American Literary Tradition,* Patricia Liggins Hill, General Editor, Houghton Mifflin, 1998, pp. 1811–1815.

- "Africana Womanism, Black Feminism, African Feminism, Womanism," in *Sisterhood, Feminisms and Power.* Obioma Nneameka, Editor, New Jersey: African World Press, 1998, pp. 149–162.
- "Self-Naming and Self-Defining: An Agenda for Survival," in *Sisterhood, Feminisms and Power,* Obioma Nneameka, Editor, New Jersey: African World Press, 1998, pp. 449–452.
- "Africana Womanism and the Critical Need for Africana Theory and Thought," in *The Western Journal of Black Studies*, Vol. 21, No. 2, Summer 1997, pp. 79–84.
- "Cultural and Agenda Conflicts in Academia: Critical Issues for Africana Women's Studies," in *The Western Journal of Black Studies* Vol. 13, No. 4, Winter 1989, pp. 185–189.
- "The Tripartite Plight of African-American Women as Reflected in the Novels of Hurston and Walker," in the Western *Journal of Black Studies* Vol. 20, No. 2, December 1989, pp. 192–207.
- "Africana Womanism, Black Feminism, African Feminism, Womanism," in *Black Studies: From the Pyramids to Pan Africanism and Beyond,* William Nelson, Jr., Editor, McGraw Hill, 2001.
- "Africana Womanism: Entering the New Millennium," in *State of the Race, Creating Our 21st Century: Where Do We Go From Here,* Jemadari Kamara and T. Menelik Van Der Meer, Editors, University of MA-Boston Press, 2001.
- "Come colour my rainbow: Themes of Africana womanism in the poetic vision of Audrey Kathryn Bullett, Ronald J. Stephens, Maureen Keaveny, Venetria K. Patton. *Journal of Black Studies* Thousand Oaks: Mar 2002. Vol. 32, Iss. 4; p. 464 (16 pages).
- "Common bonds from Africa to the U.S.: Africana womanist literary analysis, Betty Taylor Thompson. *Western Journal of Black Studies* Pullman: Fall 2001. Vol. 25, Iss. 3: p. 177 (8 pages).
- "Lucy Terry Prince: The cultural and literary legacy of Africana womanism, April Langley. *Western Journal of Black Studies* Pullman: Fall 2001. Vol. 25, Iss. 3; p. 153 (10 pages).
- "Theorizing difference within black feminist thought: The dilemma of sexism in black communities, Austin, Algernon. *Race, Gender and Class,* New Orleans: Jul 31, 1999. Vol. 6, Iss. 3; p. 52.

1. Marianne van den Wijngaard (1997). Reinventing the sexes: the biomedical construction of femininity and masculinity. Race, gender, and science. Indiana University Press. p. 171 http://books.google.com/books? Retrieved June 3, 2011.
2. Hale Martin, Stephen Edward Finn (2010). Masculinity and Femininity in the MMPI-2 and MMPI-A. U of Minnesota Press. p. 310. http://books.google.com/books? Retrieved June 3, 2011.

- Brinjikji, Hiam. (1999). Property Rights of Women in Nineteenth Century England. Unpublished manuscript, Department of English, University of Maryland, College Park, M.D. Retrieved from: http://www.umd.umich.edu/casl/hum/eng/classes/434/geweb/PROPERTY.htmhttp://webspace.ship.edu/cgboer/horney.html.
- Engler, Barbara. (2009). *Personality Theories*. 8th Ed. Houghton Mifflin Harcourt, Print.
- Horney & Humanistic Psychoanalysis: Major Concepts. International Karen Horney Society. N.p., 18JUN2002. Web. 21 Oct 2010. Retrieved from: http://plaza.ufl.edu/bjparis/horney/fadiman/04_major.html.
- Perron, Roger. Inferiority, Feeling of. Encyclopedia.com. N.p., 2005. Web. 21 Oct 2010. Retrieved from: http://www.encyclopedia.com/doc/1G2-3435300700.html.
- Lambert, Tim. (n.d.). 16th Century Women. Retrieved from http://www.localhistories.org/women.html
- Lowe, Maggie. (1989). Early College Women: Determined to be Educated. Unpublished manuscript, Department of History, State University of New York, Potsdam, NY. Retrieved from: http://www.northnet.org/stlawrenceaauw/college.htm
- The Woman Suffrage Timeline. (2007). Retrieved from: http://www.thelizlibrary.org/suffrage/
- Women in the Senate. (n.d.). Retrieved from: http://www.senate.gov/artandhistory/history/common/briefing/women_senators.htm
- Horney, K. (1967). The Flight from Womanhood: The masculinity-complex in women as viewed by men and by women. In H. Kelman (Ed.) Feminine psychology. New York: Norton.
- Schultz, D., Schultz, S. (2009). *Theories of Personality* (9th Ed.) New York: Wadsworth, Cengage Learning.
- Hansen, R., Hansen, J., Pollycove, R. (2002). *Mother nurture: a mother's guide to health in body, mind and intimate relationships*. New York: Viking Penguin.
- Kapur, M. (2005, August 5). Balancing motherhood and a career. CNN.com International. Retrieved from: http://edition.cnn.com/2004/BUSINESS/08/04/maternity.leave/index.html
- Resa, R. (2009, December 8). Give up a career or give up motherhood. The Huffington Post. Retrieved from: http://www.huffingtonpost.com/ramon-resa-md/give-up-a-career-or-give_b_383645.html
- Christine Skelton, Becky Francis, *Feminism and the Schooling Scandal*, Taylor & Francis, 2009 ISBN 0415455103, 9780415455107 p. 104.
- Sarah Hoagland, *Lesbian Ethics: toward new value*, pp. 60, 154, 294.

- Marilyn Frye, “Some Reflections on Separatism and Power.” In *Feminist Social Thought: A Reader*, Diana Tietjens Meyers (ed.) (1997) New York: Routledge, pp. 406-414.
- Chicago Women’s Liberation Union, Hyde Park Chapter. *Socialist Feminism: A Strategy for the Women’s Movement*, 1972, booklet.
- Saulnier, Christine F. Feminist Theories and Social Work: Approaches and Applications (1996) ISBN 1560249455.
- Echols, Alice. Daring to Be Bad: Radical Feminism in America, 1967-75, University of Minnesota Press, 1990, ISBN 0816617872, p.164.
- Dunbar, Leghorn. The Man’s Problem, from No More Fun and Games, Nov 1969, quoted in Echols, 165.
- Davis, Flora. Moving the Mountain: The Women’s Movement in America since 1960, University of Illinois Press, 1999, ISBN 0252067827, p. 271.
- Bunch, Charlotte/The Furies Collective, Lesbians in Revolt, in The Furies: Lesbian/Feminist Monthly, Vol.1, January 1972, pp. 8-9.
- Bunch, Charlotte. Learning from Lesbian Separatism, Ms. Magazine, Nov. 1976.
- Hoagland articulates a distinction (originally noted by Lesbian Separatist author and anthologist, Julia Penelope) between a lesbian subculture and a lesbian community; membership in the subculture being “defined in negative terms by an external, hostile culture”, and membership in the community being based on “the values we believe we can enact here.” Hoagland, Sarah Lucia. Lesbian Ethics: *Towards a New Value*, Institute for Lesbian Studies, Palo Alto, Ca.
- http://www.merriam-webster.com/dictionary/sexism?show=0&t=1308304677
- http://dictionary.reference.com/browse/sexism
- http://www.thefreedictionary.com/sexist
- http://www.encyclopedia.com/topic/Sexism.aspx
- Bradley, Martha Sonntag; Woodward, Mary Brown Firmage (1994), “Plurality, Patriarchy, and the Priestess: Zina D. H. Young’s Nauvoo Marriages”, *Journal of Mormon History* 20 (1): 84–118, http://content.lib.utah.edu/u?/jmh,17862.
- Cornwall, Marie (1994), “The Institutional Role of Mormon Women”, in Marie Cornwall, Tim B. Heaton, Lawrence Alfred Young (eds.), *Contemporary Mormonism: Social Science Perspectives*, Urbana: University of Illinois Press, pp. 239–64 .
- Foster, Lawrence (1979), “From Frontier Activism to Neo-Victorian Domesticity: Mormon Women in the Nineteenth and Twentieth Centuries”, *Journal of Mormon History* 6: 3–22, http://content.lib.utah.edu/u?/jmh,16431.

- Hanks, Maxine (1992), Women and Authority: Re-emerging Mormon Feminism, Salt Lake City, Utah: Signature Books, ISBN 1-56085-014-0, http://www.signaturebookslibrary.org/women/introduction.htm.
- Hardy, B. Carmon (1994), "Lords of Creation: Polygamy, the Abrahamic Household, and the Mormon Patriarchy", *Journal of Mormon History* 20 (1): 119–52, http://content.lib.utah.edu/u?/jmh,17897.
- Iannaccone, Laurence R.; Miles, Carrie A. (1994), "Dealing with Social Change: The Mormon Church's Response to Change in Women's Roles", in Marie Cornwall et al. (eds.), *Contemporary Mormonism: Social Science Perspectives*, Urbana: University of Illinois Press, pp. 265–86 .

Index

C

J

K

L

M

N